DEVELOPMENTAL DISABILITIES
Theory, Assessment, and Intervention

DEVELOPMENTAL DISABILITIES
Theory, Assessment, and Intervention

Edited by

Michael Lewis, Ph.D.
Institute for the Study of
  Exceptional Children
Educational Testing Service
Princeton, New Jersey

Lawrence T. Taft, M.D.
Department of Pediatrics
Rutgers Medical School — UMDNJ
Piscataway, New Jersey

SP

SP MEDICAL & SCIENTIFIC BOOKS
a division of Spectrum Publications, Inc.
New York • London

9/1983
Psych.

Published by:
SPECTRUM PUBLICATIONS, INC.
175-20 Wexford Terrace, Jamaica, N.Y. 11432

Library of Congress Cataloging in Publication Data
Main entry under title:

Developmental disabilities.

Includes index.
1. Child development deviations—Congresses. 2. Child development—Congresses. 3. Developmentally disabled children—Congresses. I. Lewis, Michael, 1937 Jan. 10–   . II. Taft, Lawrence T. [DNLM: 1. Child development disorders—Congresses. WS 350.6 D4892 1979]
RJ135.D477   618.92'8   81-8592
ISBN 0-89335-139-3   AACR2

CONTRIBUTORS

Jeanne Brooks-Gunn, Ph.D.
Institute for the Study of Exceptional
   Children
Educational Testing Service
Princeton, New Jersey

S. Buechler, Ph.D.
Department of Psychology
University of Delaware
Newark, Delaware

Earl C. Butterfield, M.D.
Mental Retardation Research Center
University of Kansas School of
   Medicine
Kansas City, Kansas

William B. Carey, M.D.
Media, Pennsylvania

Douglas Derryberry, Ph.D.
University of Oregon
Eugene, Oregon

Robert N. Emde, M.D.
University of Colorado Medical School
Denver, Colorado

Joseph F. Fagan, Ph.D.
Department of Psychology
Case Western Reserve University
Cleveland, Ohio

Peggy C. Ferry, M.D.
University of Arizona Health Sciences
   Center
Tucson, Arizona

David Belais Friedman, M.D.
Pediatric Pavilion
University of Southern California
   School of Medicine
Los Angeles, California

Theodore Gaensbauer, M.D.
University of Colorado Medical School
Denver, Colorado

Robert J. Harmon, M.D.
University of Colorado Medical School
Denver, Colorado

Alice H. Hayden, Ph.D.
Model Preschool Center for
   Handicapped Children
Experimental Education Unit
University of Washington
Seattle, Washington

Carroll E. Izard, Ph.D.
Department of Psychology
University of Delaware
Newark, Delaware

Melvin D. Levine, M.D.
Brookline Early Education Project
Brookline, Massachusetts

Michael Lewis, Ph.D.
Institute for the Study of Exceptional
   Children
Educational Testing Service
Princeton, New Jersey

Merritt B. Low, M.D.
American Academy of Pediatrics
Greenfield, Massachusetts

Robert B. McCall, Ph.D.
Center for the Study of Youth
    Development
Boys' Town
Omaha, Nebraska

Jon F. Miller, Ph.D.
Waisman Center for Mental
    Retardation and Human
    Development
University of Wisconsin
Madison, Wisconsin

Gabriella E. Molnar, M.D.
Pediatric Rehabilitation Service
Albert Einstein College of Medicine
Yeshiva University
Bronx, New York

Frank Oberklaid, M.D.
Children's Hospital Medical Center
Boston, Massachusetts

Ralph Peabody, Ed.D.
Program in Special Education
University of Pittsburgh
Pittsburgh, Pennsylvania

Isabelle Rapin, M.D.
Department of Neurology
Albert Einstein College of Medicine
Yeshiva University
Bronx, New York

Richard N. Reuben, M.D.
Department of Pediatric Neurology
New York University Medical Center
New York, New York

Mary K. Rothbart, Ph.D.
Department of Psychology
University of Oregon
Eugene, Oregon

Robert J. Ruben, M.D.
Department of Otorhinolaryngology
Albert Einstein College of Medicine
Yeshiva University
Bronx, New York

Karen Saywitz, Ph.D.
University of Wisconsin
Madison, Wisconsin

Patricia Ann Shepherd, Ph.D.
Case Western Reserve University
Cleveland, Ohio

Donald J. Stedman, Ph.D.
Department of Education
University of North Carolina
Chapel Hill, North Carolina

Lawrence T. Taft, M.D.
Department of Pediatrics
College of Medicine and Dentistry
Rutgers Medical School
Piscataway, New Jersey

Louise Cherry Wilkinson, Ph.D.
Department of Psychology
University of Wisconsin
Madison, Wisconsin

Peter H. Wolff, M.D.
Department of Psychiatry
Children's Hospital Medical Center
Boston, Massachusetts

Philip R. Zelazo
Center for Behavioral Pediatrics
    and Infant Development
Tufts New England Medical Center
Boston, Massachusetts

PREFACE

The chapters in this volume are drawn from the presentations delivered at a symposium on Developmental Disabilities in the Preschool Child. This symposium was held under the auspices of The Institute for Pediatric Service of Johnson and Johnson Baby Products. It was co-sponsored by The College of Medicine and Dentistry of New Jersey, Rutgers Medical School, and The Institute for the Study of Exceptional Children, Educational Testing Service. The symposium was held in the Fall of 1979 in Chicago, Illinois and the participants, including Ph.D.'s, Ed.D.'s, and M.D.'s, represented the interdisciplinary approach which characterized the meetings. The interdisciplinary set of speakers was matched by an equally diverse audience who represented almost every professional group concerned with the needs of disabled children and their families. Because of the successful information exchange that took place, a published volume of the proceedings was determined to be useful for others who were not able to attend. To all those who toil to help developmentally disabled children and their families we dedicate this volume.

Michael Lewis
Lawrence T. Taft

CONTENTS

INTRODUCTION

There is a well known fable about a group of blind men who were lead to an elephant. Each was permitted to touch and examine a separate part of the animal and when asked to describe what an elephant was like, gave quite a divergent picture. This story has a strong analogy to those disciplines which are concerned with the development of the young child. The health professional may focus on the child's growth, the educator on the child's IQ scores and learning, and the developmental psychologist on the problems surrounding the child's development. Each touches and examines a different aspect of the organism and the resulting description is as divergent as the blind men's around the elephant.

In order to address the problem, it is necessary to bring together the divergent disciplines surrounding early development and to try to understand their interrelationship and interaction. The problem is not easy since different concepts, languages, and models underlie the different disciplines. Not only are there cross-discipline differences in these areas but different disciplines have different goals. Although there is often considerable overlap, health professionals are mainly interested in assessment and treatment from a biological point of view; the educator is interested mainly in intervention, while the developmental psychologist is interested in issues of process.

The purpose of the symposium and this volume is to initiate an interdisciplinary approach to the study, assessment, and treatment of developmentally disabled preschool children. We wish to view a wide variety of functions of the preschool child, not restricting ourselves only to sensory or cognitive aspects. Toward this goal, we have chosen five areas of developmental functioning to focus our attention: (1) sensory functions including visual and auditory systems; (2) motor development; (3) cognitive development; (4) language development; and (5) affective/temperament development. Although we realize that the maturations of specific functions do not occur in isolation but are dynamically interdependent, it was felt for didactic purposes to present them as individual areas of development. Such a strategy, while often followed, may do a disservice to the interdependent nature of development as well as the specific functions themselves.

For each of these five areas our approach is to combine a discussion of basic processes of development with assessment technique and intervention procedures. We believe that a presentation of developmental theory can be translated into assessment techniques which can then be clinically useful and can also lead to more specific intervention strategies. Each of the five functions follows this format.

The results of the symposium have led us to believe that current developmental theory and its clinical application are, for the most part, unrelated. We suggest that there are multiple reasons for this state of the art. For one, there are useful developmental theories but there is a lag in the application of research findings into clinical use. On the other hand, research findings and theory may not have any clinical application. This is because the theories or techniques are too narrow and specific for use in a clinical setting. Although the interdisciplinary model was not fully achieved, we now recognize that such an achievement can only occur after sufficient information exchange.

The practical value of the symposium and this volume is in the start of such a dialogue. The information exchange should aid the health professionals in understanding the basic science of development, how to recognize dysfunctional development, and possible intervention approaches. The biological and clinical perspective of the health professional should provide the educator and developmental psychologist with a broader knowledge base to construct theory and intervention procedures which utilize both biology and culture.

DEVELOPMENTAL DISABILITIES
Theory, Assessment, and Intervention

PART I

Sensory Development

This section is concerned primarily with visual and auditory sensory processes. Other sensory systems have received little or no attention and except for the visual and auditory modalities, little is known about their capacities, individual differences, or developmental course. Much work still needs to be accomplished in this regard and, while the visual and auditory sensory systems have been shown to be complex and important, we should be prepared to spend more effort in learning more about the olfactory, gustatory, and kinesthetic modes. In the part to follow, only the visual and auditory systems will be considered. While this represents only a portion of the sensory systems, enough is now understood to provide an important start for study, diagnosis, and intervention in these developmental dysfunctions.

As will be apparent, theory about visual and auditory development has received considerable attention. As a result, the development of complex and empirically sound theories exists and can be used to generate useful assessment procedures. Most neglected are the intervention strategies, either because the dysfunctional sensory systems do not lend themselves to easy correction or because not enough research effort has been devoted to their consideration.

1

Handicapped Child — Facts of Life

MERRITT B. LOW

I do not need to remind my readers that the handicapped child is a subject, not an object; a person, not a thing. Likewise, variation from the norm or average can be troublesome. Many of us, through ignorance or wish-fulfillment, often do not separate healthy, normal divergence from the deviance which should be of concern. There is sometimes a thin dividing line in terms of interpretation. Powerful and interested groups are newly involved in the care of the handicapped. Society with its compassion and guilt is heavily into the act, as are government, education, science and medicine. What some people call research in this area should not be dignified by the word, and I am sure Claude Bernard with his experimental method and Koch with his postulates would turn over in their graves were they able to see some of it. On the other hand, dead certainty is the enemy of strategic gain in the therapeutic area.

I was at first going to talk about problems and pitfalls, but this seemed a rather negative approach. So I'm going to label some of my thoughts "the facts of life." We must not ignore these facts.

The first, but not necessarily the most important, is the entrance of the federal government into the arena. The Elementary and Secondary Education Act of 1965 came into being during the term of President John Kennedy who, with his family, had a long-time interest in helping the handicapped. Up to that time school districts by and large had rather complete control of their own educational activities and depended on community interest and monies to further their efforts. Since 1965, although local autonomy still receives a certain amount of lip service, the purse-strings are controlled by the federal government.

This produces an interesting situation which we could call LAP, "Local Autonomy Purse-string" interaction.

Another interaction could be described as the L & L, or Labels and Lists, situation. We are cautioned on the one hand not to use labels but are told in the next breath that we must list "the number" we have in each of certain categories. This happened with the handicapped child in the Head Start Program. As we all well know, the woods are full of early identifiers, screeners, assessors and intervention strategists—sometimes so many we can't see the trees we're trying to nourish. Screening, because it is definite and subject to statistical analysis and tabulation, is a favorite activity. Our own pediatric Early Periodic Screening Diagnosis and Treatment program (EPSDT) has indeed become stalled, mostly in screening activity. Without treatment and follow-up, screening is a rather futile exercise. Furthermore, it can cause anxiety, for many false-positives and false-negatives turn up, especially in screening the neonate and the infant and young child. The so-called at-risk concept is far from perfect. Theoretically, we ought to be able to list certain criteria that put an infant at risk, and sometimes this does work out. But, on the other hand, one-quarter to one-third of the children that turn up later at a child development clinic come from a background where it is hard to identify at-risk factors. Furthermore, there are certain problems and hazards arising from the registration and subsequent procedures involving children who are at risk and have been screened. The main problems are those of anxiety, confidentiality and privacy. Some parents find it hard to have their children on registration lists, with periodic follow-ups by persons they often consider strangers worthy of suspicion. I have already alluded to the "label" problem which can arise after screening. Also after screening we can get led into false or inaccurate promises and, although any kind of change may lead to betterment, this is not always so. Sometimes the promises cannot be kept and are too sanguine or, conversely, too gloomy.

Another problem with screening is what I call the "so what?" psychology. Even after we get a child screened and labeled, we sometimes have no definite plan. Suffice it to say that many people still are under the impression that little can be done, at least for certain problems with the handicapped, especially very early in life. This is a superficial concept but, on the other hand, it is perfectly true that early intervention has not yet been conclusively proved to be efficacious "across the board."

I answer to "so what?" questions basically by saying that there is still a lot to do about emotional interrelationships and secondary behavioral problems that arise in any handicapping condition and that it is often necessary to separate the primary and secondary factors and sometimes deal with them a bit differently.

I would like to point out, though, some of the very positive accomplishments of screening. Amblyopia is an outstanding example of how early detection may mean the difference between good vision and impaired vision in the affected eye. Early detection of so-called PKU disease, of thyroid deficiency, of genetic problems in relation to the family as a whole, are other potentially beneficial results from screening and follow-up.

Another fact of life is the matter of IEP's, the Individual Education Plans developed in each school district for each handicapped student. With regard to the handicapped child, especially one with multiple handicaps, they should be ICP's, or Individual Child Plans. There is inevitable slanting in this area. Different school systems have different capabilities and specific biases and attitudes. Special care is often thought necessary in developing an IEP, because if one does not attain what one may appear to promise, there is some threat in this modern litigious world.

I should now like to address myself to the "child find" concept and problem. There are 3.9 million children identified as handicapped from the five- to seven-year-old pool when in reality there should be five to six million. In the group from 3 to 21 years there should be eight to nine million. Why haven't we found these other handicapped children? I guess the basic reason is that we are reluctant to label and classify them partly because the numbers are so frightening. Hence we try to keep them off the rolls. Some of us also conscientiously and consciously avoid the necessary labeling and categorization for the philosophic reasons I've mentioned previously.

We also have some financial problems. We all read quotes like "twice as much or more is spent on handicapped children as on normal ones." Whereas there are indeed finite money limits to all social problems and programs, the ethical aspects here are something society must decide. Handicapped children shouldn't be the goat for education's money problems. We all know this problem has many other aspects. The phrase "related services" has to be better defined and include more fiscal notes and outlines than we presently find in PL94-142 (The Education for All Handicapped Children Act of 1975). Alternative ways of financing certainly can be developed and we are not yet taking enough advantage of these other options. "Education" as "health care provider" has to be considered and explored further. Some school setups currently do provide medical care by hiring physicians and other personnel as needed. We must consider whether this is the ideal solution for the almost universally accepted concept of a "medical home" for every child. Incidentally, I do not mean an institution! I mean a 24-hour-a-day physician's office or medical center or a physician-manned clinic. Please do not consider it pejorative if I say that the school perhaps can be a "medical store" where certain health benefits can be obtained effectively and efficiently. But this should not compromise the idea of a medical home, and it is difficult for me to see the school serving a child 24 hours a day, 7 days a week, 52 weeks a year.

We also want to be sure what we're talking about when we define education. A sensitive, compassionate father once said to me in a child development clinic, "How do you ever expect to educate my poor little son?" This was a child who would never learn to read or write or do arithmetic, but I was talking about education in terms of having the child learn to be more adequate, to improve his self-care. In this context most children can be educated, but we must be sure parents understand the goals we have in mind.

There are further facts we must address. Medical personnel must understand a lot more about the educational process and require more in-service training to help them recognize needs and opportunities and capabilities. We also must deal more realistically with priorities. Should we devote our limited financial resources to teaching the mildly handicapped? That's where the so-called "payoff" is if that's all we are interested in.

Barriers are another matter. One person's aid may be another person's barrier. Stairs, elevators, ramps and room sizes have to be tailored to individual handicaps rather than be something for everyone. Therapeutic, diagnostic and testing confusions all lead to defensive efforts. Fragmentation is rife. We use different "lingos." I-teams, interdisciplinary efforts, transdisciplinary efforts, multidisciplinary approaches, all have their defenders. My own favorite would be "codisciplinary."

The pediatrician and family practitioner have specific problems of their own regarding developmental disabilities. Knowledge, experience and training are necessary and often lacking. It is much easier to cure a strep throat than a case of rheumatoid arthritis. Physicians tend to feel more comfortable in the area of specific treatments for specific diseases and have problems with multifaceted etiologies. It is probably true that only about 10 percent of general pediatricians and other physicians who care for children have an in-depth interest in the handicapped child. More training and educational programs should be developed forthwith.

We must also face the fact that neurologic evaluations often tend to be static, whereas developmental pediatrics is a dynamic specialty. Many physicians have trouble taking the psychosocial leap; that is, they would rather deal with an approach that is didactic and well-defined for them or by them. It is sometimes difficult for a physician to develop the various risks and alternatives and then let the patient carry on from there. We also have trouble with the advocacy-adversary balance. If we lean heavily toward a child's interests, we may become a school principal's adversary, perchance inadvertently. Furthermore, there is great disarray in health education in the schools at this point.

Perhaps the day will come when SAT's in health will be used in schools and when health education will have the standing of language, social studies, science and math. Appropriate knowledge of health would appear to be a top priority for a child moving from one educational milestone to the next.

Our efforts in these matters are exciting. We are looking at frontiers of theoretical appraisals on a scientific basis. We are trying to bridge the gap between these concepts and the pragmatic approach of intervening where possible, as early as possible, supported by reason, science, compassion and the art that is part of education and medicine. As William Blake said, "Art and science cannot exist but in minutely organized particulars." Credibility and evaluation are watchwords of the day. Society is very interested and we will find that co-disciplinary activities are going to pay in every way. Handicapped children are individuals, and they need individual advocates and a medical home. From this medical home sensible programs can be developed. We must bridge our plans for the general good into the areas of minute particulars. Various disciplines to-gether can accomplish the results for which we all hope as we increase our knowledge of each other and the barriers and hostilities fade away.

2

Theoretical Issues in the Early Development of Visual Perception

JOSEPH F. FAGAN III
PATRICIA ANN SHEPHERD

Introduction

Objectives

The present chapter will provide a selective review of findings on the growth of visual pattern perception in infants ranging in age from birth to seven months. (More comprehensive reviews are readily available in Cohen and Salapatek, 1975 and Haith and Campos, 1977.) We will first present the basic measures or operational definitions of infant visual perception. One such measure is the infant's tendency to devote more fixation to some stimuli than to others. Such naturally occurring visual preferences have been used to study a number of aspects of visual perception. Two preferences particularly useful in the study of infant perception are greater attention to patterned than to plain targets and a tendency to devote more attention to a novel than to a previously seen target. Illustrations will show how a general preference for patterning has been used to study the development of visual acuity. Preferences for novelty will be considered for the information they have yielded on more subtle types of pattern perception such as the development of the infant's ability to differentiate among faces. Following a discussion of basic measures of infant visual perception, particular illustrations of the development of pattern perception from birth to seven months will be presented. The summary will begin with estimates of the infant's ability to detect patterns and a compilation of the basic visual dimensions to which infants attend in discriminating among patterns. The review will then consider pattern perception from three to seven months. Specific illustrations will elucidate the infant's development in discriminating among patterns on the basis of orientation and in making progressively more subtle distinctions among faces. Specific theoretical issues and needs for further research will be noted throughout the presentation. The final section of the chapter will include a more general discussion of practical implications and theoretical issues arising from the study of infant pattern perception.

Operational Definitions

Three major techniques are currently used to assess the visual capabilities of infants: the elicitation of optokinetic nystagmus, the measurement of visually evoked potentials, and the study of the infant's visual interest or preferential looking. Optokinetic nystagmus refers to a series of reflexive eye movements produced in response to objects moving laterally across the visual field. These movements begin with a fixation phase in which the eye follows an object across the field and end with a faster phase in which the eye moves in the opposite direction after it has followed the object as far as possible. Optokinetic nystagmus is apparently involuntary, since a seeing individual with open eyes viewing moving stripes cannot help but show the response (Gardner and Weitzman, 1967). The optokinetic response is simple to elicit in infancy. The infant is shown a moving canopy over his crib on which is printed some pattern, typically graded black and white stripes. The smallest gradation of stripes which elicits optokinetic nystagmus is assumed to yield an estimate of the infant's visual acuity. Optokinetic nystagmus responses have been used to study binocular fixation, convergence and conjugate eye movements as well as visual acuity. The chief advantage of the procedure in infants is that it is relatively simple to use and inexpensive. The major disadvantage is that the elicitation of optokinetic nystagmus limits the investigator to the study of pattern detection. The response does not readily lend itself to the study of discrimination among patterns.

Researchers using visually evoked potential look for a change in the pattern of electrical activity in the infant's brain in response to a visual stimulus. In order to record a visually evoked potential, electrodes are attached to the infant's scalp over the area of the visual cortex. The infant is then allowed to observe various patterns, and his brain's electrical signals are recorded, amplified, summed and averaged to form an encephalogram. The study of visually evoked potentials, the most recently developed visual assessment technique, has been used thus far chiefly to estimate visual acuity in infants. One advantage of this technique is that it is a direct measure of brain activity and requires no overt behavioral response on the infant's part. Its major disadvantage is its reliance on complicated, expensive equipment for recording brain activity and the necessity for skilled technicians to reduce and interpret data. Thus most investigators of infant vision are still relatively unfamiliar with the visually evoked potential technique.

Most often employed in the study of infant visual perception is the visual interest or preferential looking test originated by Fantz (1956). The test rests on the assumption that if an infant looks more at one stimulus than at another he must be able to differentiate between the two targets. Differential visual fixation is operationally defined when one of a pair of targets elicits significantly more than 50 percent of the infant's total fixation time. The procedure for determining an infant's visual fixation is relatively simple. The infant is placed in front of a "stage" on which the targets are secured. With the targets in place, an observer, looking through a peephole centered between the targets, observes the corneal reflection of a target over the pupils of the infant's eyes and records the length of fixation paid to each stimulus. This test is inexpensive and simple to use either in a laboratory setting or in the infant's home. Visual interest testing has revealed, as we shall see, that infants show selective attention to aspects of the visual surroundings from the first few days of life.

In addition to finding which targets infants prefer to look at, investigators have taken advantage of certain naturally occurring visual preferences to solve the problem posed by the fact that infants sometimes prefer to fix on one target as much as another. Such lack of differential fixation when faced with a choice between two stimuli may imply either lack of discrimination or the equal attention values of stimuli which are actually discriminable. One solution to the problem of equal visual fixation is to rely on a known visual preference to increase the salience of one of the members of a target pair. The strong and consistent preference demonstrated by infants for patterned stimuli over plain targets, for example, was employed by Fantz (Fantz *et al.*, 1962) to estimate infant visual acuity and by Fagan (1974a, 1975) to explore infant color perception.

Fantz paired patterns of black and white stripes of various widths with plain gray targets of equal brightness. Since infants prefer patterned to plain stimuli, Fantz assumed that stripes would be preferred to solid gray targets as long as the stripes are resolvable. The finest width of stripes preferred to gray indicated the infants' level of acuity. Fagan paired checkerboards composed of two differently colored Munsell papers with unpatterned targets of either paper and recorded the amount of visual fixation on patterned and unpatterned stimuli. Presumably, any preference for a checkerboard over a plain target depended on the perception of the hue differences creating the checked pattern. Color perception is not one of the concerns in the present review of infant pattern perception, and issues of infant acuity will be explored in the next section. For our present purposes, however, it is important to note that reliance on the infant's basic visual preference for patterned targets is what allowed these findings on acuity and on color perception.

Another means researchers used to test the infant's ability to discriminate between two targets evoking equal attention is to pair the targets following exposure to one of them. It is a well-documented finding that after exposure to a target infants will shift their fixation predominantly to a novel stimulus when the opportunity to do so is presented. This preference for a novel over a previously exposed target gives two kinds of information. It shows that the two targets are discriminable, and it indicates that the infant can recognize or identify one of the targets as familiar. The infant's preference for visual novelty has provided a useful tool for the study of infant visual perception, particularly, as we shall see, in charting the growth of social perception.

In summary, by observing the infant's visual behavior, especially the attentional preferences, we have been able to begin to map out the dimensions of the visual world to which the infant attends, to note which dimensions command more or less of his attention, and to observe how he grows in his differentiation of patterned stimulation in the visual world.

Pattern Detection and Discrimination

Infants, from birth, are capable of some degree of pattern perception. Specifically, neonates exhibit pattern detection by selecting patterned stimuli for visual inspection more often than unpatterned stimuli, and they evidence pattern discrimination by making consistent attentional choices among patterned stimuli.

Acuity

We will give a brief overview of the infant's ability to detect patterns and note what appears to be the most theoretically interesting direction for further research on this subject. For a more detailed exposition of studies of infant visual acuity, the reader is referred to three recent and excellent reviews by Harter, Deaton and Odom (1977), Dobson and Teller (1978), and Salapatek and Banks (1978).

Visual acuity refers to the spatial resolution capability of the visual system, the threshold value for detecting pattern detail. It is not possible to give absolute threshold values for infant pattern detection, since estimates of infant visual acuity vary according to the kind of acuity measured, the discriminative response observed and the type of pattern to be resolved. Tests of minimum visible acuity, for example, in which the detection of the finest single line on a blank field is estimated, yield lower thresholds for both infants and adults than estimates of minimum separable acuity, which are based on the finest width of black and white stripes preferred to a plain gray field of equal brightness (Fantz *et al.,* 1975). In addition, estimates of acuity based on the recording of visually evoked potentials typically yield lower thresholds than do estimates based on optokinetic nystagmus or preferential fixation (Harter *et al.,* 1978). Finally, infants show better minimum visible acuity when asked to detect a curved line than a straight line (Fantz *et al.,* 1975) and, like adults, are better able to resolve horizontal or vertical stripes than oblique stripes (Leehey *et al.,* 1975).

Despite these variables affecting acuity estimates, it is possible to identify trends in the early development of pattern detection and to estimate ranges of infant acuity at various ages. Investigators agree that acuity develops most rapidly from birth to six months with a slower rate of improvement to one year. Estimates (in Snellen equivalents) range from 20/800 to 20/200 at birth, from 20/160 to 20/20 (adult acuity) at six months and 20/66 to 20/20 by one year. In more operational terms one can safely assume that the average infant, at birth, is able to resolve the pattern contained in a set of 1/8-inch black and white stripes held about nine inches from his eyes. By six months he can perceive at a distance of 12 inches the detail produced by 1/64-inch stripes.

The most interesting direction for further research on infant pattern detection appears to lie in the measurement of infant acuity via contrast sensitivity functions and the application of Fourier's theorem and linear systems analysis to the description of patterns. An extensive exposition of the merits of plotting contrast sensitivity functions for infants and of obtaining sophisticated descriptions of the patterns is contained in articles by Salapatek and Banks (1978) and Banks and Salapatek (1979) along with a review of studies which have obtained such estimates of infant acuity. Briefly, contrast sensitivity is found by presenting the infant with test patterns composed of light and dark stripes paired with plain targets of equal brightness. The patterned targets employed, however, vary not only in the width of the stripes but in the brightness between the stripes. In effect, various shades of gray are employed to create a striped pattern at each stripe width. Thus, the question becomes: what is the smallest discernible difference in brightness given a particular width? Contrast sensitivity functions are plotted as a function of threshold contrast sensitivity at various widths, and acuity is estimated by extrapolation.

Estimates of visual acuity derived from contrast sensitivity functions are somewhat higher for both infants and adults than those derived solely from visual discriminations of high-contrast (black-white) patterns. These lower thresholds are to be expected, since differences in spatial frequency (stripe separation) are more easily detected in patterns containing intermediate light-dark contrast than in those with very high or very low contrast. Hence, one may obtain more accurate and lower threshold estimates of acuity as well as some measure of sensitivity to contrast simply by employing targets which vary in brightness as well as in stripe width.

It is also possible, by applying Fourier's theorem and linear systems analysis, to describe patterns in terms of their internal spatial frequencies and brightness contrasts. In effect, if one knows the infant's contrast sensitivity function and the description of the pattern, one can predict the visibility or detectability of that pattern for the infant. Hence, one can estimate which patterns may be above or below the threshold for detection for infants at various ages. It is also possible to equate different patterns for detectability and to note the extent to which targets may vary in visibility. The combination of more accurate acuity estimates and more sophisticated pattern description promises to go far in reconciling diversities among studies of infant acuity which vary in the kind of acuity estimated and the type of stimulus shown. A recent study by Banks and Salapatek (1979) recounted successful attempts to effect such reconciliation.

Basic Dimensions

Infants, from the first few days of life, are able not only to detect the presence of pattern but also to discriminate among patterns. Such differentiations among patterns may be based on variations between patterns in the size, number or form of their elements. Initial experiments on newborn visual preferences by Fantz (1963), Hershenson (1964) and Stechler (1964) demonstrated an early ability to distinguish among patterns. In the Fantz study infants were shown six test objects one at a time. All the stimuli were flat discs; three were patterned (face, bull's-eye, newsprint) and three unpatterned (red, fluorescent yellow and white). The length of fixation on each of the stimuli was timed. The results showed that patterned were preferred to unpatterned stimuli and that among the patterned stimuli the strongest visual preferences were for the face-like objects. Stechler found that neonates spent more time viewing a schematic face than an array of dots, and Hershenson demonstrated that newborns clearly preferred some checkerboards to others.

The fact that some patterns attract more of the newborn's attention than others led to an examination of what specific differences between patterns may mediate these preferences. For example, to discover if variations in the size or number of elements from one pattern to another could determine such preferences, Miranda and Fantz (1971) studied the distribution of visual attention by newborn infants among a set of nine patterns varying in size and number of details in a pattern. Targets were paired in all possible combinations and fixation times were noted. The total times spent looking at each target showed that where number of elements was the same, newborns preferred larger to smaller elements. When patterns contained elements of equal size, attention was given to patterns with more elements. One set of three patterns which Miranda and Fantz employed varied both size and number of elements while holding overall light reflectance (area of black) equal, much like a series of checkerboards. Here there was a reliable preference for the pattern with fewest elements but largest size over the other two patterns, which indicated that for newborns size seemed to dominate over number when the two dimensions were opposed. In short, size and number of elements in a pattern can each serve as a basis for newborns' preferences among a series of patterned targets.

Thus far, we have presented evidence to show that newborns are sensitive to the presence and quantity (size or number) of patterning. Fantz and Miranda (1975) demonstrated that newborns are also sensitive to differences in form. They employed four pairs of forms in which the members of each pair were equated for total contour length, brightness and number of elements. The targets differed in form, with one member of each pair being curved and the other being straight. Observations of 44 infants showed that the curved member of three of the four pairings elicited about 63 percent of total fixation time, significantly more than the straight.

In summary, the newborn infant is selectively attentive to aspects of the visual surroundings. Patterned surfaces are detected and preferred to unpatterned ones, and some patterns elicit more attention than others. Preferences among patterns are mediated by variations along specific dimensions. These dimensions include, but are not limited to, size and number of elements and form of contour.

There is ample evidence that during the first three months of life infants continue to base discriminations among patterns on quantitative features such as size (Fantz and Fagan, 1975; Ruff and Turkewitz, 1975; Milewski, 1978), number (Ruff and Birch, 1974; Fantz and Fagan, 1975), and contour density (Maisel and Karmel, 1978) and on qualitative aspects such as form (Ruff and Birch, 1974; Ruff, 1976; Milewski, 1978) or configuration (Ruff and Birch, 1974; Ruff and Turkewitz, 1975; Maisel and Karmel, 1978; Milewski, 1979). In addition, investigators frequently point to shifts in preferred dimensions over age. Fantz and Fagan (1975), for example, noted that relatively greater attention is paid to number than to size of elements after 10 weeks of age; and Ruff and Turkewitz (1974) and Maisel and Karmel (1978) found interactions between age and the dimensions of the stimulus (size or contour density versus configuration) mediating discrimination among patterns.

Much theoretical activity has focused on attempts to explain early visual preferences and shifts in preference over age on the basis of some single underlying dimension such as "complexity" (e.g., Brennan *et al.,* 1966) or "amount of contour" (Karmel, 1969). Such reductionism is difficult to maintain in the light of the many stimulus variations now known to provide an effective basis for infants' discriminations among patterns. In fact, explanations that age-related discriminative shifts within even limited sets of patterns (e.g., patterns varying in size or number of elements) are due to shifts in complexity or amount of contour have not proved adequate (see Fantz and Fagan, 1975).

Furthermore, the task of explaining shifts in visual preferences over age is complicated by the fact that what appear to be shifts in perceptual preferences may actually reflect maturational changes in sensory-motor functioning. Changing preferences for size, number, contour density and form may, to some extent, be due to the rapid development of acuity; that is, such changes in preference may be a function of how resolvable a pattern is from age to age.

Changes in the manner in which infants scan targets may also account for what appear to be shifts over age from an attentional reliance on one dimension to another. The two-month-old infant is more apt to scan the internal features of a target than is the one-month-old infant (Maurer and Salapatek, 1976). Infants under two months tend to focus their gaze on the outer contours of a target. These shifts over age in how infants scan targets may help to explain why a number of investigations have found that form or configuration plays an important role in pattern discrimination for infants at two to three months but has little or no effect earlier (e.g., Ruff and Turkewitz, 1975; Ruff, 1976; and review by Fantz et al., 1975). In such investigations form variations are typically accomplished by presenting the infant with two white cards providing a background for two black forms (e.g., curved versus straight lines); that is, the infant is shown two cards whose external contour is identical but whose internal pattern varies from card to card. However, Fantz and Miranda (1975), as we noted earlier, found that even newborns could discriminate curved from straight forms. In fact, the neonates in the Fantz and Miranda study only made such discriminations when the forms were not embedded in cards with identical outer contours but rather were presented on a large homogeneous background. Moreover, Fantz and Miranda also found that the same neonates could no longer discriminate among these forms when they were encased in cards that had identical outer contours (i.e., presented in the midst of a white square). Thus, infants at various ages can discriminate on the basis of form if the patterns are readily scannable.

In brief, further attempts at explaining the early growth of visual perception must take into account variations in sensory-motor ability from age to age. Perhaps the greatest empirical need now is for longitudinal studies of discrimination on the basis of dimensions such as size, number and form or configuration, with patterns that are suprathreshold and scannable at each age.

Orientation Perception

During the first four months infants can distinguish one pattern from another. Early distinctions among patterns are made on the basis of variations in the size or number of elements composing the patterns or by attention to differences in the form of the elements comprising the patterns. From four months infants clearly demonstrate the ability to perceive differences among patterns equated for size and number of elements as well as for the form of internal elements. Such distinctions are most obvious when the infant proves able to discriminate a pattern from itself in a different orientation.

Abstract Figures

The infant, from at least four months of age, can discriminate one orientation of a figure from another. Studies by McGurk (1972), Cornell (1975) and Fagan (1979a) have provided examples of distinctions among various rotations of abstract patterns. McGurk (1972) allowed six-month-old (26 week) infants to view a simple stick figure, ?, over successive presentations during which looking time declined. Following habituation, the infants were shown a 180° rotation of the figure, and looking time returned to its original level. Such recovery or dishabituation indicated discrimination of the novel from the previously seen orientation. Cornell (1975) found that infants as young as 18 weeks could distinguish among 180° rotations of collections of small triangles arranged to form an overall pyramidal shape (e.g., △ vs.▽). Specifically, the infants in Cornell's study paid more attention to a novel presentation when a novel and a previously exposed orientation were paired. Fagan (1979a) also took advantage of the infant's tendency to fix more on a novel target in a paired-comparison test and demonstrated that 22-week-old infants could distinguish a ⌐-shaped collection of small squares from a 90°rotation (i.e., ⌐ vs. ⌐).

   While the experiments noted above demonstrate that four- to six-month-old infants perceive pattern orientation, a thorough, parametric study of their ability to distinguish among the various orientations of particular abstract patterns remains to be done. Of most importance in future studies would be the kind of patterns employed. Patterns should be chosen on the basis of relevance to perceptual theory. For example, the forms employed by Fagan (1979a) noted earlier were modeled after patterns described and studied extensively by Garner (1974) in experiments with adults. Garner notes that a pattern when rotated in 90° steps or reflected may produce either a smaller or a larger number of alternative forms. An X, for example, remains an X when rotated or reflected while a ⌐ produces four different forms (⌐, ⌐, ⌐, ⌐), and an F yields eight forms (F, ⌐, ⌐, ⌐, ⌐, ⌐, ⌐, ⌐). Garner (1974, Fig. 2.1) notes that adults find it easier to discriminate one orientation from another when the number of alternatives in the set is smaller rather than larger (e.g., ⌐ from ⌐ would be easier than F from ⌐). The inference is that adults are sensitive not only to the pattern they are seeing but also to the alternatives contained in the set to which a pattern belongs. Would infants also display such variations in ease of discrimination? Might we then infer some developmentally early sensitivity to the number of alternatives available in a pattern? Perhaps, but the questions await study and serve here to illustrate how the infant's orientation perception may be studied with patterns linked to perceptual theory.

Faces

Thus far, we have discussed the infant's perception of the orientation of abstract patterns and, in particular, abstract patterns which may or may not have a customary orientation. By customary orientation we mean patterns that adults would label upright in one orientation and nonupright in another. Faces are perhaps the most prominent example of patterns having a customary orientation. The study of the infant's ability to discriminate among various orientations of patterns with a customary orientation, such as faces, is of particular interest, since Braine has recently advanced a theory (in press) which assumes that orientation perception proceeds in a particular sequence with development. Specifically, she assumes that identifying the orientation of a familiar object such as a face develops in three stages. Initially, the child distinguishes an object in its upright position from the same object positioned either upside down or sideways. Distinctions among nonupright orientations, such as upside down from sideways, occur in the second stage. The third stage is characterized by the distinction of left from right. Braine cites the performance of two- to three-year-olds on discrimination learning tasks to support her main assumption that the sequence in which identifications among orientations are made does develop from a differentiation of upright from nonupright to distinctions among non-uprights and, finally, to left-right discriminations.

It is entirely possible, however, that the sequence of orientation perception outlined by Braine is quite basic, occurring in the early months rather than in the early years of life. On the basis of novelty preferences we know, for example, that four- to five-month-old infants can identify which face orientation they have seen before when an upright and an upside down face serves as either a novel or as a previously exposed target (McGurk, 1970; Fagan, 1972; Caron et al., 1973; Caron et al., 1977). In fact, an early study by Watson (1966), which monitored smiling time to various orientations of a face, demonstrated that four-month-old infants differentiate upright from either upside down or from sideways faces but may not distinguish upside down from sideways faces.

In an attempt to confirm and extend such observations Fagan and Shepherd (1979) undertook a recent study which explored the development from four to six months of the infant's ability to recognize the orientation of a face. Recognition was inferred from the infant's visual preference for a novel over a previously seen target. The particular orientations the infants were asked to identify were chosen to test Braine's theory of the development of orientation perception. As we have seen, Braine's theory predicts that at whatever age a differentiation between upright and upside down is made, a similar distinction should be possible between upright and sideways. Since a number of investigators have shown that four- to five-month-old infants can discriminate an upright face from itself upside down but only Watson (1966) provides evidence of a distinction between upright and sideways at four months, a sample of infants at four to five months were tested in the Fagan and Shepherd study on pairings of a woman's face upright and sideways.

Theoretically, distinctions between two nonuprights, such as upside down from sideways, should be more difficult at an early age than those between the upright and a nonupright. Again, we have only Watson's demonstration of the four-month-old infant's failure to smile more at an upside down than at a sideways face to confirm such a prediction. Hence, Fagan and Shepherd tested a group of four- to five-month-old infants on the distinction between upside down and sideways to determine if they could identify the familiar member of a pair of two nonuprights. Fagan and Shepherd also tested the differentiation of upside down from sideways at five to six months as well as the differentiation of right from left, presumably the most difficult discrimination.

Figure 1, which is based on the results of Fagan and Shepherd as well as earlier studies, provides a summary illustration of the distinctions among facial

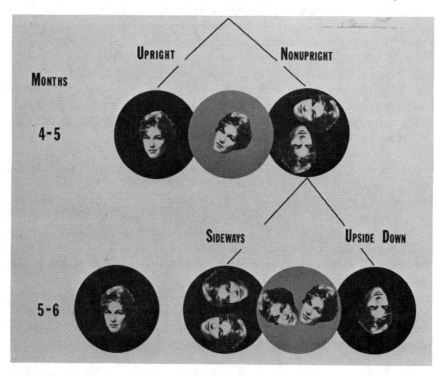

FIG. 1.   Early development of facial orientation perception.

orientations which are or are not accomplished from four to six months of age. In Figure 1 nonoverlapping black circles contain distinguishable orientations. Thus, at four to five months upright and upside down faces inhabit two different black circles since, as we have noted, upright and upside down are discriminable at these ages. In agreement with Watson's (1966) findings and with Braine's prediction that a similar distinction should be possible between upright and sideways at four to five months, Fagan and Shepherd's four- to five-month-old subjects distinguished upright from sideways and fixed more significantly on the novel orientation on recognition testing. Orientations contained within a circle in Figure 1 represent discriminations in which infants gave no evidence of having identified the previously seen member of two orientations.

Hence, at four to five months the upside down and sideways orientations are pictured in the same circle, since the percentage of fixation to the novel target for Fagan and Shepherd's four- to five-month-old infants did not depart from chance. The failure of the younger infants in this study to distinguish upside down from sideways replicates Watson's earlier results and confirms Braine's prediction that distinctions between two nonuprights should be more difficult at an early age than those between upright and nonupright.

By five to six months, however, a differentiation between upside down and sideways as distinct orientations within the class of nonuprights had taken place for the Fagan and Shepherd infants. Moreover, Fagan and Shepherd found, as predicted, limitations on orientation identification at five to six months in the failure of the older infants to distinguish right from left. In short, the results taken together with earlier work confirm Braine's main assumption that orientation identifications develop in a sequence in which a differentiation of upright from nonupright precedes distinctions among nonuprights which, in turn, are solved earlier than left-right discriminations.

Braine suggests that a diagonal may be seen as a nonupright that is neither upside down nor sideways. If so, the diagonal should, at some point in the development of orientation perception, be difficult to distinguish from either sideways or upside down (since both are nonupright positions) while being readily differentiated from the upright. Fagan and Shepherd included a number of recognition tests in which the diagonal was paired with upright and with upside down or sideways orientations at both four to five and five to six months to explore the role of diagonality in the early development of orientation perception (Figure 1).

The infants in Fagan and Shepherd's study did not reliably differentiate upright from diagonal or upside down from diagonal at four to five months. Hence, the status of the diagonal as an upright or as a nonupright must be considered indeterminate at this age as signified in Figure 1 by the gray circle which contains the diagonal and which overlaps the black circles containing upright and nonupright, respectively.

By five to six months Fagan and Shepherd found that the place of the diagonal in the infants' perception of orientation had become more articulated. Infants at five to six months readily differentiated the diagonal from the upright, but failed to distinguish the diagonal from nonuprights, either from the sideways or from the upside down. Thus, it seems that at four to five months the diagonal is seen as an orientation that may be upright or nonupright. In accordance with Braine's suggestion, at five to six months the diagonal is seen as a nonupright; it is readily differentiated from the upright, but is not clearly identified within the nonupright category as distinct from upside down or sideways.

In summary, studies tracing the development from four to six months of the infant's ability to identify the orientation of a face confirm the main assumptions of Braine's theory of the development of orientation perception. Specifically, infants make an initial distinction of upright from nonuprights at four to five months and then differentiate among nonuprights at five to six months. But they give no evidence of the ability to make left-right identifications at five to six months, an age at which they are able to distinguish among nonuprights. Further, infants at four to five months initially confuse the diagonal with both upright and nonupright orientations and later, at five to six months, see the diagonal as a nonupright that is neither upside down nor sideways. When infants can first identify right and left and when the diagonal is first differentiated from other nonuprights are questions to be investigated in future research.

Experimental considerations of the development of orientation perception during infancy have yielded a number of theoretical implications and directions for further study. One is that it is useful if not necessary to invoke a frame of reference (up, down, side, etc.) to interpret the infant's discrimination of facial orientations. The need to infer categories like upright and nonupright becomes quickly apparent ·when one realizes that attempts to explain the Fagan and Shepherd results on the basis of sheer rotation differences among the stimuli may be easily dismissed. Put simply, there are instances in which the same differences in degree of rotation either do or do not lead to identification. For example, infants at four to five months discriminate upright from sideways (a 90° difference) but not upside down from sideways (also a 90° difference). Similarly, at five to six months infants distinguish upright from diagonal, sideways from upside down, and upright from upside down (differences of 45°, 90° and 180°, respectively) but fail to differentiate sideways from diagonal, diagonal-left from diagonal-right, or sideways-left from sideways-right (also variations of 45°, 90° and 180°).

One might argue, of course, that the need to infer categories such as upright and nonupright to explain the development of orientation perception is limited to the explanation of facial perception. It is possible to decide if such an argument is valid. Since there do exist various abstract figures which, for older children and adults, are considered upright in one orientation but not in others (see Braine, in press, for a review of research on such figures), it should be possible to test the infant's distinctions among various orientations of abstract figures having clear "focal points" in the same manner as facial orientation has been tested. Should orientation perception for abstract figures also develop from an initial distinction of upright from nonupright to differentiations within non-uprights and then to left-right discriminations, as is true for faces, then one might feel justified in rejecting the need for two explanations of orientation perception, one for abstract figures and one for faces. The research remains to be done.

A second important implication, and the final one to be noted here, is that the results support Braine's (in press) assertion that the main stages of orientation perception outlined in her theory exist not only as a sequence of developmental periods but represent different levels for the processing of orientation information at any age. Evidence from preschool children's solution of discrimination tasks and adults' judgments of previously seen objects in various orientations is presented to support her assertion. The infant work noted above underscores the validity and generality of Braine's outline of the basic stages of orientation perception by noting the manner in which infants at four to six months, presented with the same face in different orientations, distribute their visual fixation to novel and previously exposed targets. This preference is akin to the behavior of two- to three-year-olds on two-choice discrimination tasks and follows the same course as the distribution of reaction times by adults asked to identify the orientation of figures in various contexts.

One specific question generated by this similarity of processing orientation information from age to age is the role of the diagonal in the perception of children and adults, a question that has received little study. Specifically, given the similarity of infants, children and adults in finding certain identification tasks involving upright, upside down and sideways orientations as more or less difficult to solve, it is also possible that the order in which infants make identifications involving the diagonal remains invariable at different ages. Whether or not the infant speaks for the child and the adult on this issue remains an interesting empirical question.

Facial Pattern

As we have noted, the growth of facial pattern perception involves four successive differentiations among faces, each more refined than the next. The first two stages appear to reflect the perception or identification of faces in general and the second two of faces in particular. The initial differentiation made in the first two weeks of life, is a general discrimination of facelike from nonfacial patterns.

A distinction of proper from altered facelike patterns appears at four to five months. By five to six months differentiations among individual faces are easily accomplished as long as the faces vary by age or sex (e.g., man from baby or man from woman). Finally, at six to seven months a distinction is made among faces of the same age or sex (e.g., one man from another). Much of the material in this section is based on a recent and extensive review of the origins of facial pattern recognition by Fagan (1979a).

General Distinctions

In the first few weeks of life the infant can discriminate a facelike pattern from other patterns that differ widely from a face, such as a bull's-eye. Before about four months infants do not discriminate between two facelike patterns which differ only in arrangement of internal elements, e.g., a schematic face from a version of itself made by rearranging features. Specifically, early findings by Fantz (1961, 1963) that patterns representing the human face elicit more fixation than nonfacial patterns, even by newborns, provoked a number of studies which focused on the extent to which patterns varying in degree of resemblance to a face controlled infant attention.

In general, these reports may be divided into experiments where little effort was made to control differences between patterns other than facial configuration which might also determine visual preference (e.g., brightness, size and number and form of elements) and those reports that did attempt such control. Studies with uncontrolled extraneous factors provided one quite uniform result: infants prefer faces to nonfaces. This is true both for newborns (Stechler, 1964; Fantz, 1966) and for older infants (Kagan and Lewis, 1965; Kagan *et al.*, 1966; Fantz, 1966; Fantz, 1967; McCall and Kagan, 1967; Moss and Robson, 1968). This is also true when faces are compared to patterns containing fewer elements (Stechler, 1964; Fantz, 1966; Kagan *et al.*, 1966), to a variety of patterns such as bull's-eyes and checkerboards (Kagan and Lewis, 1965; Moss and Robson, 1968), to random shapes (McCall and Kagan, 1967), and to relatively complex, unfamiliar objects (Fantz, 1967). Consistent as these results may be, however, they do not prove that facial configuration is a prepotent stimulus characteristic for the infant, since in each case other features may have covaried with facial resemblance and mediated the final preference.

The relative attention value of facial configuration for infants from birth to four months was more systematically assessed by comparing schematic faces with rearrangements of the same elements contained in the faces, either "scrambled" or rotated versions of faces. Given such control over extraneous factors, the attentional superiority of facial configuration breaks down (see review by Fagan, 1972), and no strong support emerges for preferences for schematic over scrambled faces, at least within the first four months.

Thus, in the first few weeks of life the infant distinguishes facelike from nonfacelike patterns. Since neonates are visually responsive to gross aspects of patterning such as the size, number and form of pattern elements (Fantz *et al.,* 1975, pp. 279–287 and section II-B of the present chapter), the newborn's distinctions between faces and nonfaces are likely based on such elementary characteristics rather than on the configuration we call a face. This simple explanation of the basis of neonatal preferences for faces gains support from the fact already noted that infants before about four months do not discriminate between two facelike patterns (e.g., face and scrambled face) which differ only in arrangement of internal elements.

Following the initial differentiation of facelike patterns from nonfacelike patterns, the next three perceptual accomplishments occur successively in the four- to seven-month period. Figure 2 illustrates the main results of experiments aimed at charting the development of recognition and differentiation among faces during the fourth to seventh months of infancy. On the left are face identifications possible at ages four to five, five to six, and six to seven

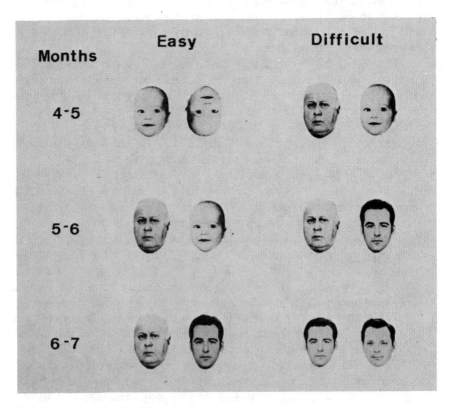

FIG. 2.   The growth of facial recognition.

months. On the right are identifications which are more difficult to make at these ages.

By four to five months, as Figure 2 indicates, the proper arrangement of facial elements can be differentiated from an improper arrangement of the same elements. Specifically, by 16 weeks the proper arrangement of facial elements can be discriminated from a scrambled pattern (Haaf and Bell, 1964; McCall and Kagan, 1967; Haaf, 1977) or, as pictured, from a rotated face (Watson, 1966; McGurk, 1970, Experiment II; Fagan, 1972, Experiment II). At the same time, the four-month-old infant appears limited to a general discrimination of proper from improper face patterning, since more subtle discriminations of one face from another are not evidenced at 16 weeks (Fagan, 1972, Experiment II). As this discussion continues, it should be noted that the ages stated for particular discriminations are approximations. The fact, for example, that studies allowing subjects relatively brief study of achromatic photos of unfamiliar faces have failed to find evidence of discrimination among faces prior to 20 weeks (Fagan, 1972; Cornell, 1974; Miranda and Fantz, 1974) does not mean that such discriminations are not possible somewhat earlier. It is quite likely that highly familiar instances or representations with more fidelity than achromatic photos might be discriminated from novel ones before five months. Cohen *et al.* (1977) found recovery of response to a novel target following habituation to criterion when chromatic photos of women, men and babies were presented to 18-week-old infants. The point we wish to make is simply that the differentiation of a proper arrangement of facial features from an improper arrangement appears to precede the distinction of one face from another, and both developments likely occur in the four- to five-month period.

Individual Faces

By five to six months a third step in the development of facial perception is taken: one face can easily be discriminated from another if the two faces vary in age or in sex. Faces differentiated from each other by five-month-old infants are illustrated in the middle row of Figure 2. These stimuli are typical of those employed in a series of studies by Fagan (1972, 1973, 1974b, 1977) in which 22-week-old infants preferred whichever target served as the novel member of a pair of faces when distinctions were to be made between a man and a woman, a man and a baby (as pictured), and a woman and a baby. Independent confirmation of the five-month-old infant's ability to differentiate among face photos is provided in studies by Cornell (1974) and by Dirks and Gibson (1977), who presented faces of men and women, and by Miranda and Fantz (1974), who used a woman's and a baby's face as discriminanda.

In short, at about five months a man can be differentiated from a woman or, as pictured, a man from a baby. But there is little evidence of such discrimination at five to six months for faces of the same sex. For example, one man is not readily discriminated from another (Fagan, 1979b; Dirks and Gibson, 1977) even when simple physical differences (e.g., hair length, shape of face, etc.) between the men's faces are maximized, as shown in the middle row of Figure 2. Fagan and Singer (1979) recently used the faces of the bald man and the dark-haired man in a study which explored the influence of the number of simple feature differences among faces on the five- to six-month-old infant's ability to discriminate among photographs of faces.

Although infants at five to six months can differentiate among faces as long as these vary in age or in sex, there is little evidence of such differentiation when, for example, one man is to be discriminated from another. Fagan and Singer thus asked if it is fair to assume that infants base their discrimination on those features which define the sex or age of a face. Such an assumption may or may not be warranted. Adult males, for example, tend to have full heads of hair, defined eyebrows and oval faces, while babies are bald and more round-faced. These simple differences alone may be sufficient to account for the five- to six-month-old infant's ability to distinguish a man from a baby. Similar examples might be drawn for the differences between a man's face and a woman's face.

While it is not possible to specify exactly what feature or feature combinations define sex and age, it is possible for adults to judge faces of men, women and babies as more or less similar for specific aspects such as hair length, eye separation, nose length, mouth width, etc. Thus, Fagan and Singer employed faces which differed greatly in age but were physically similar (e.g., a man and a baby both round-faced and bald) and asked whether such a similarity in simple features would prevent the five- to six-month-old infant's recognition of a previously seen face. Similarly, they asked if the infant's recognition would be facilitated by increasing the number of simple feature differences between two faces of the same sex. The general question of their study, then, was whether distinctions among faces at five to six months is primarily accomplished by an analysis of the particular information defining sex or age or by a reliance on the more obvious physical differences along certain face features which happen to covary with age or sex.

Fagan and Singer employed a paired-comparison test of novelty preference and asked some five- to six-month-old infants to recognize which of two faces they had seen before when the two faces were different in age or in sex but had been judged by adults as being highly similar in physical features. Other infants were asked to identify which face was new when the two faces were alike in sex and in age but had been judged by adults as being physically quite disparate.

The achromatic face photos employed in the Fagan and Singer study are illustrated in Figure 3. The three pairings in the left column, the baby and the

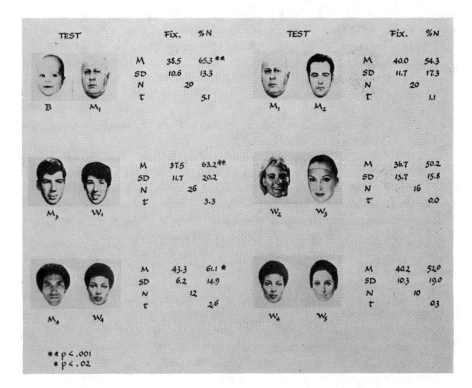

FIG. 3. Differentiation among faces varying in age or sex on the part of five-month infants.

bald man, the white man and white woman (in actuality, brother and sister) and the black man and black woman had been rated by adult judges as having relatively few physical feature differences between the pair members. The two members in each of the three remaining pairs, the two men, the two white women, and the black woman and white woman pictured in the right column, although the same sex, were judged quite dissimilar. Figure 3 also lists the percentages of total fixation paid to the novel target on recognition testing for each of the six groups of infants. The *t* values in Figure 3 represent the departure of the mean %N score from a chance value of 50 percent; such a departure indicates discrimination.

As one can see from Figure 3, faces disparate in age or sex but judged similar along many features (the bald man and the baby, the brother and sister, the black man and the black woman) were easily discriminated as demonstrated by high and reliable preferences for novelty. Infants gave no evidence, however, of having recognized which of two highly dissimilar men or women had previously been seen, as indexed by visual preferences which did not depart from a chance value of 50 percent. In effect, the Fagan and Singer results imply that whatever the features constituting the differences between a baby and a man or between a man and a woman, these attributes seem to be sufficient for the five- to six-month-old infant's recognition. Moreover, it would appear that extensive physical differences without accompanying differences in age or sex are not sufficient for discrimination at these ages.

By six to seven months the infant reaches the fourth step in his perceptual differentiation of faces and is able to discriminate between same-sexed faces. In addition, by six to seven months the number of simple feature differences between faces now aids the infant in differentiating between, for example, two male faces, with distinctions more easily made between very different than between very similar men (as shown in the bottom row of Figure 2).

The evidence for these statements comes from a study by Fagan (1976) which examined the ability of a six- to seven-month-old (29 week) infant to make rather fine discriminations among photos of adult male faces. Fagan (1976) used pairs of faces judged by adults as more or less similar to discover if the infant would find certain faces more difficult to discriminate than others. The faces were slightly modified versions of four men, two of which had been judged as most similar and two at least similar from all possible pairings of photos of 255 male faces shown to adults in a study by Goldstein et al. (1971). As an additional feature of the Fagan experiment, infants were required to differentiate between two men when shown in full-face, three-quarter or profile views. The question was whether the features peculiar to some poses would facilitate the infant's discrimination among faces.

The faces judged highly discriminable by adults were easily differentiated by the seven-month-old infants with high and reliable preferences for novelty regardless of the pose. Infants had some difficulty, however, with faces judged as being of low discriminability. Only performance on the three-quarter poses was at a level with that for faces of high discriminability. In short, data from six- to seven-month-olds in the Fagan (1976) study indicates that some of the features which adults use in discriminating among faces may be quite basic, with infants' "judgments" of discriminability following a similar course. In addition, infants seem to find three-quarter poses more informative than full faces or profiles when discriminations between highly similar faces are called for.

Summary

We can roughly approximate the growth of facial identification during the first seven months of life and specify important age periods and developments in this progression. In general, it appears that progressively more refined feature combinations succeed one another over age as the basis of the infant's differentiation of faces. The succession begins in the first month with those gross features which distinguish a face from a nonface and proceeds, at four to five months, to those features which signal proper arrangement of facial features. At five to six months the features defining the sex or age of a face are most informative. Finally, at six to seven months the feature differences between same sex faces prove useful for discrimination.

Theoretically, what we are observing is that infants can abstract the distinctive or invariant features common to three-dimensional, chromatic, moving, real faces and can then apply their perceptual knowledge to accomplish discriminations among two-dimensional, achromatic, still representations of faces, such as photos. Initially, the face, as a pattern, possesses stimulus characteristics which elicit the neonate's attention, i.e., large elements, numerous elements, many curved contours, and elements of sufficient contrast and separation. Attention to these attractive patterns results in the abstraction of the customary arrangement of the elements by four months. As a third step, it would appear that particular features or feature combinations, such as those defining the sex or age of a face, are abstracted and relied on for recognition. Of most interest is the fact that the detection of feature combinations defining age or sex occurs earlier in development than does the reliance on differences along what would appear to be more easily observed facial features, such as presence or absence of hair. In fact, it is not until about seven months that the number of simple feature differences aids the infant in differentiating between faces. Certainly, one of the most interesting conceptual and empirical areas for further study is the specification of exact characteristics which define the sex or age of a face for the infant.

Summary and Discussion

From birth infants are able to detect the presence of pattern and to discriminate among patterns. Rapid growth in the ability to resolve pattern detail occurs during the first six months, and greater pickup of pattern detail is a likely consequence of the development of scanning ability over the first three months. The extent to which the neonate's preferences for one pattern over another and the manner in which changes in such preferences over the first three months may be related to early sensory-motor development are empirical matters, particularly with regard to pattern discriminations made on the basis of quantity (e.g., size, number, length of contour). Variations in form, however, provide a basis for pattern discrimination from birth, at least for resolvable and scannable forms. Differences in form or configuration appear to play an important role in pattern perception throughout the early months of life.

Certain patterns, most notably the human face, contain features of a particular size, number and form that attract the infant's attention from birth and thus are readily differentiated from other patterns whose features are less attractive. From about the fourth month subtle differences between patterns equated for size, number and form provide a basis for pattern discrimination. Differences in a pattern's orientation, for example, are recognized. Moreover, the growth of differentiation of one orientation from another among patterns having a customary orientation, such as the human face, follows a theoretically predictable course from four to seven months. Concurrent with the development of orientation perception is a growing differentiation among properly oriented faces. Initially, one face is distinguished from another on the basis of features defining age or sex and then by feature differences between same-sex, same-age faces.

In closing, we would like to comment on the relation between early visual pattern perception and early and later cognitive functioning, a general issue of both practical and theoretical import. Evidence suggests that early individual differences in pattern perception and identification reflect individual differences in cognitive functioning. As we have seen, discrimination of patterning and identification of familiar patterns can be tested by pairing previously exposed and novel targets. The infant's ability to recognize a previously seen pattern as measured by his preferences for novel targets appears to be related to his later cognitive functioning. Specifically, samples of infants who are highly likely to differ in measured intelligence later in life, such as Down's syndrome and normal infants, also differ in their ability to recognize familiar visual patterns within the first eight months of life (Miranda and Fantz, 1974). Presumably, such group differences early in life indicate differences in visual recognition memory among individual infants, differences which may be valid estimates of current and later intelligent functioning. Recent work by the senior author of the present chapter has been aimed at estimating the predictive validity of tests of infant visual recognition memory for patterns as measures of intelligence. Preliminary results have been encouraging. Differences in visual fixation to novel visual patterns on the part of children initially tested from four to seven months of age are reliably correlated with later intelligence between four and seven years, i.e., with performance on vocabulary tests and vocabulary subtests of standard intelligence tests (Fagan, 1979b).

In effect, there is support for the assumption that variations in early visual pattern perception and memory both reflect and predict variations in intelligent functioning. Practically, the development of refined tests of infant memory for patterns may accomplish what years of research on infant sensory-motor abilities have not done, i.e., predict later intellectual functioning. When developed, such tests would be useful to screen infants suspected to be at risk for lower cognitive functioning due to various prenatal or perinatal factors. Such tests could also determine the short-term effects of intervention programs. Theoretically, the demonstration of continuity between early visual recognition memory and later intelligence raises the question of the basis for the continuity. McCall *et al.* (1977), for example, point out that continuity from one age to the next might be found because individual differences in rate of development for one behavior at an early age may be the same for an entirely different behavior at a second age (e.g., the early walker may be the early reader); or continuity might reflect individual differences in conceptually related skills from age to age (e.g., the infant with advanced perceptual and memory skills may be the child with such advanced skills). In other words, we might ask if continuity is due to consistent individual differences in general rate of development, assuming no relation between early and later functions. Or we might ask if the continuity lies in the fact that the same kind of function is tapped from age to age, with individuals retaining their relative standing on a particular skill over age.

A lengthy discussion of the basis for continuity is beyond the scope of this chapter. We feel that the hypothesis of continuity in kind, rather than in rate, provides the more heuristic working assumption. Thus, the task becomes specifying similarities in the informational character and the solution processes between early pattern perception and memory tasks and later intelligence tests. For the present, however, it is sufficient to note that the demonstration of links between early visual perception and memory and later intelligence raises the issue of the basis of such continuity, an issue we consider of great importance for the further study and analysis of infant pattern perception.

Acknowledgments

The preparation of this chapter was supported by Multiple Research Project Grant HD-11089 from the National Institute of Child Health and Human Development, and by a grant from the National Foundation–March of Dimes. Author Fagan's address: Department of Psychology, Case Western Reserve University, Cleveland, Ohio 44106.

References

Banks, M.S. and Salapatek, P. Infant pattern vision: A new approach based on the contrast sensitivity function. Unpublished manuscript (1979).

Braine, L.G. Early stages in the perception of orientation, in Bortner, M. (ed.), *Cognitive development and growth* (in press).

Brennan, W.M., Ames, E.W. and Moore, K.W. Age differences in infants' attention to patterns of different complexities. *Science*, 151:355–356 (1966).

Caron, A.J., Caron, R.F., Caldwell, R.C. and Weiss, S.E. Infant perception of the structural properties of the face. *Devel. Psychol.*, 9:385–399 (1973).

Caron, A.J., Caron, R.F., Minichiello, M.D., Weiss, S.J. and Friedman, S.L. Constraints on the use of the familiarization-novelty method in the assessment of infant discrimination. *Child Devel.*, 48:747–762 (1977).

Cohen, L.B., Deloache, J.S. and Pearl, R.A. An examination of interference effects in infants' memory for faces. *Child Devel.*, 48:88–96 (1977).

Cohen, L.B. and Salapatek, P. (eds.) *Infant perception: From sensation to cognition. Vol. 1. Basic visual processes.* New York: Academic Press (1975).

Cornell, E.H. Infants' discrimination of photographs of faces following redundant presentations. *J. Exper. Child Psychol.*, 18:98–106 (1974).

Cornell, E.H. Infants' visual attention to pattern arrangement and orientation. *Child Devel.*, 46:229–232 (1975).

Dirks, J. and Gibson, E. Infants' perception of similarity between live people and their photographs. *Child Devel.*, 48:124–130 (1977).

Dobson, V. and Teller, D.Y. Visual acuity in human infants: A review and comparison of behavioral and electrophysiological studies. *Vision Res.*, 18:1469–1483 (1978).

Fagan, J.F. Infants' recognition memory for faces. *J. Exper. Child Psychol.*, 14:453–476 (1972).

Fagan, J.F. Infants' delayed recognition memory and forgetting. *J. Exper. Child Psychol.*, 16:424–450 (1973).

Fagan, J.F. Infant color perception. *Science*, 183:973–975 (1974a).

Fagan, J.F. Infant recognition memory: The effects of length of familiarization and type of discrimination task. *Child Devel.*, 45:351–356 (1974b).

Fagan, J.F. Infant hue discrimination. *Science*, 187:277 (1975).

Fagan, J.F. Infants' recognition of invariant features of faces. *Child Devel.*, 47:627–638 (1976).

Fagan, J.F. The origins of facial pattern recognition, in Bornstein, M. and Kessen, W. (eds.), *Psychological development from infancy.* Hillsdale, New Jersey: Lawrence Erlbaum Associates (1979a).

Fagan, J.F. Infant recognition memory and later intelligence. Paper presented at the Society for Research in Child Development Meeting, San Francisco, March 16 (1979b).

Fagan, J.F. and Shepherd, P.A. Infants' perception of face orientation. *Infant Behav. and Devel.*, 2:227–234 (1979).

Fagan, J.F. and Singer, L.T. The role of simple feature differences in infants' recognition of faces. *Infant Behav. and Devel.*, 2:39–45 (1979).

Fantz, R.L. A method for studying early visual development. *Percept. and Motor Skills*, 6:13–15 (1956).

Fantz, R.L. The origin of form perception. *Sci. Amer.*, 204:66–72 (1961).

Fantz, R.L. Pattern vision in newborn infants. *Science*, 140:296–297 (1963).

Fantz, R.L. Pattern discrimination and selective attention as determinants of perceptual development from birth, in Kidd, A. and Rivoire, J.L. (eds.), *Perceptual development in children.* New York: International Universities Press (1966).

Fantz, R.L. Visual perception and experience in early infancy: A look at the hidden side of behavior development, in Stevenson, H.W., Hess, E.H. and Rheingold, H. (eds.), *Early behavior: Comparative and developmental approaches.* New York: Wiley (1967).

Fantz, R.L. and Fagan, J.F. Visual attention to size and number of pattern details by term and preterm infants during the first six months. *Child Devel.*, 46:3–18 (1975).

Fantz, R.L., Fagan, J.F. and Miranda, S.B. Early perceptual development as shown by visual discrimination, selectivity, and memory with varying stimulus and population parameters, in Cohen, L. and Salapatek, P. (eds.), *Infant perception: From sensation to cognition. Vol. 1. Basic visual processes.* New York: Academic Press (1975).

Fantz, R.L. and Miranda, S.B. Newborn infant attention to form of contour. *Child Devel.*, 46:224–228 (1975).

Fantz, R.L., Ordy, J.M. and Udelf, M.S. Maturation of pattern vision in infants during the first six months. *J. Compar. and Physiol. Psychol.*, 55:907–917 (1962).

Gardner, R. and Weitzman, E. Examination for optokinetic nystagmus in sleep and waking. *Arch. Neurol.*, 16:415–420 (1967).

Garner, W.G. *The processing of information and structure.* Potomac, Maryland: Lawrence Erlbaum Associates (1974).

Goldstein, A.J., Harmon, L.D. and Lesk, A.B. Identification of human faces. *Proceedings of the IEEE*, 59:748–760 (1971).

Haaf, R.A. Visual responses to complex facelike patterns by 15- and 20-week-old infants. *Devel. Psychol.*, 13:77–78 (1977).

Haaf, R.A. and Bell, R.Q. A facial dimension in visual discrimination by human infants. *Child Devel.*, 38:893–899 (1966).

Haith, M.M. and Campos, J.J. Human infancy. In *Annual review of psychology.* Palo Alto: Annual Reviews Inc. (1977).

Harter, M.R., Deaton, F.K. and Odom, J.V. Pattern visual evoked potentials in infants, in Desmedt, J.E. (ed.), *Visual evoked potentials in man: New developments.* Oxford: Clarendon Press (1977).

Hershenson, M. Visual discrimination in the human infant. *J. Compar. and Physiol. Psychol.*, 58:270 (1964).

Kagan, J., Henker, B.A., Hen-Tov, A., Levine, J. and Lewis, M. Infants' differential reactions to familiar and distorted faces. *Child Devel.*, 37:519–532 (1966).

Kagan, J. and Lewis, M. Studies of attention in the human infant. *Merrill-Palmer Quart.*, 11:95–127 (1965).

Karmel, B.Z. The effects of age, complexity, and amount of contour on pattern preferences in human infants. *J. Exper. Child Psychol.*, 7:339–354 (1969).

Leehey, S., Moskowitz-Cook, A., Brill, S. and Held, R. Orientational anistropy in infant vision. *Science*, 190:900–902 (1975).

Maisel, E.B. and Karmel, B.Z. Contour density and pattern configuration in visual preferences of infants. *Infant Behav. and Devel.*, 1:127–140 (1978).

Maurer, D. and Salapatek, P. Developmental changes in the scanning of faces by young infants. *Child Devel.*, 47:523–527 (1976).

McCall, R.B., Eichorn, D.H. and Hogarty, P.S. Transitions in early mental development. *Monographs of the Soc. for Res. in Child Devel.*, 42, No. 3 (1977).

McCall, R.B. and Kagan, J. Attention in the infant: Effects of complexity, contour, perimeter, and familiarity. *Child Devel.*, 38:939–952 (1967).

McGurk, H. The role of object orientation in infant perception. *J. Exper. Child Psychol.*, 9:363–373 (1970).

McGurk, H. Infant discrimination of orientation. *J. Exper. Child Psychol.*, 14:151–164 (1972).

Milewski, A.E. Young infants' visual processing of internal and adjacent shapes. *Infant Behav. and Devel.*, 1:359–371 (1978).

Milewski, A.E. Visual discrimination and detection of configurational invariance in 3-month infants. *Devel. Psychol.*, 15:357–363 (1979).

Miranda, S.B. and Fantz, R.L. Distribution of visual attention of newborn infants among patterns varying in size and number of details. Proceedings, American Psychological Association, Washington, D.C. (1971).

Miranda, S.B. and Fantz, R.L. Recognition memory in Down's Syndrome and normal infants. *Child Devel.*, 45:651–660 (1974).

Moss, H.A. and Robson, K.S. Maternal influences in early social visual behavior. *Child Devel.*, 38:401–408 (1968).

Ruff, H.A. Developmental changes in the infant's attention to pattern detail. *Percept. and Motor Skills*, 43:351–358 (1976).

Ruff, H.A. and Birch, H. Infant visual fixation: The effect of concentricity, curvilinearity, and number of directions. *J. Exper. Child Psychol.*, 17:460–473 (1974).

Ruff, H.A. and Turkewitz, G. Developmental changes in the effectiveness of stimulus intensity on infant visual attention. *Devel. Psychol.*, 11:705–710 (1975).

Salapatek, P. and Banks, M.S. Infant sensory assessment: Vision, in Minifie, F.D. and Lloyd, L.L. (eds.), *Communicative and cognitive abilities: Early behavioral assessment.* Baltimore: University Park Press (1978).

Stechler, G. Newborn attention as affected by medication during labor. *Science*, 144:315–317 (1964).

Watson, J.S. Perception of object orientation in infants. *Merrill-Palmer Quart.*, 12:73–94 (1966).

3

Clinical Appraisal of Vision

RICHARD N. REUBEN

Introduction

Except for the reflex pupillary reaction to light, responses to visual stimuli are considered to be indicative of cortical function in man. The pupillary constriction on exposure to a flash of light is automatic and even occurs in drowsiness and in sleep. This reflex is mediated by the mid brain and does not depend on cerebral hemisphere function. In contrast, all other responses to a visual stimulus, whether it be simply turning of the eyes towards a flash or reading a paragraph of printed material, involve the entire visual pathways in the brain including the visual cortex. To elicit the maximal reaction to a perceived light stimulus, the subject must be alert, interested and able to respond in a meaningful way.

Tests of visual acuity and visual perception in older children and adults require not only alertness and attention but the ability to vocalize the answers. For example, the 6-year-old child is expected to name the number or letter indicated on the eye chart. The accuracy of his response is easily determined. In younger children, hand gestures or affirmative or negative responses serve almost as well. In very young children and in infants, reliance must be placed on indirect means of evaluating vision (gaze preference, eye movement or electrically recorded cerebral responses) since the subject may not comprehend the task set for him or may be unable to respond appropriately. In this sense, the immaturity of general brain function may hamper the appraisal of a specific (visual) function.

Visual Responses in the Newborn Period
(First 28 days of life)

The pediatrician frequently hears from the parents of a very young infant that the baby does fix his gaze on the parents' face and that he may open his mouth, wrinkle his forehead or purse his lips in response to movement of the parents' head or change in the parents' facial expression. These responses to visual contact may be reinforced by the parents' voice and by touching.

Such visual responses are typically elicited when the infant is awake and comfortable and neither hungry nor satiated, usually two or three hours after feeding. The hungry, vigorously crying child is less accessible and the same is true for the drowsy infant who has just been fed.

In defense of the pediatrician who may express some skepticism concerning the parents' report of the visual competency of their 2-week-old child, one must recall the circumstances of the usual newborn medical examination conducted in the hospital nursery. There, the infant may be aroused from sleep, transferred from his warm crib to a cooler examining table, stripped of his clothing and bathed in bright light. Hardly the circumstances conducive to quiet visual communication! In fact, little or no effort may be given to evaluate anything more than the pupillary reflex to light (if the usually puffy lids can be separated) or perhaps the blink or grimace induced by the bright light. Even the follow-up examination at 6 weeks of age may include little attention to vision. A variety of measurements, a note about the fontanel, a comment about nursing or formula and advice to the parent may preempt all attention. If the infant should inadvertently smile in the direction of the physician, this might deserve a separate notation.

In regard to the newborn's ability to attend to visual stimuli, the following excerpts from the work of Andre Thomas in the early part of this century are offered.

> In the first 10 days, the head and eyes turn towards a light . . . . At about a fortnight, the infant's eyes intermittently follow a near object for a short distance if it is moved horizontally. . . . At about one month, the baby looks intermittently at the examiner's face; at about 6 weeks, he first smiles at seeing his mother. (Thomas *et al.*, 1960)

In the same monograph, the observation is offered that "reactions are distinguished from reflexes by their greater complexity and the inconstancy of the response . . . being hungry or well-fed affects the response . . . crying inhibits some reaction."

The importance of noting the physiologic state of the infant has been emphasized and elaborated upon by Prechtl (1977) and by Brazelton (1973) in the latter's monograph. Elucidation of the infant's response to inanimate (red ball) and animate (face) visual stimuli depended on the infant's "state." The desirable state was described as "alert with bright look; seems to focus attention on source of stimulation, such as an object to be sucked, or a visual or auditory stimulus; impinging stimuli may break through, but with some delay in response. Motor activity is at a minimum."

This "bedside approach" to the demonstration of newborn visual competency has been supplemented by other methods.

(a) Optokinetic Nystagmus

As long ago as 1930 (McGinnis, 1930), there was an account of optokinetic nystagmus elicited in a newborn infant by placing him inside a large rotating drum painted with alternating stripes of black and white. This observation has been confirmed many times and the procedure has been refined to the point where it may be used as an index of visual acuity (Gorman et al., 1957). In this respect, the discrimination of the individual black and white stripes depends on the width of the stripes and the visual acuity of the subject (assuming that other variables such as lighting and rotary speed are held constant). Again the state of the infant must be appropriate for the test procedure.

(b) Computer Recording of Visual Cortex Evoked Responses

Following the development of computer techniques and equipment, investigation of cortical potentials evoked by sensory stimuli was undertaken in many centers (Whipple, 1964). Visually evoked responses could not previously be reliably recorded by the ordinary scalp electroencephalogram without the magnification and isolation of the induced response by the new method. In contrast, electrical recordings of induced retinal potentials had already been well demonstrated. Early efforts at recording the sensory evoked cortical response employed a simple stimulus, namely, exposure to a repetitive flash of light. Investigators were able to show that a visually evoked cortical response could be elicited from newborn infants and even a primitive response from premature infants. One such study demonstrated the electroretinogram to be identical in form with the adult response whereas the evoked cortical potentials changed considerably with maturation (Fogarty and Reuben, 1969). More sophisticated techniques employed exposure to complicated visual stimuli in the form of patterns of different types.

(c) Pattern Vision in Newborn Infants

The newborn infant's visual attention may be attracted not only by a bright object or by the examiner's face, but by patterns of varying shape and size (Fantz, 1963). Infants do show a preference for certain features such as stripes or curved lines over equally lit but homogeneous or purely monochromatic surfaces. This ability to discriminate between two targets as demonstrated by a preference in gaze time has served as further evidence of cortical visual function.

Development of Vision in Infants and Children

In the first month of life, the infant is expected to regard his mother's face and smile responsively by six weeks of age. 75% of newborn infants will follow a target from the side to the midline and most will follow it past the midline by two months of age. Between two and eight months of age, there are indications of increasing attention to details, to smaller objects, to recognition of the familiar versus the strange and increasing eye-hand coordination. By 18 months of age, 75% of infants will be able to build a two block tower. The ability to place a round block into an appropriate space is evident at 2½ years or before and the capacity to copy a circle with a pencil and paper, between 2½ and 3 years. Recognition of colors, letters and numbers is established between 4 and 5 years of age (Frankenberg and Dodds, 1969).

The maturation of vision is dependent on the intimate relationships between visual acuity, visual perception and visual motor integration. Deficits in either visual acuity or visual processing will interfere with the orderly development of visually related activities. Abnormal vision in both eyes is more readily recognized than even total loss of vision in one eye. Diminished vision may be appreciated in terms of poor fixation, inattention to small objects, failure of visual recognition of familiar objects or faces and the development of nystagmus or strabismus. Loss of vision in one eye may not be suspected at all until it deviates from the normal parallel position with its mate or when the good eye is inadvertently occluded and it becomes evident that the child cannot see. More commonly, the strabismus is the primary disorder and failure to take corrective measures leads to the development of amblyopia in the constantly deviating eye. Failure to encourage the use of this eye before five or six years of age will cause normal vision to become irretrievable.

Children at risk for disorders of vision include those whose mothers had a prenatal infection with Rubella, Herpes, Toxoplasmosis or Cytomegalic virus disease. In these diseases, the infant's eye may be affected by a cataract or retinal defect. Congenital anomalies including those with chromosomal abnormalities are frequently associated with defects in formation of the eye. Metabolic disorders may affect the lens or retina. Premature birth was once a great risk because of retrolental fibroplasia.

It should be noted that diseases or injuries of the brain may be accompanied by optic atrophy and poor vision. More often, the mental retardation and the lack of visual interest in surroundings or response to stimuli may be mistaken for some obscure cause of blindness. In time, the presence of normal visual function initially masked by the retardation will become evident.

Evaluation of Visual Acuity

The most familiar and certainly the most widely accepted means of testing visual acuity is the Snellen Chart. Its standard construction calls for the letter E to subtend an angle of five minutes. Each of the three arms of the E subtend an angle of one minute as do the two spaces between the arms. That other letter which most closely approximates the E is the B. Distinguishing the B from the E might be considered a test of visual acuity in the same fashion that a C and an O may be distinguished from each other. The issue here is to discriminate whether the two figures are the same or different, a problem of what has been termed "resolution acuity." There will be a point where the progressive diminution in size of the letters no longer allows the subject to distinguish one from the other. Most of the other letters on the Snellen Chart involve the function of visual recognition and this is not exactly the same as acuity. Furthermore, not all the letters are equal in ease of recognition or familiarity.

It is frequently possible to obtain a better "visual acuity" with the illiterate E chart than with the formal Snellen Chart itself. This is particularly true of children around the kindergarten age. There are other factors in the use of the Snellen Chart of which we should be aware. Young children may "see" better if the letters are presented individually rather than five or six on a line. Furthermore, it is frequently easier for a child to focus his attention on a single line presented by itself rather than pulled out of the background of the entire Snellen Chart. Nevertheless, in spite of these objections, the Snellen Chart does employ familiar targets, letters or numbers, and requires little preparation for the subject to be tested.

The downward extension of the Snellen principle, the recognition of familiar letters, has been found useful for younger children. The illiterate E chart requires the 4-year-old only to point his hand in the same direction as the open end of the letter E. The test may be facilitated by actually supplying a three-dimensional E form and asking the child to rotate it into the same direction as the target E. An alternative test is the substitution of the picture of a hand for the letter E and the child is then asked to move his own hand in the same direction as the target.

The last two tests described depend on the ability of the child to match the orientation of the target with his hand or an object held in his hand. He is not required to name or identify anything. There is another test designed for small children which involves matching of small toys at a distance of ten feet. The abbreviation STYCAR stands for Screening Test for Young Children and

Retardates (Savitz, Valadian and Reed, 1964). A similar test, the Allen Cards, requires the subject to match pictures of common objects.

Visual acuity as tested by these various measures is reported to develop from 20/70 at 2 years of age to 20/30 at 5 years of age and 20/20 at 7 years of age.

Tests of visual acuity for newborn and young infants depend on indirect responses in the sense that the subject does not indicate the answer or participate in the sense that he must understand what is being asked of him. These tests include the induction of optokinetic nystagmus by alternating black and white stripes and by the measurement of visually evoked cortical responses by different sized and different colored stimuli (Sokol, 1978; Dobson and Teller, 1978).

Summary

Reliable visual responses have been observed in newborn infants. Early evaluation of vision may be undertaken indirectly by methods which do not require active participation by the infant. A variety of methods have been described which do depend on the cooperation and response of the child and in this sense test his vision directly.

Brief comments on children at risk and early warning signs have been given.

References

Brazelton, T.B. *Neonatal Behavioral Assessment Scale*. Philadelphia, Pa.: J.P. Lippincott Co. (1973).

Dobson, V. and Teller, D. Assessment of visual acuity in infants, in Armington, J.C., Krauskopf, J., and Wooten, B.R. (eds.), *Visual Psychophysics and Physiology*. New York: Academic Press (1978).

Fantz, R.L. Pattern vision in newborn infant. *Science*, 140:296–297 (1963).

Fogarty, T. and Reuben, R. Light-evoked cortical and retinal responses in premature infants. *Arch. Ophthal.*, 81:454 (1969).

Frankenberg, W.K. and Dodds, J.B. *Denver Developmental Screening Test*. Boulder, Co.: University of Colorado Medical Center (1969).

Gorman, J.J., Cogan, D.G. and Gillis, S.S. An apparatus for grading the visual acuity on the basis of optokinetic nystagmus. *Pediatrics*, 19:1088–1092 (1957).

McGinnis, J.M. Eye-movements and optokinetic nystagmus in early infancy. *Genetic Psychology Monographs*, 8:321 (1930).

Prechtl, H.F.R. *The Neurological Examination of the Full Term Newborn Infant*. Philadelphia, Pa.: J.B. Lippincott Co. (1977).

Savitz, R., Valadian, I. and Reed, R. *Vision Screening of the Pre-School Child*. Children's Bureau Publication No. 414, U.S. Dept. of Health, Education & Welfare, Washington, D.C. (1964).

Sokol, S. Measurement of infant visual acuity from pattern reversal evoked potentials. *Vision Research*, 18:33–39 (1978).

Thomas, A., Chesni, Y. and Dargassies, S. "The Neurological Examination of the Infant." MacKeith, Polani & Clayton-Jones (eds.), National Spastics Society, London W.I. U.K. (1960).

Whipple, H. Sensory evoked response in man. *Annals of New York Academy of Sciences*, 112:1–546 (1964).

4

Early Visual Impairment: Research and Assessment

JEANNE BROOKS-GUNN

One of the issues repeatedly raised concerning developmental disabilities in the preschool child, and I think the most important one, is how the knowledge bases of different professional groups may be integrated, rather than existing independently or even competitively, to serve the handicapped young child. Each of us, schooled in our various disciplines, often sees a child quite differently and consequently we do not treat the child but treat the "problem." For example, a mother tells us she is worried because her son shows little interest in his surroundings. As anticipated from her report, the 3-month-old is unable to track an object that moves slowly across the visual field, although he seems to fixate on stationary objects. How do different professionals interpret this observation? One observer might focus on neurological problems indicating visual impairment of some type; another might postulate a modality preference with no neurological impairment (since further testing shows the infant to be more interested in auditory than visual stimulation); another might concentrate on the infant's physical coordination, decreases in reflexive behavior, and increased muscle strength; yet another might cue in on the fact that the infant prefers social to nonsocial stimuli (since further testing shows the infant readily tracking a person's face but not a brightly colored ball); someone else might notice that the child is not very alert, spending a great deal of time (relative to other infants his age) asleep or drowsy; yet another hypothesizes that the child needs extra stimulation to elicit a response such that providing a moving face coupled with a voice or a rattle results in tracking while auditory or visual stimuli alone do not; another postulates acuity deficits since that tracking will occur at certain distances but not others; and someone else notices that the mother interacts by relying on vocalizing to her infant and does not provide much visual stimulation (thereby making his disinterest in visual stimulation more understandable from a social viewpoint).

From this simple description, it is clear that different professionals—in this case clinical psychologists, ophthalmologists, neurologists, pediatricians, developmental psychologists, special educators, and physical therapists—may focus on different aspects of the problem rather than on multiple dimensions of the child. Without an interdisciplinary and holistic approach, we will continue to treat disabilities rather than children.

As the opening example of the infant who did not visually track objects illustrated, our knowledge about visual functioning is enhanced by acknowledging the interaction of the different disciplines. Aspects of the visual system do not act separately, but covary in complex ways. The efficacy of physical eye exercises needs to be examined not just in terms of remediating the physiological deficit but in improving visual perception and perhaps even reading ability. The development of corrective lenses for young infants and children has vast implications for the development of visual perception and ultimately knowledge of the social world. And the prediction of later visual deficits from early psychological and medical experience is of concern for such issues as the relationship of anoxia at birth with later blindness and the ability of measures of infant visual perception to predict preschool cognitive functioning.

In order to better understand the interaction of domains, we shall explore the research on visual impairment, assessment of the visual dysfunction, and the links between research, detection, and intervention on vision.

Research on Vision

Need for Research

The importance of an intensive and extensive research effort on developmentally delayed young children cannot be overemphasized. While the past decade has witnessed an explosion of research on normal infant visual development, there has been no corresponding movement in the study of visual development in at risk and handicapped populations. The research involving these populations which has been done to date has treated only the most obvious issues, e.g., the relationship of blindness to supplementary oxygen therapy in anoxic and premature infants (Reed and Stanley, 1977), the efficacy of physical eye exercise for success in reading and perception (Heath *et al.*, 1976), and the developmental deficits and strengths associated with being blind from birth, specifically the cognitive, affective, and social relational concomitants of blindness in infancy and early childhood (Adelson and Fraiberg, 1974; Burlingham, 1975; Dubose, 1976; Fraiberg, 1974, 1971, 1968). Much more needs to be done, in terms of these issues as well as in terms of other aspects of visual development (see the other chapters on vision in this volume).

Role of Research in Assessment

Not only can the need for research be demonstrated, but an examination of the major infant assessment techniques reveals that research, in fact, has been an integral part of the development of these measures. Research enters into the evolution of an assessment tool in one of two ways. First, a research paradigm designed to gather normative data may be adapted to collect such data on deviant development. Second, a clinical tool may be developed and validated through research on normal and deviant infant populations. For example, the first paradigm was used by Lewis (1969, 1975) who developed a measure of visual attention and information processing and later used this measure to study visual attentional deficiencies in at risk populations (Lewis, 1971; Zarin-Ackerman *et al.*, 1977). The second paradigm was used by Brazelton (Neonatal Behavioral Assessment Scale) who developed a clinical neonatal assessment scale, then refined the scale by testing a large number of normal infants, and finally used the scale to detect differences between at risk and normal populations (Brazelton, 1973). Both methodologies are essential in any research effort, especially with regard to the development of assessment instruments.

Research Design

Not only do we need more systematic research on vision, but more systematic and rigorously designed studies are required. Without careful planning, many studies do not provide the information necessary to answer the original question. This problem may be illustrated by looking at the effect of physical eye exercise upon reading scores. The interest in this topic has generated much debate, but little research (cf. Heath *et al.*, 1976). This topic will be used to highlight some principles of research design.

First, the children to be given such exercise must be identified: are these children chosen because they have reading, reading readiness, or visual perceptual deficits, because they have physiological eye problems, or because of some combination of these? Second, before examining the hypothesis that physical eye exercises are related to reading success we need to ask, in a normative sense, if the converse is true: i.e., do children with eye problems have more difficulty learning to read, and if so, how much more difficulty (i.e., are they delayed throughout elementary school, do they lag in initial reading ability but "catch up" fairly rapidly, are they frustrated by their impairment and therefore exhibit behavioral problems that lead to or exacerbate the reading problem, and so on)? Third, once an investigator identifies a sample and determines that eye problems are related to reading difficulties, the choice of treatment must be specified. Here again, many strategies may be employed. At the very least, the type and length of exercise should be specified in great detail. At the very best, several different levels of the treatment would be given to separate groups in order to explicate the issues of how much, what type, and when treatment is effective. As an aside, in many treatment studies, the use of a control group is problematic. If a treatment is believed to be successful, then providing no treatment to a control sample is unethical. Because of this, the use of no treatment control groups has diminished in recent years. In its place has arisen differential treatment or treatment level designs. Different levels of treatment may be given to groups of subjects; using our example, one group may receive eye exercise sessions three times a week, another every day (treatment amount); or one group may participate in exercise sessions four months, another group eight months (treatment length); or one group may begin eye exercises at an earlier age than another group (age of treatment onset). Another design involves differential treatments for several groups, who would receive the same amount of different treatments in order to test the efficacy of different treatment strategies.

Fourth, the outcome measures must be specified. The fact that treatments might be equally effective but may lead to different outcomes must be considered when choosing outcome measures. For example, if an intervention program for the partially sighted stresses social adaptability, then only testing for the cognitive success would be an unfair test of program success, just as only testing for social skills in a cognitively-oriented program would be inappropriate. Also, treatment may have indirect effects or unanticipated outcomes: a program aimed at facilitating visual perception may reduce classroom or home behavioral problems as frustration decreases and self-confidence increases with regard to school success. For these reasons, narrow definitions of success (i.e., intelligence or reading test scores) are likely to limit the outcomes of the study and the understanding of the phenomenon.

Fifth, reliance on group data analyses also may place a limit on the information gathered from a study. In many cases, no significant main effects may be found, even though individuals benefited from the treatment. For example, in most intervention programs, some children will be shown to improve while others will not, or some children will excel in certain domains, some children in other domains. Taking an individual difference approach dictates that the characteristics of those who benefit and those who do not be taken into account. These factors may not always be biological (i.e., those with less severe physical impairment meet with more success), but may be psychological (i.e., those who are more motivated, curious, or interested in their environment may be influenced) or environmental (i.e., those who have parents or siblings who encourage them, spend time teaching them at home, or provide appropriate educational materials in the home have more success in an intervention program). In all likelihood, all three factors covary such that the success of a program or treatment is multicausal and multidirectional (i.e., not only does the more curious child encourage parental interaction but the parent who interacts with her child more facilitates the development of curiosity). In brief, a multicausal model needs to be developed and tested in order to answer adequately questions where psychology, environment, education, and biology interface.

Finally, the expectations concerning the efficacy of treatments may influence the study's outcome. Adult expectations are especially important when studying children, as expectations can influence another's behavior in a kind of self-fulfilling prophecy. The best known example involves the Rosenthal and Jacobson study (1968) of teachers' expectations for their pupils: students who were expected to "bloom" academically did so, even though subjects were randomly assigned to be "bloomers." Although methodological issues have been raised about this procedure, others have found expectations to be salient in a teaching setting (Rosenthal, 1971; Seaver, 1973).

In summary, then, careful consideration of research design issues is crucial, as is the critical evaluation of design in order to determine whether or not a study has answered the initial question or an altogether different one.

Case History Research

As stated earlier, there are at least two separate research methodologies which have been developed, each with different functions, aims, and outcomes. The one that has been discussed at length in the preceding section is hypothesis testing. The other might be termed hypothesis generation, which is the realm of clinical and case history approaches. This approach may be very valuable in that potential hypotheses may be discovered via the observation of individual cases, which may then be tested in a more formal manner.

As an example of the case history approach, the recent study by Enoch and Rabinowitz (1976) may be cited. After a newborn with a congenital dense unilateral cataract had the condition corrected at four days of age, the child's visual acuity in both eyes was assessed for over four months. While the normal eye exhibited the expected developmental increases in visual acuity over the first four months, the aphakic eye did not until acuity was corrected. Even then, the aphakic eye lagged behind the normal eye with respect to acuity. This case provides a clue to the relationship of early visual experience to later visual acuity, and suggests that young children with congenital cataracts should be assessed for visual acuity even after correction has taken place.

Assessment of Visual Impairment

Problems with Assessment Techniques

Current assessments of visual functioning in infancy and early childhood are inadequate for many reasons. First, some of the most widely used psychological detection measures yield nothing more than a description of the young child's level of functioning, usually represented by a single score. In terms of vision, this translates into a categorization of blind versus partially-sighted versus normal, rather than an assessment of amount and type of dysfunction (i.e., visual acuity, visual accommodation, astigmatism, color sightedness). Such a tripartite categorization, in the case of the child who is not classified as blind, gives no information about the nature of the child's deficit or specific strengths and weaknesses, and therefore is of limited use in designing curricula.

Second, many visual detection psychological measures focus on developmental milestones that include other skills. For example, visually following another person's face in part is related to interest in the social environment, while being visually interested in one's own hand movements is related to physical skill (i.e., ability to move the hand through space and being able to control head movements). Although failure on either of these tasks tells us something about the visual system, it is not indicative of visual dysfunction in and of itself. Furthermore, using a milestone approach leads to the visual deficit being detected quite late.

Third, the predictive power of most tests has not been demonstrated. Although not a problem for the diagnosis of blindness, it is a problem for a diagnosis of poor or partial sightedness. Recent vision research suggests that acuity is quite poor at birth (about 20/400 using Snellen equivalents), increasing rapidly through the first six months of life. As another example, the incidence of astigmatism is much higher (ten times) in infants than in older children with the incidence remaining high through six months and declining thereafter, at least through three years (Howland et al., 1978; Mohirdra et al., 1978). These investigators are now following some of their subjects in order to see whether early astigmatism is related to the development of meridional amblyopia.

Innovations in the Assessment of Visual Impairment

Recent research suggests that early visual problems, such as myopia and astigmatism, are related to later visual deficits, *even with* correction. For example, adults who had early myopia have lower visual acuity than normal adults even after the myopia had been corrected (Florentini and Maffei, 1976). A more dramatic example involves the presence of congenital cataracts; after they have been removed, visual problems still occur (von Senden, 1960).

Given these suggestive studies, it seems imperative that norms for visual functioning be developed in order to identify those children who are at risk for later visual deficits and who may benefit from early correction. It is clear, from the preceding discussion, that early assessment must become a priority. In the past decade, a great deal has been learned about the infant's visual system, several visual assessment techniques have been developed or perfected, and norms for visual acuity and astigmatism are being compiled. Several excellent reviews of these advancements have appeared (Haith and Campos, 1977; Maurer, 1975; Salapatek, 1975; Salapatek and Banks, 1978). Only a few of these innovations and findings will be presented here; all are important in terms of assessing visual deficits.

The development of three eye movement systems has been examined extensively in the first months of life. These three are saccadic eye movements (sudden changes in eye position as the eye fixates on different objects in succession), smooth pursuit movements (slow and smooth movements of the eye as the eye follows a slow moving object), and vergence movements (the two eyes converge or diverge in order to fixate on one object in the visual field). All three systems exist at birth but are immature. For example, when following a target, newborns do not exhibit smooth pursuit movements, but exhibit more saccadic movements. Smooth pursuit movements begin to be seen about two months of age, and the movements become smoother over the first year of life (Dayton and Jones, 1964). Saccadic movements in the first few months of life tend to undershoot the target, and multiple saccades are needed to locate the target (Aslin and Salapatek, 1975). The vergence system is also immature, reaching adult competency between three and six months of age (Salapatek and Banks, 1978).

Young infants also show acuity deficits due to immaturity in the first year of life, with visual acuity increasing rapidly in the first six months. Several different techniques have been developed (see Dobson and Teller, in press, and Salapatek and Banks, 1978, for reviews of these techniques). Typically high contrast, black and white patterns are used as the stimuli, and the width of separate stripes that are able to be detected is the measure of acuity. Either two lines separated by a gap or black and white stripes of equal width are used, the latter being called a square-wave grating. Different stripe widths are compared to see when the stripes are discriminable. Stripe widths may be translated into minutes of the arc, spatial frequencies, or approximate Snellen equivalents. Three different responses have been employed to measure visual acuity in the infant—optokinetic nystagmus (OKN), visually-evoked cortical potentials (VEP), and preferential looking.

The preferred method for eliciting OKN involves a rotating drum or canopy that presents stimuli that cover the infant's entire visual field. Rhythmic eye movements are measured as a function of different stripe widths, with discriminable stripe widths eliciting OKN. At one month of age, the Snellen equivalents are approximately 20/400, at six months about 20/100 (cf. Enoch and Rabinowitz, 1976; Fantz *et al.*, 1962).

The visually evoked potential (VEP) technique examines the infant's EEG patterns when different stripe width square-wave gratings are flashed in front of the infant. Snellen equivalents at one month of age are approximately 20/400 and at six months 20/50 to 20/25 (Marg *et al.*, 1976; Sokol and Dobson, 1976).

In the original preferential looking technique developed by Fantz *et al.* (1962), a pair of stimuli are presented simultaneously; one stimulus is a gray field, the other a stripe pattern. When the child looks at the stripe pattern longer than the gray field, it is assumed that the child is differentiating between the gray field and stripe pattern. Visual age acuity estimates are computed in terms of the age at which 75% of the infants exhibit a preference for a particular stripe width or infants exhibit preferential looking 75% of the time. At one month of age, Snellen equivalents are approximately 20/800 to 20/400, while at six months the Snellen equivalent is 20/100. Similar acuity estimates are reported by Dobson and Teller (in press), who have developed a slightly different preferential looking procedure.

Within the three techniques, the visual acuity age estimates are quite similar, although some differences occur across techniques. These are probably a reflection of the different criteria used to estimate acuity, with the stricter criteria being applied in the preferential looking and OKN techniques than in the VEP studies (Dobson and Teller, in press).

These studies suggest that visual acuity may be assessed with accuracy in the first year of life. Given the importance of early visual experience upon later visual deficits and upon learning, the early assessment of visual impairment and correction or remediation must be initiated as early as possible.

Links Among Research, Assessment and Intervention

Research, assessment and intervention are related in several ways with each contributing to knowledge gained in other areas. Illustrations from the field of vision serve to exemplify this point.

In order to identify children at risk for visual impairment and to assess those with known impairments but whose extent of delay is unknown, continuous basic research must be applied to issues of detection. In the field of vision, research methodologies used to learn about early visual preferences, development, and habituation are being applied to test acuity, to examine differences between at risk and normal infants, to predict cognitive dysfunction, and to provide multiple measures of visual impairment. Some of the instruments discussed in the last section are examples of this movement.

Research and intervention also are related; in order to develop appropriate intervention strategies, information about the sequence of development is necessary. Not only does research feed into intervention, but knowledge about what intervention strategies are appropriate provides information about development and hypotheses for testing. In addition, the fact that individualized approaches to intervention have proved more successful than group approaches suggests that research designs also must become more individualized, as was discussed earlier.

Detection and intervention are obviously intertwined, as intervention cannot be conducted without identification. Unfortunately, identification does not always lead to intervention. Of the 70,000 children from birth to 19 who were diagnosed as visually impaired in 1974, only 34 percent were being served educationally (Hobbs, 1975).

Another issue related to the link between detection and intervention has to do with the nature of the diagnosis. The federal definition for visually handicapped is "a visual impairment which, even with correction, adversely affects a child's educational performance. The term includes both partially seeing and blind children" (Public Law 94-142, section 126.5).

As with other handicapping conditions, the federal definition is educational, even though visually handicapped is traditionally defined as "visual acuity in the better eye with correction of not more than 20/200, or a deficit in the visual field so that the widest diameter of vision subtends an angle of no greater than 20°" (Newkirk *et al.*, 1978). This medical definition is used by 26 states, and one-quarter of all of the states do not mention *any* educational component in their definition (Newkirk *et al.*, 1978). One problem with the medical definition is that the range of competencies within those identified as visually impaired is great. For example, two children classified as blind may be totally different: one may be able to read Braille, the other printed material (Gearhart and Weishahn, 1976). Thus, medical definitions need to be replaced by classification systems that include educational components, if we are to provide the most appropriate service to the visually impaired.

Finally, all factors interact since they feed into one another. For example, let us look at the visual attention paradigm. Studies suggest that early visual attention is an indication of visual acuity as well as a predictor of later intellectual development, whether adaptive or dysfunctional (Lewis, 1969, 1971, 1975; Lewis and Brooks-Gunn, 1981). For this reason, the attention task is considered an effective identification/assessment/diagnostic instrument. Thus, basic research leads to detection measures. After the attention task is used to identify and assess, intervention strategies which specifically address the dysfunction indicated by task performance are implemented. Thus, information from a detection measure is used as the basis for specific intervention techniques. During the course of intervention, the attention instrument is used again, to assess and to evaluate. A performance change is a measure of progress and is an evaluation of the intervention strategy and leads to specific modifications of that strategy. The cycle continues until the visual dysfunction has been eliminated or remediated to the fullest extent possible. Meanwhile, research on group data from a large number of these research detection-intervention sequences adds to our knowledge about the predictive power of the attention task as an identification/assessment measure and about the effectiveness of certain intervention techniques.

References

Adelson, E. and Fraiberg, S. Gross motor development in infants blind from birth. *Child Devel.*, 45(1):114–126 (1974).

Aslin, R.N. and Salapatek, P. Saccadic localization of peripheral targets by the very young human infant. *Percept. Psychophysiol.*, 17:293–302 (1975).

Brazelton, T.B. Neonatal behavioral assessment scale. *Clinics in Developmental Medicine, No. 50.* Philadelphia, Pa: Lippincott (1973).

Burlingham, D. Special problems with blind infants: Blind baby profile. *Psychoanal. Study of the Child*, 30:3–13 (1975).

Dayton, G.O., Jr. and Jones, M.H. Analysis of characteristics of fixation reflexes in infants by use of direct current electroculography. *Neurology*, 14:1152–1156 (1964).

Dobson, V. and Teller, D.Y. Assessment of visual activity in human infants: A review and comparison of behavioral and electrophysiological studies. *Vision Research*, in press.

Dubose, R. Developmental needs in blind infants. *New Outlook for the Blind*, 70(2):49–52 (1976).

Enoch, J.M. and Rabinowitz, I.M. Early surgery and visual correction of an infant born with unilateral eye lens opacity. *Documents in Ophthalmol.*, 41:371–382 (1976).

Fantz, R.L., Ordy, J.M. and Udelf, M.S. Maturation of pattern vision in infants during the first six months. *J. Compar. Physiol. Psychol.*, 55:907–917 (1962).

Florentini, A. and Maffei, L. Spatial contrast sensitivity of myopic subjects. *Visual Res.*, 16:437–438 (1976).

Fraiberg, S. Parallel and divergent patterns in blind and sighted infants. *Psychoanal. Study of the Child*, 23:264–300 (1968).

Fraiberg, S. Separation crises in two blind children. *Psychoanal. Study of the Child*, 26:355–371 (1971).

Fraiberg, S. Blind infants and their mothers: An examination of the sign system, in Lewis, M. and Rosenblum, L. (eds.), *The Effect of the Infant on Its Caregiver.* New York: Wiley (1974).

Gearhart, B. and Weishahn, M. *The Handicapped Child in the Regular Classroom.* St. Louis: C.V. Mosby (1976).

Haith, M.M. and Campos, J.J. Human infancy. *Ann. Rev. Psychol.*, 28:251–293 (1977).

Heath, E.J., Cooke, P. and O'dell, N. Eye exercises and reading efficiency. *Academ. Ther.*, 11(4):435–445 (1976).

Hobbs, N. *The Futures of Children.* San Francisco, CA: Jossey-Bass (1975).

Howland, H.C., Atkinson, J., Braddick, D. and French, J. Infant astigmatism measured by photorefraction. *Science*, 202/4365:331–333 (1978).

Lewis, M. Infants' responses to facial stimuli during the first year of life. *Develop. Psychol.*, 1:75–86 (1969).

Lewis, M. A developmental study of the cardiac response to stimulus onset and offset during the first year of life. *Psychophysiology*, 8(6):689–698 (1971).

Lewis, M. Mothers and fathers, boys and girls: Attachment behavior in the one-year old, in Monks, F.J., Hartup, W.W. and deWit, J. (eds.), *Determinants of Behavioral Development*. New York: Academic Press (1972).

Lewis, M. The development of attention and perception in the infant and young child, in Cruickshank, W.M. and Hallahan, D.P. (eds.), *Perceptual and Learning Disabilities in Children* (Vol. 2). Syracuse: University Press, pp. 137–162 (1975).

Lewis, M. and Brooks-Gunn, J. Attention and intelligence. *Intelligence*, 1981(*s*), 3.

Lewis, M. and Rosenblum, L. Introduction, in Lewis, M. and Rosenblum, L. (eds.), *The Effect of the Infant on Its Caregiver: The Origins of Behavior* (Vol. 1). New York: Wiley (1974).

Lewis, M. and Scott, E. A developmental study of infant attentional distribution within the first two years of life. Paper presented at a Symposium on Learning in Early Infancy, at the XX International Congress of Psychology, Tokyo, Japan, August (1972).

Maurer, D. Infant visual perception: Methods of study, in Cohen, L.B. and Salapatek, P. (eds.), *Basic Visual Processes: Infant Perception: From Sensation to Cognition* (Vol. 1). New York: Academic Press (1975).

Marg, E., Freeman, D.N., Peltzman, P. and Goldstein, P.J. Visual acuity development in human infants: Evoked potential measurements. *Investigative Ophthalmology*, 15: 150–153 (1976).

Mohirdra, I., Held, R., Gwiazda, J. and Beill, S. Astigmatism in infants. *Science*, 202/4365: 329–331 (1978).

Newkirk, D., Bloch, D. and Shrybman, J. An analysis of categorical definitions, diagnostic methods, diagnostic criteria and personnel utilization in the classification of handicapped children. The Council for Exceptional Children, March (1978).

Reed, P. and Stanley, F. (eds.) *The Epidemiology of Prematurity*. Baltimore: Urban & Schwaizenberg (1977).

Rosenthal, R. Teacher expectations, in Lesser, G.S. (ed.), *Psychology and the Educational Process*. Glenview, Illinois: Scott Foresman (1971).

Rosenthal, R. and Jacobson, L. *Pygmalion in the Classroom: Teacher Expectation and Pupil's Intellectual Development*. New York: Holt, Rinehart & Winston (1968).

Salapatek, P. Pattern perception in early infancy, in Cohen, L.B. and Salapatek, P. (eds.), *Basic Visual Processes: Infant Perception: From Sensation to Cognition* (Vol. 1). New York: Academic Press (1975).

Salapatek, P. and Banks, M.S. Infant sensory assessment vision, in Minifie, F.O. and Lloyd, L. (eds.), *Communications and Cognitive Abilities: Early Behavioral Assessment*. Baltimore: University Press (1978).

Seaver, W.B. Effects of naturally induced teacher expectancies. *J. Person. and Soc. Psychol.*, 28:333–342 (1973).

Sokol, S. and Dobson, V. Pattern reversal visually evoked potentials in infants. *Investig. Ophthalmol.*, 15:58–62 (1976).

von Senden, M. *Space and Sight*. Translated by P. Heath. New York: Methuen (1960).

Yoshida, R.K., Lewis, M., Schimpler, S., Ackerman, J.Z., Driscoll, J. and Koenigsberger, M.R. The distribution of attention within a group of infants "at risk." Research Bulletin 74-41, Princeton, N.J.: Educational Testing Service (1974).

Zarin-Ackerman, J., Lewis, M. and Driscoll, J. Language development in two-year old normal and risk infants. *Pediatrics*, 59,6(supplement):982 (1977).

5

Intervention Strategies and the State of Education for the Visually Handicapped

RALPH PEABODY

Twenty-five years ago my wife and I were hired to start a public day school program for blind preschool children. Recently, I met a member of that first class. Rob had a profound hearing loss as well as being blind. For several years we could not get appropriate service for him because of his hearing loss. Another of our first students, Ken, is a graduate of Michigan State University presently working for the federal government. Ken was originally diagnosed as mentally retarded, and his parents were urged to commit him to a state institution.

Twenty-five years ago our public school program for blind children was rare. It still is today in many parts of our country. Prior to the 1968 federal Handicapped Children's Early Education Program, it was estimated that of the one million handicapped, preschool children 75 percent were not receiving needed educational services (HEW, 1978). This act, along with incentive funds from P.L. 94-142, has helped to alleviate but not change the situation. Ironically, the critical shortage of services is in some places due to legislative restrictions. For example, Pennsylvania has neither mandatory nor permissive legislation for preschool education for the handicapped. Therefore, no local or state school funds can be used for this purpose, and services are limited by the amounts of federal and private funds available. This is in contrast to Michigan which has mandatory education for the handicapped from birth to age 25.

This lack of services is further compounded by the serious shortage of professionally prepared teachers of the visually handicapped and the number of children not receiving service. Josephine Taylor (1977) of the Bureau of Education for the handicapped wrote:

> ... There may be 58 to 60 thousand children out there needing service. We may assume that we need six thousand teachers tomorrow. For the past several years we have been graduating 250 to 300 teachers a year. We are not even taking care of the attrition rate.

Yet, a preschooler today might have better services than we were able to offer 25 years ago. A network of regional services for the deaf-blind has been established throughout the country, and the Bureau of Education for the Handicapped has funded professional preparation programs for teachers. Multiply handicapped children, including those with severe problems, now have a right to an education.

Twenty-five years ago, the delay in services to a student like Rob was due to another problem, lack of appropriate diagnosis. The clinic's otolaryngologist was actually reluctant to add to the parents' burden the knowledge of deafness in addition to blindness. Relations and cooperation with the parents became extremely strained as I insisted on further diagnostic work at a different hospital. In the meantime, we could not provide the appropriate educational program. Today, both parents and schools have due process rights, unheard of then. When no agreement can be reached during the mandatory Individual Education Program conferences with parents, these rights can be exercised through a hearing.

Now let's examine the situation of Ken in today's terms. He had been identified as mentally retarded on the basis of an IQ score of 79. I shall not go into the safeguards against discriminatory testing in P.L. 94-142. But, one should consider that, "like the IQ scores of culturally and economically dissimilar youngsters, the scores of physically disabled youngsters may not be appropriate measures of those youngsters' learning potential" (Scherr, 1979). In Ken's case, the test was inappropriate. He was mislabeled and excluded from a suitable program. Only through his parents' perseverance was he enrolled in our program, without our knowledge of the previous diagnosis.

Another factor inhibited his development. He had been fitted with cosmetic prostheses in both eyes when quite young. One day during play one prosthesis fell out and was not immediately replaced. We then observed that he seemed to be moving about with more confidence. After some probing and discussion, Ken affirmed that "maybe" he could tell where things were a little better without the prosthesis. Granted, he could at most only perceive shadows. But this was useful vision and he had not been receiving any visual efficiency training. At approximately that time Barraga was conducting research which showed visual efficiency training to be effective in increasing visual functioning (Barraga, 1964).

There are interesting aspects to this "discovery" of visual ability. First, and very significant, Ken could not tell us he had any visual functioning. He did not know it! A child with a congenital deprivation, having no notion of normalcy, cannot describe his own situation. In working with low-vision or partially seeing children we can make no *assumptions*. We must discover with the child his functional abilities through learning and observation.

Second, it was unknown through examination that there was some usable vision. This is not at all uncommon, nor is the improvement of visual efficiency with training.

A great deal of harm and unnecessary deprivation in normal development has occurred from the assumption that a child lacks useful vision. This has also caused parents a great deal of anguish and despair. It is most important that specialists explain the implications of residual vision to them at the time of diagnosis. We cannot assume that people understand that most of the blind can see. It has been very wisely stated that "more people have been blinded by definition than any other cause" (Greenwood, 1963).

In terms of the idea of "possibilities of normal development," there are some cautions we must exercise. Over the past few decades sensitive observations have been made of the growth and development of visually handicapped infants. Gathered together (Warren, 1977), they form much of the basis of our knowledge. We do not have a large bank of research data, as our population is not only small but our children are frequently so dissimilar to each other that we must carefully scrutinize any generalizations.

Consider briefly the effects of the age at onset of the visual disability on growth and development. The congenitally blinded person will have no visual memory or references. Everything must be learned assuming no previous visual experiences. Therefore, all concepts the person forms will have to be carefully constructed, learning small parts and putting them into a whole. On the other hand, the adventitiously blinded person may be able to visualize new learning tasks based on previous experiences. The amount of experiences, of course, will vary with the age at the time of impairment.

Gruber has spoken of blindness as occurring when one is "unable to manage life by visual means." This is rather understandable when the person is totally blind, a rare condition among our child population, most of whom have *some useful residual vision.* For these students with some vision, it is even more important to examine Gruber's statement. The implication is that people with limited vision (partially seeing) will be able to manage their lives with visual means in some environments or for some tasks and be unable to do so in others. Therefore, the totally blind person lives with a visual "constant" and the person with limited vision lives with a visual "variable." This is important in understanding that a person may be "blind" at one moment and not the next, depending on the environment and/or the task. It is also extremely important to consider this visual variability in educational assessment and planning (Gruber, 1966).

Our professional literature shows that blind children appear to develop along the same pattern as normal children, but not at the same rate. We can expect all the developmental stages and levels identified for normal children, but we cannot expect them at the same ages. Because of the age discrepancies, the literature frequently refers to blind children's "developmental lags."

At this point I part company with many of my colleagues. If it is *normal* for the blind child to accomplish developmental levels at a later age, then that should not be considered a developmental lag but normal development. When parents and others hear of developmental lags, they expect them and can easily not be attuned to measures to help prevent them. What must be done is to understand visually related development in order to appreciate the idiosyncrasies of the blind child's development. For example, studies show that blind children walk considerably later than sighted children. Fraiberg (1977) has shown that self-initiated mobility follows the ability to reach out on a sound cue. While sound alone probably does not have the motivation or incentive of a visual cue, Fraiberg's intervention program, establishing sound and touch relationships, has had infants walking at much earlier ages. This is but one example of a visually related development and its effect on the blind infant.

A discussion of young blind children must include some consideration of stereotypic behavior which is quite common among congenitally blind children. "Blindisms," as they are sometimes called, are large or small body movements which are considered a form of sensory stimulation. They may include head shaking, shaking of the hands, rocking, swaying or eye poking, to name but a few. They resemble the same types of mannerisms displayed by autistic children. This similarity has often led to the belief that the blind child may also be disturbed or autistic, while in fact such is not the case. Many explanations have been advanced for this behavior (Warren, 1977). The prevailing theory is that it is a compensatory stimulation to the lack of visual stimulation. It is possible that the behavior originated out of a need. It is of concern to us because when the child is indulging in this self-stimulating behavior, he is not interacting with, manipulating or learning about his environment. He is, in fact, withdrawing. Under stress conditions, the behavior increases, leading to concern about the child's coping mechanisms. This behavior should be prevented as much as possible through early intervention programs, not merely because it is socially unacceptable, but because it obviously impedes the "possibilities for normal growth and development." When it is already ingrained in the child's behavioral repertoire, behavior modification programs have helped eliminate this stereotypic self-stimulation.

In determining specific intervention strategies, we must look carefully at the task in relation to the individual and the environment. Consider this child:

Mike is an albino, eight-year-old boy with extreme sensitivity to bright light (photophobia). Although somewhat near-sighted (myopic), he functions quite well in the classroom at his desk (functions like a person with normal sight). He does have some problems with seeing the blackboard from his seat and seeing the teacher when the teacher stands in front of the windows to talk (Mike is now functioning as a person with limited or partial vision). Mike has extreme trouble when leaving the school to go to the playground on a bright sunny day (at this point he may be functioning as a blind person).

Now consider a preschool child who does not seem to be progressing appropriately in language development and in exploring the environment as much as might be desired. The parents report that they have complied with suggestions for working with the child. On each visit to the child's home, the teacher realized that the television was playing rather loudly. The mother let it be known that she keeps the television on for company. Think now of the child, totally blind. With the television on, the child was also "deaf" to meaningful and normal language and environmental sounds as they were masked out. So, although there was nothing wrong with the child and the intervention tasks were appropriate, the environment prohibited learning.

Now let us consider areas in which the teacher is likely to initiate intervention strategies. I have taken two sources directly from the literature: *Alive ... Aware ... A Person,* by Rosemary O'Brien (1976) and *Vision Up* by Croft and Robinson (1976). Both of these are developmentally based, carefully sequenced and age-referenced.

O'Brien's areas include: motor development, language development, sensory/perceptual development, self and social awareness and cognitive/creativity. Similarly, *Vision Up* includes: self-help; physical development; the home; social, personal and intellectual development; and language development.

These two resources are very valuable tools, but sensitivity must be exercised when using a prepared curriculum. Think of the two children described above. If these curriculum tasks were taught without an awareness of the environment as well as unique characteristics of the child, learning might be impeded. We professionals are part of a child's ecological system.

> This system consists of the child and the settings and the individuals within these settings that are a part of the child's early life. All parts of the system influence all other parts of the system. Physical and psychological as well as social factors are involved. Thus assessments and interventions focus on the exchange between the child, the settings in which he participates, and the significant individuals who interact with him. Each child's ecological system is unique. The objective is not merely to change or improve the child but to make the total system work. Change in any part of the system, or in several parts, may accomplish this purpose. And changes may be brought

about through interventions affecting physical, psychological, or social functioning of one or more of the components of the system (Hobbs, 1975, p. 114).

We are also part of a team.

Each team is a unique blend of the professional and personal characteristics of its members, its effectiveness determined in large part by the dynamics of that configuration. The similarities, differences and areas of overlap among the various professionals provide a source of potential conflict and misunderstanding. . . (Ducanis and Golin, 1979, p. 9).

These conflicts and misunderstandings can be eliminated through greater personal contact and discussion. For example, a familiar teacher assessing a child in his familiar home surroundings may observe the child functioning on quite a different level than in a strange clinic. Professionals talking to parents independently may inadvertently give quite contrasting impressions.

Another misunderstanding may occur when a child is referred to another professional. We can easily assume that a certain service will be provided, which that person may not see as his role. We need to know much more about each other to develop the most appropriate and effective intervention strategies. On behalf of all teachers I would like to issue each of you an invitation to contact us about any child with whom we are both concerned.

References

Barraga, N.C. *Increased Visual Behavior in Low Vision Children*. New York: American Foundation for the Blind (1964).

Croft, N.B. and Robinson, L.W. *Project Vision-Up Curriculum. A Training Program For Preschool Handicapped Children*. Boise, Idaho: Educational Products Training Foundation (1976).

Ducanis, A.J. and Golin, A.K. *The Interdisciplinary Health Care Team*. Germantown, MD: Aspen Systems Corporation (1979).

Federal Aid to Preschool Education, Programs for the Handicapped, Office for Handicapped Individuals, H.E.W., Washington, D.C. (1978).

Fraiberg, S. *Insights from the Blind*. New York: Basic Books (1977).

Greenwood, L.H. Shots in the Dark, in Schloss, I.P. Implications of Altering the Definition of Blindness. *American Foundation for the Blind, Research Bulletin No. 3*. New York: American Foundation for the Blind, 111 (August (1963).

Gruber, K.F. Self concept of the visually impaired. Symposium presented at a meeting for *The Special Education and Vocational Rehabilitation of the Visually Impaired*. New York: Teachers College, Columbia University (1966).

Hobbs, N. *The Futures of Children*. San Francisco, Ca.: Jossey-Bass, Inc. (1976).

O'Brien, R. *Alive . . . Aware . . . A Person.* Rockville, Md.: Montgomery County Public Schools (1976).

Norris, M., Spaulding, P. and Brane, F. *Blindness in Children.* Chicago, Ill.: The University of Chicago Press (1957).

Scherr, J.E. Danger—testing in progress. *Amicus,* Vol. 4, No. 2, National Center for Law and the Handicapped, March/April (1979).

Taylor, J.L. Competency based programs: a national perspective. *J. Visual Impairment and Blindness.* New York, May (1978).

Warren, D.H. *Blindness and Early Childhood Development.* New York: American Foundation for the Blind (1977).

6

Theoretical Issues in the Development of Audition

ROBERT J. RUBEN
ISABELLE RAPIN

Introduction

Audition is the process of hearing or listening. The development of this ability in all species examined depends upon a number of sequential events. They include the development of a normal anatomic transformer (middle ear) and transducer (inner ear); a central nervous system and its auditory afferent and efferent connections; and, in birds and mammals, exposure to appropriate auditory stimuli—an essential component of the normal development of audition. Failure either in the formation of any structural part or in the exposure to sound stimuli will result in deviant auditory function for a particular individual. There are at least three types of developmental errors of exposure to sound which can result in abnormal audition in the developing organism: in the quality, the quantity and the timing of the sound stimulus.

Adequate auditory development in man, and perhaps some other species with a complex and sophisticated auditory communication system that substantively affects genetic fitness determines, the individual's ability to use this modality of communication. Inadequate auditory communication is highly detrimental. The more the species relies on complex auditory communication, the greater the detriment of abnormal audition. Thus, a human society based on manual skills, e.g., the farming economy of Europe in the 14th century, can tolerate a high rate of illiteracy and marginal verbal communication skills without detriment. In a society based on communicative skills, e.g., the contemporary, service-oriented, North American society, individuals with even minor difficulties in auditory and verbal communication will be at a great disadvantage. Abnormalities of audition and communication skills, other than total deafness, would not have been recognized in the Middle Ages and if recognized would not have been significant for the population. Today the same abnormalities are recognized and are highly significant for the fitness of the individual and consequently the society.

Development — Anatomic

The basic histologic outline for the anatomic development of the ear has been known since the last half of the 19th century (Boettcher, 1869; Retzius, 1881, 1884). More recently Bast and Anson (1949), Bredberg (1968) and Sher (1971) have refined these original observations. The mammalian cochlea initially forms from an otic placode on the dorsolateral anterior aspect of the head region of the embryo. The placode invaginates to form an otic cup and this process continues until an otic cyst is formed. Studies by Li *et al.* (1978) have shown in the mouse that the cells of the otocyst that have formed the ventral portion will become the cochlea. The otocyst then begins to take on the shape of the mature labyrinth and in man is anatomically mature at approximately the fifth or sixth month of fetal life.

The epithelium of the cochlea, the organ of Corti, consists of a number of different cell types, some of which are primary receptor cells, the hair cells, and other supporting cells, Hensen's cells, Deiters' cells, etc. These cells have been found to be end-state cells (Ruben, 1967) in that in the mature animal they are not increased or replaced. In the mouse these cells undergo their terminal mitosis during the 13th and 14th days of gestation. There are no comparable data for man, but while extrapolation from mouse to man is imperfect, one can surmise that the cells comprising the organ of Corti in man probably undergo their terminal mitosis by the end of the second month of fetal life. Thus, the receptor cells which serve to transduce sound are laid down early in fetal life and must serve the organism until death. Any loss of these cells, either during fetal life or postpartum, will result in hearing loss.

The histologic differentiation of these cells occurs at various times after terminal mitosis. It appears to start near the base of the cochlea (the high-tone transducer area) and spread apically (the low-tone transducer portion of the cochlea) with the cells of the apex differentiating last. The inner hair cells differentiate before the outer hair cells.

Studies in the kitten (Pujol *et al.*, 1978) reveal that initially the inner hair cells are innervated by both afferents and efferents with very little afferent innervation of the outer hair cells. As the kitten matures, there is an increase in afferent and efferent innervation of the outer hair cells with decreased efferent innervation of the inner hair cells. The process of innervation of the inner hair cells coincides with the first physiologic and behavioral responses to sound (Pujol, 1972).

The mechanisms which control the process of differentiation from the otic placode to the mature cochlea are now being defined (Van De Water *et al.,* in press). It would appear that in the mouse the neural tube and the cephalic mesenchyma are essential for the development of the early otocyst. The neural tube is needed first but is gradually supplanted by the action of the cephalic and then the periotic mesenchyma. Deol, who has studied a number of mutant mice, demonstrated the abnormalities of the developing neural tube will result in abnormalities of the structure of the inner ear (Deol, 1978). Organ culture studies indicate that an abnormally programmed neural tube may transmit an abnormal message to a normal mouse otocyst. The converse also appears to obtain in that a normal neural tube may lessen the abnormalities in an abnormal otocyst (Van De Water, personal communication).

Many questions remain to be answered concerning the development of the mammalian inner ear at the tissue and cellular levels. Among those questions pertinent to an understanding of audition are the factors controlling the peripheral innervation of the cochlea. Studies have shown that peripheral innervation is not necessary for the development of the sensory structures of the otocyst and do not appear to be necessary for the maintenance of the sensory structures in the adult (Ruben *et al.,* 1963; Van De Water, 1976). The factors that cause each nerve fiber to connect with specific hair cells and to a specific cell in the cochlear nucleus complex are being studied. Experiments in which one statoacoustic ganglion complex is placed between two growing otocysts have been carried out in our laboratory, and our preliminary results show that nerve fibers will grow to both otocysts. There are, as expected, mechanisms which control this neuronal specificity. In what way these patterns of growth occur and how they are regulated are, at present, unknown.

It is known that in the cat the pattern of peripheral innervation is not completed until after physiologic and behavioral evidence of hearing. Whether or not the same is true of central connections is not entirely known. Mlonyeni (1967) states that in the mouse the number of differentiated neurons in the ventral part of the cochlear nucleus reaches adult values on the 11th postnatal day, but in the dorsal portion not until the 16th day. Webster (in press) showed that the soma of the neurons of the brain stem auditory nuclei achieve adult size by the 12th postpartum day. There is no information about the formation of synapses or the development of dendritic arborization in the central nuclei.

Thus, it would appear that the ear in mammals may not be committed to a fixed pattern of peripheral innervation until after it is functional, which leaves the possibility of environmental sound causing a change in the neural pattern of auditory input. It is also known that the primary auditory nuclei of the cochlear nucleus complex in the mouse show evidence of maturation of cell and soma size during the period of postfunctional development. Thus, there may also be changes in the pattern of brain stem innervation during environmental exposure to sound.

A number of studies indicate that both the developing and mature auditory central nervous system show a certain amount of anatomical plasticity (Ruben, in press). The first of these studies was by Levi-Montalcini (1949), later expanded by Parks (1979). The studies consisted in removing the otocyst of the developing chick unilaterally, allowing the embryo to continue to develop. The central auditory nervous system of embryologically deafferentated chicks was examined and found to have on the ablated side anatomical differences in the primary auditory nuclei. These differences were a decrease in the size of the nuclei and in the number of cells composing the nuclei, alteration in shape of the nuclear mass, and a different position of the primary auditory nuclei within the brain stem. These studies have shown, in the developing chick, that the auditory afferents exert control over the development of the primary portion of the central auditory nervous system.

Experiments assessing the effects of destruction of the mature cochlea and its afferents show that there is degeneration in both primary and secondary central auditory nuclei (Ruben, in press). Van den Pol et al. (1979) stated that in the posthatched chick degeneration in secondary and tertiary auditory nuclei occurs after removal of the inner ear. In a series of studies Gulley et al. (1978) found significant changes in the pre- and post-synaptic organelles of the primary (anteroventral cochlear nucleus) brain stem auditory nuclei in the waltzing guinea pig (an autosomal dominant, mutant, guinea pig in which there is primary hair cell degeneration with a minimal amount of neural degeneration).

Several experiments have been carried out to explore the possibility that degeneration in central auditory nuclei may result from a diminution of auditory stimulation without disruption of the transducer or primary afferents. Coleman and O'Connor (1979) removed the middle ear ossicles from rat pups and found a decrease in the size of the spherical cells in the anteroventral cochlear nucleus. The effect was only noted in the monaural preparations and not in animals whose ossicles had been removed from both ears (these data are congruent with the physiologic data of Clopton; see section on physiology, Clopton and Silverman, 1977). Webster and Webster (1977 and in press) found that in young mice sound deprivation or occlusion of the middle ear resulted in a statistically significant decrease in the size of various cell groups in primary and secondary central auditory nuclei. The Websters also noted that the decrease did not result if the auditory deprivation occurred later in the animal's life, nor could the effect be reversed by exposure to auditory stimuli after a period of deprivation.

This information shows that the central and peripheral auditory systems exert reciprocal control over each other. Early in embryonic life the major inducer for the inner ear is the developing rhombencephalon. As the inner ear matures, its input is necessary for the organization of at least part of the central auditory nervous system. As the organism matures to a state in which the peripheral auditory system is functional, input from this system appears to be necessary to control of maturation and innervation of portions of the central auditory system. In the mouse and the rat sensory input will affect the anatomic configuration of the auditory central nervous system.

Studies of human material in this area are difficult because of many confounding variables. Studies of the brains of deaf patients are being undertaken, but one must be sure that the peripheral lesion occurred before the central lesion, as would be the case in postnatally acquired deafness. In other cases, e.g., rubella embryopathy or Waardenburg's syndrome, the same teratogen may have affected both sites independently. Some data (Marx, 1925) correlate the effects of anencephaly, a massive anomaly of the skull and brain, with abnormal formation of the inner ear. Our own clinical experience indicates that severe central nervous system malformations other than anencephaly may be associated with normal inner ears, at least as assessed by x-ray or auditory evoked potential testing. Minor abnormalities of the bony structure of the inner ear have also been found in infants without obvious CNS malformation.

Development — Electrophysiologic

The electrophysiologic development of the cochlea and the VIIIth nerve has been studied in a number of different mammals including the mouse, rat, opossum, rabbit, cat, and hamster (Alford and Ruben, 1963; Anggard, 1965; Brugge et al., 1978; Clopton and Winfield, 1976; Finck et al., 1972; Konishi, 1970; Larsell et al., 1935; Mair et al., 1978; McCrady et al., 1937, 1940; Mikaelian and Ruben, 1965; Pujol, 1972). These studies found that the functional development of hair cells, as measured by the cochlear microphonic, appears to start near the base and extend to the remainder of the base and to the apex of the cochlea. There is an increase both in sensitivity and in the range of frequencies to which they respond. These physiologic changes parallel the anatomic changes in the organ of Corti (Pujol and Hilding, 1973), although no one specific change in the organ of Corti has been found to be responsible for reactivity of the hair cells. The two D.C. potentials, the summating potential and the endocochlear potential, have been shown to develop in conjunction with the development of the cochlear microphonic (Anggard, 1965). The ability of the VIIIth nerve to transmit messages from the cochlea parallels cochlear development (Konishi, 1970).

Pujol (1972) has shown that the various auditory centers of the central nervous system, including the cochlear nucleus, inferior colliculus, medial geniculate body, and auditory cortex, have a centripetal pattern of maturation. Studies of the latency of auditory evoked responses indicate that maturation proceeds from the periphery to the cortex. Pujol (1972) also examined other physiologic patterns of cell reactivity. He recorded from single units within the cochlear nucleus, inferior colliculus and medial geniculate body in the developing kitten. He found that initially cells in the central auditory nuclei are capable of "on" responses. They then developed rhythmic responses which are followed by the mature pattern of firing throughout stimulation. He also examined the development of inhibitory mechanisms. His tentative conclusion was that they make their appearance first in the inferior colliculus and medial geniculate body; their onset is relatively late in the maturational process.

Aitken *et al.* (1975) showed that at first the turning curves of single units in the pericentral portion of the cochlear nucleus of the kitten are broader than those of cells in its central portion. The threshold of these units drops from 100 dB at the 6th to 11th day of life to near 40 dB in the adult. This marked drop in threshold occurs from the 11th to the 21st postpartum days, and tonotopic organization of the central nucleus of the inferior colliculus is observable by the 11th day. The investigators felt that some of these findings could be accounted for by anatomic maturation of the central nervous system. Several observers (Hassmannova and Myslivecek, 1967; Marty and Thomas, 1963) have found that the central nervous system may be capable of processing auditory information before the cochlea matures. The investigations included a series of studies in which developing animals, cats and rats, had their medial geniculate bodies stimulated electrically before there was evidence of hearing based on the ability to record evoked potentials from the VIIIth nerve. Potentials were evoked within the cortex by electrical stimulation of the medial geniculate. These studies concluded that the central auditory system can transmit information before the end organ and VIIIth nerve are able to transmit it to the central nervous system.

Electrophysiologic studies of the development of audition have been carried out (Ohlrich *et al.*, 1978; Schulman-Galambos and Galambos, 1975, 1979; Starr *et al.*, 1977) in both premature and term infants by recording brain stem and cortical auditory evoked potentials. Starr *et al.* (1977) found a decrease in latency and an increase in amplitude of brain stem potentials with age. The earliest studies were performed in infants at 25 weeks gestational age. The largest shift occurred at 34 weeks gestational age. Wave forms recorded by this technique are felt to represent the evoked responses from the various auditory relays. The first wave is thought to originate from the VIIIth nerve and the V wave from the region of the inferior colliculus. Wave I, purportedly from the VIIIth nerve, has been observed to mature earlier (at approximately five to seven months depending on the stimulus used) (Hecox, 1975; Salamy *et al.*, 1975) than wave V, which is more central. It would appear that in man, as well as in the rodent species studied, there is a peripheral to central pattern of physiologic development. However, Graziani *et al.* (1968) and Starr *et al.* (1977) also noted that a cortical response could be recorded in infants of less than 28 weeks gestational age at a time when the same sound stimulus did not elicit a recordable brain stem auditory evoked potential (Starr *et al.*, 1977). This discrepancy may reflect the small amplitude of waves generated by the brain stem because of poorly synchronized firing or of some other factor in the organization of the developing central auditory nervous system in man.

Maturation of the electrophysiologic response in man appears to depend upon anatomic maturation of the inner ear (Bredberg, 1968). Keith (1975) examined the possibility that the middle ear may be responsible for decreased sensitivity of auditory acuity in newborns. He found that term infants 2½ to 20 hours after birth have normally functioning middle ears when assessed by measures of middle ear compliance, tympanometry and middle ear pressure. The electrophysiologic data suggest that the term infant has anatomically mature middle and inner ears and that the maturation of the remainder of the auditory system takes place over the next 18 months.

Auditory deprivation has been shown in animals to have electrophysiologic consequences both in the periphery and centrally. In two strains of mice with genetically determined progressive inner ear deafness, recordings of the cochlear microphonic and VIIIth nerve action potential (Mikaelian *et al.*, 1965; Mikaelian and Ruben, 1964, 1965) demonstrated increased sensitivity and narrowing of the frequency range. Central effects (Henry and Lepkowski, 1978) of progressive hearing loss were found at the level of the inferior colliculus.

Electrophysiologic changes in the colliculus were found in rats who had been sound deprived for a number of weeks or months starting at birth or soon afterwards. Batkin *et al.* (1970) showed that rats deprived for eight months had a 20 dB increase in threshold when tested by auditory evoked potentials.

The consequences of unilateral auditory deprivation have been studied in the rat (Clopton and Silverman, 1977; Silverman and Clopton, 1977). There is a decrease in the number of units in the inferior colliculus that respond when the deprived ear is stimulated. The normal inhibition that occurs when sound is presented binaurally does not occur in animals who sustained unilateral deprivation. This effect is not present when the deprivation was binaural. Deprivation has to occur between the 10th and 60th days after birth in order to produce these effects; there is no effect if deprivation occurred later than the 60th postpartum day.

The pattern of sound stimulation experienced by young rats during the first four months of life was found to influence the pattern of response at the collicular level (Clopton and Winfield, 1976). The firing rate of single units in the inferior colliculus increased selectively when stimulated with a familiar sound pattern compared to their firing rate with a novel sound pattern. This evidence indicates that in the rat the responsivity of cells at the level of the inferior colliculus can be modified by auditory experience.

Science has just started to outline the electrophysiologic patterns of auditory development in various species. As a general principle, they appear to mature centripetally, starting from the periphery and occurring last at the cortical level. Thus far, most of the investigators have examined sensitivity and frequency selectivity, and only one study has looked at the development of integrative function in the auditory system. The physiologic effects of loss of the peripheral system are not well known.

The physiology of the auditory system is modified by environmental sound, judging by the deprivation studies and the one study (Clopton and Winfield, 1976) in which the reactivity of units was modified based on their previous pattern of sound exposure. Both the anatomic and physiologic studies thus indicate that deprivation appears to be effective in the rodent only during the immediate postpartum period. Whether or not these findings apply to man is not known, but one would be surprised if the same were not true for man since his central nervous system also continues to develop after birth. Plasticity is likely to play a more important role for the premature than the term infant because of greater immaturity of the central nervous system. The extent to which sound controls the development of the auditory system is unknown except for the changes in sensitivity to loudness and loss of binaural interaction just described and the one experiment showing modification of the sensitivity of single units in response to changes in sound patterns.

Development — Behavioral

Study of the behavioral correlates of auditory development is limited by the methodologies available to assess this behavior. It is particularly difficult when working with immature organisms, be they birds, rats, mice or children. Many kinds of measurements have been used in an attempt to correlate the organism's response to a particular stimulus. Some studies have relied on performed behavioral patterns occurring in response to sound.

The ontogeny of behavioral responses to sound correlates well with the physiologic data (Ehret, 1976, 1977; Warfield et al., 1968). Ehret's studies in the mouse show that even after physiologic and anatomic maturation of the ear and VIIIth nerve are complete, threshold for pure tones and masked threshold continue to decrease. These findings were attributed to the late maturation of the central auditory system in this species. The data imply that final maturation of audition in the mouse may depend upon central mechanisms and that these maturational processes are centripetal. This theory agrees with the known anatomic and physiologic information obtained from this and other species.

In man the development of behavioral responses to sound appears to occur as early as the 20th fetal week (Eisenberg, 1976; Northern and Downs, 1974). That the premature infant will respond behaviorally to sound has also been well documented. There is little information about the frequency range, loudness and difference limens of the premature infant's responses to sound.

The term infant responds to a variety of auditory stimuli, depending upon his level of arousal, the repetition rate and the character of the stimulus. Threshold for behavioral responses to sound decreases during the first two to three years of life. These changes and other factors must be taken into account before any statement is made about an absolute behavioral threshold in the infant.

Ability to discriminate among speech sounds occurs early in the normal human infant. Kuhl (1976) states that one- to three-month-old infants can discriminate all of the speech sounds phonologically relevant in the English language. Skinner (1978) has summarized available information concerning infants' perception of speech sounds. At two weeks of age the infant can recognize the overall rhythmic pattern of speech. The ability to discriminate between a statement and a question which used the same words but a different intonational pattern is apparent at eight months. Menyuk (1977) discussed another aspect of the development of audition, the more complex interaction between the perception and mechanisms of speech production, that is, between hearing and vocalization. This can be measured by studying the effects of delayed auditory feedback. In the adult, delaying the auditory feedback of an individual's voice will slow the rate of his speech. This effect was reported not to be seen in children at one year, nine months of age. It began at two years and four months and was at four years of age similar to the adult response, indicating that the complex operations required for central auditory processing may take a number of years to be fully developed in man.

The nature of environmental sound to which the developing organism is exposed seems to determine, in part, its eventual auditory capabilities. Most of the studies have used various types of sensory deprivation. Gottlieb (1976) showed that if a duckling is deprived of its own voice immediately before hatching it will not be able to discriminate its mother's call as would ducklings not deprived of their own cries. Further experiments showed that the deficit involves a decrease in the ability to attend to the high-frequency component of the maternal call. Exposure to other sounds in the high-frequency range compensates in part for the deprivation. The effect persists up to 65 hours after hatching.

Kerr (in press) plugged the ears of prehatched, 18½-day-old chick embryos. This resulted in a 40-dB attenuation of sound which was maintained to the third or fourth day posthatching. The ability of the deprived chicks to discriminate among auditory stimuli was decreased when compared to normal.

One of the earliest studies on the behavioral effects of auditory deprivation in animals was carried out by Wolf (1943) in the rat. He raised rats with either visual or auditory deprivation. Animals deprived of auditory stimulation competed better for food when visual cues were used than with auditory cues. The visually deprived animals did better in food competition tasks when attending to auditory stimuli than to visual stimuli.

Tees (1967) noted that rats who underwent auditory deprivation after birth took longer to discriminate between patterns, and discriminations were poorer than in normal rats. He felt that auditory deprivation damaged the development of auditory acuity in these animals. Thus, it would appear that in the rat ability to process auditory patterns depends to some degree on sensory input.

The effect of auditory trauma producing hearing loss has been investigated in certain strains of mice (Saunders and Bock, 1978). It appears that a partial loss of peripheral auditory function during the early postpartum period in these mice increases the responsiveness of the central auditory nervous system, since later exposure to noise will result in epileptic seizures. "Disuse supersensitivity" has been hypothesized to account for this effect. Henry *et al.* (1975) studied this problem by comparing mice with a genetic hearing loss to mice with experimentally produced conductive hearing loss. They found that audiogenic seizures could be induced in both groups. This evidence further supports the occurrence of disuse supersensitivity during early periods of development. These studies of priming for audiogenic seizures provide evidence that environmental sound can alter the behavioral responsiveness of the central nervous system.

Studies of the behavioral effects of the acoustic environment in maturing infants have followed several lines of research. Perhaps the most obvious was to investigate the behavioral consequences of congenital hearing loss (Rapin, 1979). The effects of severe to profound sensory neural hearing loss on the individual are pleomorphic. Most congenitally deaf individuals exhibit substantial deficits in linguistic skills and are subject to profound experiential deprivation (Conrad, 1979). They are deficient economically and socially (Schein and Delk, 1974). The well-known difference between the consequences of severe to profound deafness acquired before the age of two compared to deafness acquired later in life can be attributed to the better linguistic ability of this latter group (Lenneberg, 1967; Rapin, 1979; Schein and Delk, 1974).

The effect in man of auditory deprivation unassociated with loss of end organ function has also been examined. Perhaps the earliest study was described by Herodotus (1946 edition). He reported that Pharaoh Psammetichus had two infants raised in total isolation from human speech and nursed by goats. Their first recorded utterance, at the age of two, was "becos," which Itard (1821) conjectures was an imitation of the bleeting of the goat.

There have been other children whom circumstances caused to be raised with little or minimal exposure to speech. The best known are the boy, Victor (Lane, 1976), and the girl, Genie (Curtiss, 1977). Many confounding variables exist in both these cases, such as the possibility of mental retardation and the lack of complete history to determine when they were isolated from speech. As far as can be ascertained, both children could hear normally. Both had no language when they were first brought to professional attention. Victor did not develop speech but was able to communicate to a modest extent by gesture. Genie did develop some rudiments of spoken language, but at the time of the report her language was still grossly immature. These cases underscore that prolonged exposure to spoken language at the right age is required for normal language acquisition.

A large number of infants and children because of otitis media, have undergone a modest amount of auditory deprivation during their first few years of life. Many studies attempted to show that children who had otitis media suffered a cognitive deficit as a direct or indirect consequence of deficient linguistic skills secondary to their auditory deprivation (Rapin, 1979, in press). All of these studies suffer from various difficulties in their design. Some use esoteric groups, e.g., Australian aborigines. Others may not provide information on the extent or duration of the hearing loss, include normal controls, or indicate the child's hearing level at the time of testing. Nevertheless, when the entire body of data is considered, there would appear to be a correlation between modest auditory deprivation during the first two years of life and a deficit in linguistically determined cognitive function during later childhood and adolescence. Whether or not these effects are permanent and invariably present is not known.

One of the earliest clinical descriptions of the effects of middle ear effusion is that of a seven-year-old who had middle ear infections up to the age of three (Eisen, 1962). Clinical examination of this boy at age seven, when his hearing was normal, showed him to be behaving like a hearing-impaired child: He had difficulty localizing sound and determining where background sounds came from; he did not discriminate words clearly; his fund of general knowledge was impoverished; he could not find words to express his thoughts; he had difficulty with tasks requiring abstraction and conceptualization; he could not understand what was expected of him in social situations and he did not understand other peoples' social behavior. There was a delay between his being asked a question and his answer, as if he were thinking over the question. Which of these effects were due to the hearing loss before the age of three and what is the role of other intrinsic and extrinsic factors are not known.

Needleman (1977) examined speech and language development in a small group of children between ages three and eight in whom otitis media had been documented before 18 months of age and had persisted for at least two years. She found that children who had had otitis media did significantly worse in word articulation, articulation of connected speech and in the use of word endings than normal children. While the study group was small and long-term effects were not known, there were clear deficiencies in the children's ability to discriminate some types of speech sounds.

Available studies of the impact of auditory deprivation have shown that there is a correlation between the anatomic and physiologic effects of deprivation and their behavioral consequences. Behavioral effects of both partial and total auditory deprivation appear to be significant in the species examined. They impair the ability of the organism to make fine discriminations and in man jeopardize the child's linguistic development. The impact of this impairment is not only cognitive but also social and psychological.

Summary and Conclusions

Plasticity of the auditory system is one of the dominant theoretical issues in the development of audition. There is evidence indicating that early in embryonic life the central nervous system plays a major role in the orderly development of the inner ear. The developing inner ear in turn appears to control the anatomic formation of the central auditory nervous system. As the animal matures, auditory stimulation governs the organism's physiologic, behavioral and auditory abilities. The effects of environmental sound in shaping the organism's ability to hear appear to occur before the central auditory nervous system matures. Available information would indicate that the maturation of the auditory system is centripetal, proceeding from the inner ear to the auditory cortex. Environmental sound would appear to have its greatest effect in shaping auditory ability from the time the inner ear and VIIIth nerve first become functional to the time when maturation of the central nervous system is achieved. Major theoretical questions to be answered are the extent to which environmental sounds are able to shape the developing auditory system and the long-term effects of various acoustical environments on the organism's auditory ability.

These problems are important to the prevention and care of auditory disease. The issue is clearest for the child who is born with a significant hearing loss. All available information suggests that the infant should be placed in as near a normal hearing environment as possible, as early as possible. In most cases this would mandate the use of hearing aids. But even with hearing aids the child's acoustic environment is abnormal. Other interventions must be developed to mitigate these deficits.

Another problem, which affects a population much larger than those with severe to profound hearing loss, is what, if anything, should be done to normalize the auditory environment experienced by the many young infants and children with modest, intermittent, fluctuating hearing losses due to persistent middle ear effusion. The solution is not as clear as the answer for the severely to profoundly deaf. Evidence in man indicates that diminution of sound stimulation during maturation of the central nervous system does result in aberrant auditory function. However, the significance and sequelae of these abnormalities are not known. They probably depend not only upon the extent and duration of the auditory impairment but also on numerous other intrinsic (genetic) and extrinsic (environmental) factors. The answers to these questions are important because there is evidence to suggest that these effects may be significant to the total function of a person, especially in a society which is based to a large extent on auditory communication and auditory based language skills.

Acknowledgments

This work is supported by N.I.H. Grant #N.I.H. 5R01NS0A365-12CMS and #GM-19100, Deafness Research Foundation, National Foundation — March of Dimes #1372 and #6-234, C.H.E.A.R. and the Manheimer Fund.

References

Aitkin, L.M. and Moore, D.R. Inferior colliculus II. Development of tuning characteristics and tonotopic organization in central nucleus of the neonatal cat. *J. Neurophysiol.,* 38:1208–1216 (1975).

Alford, B.R. and Ruben, R.J. Physiological, behavioral and anatomical correlates of the development of hearing in the mouse. *Ann. Otol. Rhinol. Laryngol.,* 72:237–247 (1963).

Anggard, L. An electrophysiological study in the development of cochlear function in the rabbit. *Acta Otolaryngol.* (Stockh.) Suppl. 203:5–66 (1965).

Bast, T.H. and Anson, B.J. *The Temporal Bone and the Ear.* Springfield, Ill: Charles C. Thomas (1949).

Batkin, S., Groth, H., Watson, J.R. and Ansbery, M. Effects of auditory deprivation on the development of the auditory sensitivity in albino rats. *EEG in Clin. Neurophysiol.,* 28:351–359 (1970).

Boettcher, A. *Uber Entwicklung und Bau des Gehörlabyrinths.* Dresden: Blockmann, Soba and Schultze (1869).

Bredberg, G. Cellular pattern of nerve supply of the human organ of corti. *Acta Otolaryngol.* (Stockh.) Suppl. 236 (1968).

Brugge, J.F., Javel, E. and Kitzes, L.M. Signs of functional maturation of peripheral auditory system in discharge patterns of neurons in anteroventral cochlear nucleus of kitten. *J. Neurophysiol.,* 41:1557–1579 (1978).

Clopton, B.M. and Silverman, M.S. Plasticity of binaural interaction II. Critical period and changes in midline response. *J. Neurophysiol.,* 40:1275–1280 (1977).

Clopton, B.M. and Winfield, J.A. Effects of early exposure to pattern sound on unit activity in rat inferior colliculus. *J. Neurophysiol.,* 39:1081–1089 (1976).

Coleman, J.R. and O'Connor, P. Effects of monaural and binaural sound deprivation on cell development in the anteroventral cochlear nucleus of rats. *Exp. Neurol.,* 64:553–566 (1979).

Conrad, R. *The Deaf School Child*. London: Harper ana Row (1979).

Curtiss, S. Genie, *A Psycholinguistic Study of a Modern Day "Wild Child."* New York: Academic Press (1977).

Deol, M.S. Deficiencies of the inner ear in the mouse and their origin, in Colloques Internationaux C.N.R.S., #266 Mechanisms of the embryogenesis of the organs of vertebrate embryos, pp. 163–177 (1978).

Ehret, G. Development of absolute auditory thresholds from the house mouse (Mus Musculus). *J. Amer. Audiol. Soc.*, 1:179–184 (1976).

Ehret, G. Postnatal development of the acoustical system of the house mouse in light of developing masked thresholds. *J. Acoustic Soc. Am.*, 62:143–148 (1977).

Eisen, N.H. Some effects of early sensory deprivation on later behavior: the quodam hard of hearing child. *J. Abnormal and Soc. Psychol.*, 65:338–342 (1962).

Eisenberg, R.B. *Auditory Competence in Early Life, Roots of Communicative Behavior*. Baltimore: University Park Press (1976).

Finck, A., Schenck, C. and Hartman, A.F. Development of cochlear function in the neonate mongolian gerbil (Meriones Unguiculatus). *J. Comp. and Physiol. Psych.*, 78:375–380 (1972).

Gottlieb, G. Early development of species specific auditory perception in birds, in Gottlieb, G. (ed.), *Studies in the Development of Behavior and the Nervous System, Vol. III, Neural and Behavioral Specificity*. New York: Academic Press, pp. 237–280 (1976). 280 (1976).

Graziani, L.J., Weitzman, E.D. and Velasco, M.S.A. Neurologic maturation and auditory evoked responses in low birth weight infants. *Pediatrics*, 41:483–494 (1968).

Gulley, R.L., Wenthold, R.J. and Neises, G.R. Changes in synapses of spiral ganglion cells in the rostral anteroventral cochlear nucleus of the waltzing guinea pig following hair cell loss. *Brain Res.*, 158:279–294 (1978).

Hassmannova, J. and Myslivecek, J. Maturation of the primary cortical response to stimulation of the medial geniculate body. *EEG and Clin. Neurophysiol.*, 22:547–555 (1967).

Hecox, K. Human brainstem evoked potentials: Acoustical, pathological and developmental dependencies. Doctoral dissertation, University of California, San Diego: 76-2300 Xerox University Microfilms (1975).

Henry, K.R., Haythorn, M. Auditory similarities associated with genetic and experimental acoustic deprivation. *J. Comp. Physiol. Psych.*, 89:213–218 (1975).

Henry, K.R. and Lepkowski, C.M. Evoked potential correlates which note a progressive hearing loss: Age related changes from the ear to the inferior colliculus of the C-57BL/6 and CBA/J mice. *Acta Otolaryngol.* (Stockh.) 86:366–374 (1978).

Herodotus. *History*, trans. Rawlinson, G. and Komorff, N. (eds.), New York: Turdo Publishing Co., pp. 81f (1946).

Itard, J.M.G. *Traité des Maladies de l'Oreille et de l'Audition*. Paris: Meguignon-Marvis (1821).

Keith, R.W. Middle ear function in neonates. *Arch. Otolaryngol.*, 101:376–379 (1975).

Kerr, L.M., Ostapoff, E.N. and Rubel, E.W. The influence of acoustic experience on the otology of frequency generalization gradients in the chicken. *J. Exp. Psych. in Animal Behavior Proc.*, in press.

Konishi, M. Development of auditory responses in avian embryos. *Proc. Nat. Acad. Sci. USA*, 70:1795 (1970).

Kuhl, P.K. Speech perception in early infancy: The acquisition of speech sound categories, in Hirsch, S.K., Eldridge, D.H., Hirsch, I.J. and Silverman, S.R. (eds.), *Hearing and Davis: Essays Honoring Hullowell Davis*. St. Louis: Washington University Press, pp. 265–276 (1976).

Lane, H. *The Wild Boy of Aveyron.* Cambridge: Harvard University Press (1976).

Larsell, O., McCrady, E., Jr. and Zimmerman, A.A. Morphology of functional development of the membranous labyrinth of the opossum. *J. Comp. Neurol.,* 63:95–119 (1935).

Lenneberg, E. *Biological Foundations of Language.* New York: John Wiley and Sons (1967).

Levi-Monatalcini, R. Development of the acousticovestibular centers of the chick embryo in absence of the afferent root fibers and of descending fiber tracts. *J. Comp. Neurol.,* 91:209–242 (1949).

Li, C.W., Van De Water, T.R. and Ruben, R.J. The fate mapping of the 11th and 12th day mouse otocyst: An in vitro study of the sites of origin of embryonic inner ear sensory structures. *J. Morphology,* 157:249–268 (1978).

Mair, I.W.S., Elverland, H.H. and Laukli, E. Development of early auditory-evoked responses in the cat. *Audiol.,* 17:469–488 (1978).

Marty, R. and Thomas, J. Réponse électro-corticale à la stimulation du nerf cochléaire chez le chat nouveau-né. *J. de Physiolog.* (Paris), 55:165–166 (1963).

Marx, H. Die Missbildungen des Ohres, in Henke, F. und Lubarsch, O. (eds.), *Handbuch der Speziellen Pathologischen Anatomie und Histologie Gehörorgan.* Berlin: Springer, Bd 12:609–729 (1925).

McCrady, E., Jr., Weaver, E.G. and Gray, C.W. Development of hearing in the opossum. *J. Exp. Zool.,* 75:503–515 (1937).

McCrady, E., Jr., Weaver, E.G. and Gray, C.W. Further investigation in the development of hearing in the opossum. *J. Comp. Psychol.,* 30:17–21 (1940).

Menyuk, P. Effect of hearing loss on language acquisition in the babbling stage, in Jaffe, B. (ed.), *Hearing Loss in Children.* Baltimore: University Park Press, pp. 621–629 (1977).

Mikaelian, D., Alford, B. and Ruben, R.J. Cochlear potentials and VIII nerve action potentials in normal and genetically deaf mice. *Ann. of Otol. Rhinol. Laryngol.,* 74: 146–158 (1965).

Mikaelian, D. and Ruben, R. Development of hearing in the normal CBA/J mouse. *Acta Otolaryngol.* (Stockh.) 59:451–461 (1965).

Mikaelian, D.O. and Ruben, R.J. Hearing degeneration in the shaker I mouse. *Arch. Otolaryngol.,* 84:418–430 (1964).

Mlonyeni, M. The late stages of the development of the primary cochlear nuclei in mice. *Brain Res.,* 4:334–344 (1967).

Needleman, H. Effects of hearing loss from early recurrent otitis media on speech and language development, in Jaffe, B. (ed.), *Hearing Loss in Children.* Baltimore: University Park Press, pp. 640–649 (1977).

Northern, J.L. and Downs, M.P. *Hearing in Children.* Baltimore: Williams and Wilkins Co. (1974).

Ohlrich, G., Barnet, A., Weiss, I. and Shanks, B. Auditory evoked potential development in early childhood: A longitudinal study. *EEG and Clin. Neurophysiol.,* 44:411–423 (1978).

Parks, T.N. Afferent influences of the development of the brainstem auditory nuclei of the chicken: Otocyst ablation. *J. Comp. Neurol.,* 183:665–677 (1979).

Pujol, R. Development of toneburst responses along the auditory pathway in the cat. *Acta Otolaryngol.* Stockh.) 74:383–391 (1972).

Pujol, R., Carlier, E. and Devigne, C. Different patterns of cochlear innervation during the development of the kitten. *J. Comp. Neurology,* 177:529–536 (1978).

Pujol, R. and Hilding, D. Anatomy and physiology of the onset of auditory function. *Acta Otolaryngol.* (Stockh.) 76:1–10 (1973).

Rapin, I. Effects of early blindness and deafness on cognition. *Res. Publ. Ass. Res. Nerv. Ment. Dis.,* 57:189–245 (1979).

Rapin, I. Conductive hearing loss effects on children's language and scholastic skills, in Ruben, R.J. and Hansen, D. (eds.), *Workshop on Otitis Media: Annal. Otol. Rhinol. Laryngol.* (1979) in press.

Retzius, M.G. *Das Gehorogan der Wirbelthiere.* 2 vols. Stockholm: Samson and Wallin, (1881, 1884).

Ruben, R.J. Development of the inner ear of the mouse: A radioautographic study of terminal mitoses. *Acta Otolaryngol.* (Stockh.) Suppl. 220 (1967).

Ruben, R.J. A review of transneuronal changes of the auditory central nervous system as a consequence of auditory defects. *International Journal of Pediatric Otorhinolaryngology,* in press.

Ruben, R.J., Hudson, W. and Chiong, A. Anatomical and physiological effects of chronic section of the eighth nerve in cats. *Acta Otolaryngol.* (Stockh.) 55:473–484 (1963).

Salamy, A., McKean, C.M. and Buda, F.B. Maturational changes in auditory transmission as reflected in human brainstem potentials. *Brain Res.,* 96:361–366 (1975).

Saunders, J.C. and Bock, G.R. Influence of early auditory trauma on auditory development, in Gottlieb, G. (ed.), *Studies of Behavior in the Nervous System. Early Influences.* New York: Academic Press, pp. 249–287 (1978).

Schein, J.D. and Delk, M.T., Jr. *The Deaf Population of the United States.* Silver Spring: National Association for the Deaf (1974).

Schulman-Galambos, C. and Galambos, R. Brainstem auditory evoked potentials in the premature infant. *J. of Speech and Hearing in Res.,* 18:456–465 (1975).

Schulman-Galambos, C. and Galambos, R. Brainstem evoked response audiometry in newborn hearing screening. *Arch. Otolaryngol.,* 105:86–90 (1979).

Sher, A.E. The embryonic and post-natal development of the inner ear of the mouse. *Acta Otolaryngol.* (Stockh.) Suppl. 285 (1971).

Silverman, M.S. and Clopton, B.M. Plasticity of binaural interaction I. Effect of early auditory deprivation. *J. Neurophysiol.,* 40:1266–1274 (1977).

Skinner, M.W. The hearing of speech during language acquisition. *Otolaryngol. Clin. of North America,* 11:631–650 (1978).

Starr, A., Amlie, R.N., Martin, W.H. and Sanders, S. Development of auditory function in newborn infants revealed by auditory brainstem potentials. *Pediatrics,* 60:831–839 (1977).

Tees, R. The effect of early auditory restrictions in the rats on adult pattern discrimination. *J. Comp. Physiol. Psychol.,* 63:389–393 (1967).

Van den Pol, A.N., Kliot, M. and Kuritzkes, R. Responses of second and third order auditory neurons to deafferentation. Abstract, Society of Neurosciences, 1979, in press.

Van De Water, T.R. Effects of removal of the statoacoustic ganglion upon the growing otocyst. *Ann. Otol. Rhinol. Laryngol.* Suppl. 33 (1976).

Van De Water, T.R., Li, C.W., Ruben, R.J. and Shea, C.A. Ontogenic aspects of mammalian inner ear development, in Gorlin, R., Ruben, R.J. and Schuknecht, H. (eds.), *NFMD Original Article Series – Birth Defect Symposium on the Ear.* In press.

Van De Water, T.R. Personal communication.

Warfield, D., Ruben, R.J. and Makelian, D.O. Behavior measurements of pure tone thresholds in normal CBA-J mice. *J. Aud. Res.,* 8:459–468 (1968).

Webster, D.B. and Webster, M. Mouse brainstem auditory nuclei development. *Ann. Otol. Rhinol. Laryngol.* Suppl. *Recent Advances in Otitis Media,* in press.

Webster, D.B. and Webster, M. Neonatal sound deprivation affects brainstem auditory nuclei. *Arch. Otolaryngol.,* 103:392–396 (1977).

Webster, D.B. and Webster, M. Auditory brainstem: Sound deprivation and critical period. *Ann. Otol. Rhinol. Laryngol.,* 1979, in press.

Wolf, A. The dynamics of selective inhibition of specific function in neurosis. *Psychosomatic Med.,* 5:27–38 (1943).

7

Appraisal of Auditory Function in Children

ISABELLE RAPIN
ROBERT J. RUBEN

The most important disorder to detect and diagnose early is loss of hearing. Among communication disorders hearing loss is both the most common and the most remediable, if not medically, then by the use of amplification and special education. The need for early detection is stressed since the small child is a developing organism. There is evidence that language acquisition begins at birth and the ability to acquire language decreases over the first few years of life (Lenneberg, 1967).

Who Needs a Hearing Evaluation?

The age of the patient should be considered in deciding whom to refer and where (Table 1).

In *infancy* the main concern is to detect children with serious or profound hearing losses and to make sure that 1) reliable hearing testing has been provided. This always requires referral to a tertiary speech and hearing (S&H) center capable of adequate testing; 2) the etiology of the hearing loss has been given adequate consideration; 3) associated deficits have been detected; 4) genetic counseling has been provided; and 5) amplification, parental counseling, and habilitation measures have been started. The main focus is on infants on the high-risk register (Table 2), those who have failed routine behavioral screening at birth or in the well baby clinic, and those whose mothers express the fear that the baby does not hear adequately. Mother's worry about hearing mandates

TABLE 1 Hearing Problems at Different Ages

Age	Main Problems	Alerting Signs
Infant-Toddler	Congenital severe sensory neural HL (genetic or acquired)	High-risk registry (Table 2) Mother's complaint Failure to pass auditory screen
	Malformation syndromes Perinatal problems Middle ear effusion Post meningitic HL Follow-up care of hearing-impaired child	— in newborn nursery (Crib-o-gram) — in well baby clinic or doctor's office
Preschooler	Middle ear effusion Progressive HL High-tone loss Undiagnosed HL Postmeningitic HL Verbal auditory agnosia HL complicating mental retardation, brain damage or autism Follow-up care of hearing-impaired child	Lack of speech Speech delayed or sparse Articulation deficit Loss of speech Inattentiveness to sound "Autistic" behavior Failure to pass school screen
School-age child and adolescent	Middle ear effusion Progressive HL Unilateral HL Acquired HL Follow-up care of hearing-impaired child	Otologic complaint Failure to pass school screen School failure

behavioral screening of the infant and almost always referral to a speech and hearing center (Cunningham, 1971; Gerber, 1977a).

In *toddlers and preschoolers* the emphasis shifts from profound loss of hearing to less severe losses, although the pediatrician needs to remain alert for children with progressive losses and those who have slipped through hearing screens during infancy. He will also need to make sure that infants who had meningitis had their hearing checked before discharge, since profound sensory neural hearing loss with vestibular impairment is a fairly frequent sequela (Nadol, 1978). Inadequate acquisition of language is the main symptom that should attract attention in this age group. The physician will be looking for children with conductive hearing losses, in particular those with middle ear effusion, and those with moderate mixed hearing losses, high-tone losses and progressive losses (Ruben, 1979). He will need to differentiate hard-of-hearing children from children with primary developmental language disorders, with mild or moderate mental retardation and with more severe brain damage or autistic features in whom a hearing loss may complicate the clinical picture

(Rapin and Wilson, 1978). Except for toddlers with uncomplicated serious otitis media, all others require referral to a specialized speech and hearing center for appropriate diagnosis and management.

In *school-age children and adolescents* profound sensory neural hearing loss moves out of the limelight. Progressive genetic hearing loss, unilateral hearing loss resulting from infection (mumps, meningitis), trauma or neoplasm (acoustic neurinoma) enters the picture, as does the very rare ototoxic deafness. Middle ear effusion continues to be a problem but is less likely to be overlooked, although school failure occasionally reflects undetected mild or mild to moderate hearing loss with resultant inadequacy of language acquisition (Needleman, 1977). Although complex cases will still require referral to a tertiary speech and hearing center, others may appropriately be referred to an otologist for further care.

TABLE 2 High-Risk Registry for Deafness

1. Family history of deafness
2. Consanguinity
3. Malformed ears
4. Cleft palate, choanal atresia, other midfacial malformation
5. Prematurity
6. Hyperbilirubinemia, exchange transfusion
7. TORCHES intrauterine infection
   (*to*xoplasmosis, *r*ubella, *c*ytomegalovirus, *h*erpes simplex, *s*yphilis)
8. Meningitis
9. Other malformation syndrome, trisomy, etc.
10. Ototoxic drugs
11. Failure to pass newborn hearing screen or well baby hearing screen

Medical Evaluation and Care by the Primary Physician (Table 3)

Newborn and Infants

The most critical information the physician can collect is the history, including all items in the high-risk register (Table 2) and responses to questions about the infant's hearing behavior. Reports that the infant does not awake to loud sound or that he does not smile until he can see the mother when she enters the room should be heeded as should reports of less frequent or less varied babble.

The physician then needs to examine the child's ears, tympanic membranes and palate carefully. Malformations of the pinna, preauricular tags or pits,

TABLE 3   Investigation of Child Suspected of Hearing Loss

Type	Children	Age	Where
Medical – Pediatric	All	Any	Physician's office or OPD
ENT	All	Any	Office, OPD, or S and H Center
Ophthal- mology	Severe SNHL	Any	Office or OPD
Neurology	Multiply handicapped	Any	Office or OPD
Laboratory tests, x-rays, etc.	Selected	Any	OPD
Audiometry – behavioral	All	Toddler and up	S and H Center
evoked response	All young and hard to test	Any	Tertiary S and H Center
complex behavioral (e.g., central battery etc.)	Selected	Childhood and up	Tertiary S and H Center
Tympanometry	All	Any	OPD, otologist, S and H Center
Vestibular (ENG)	All with SNHL	Any	Tertiary S and H Center, some otologists
Speech and language evaluation	Selected	Toddler and up	S and H Center
Cognitive	Selected	Preschool and up	S and H Center

and stenosis or atresia of the external auditory canal are often associated with malformations of the middle ear and less often of the inner ear. They may be part of a complex malformation syndrome involving the gastrointestinal, genitourinary, cardiovascular and skeletal systems (Gorlin et al., 1976; Rapin and Ruben, 1976). Detailed examination of the tympanic membrane with a pneumatic otoscope is essential. The normal tympanic membrane is translucent and permits visualization of the following features: (1) the shadow of the eustachian tube located anterosuperiorly; (2) the manubrium of the malleus in the center of the drum; (3) the long process of the incus immediately posterior to the malleus and parallel to it; (4) the crus of the stapes and the stapedial tendon immediately below the long process; (5) the chorda tympani crossing the long process of the incus horizontally and superiorly; (6) the dark shadow of the niche of the round window inferiorly and posteriorly to the stapes.

The palate should be checked next for a cleft or a submucous cleft associated with a bifid uvula and/or bony notching of the posterior margin of the hard palate. Patients with extremely high-arched palates are also suspect for a submucosal cleft. A nasal voice points to an incompetent soft palate. Children with an anomaly of the posterior palate can be assumed to have eustachian tube dysfunction causing middle ear effusion and a conductive hearing loss.

Other findings relevant to hearing in the physical examination include pigmentary changes (white forelock, heterochromia of the iris, leukoderma, multiple lentigines, albinism), abnormalities of the eyes (colobomas of the lids or of the retina, epibulbar dermoids, nystagmus, oculomotor palsies, chorioretinitis or retinitis pigmentosa), goiter, congenital heart disease, genitourinary abnormalities and anomalies of the spine and limbs (Fraser, 1976; Gorlin *et al.*, 1976; Konigsmark and Gorlin, 1976; Rapin and Ruben, 1976). Screening laboratory tests should be ordered to assist in the diagnosis. The clue to a specific etiology for the child's hearing loss is usually found outside the ear. The importance of an etiologic diagnosis for genetic counseling need hardly be emphasized. Responsibility for this aspect of the child's care clearly rests with the primary physician who must also assess the child's development and refer him for neurologic evaluation if there is any suspicion of brain dysfunction or frank neurologic impairment.

Screening tests of hearing performed in the office are of such limited value that the slightest suggestion of a hearing loss in an infant mandates immediate referral to a tertiary speech and hearing center capable of making a definitive diagnosis in that age group. Every infant must be seen by an otologist skilled in evaluating small children. He will want to follow the child meticulously throughout childhood for middle ear effusion, since it can transform a hard-of-hearing child into a deaf one (Ruben and Math, 1978), and for otitis externa brought about by a poorly tolerated earmold. He will look for signs of mastoid disease or vestibular dysfunction. He will also want to review the child's audiogram at appropriate intervals to make sure the hearing loss is not progressing and that the child's hearing aids are still optimal.

Hearing-impaired children need yearly examinations by an ophthalmologist in order to rule out refractive errors that might impair their ability to read lips and manual language clearly. Their retinas must be examined carefully for the chorioretinitis of some intrauterine infections and the retinitis pigmentosa of Usher's syndrome (profound recessive childhood sensory neural hearing loss with vestibular impairment and retinitis pigmentosa developing in later childhood; Halgren, 1959). The diagnosis of Usher's syndrome needs to be confirmed with electroretinography not only because of its genetic implications but also because evolution into deaf-blind adulthood has profound consequences for education and choice of an occupation.

Part of the physician's examination is to take a detailed family history and draw up a family tree. In case of severe sensory neural hearing loss of unknown etiology, parents and siblings should be tested in order to rule out unsuspected hearing losses that might provide crucial data for genetic counseling. We shall mention here that all parents of all children with sporadic sensory neural hearing loss of undefined etiology are advised that autosomal recessive inheritance cannot be ruled out.

Preschool Children

Ideally, all but progressive sensory neural hearing loss and acquired hearing loss, whether conductive (e.g., serous otitis media) or sensory neural (e.g., postmeningitic), should have been diagnosed earlier. This is not always the case. The main symptom in this age group is delayed or absent speech or speech that is sparse, unintelligible or poorly articulated. (The corollary of this statement is that all preschoolers with speech and language problems need to have their hearing tested, even if they act as though they can hear.) Other symptoms to look for are inconsistent responsiveness to sound and repeated bouts of otitis media (Table 1). Hearing loss should be ruled out in all children in whom mental retardation, brain damage or autistic behavior is thought adequate explanation for lack of language development, since hearing loss is more likely to be present and overlooked in them than in a normal child and may contribute to the communicative disorder (Lloyd and Reid, 1967; Vernon, 1969).

Two of the most deceptive syndromes in this age group are high-tone loss, and verbal auditory agnosia. Children with *high-tone losses* respond normally to the low-pitch component of complex acoustic signals and do not appear deaf, yet their language acquisition is delayed, their vocabulary sparse, their syntax inadequate for age and their production of consonants distorted (Matkin, 1968). The adequacy of their language skills depends on the steepness of their hearing loss but also on environmental factors such as the intensity and quality of their exposure to language.

Verbal auditory agnosia or word-deafness is often mistaken for hearing loss because of very erratic responses to sound and more or less complete loss of whatever linguistic skills had already developed (Rapin, 1977). The later and more abruptly the syndrome develops, the easier it is to diagnose. It is always manifested by loss of speech as well as inability to comprehend. In contrast to autistic children, those with verbal auditory agnosia have an effective gesture language and demonstrate inner linguistic skills by their play and appropriate use of toys. A frequent hallmark of this disorder is an abnormal EEG, usually with bilateral spike and wave discharges, although abnormality limited to the dominant, usually left side may be encountered. Staring spells or other clinical seizures may or may not occur. This condition mandates a neurologic workup, the administration of anticonvulsants and an educational approach using total communication similar to that appropriate for a deaf child, stressing the visual-manual presentation of language to supplement oral speech. Prognosis for recovery from this disorder is guarded. Its etiology is probably varied, but in at least one case it resulted from a chronic inflammatory lesion in the temporal lobe (Lou *et al.*, 1977).

Workup of preschoolers with suspected severe hearing loss is similar to that of infants. Mild or moderate hearing loss is more likely to be diagnosed now than earlier. Testing with an electroacoustic impedance bridge, the most sensitive test for detecting middle ear effusion, should be carried out periodically. Behavioral testing becomes reliable in a proportion of the children so that electrodiagnostic techniques are needed less often. EEGs should be ordered for children suspected of verbal auditory agnosia, children with autistic behavior, and for those with severe brain damage, all of whom also need referral for neurologic consultation.

School-Age Children and Adolescents

Newly diagnosed communication disorder is relatively infrequent and is usually accompanied by an otologic complaint such as hearing loss, fullness in the ear, vertigo, pain or otorrhea. Detailed ear, nose and throat examination and reliable behavioral testing are possible in all but a few multiply handicapped children and in the rare child with a nonorganic hearing loss. Mild or moderate hearing loss must be ruled out as a possible explanation for school failure. Referral to the otologist rather than a comprehensive speech and hearing center may now be appropriate, which rarely was the case in younger children.

Counseling by the physician will now need to be directed at the child as well as his parents. Items that may come up include social problems with peers, teachers and parents, and rebellion against the wearing of hearing aids. These may be considered stigmatizing by children with moderate or unilateral hearing losses and of marginal utility by the profoundly deaf. The physician will need an interpreter to communicate effectively with his deaf patient, since most deaf children and adolescents have oral skills inadequate for discussing complex matters without manual signs to supplement speech. Eventually, the deaf adolescent or young adult will want to know the cause of his deafness and will need adequate genetic counseling (Fraser, 1976; Konigsmark and Gorlin, 1976). Most deaf persons marry the deaf (Schein and Delk, 1974). While many would prefer to have hearing children, they do not consider deafness in their children nearly as catastrophic as do hearing parents (Altschuler, 1963). They need to be made aware that reliable testing of hearing is available for all ages and that it is indicated for each of their children soon after birth.

Laboratory Tests (Table 4)

Since hearing loss is not a diagnosis but a symptom, the physician will need to obtain laboratory tests that will help detect anomalies in other organ systems. These may uncover symptoms requiring therapy or shed light on the etiology of the hearing impairment. No list can be exhaustive and no test should be carried out routinely without a good reason. The list in Table 4 is meant as a guideline for what is needed in all but children with uncomplicated middle ear effusions.

TABLE 4 Laboratory Tests

Test	Indication
Urinalysis (UA), BUN, creatinine	Malformed ears, sensory neural hearing loss (SNHL)
Intravenous pyelogram	Malformed ears, abnormal UA, high BUN, etc.
TORCHES titers	SNHL in infant, suggestive stigmata
EKG	SNHL, malformation syndrome
EEG	Seizures, receptive deficit for speech, autistic behavior, severe brain damage
ERG	Retinitis pigmentosa, SNHL with impaired vestibular function
ENG (vestibular)	SNHL, vertigo, late sitting and walking
Mastoid x-rays	Malformed ears, chronic middle ear infection, SNHL
Laminograms of temporal bone	Malformed ear, middle ear anomaly

Tests for Anomalies in Other Organ Systems

Children with malformed external and middle ears have a high incidence of genitourinary anomalies, and several syndromes with profound sensory neural hearing loss are associated with renal pathology (e.g., Alport syndrome, renal tubular acidosis). A urinalysis, including the microscopic examination of the sediment and screening tests for renal function like the blood urea nitrogen and creatinine level, are indicated in all children with ear anomalies and in those with sensory neural hearing loss. All children with malformed pinnas deserve an IVP since the yield of genitourinary abnormalities is high (Longenecker *et al.*, 1965). Those with abnormal sediment or renal function must be referred to nephrologists for further testing. Children with selected complex malformation syndromes may require x-rays of the skull, spine, long bones or gastrointestinal tract, and even cardiac catheterization (see Gorlin *et al.*, 1976; Rapin and Ruben, 1976, for examples of such syndromes).

Titers for intrauterine TORCHES infections (toxoplasmosis, rubella, cytomegalovirus, herpes simplex and syphilis) should be obtained at birth or in infancy in stigmatized infants or in those with deafness suspected soon after birth. They lose some but not all of their value in older children who may have been exposed to these infections postnatally or have received vaccine. Passive transfer of maternal antibodies can be evaluated by serial testing of the relative proportion of immunoglobulins M and G.

Electrical Studies

Electrocardiograms (EKG) are useful for detecting children who may have suffered from intrauterine rubella and thus have congenital heart disease. The rate syndrome of Jervell and Lange-Nielsen (1957), in which an unsuspected conductive defect may be fatal, can be ruled out with an EKG. *Electroretinography* (ERG), a sensitive test for ritinitis pigmentosa even before visible retinal pathology appears, enables a clear distinction to be made between retinitis pigmentosa and chorioretinitis. *Electroencephalograms* (EEG) are indicated in any nondeaf child with a severe receptive speech deficit, with or without autistic features. It is, of course, indicated for a history suggestive of staring spells or other seizures.

Tests of Vestibular Function

All children with sensory neural hearing loss, especially those with delayed motor milestones require vestibular tests. Lack of vestibular function produces less drastic consequences than lack of hearing, even though orientation in space is obviously crucial for station, locomotion and the control of eye and limb movement. In fact, spatial orientation is so crucial that it depends on vision and proprioception as well as on the labyrinth. Under most circumstances proprioception and vision can compensate for virtually all the signs of lack of vestibular input. Loss of vestibular function may result in late sitting and walking (Rapin, 1974a; Eviatar *et al.*, 1979), often mistakenly attributed to nonexistent brain damage. It also produces disorientation when swimming under water and has been responsible for some children drowning. Some causes of deafness are more likely than others to impair vestibular function. The presence or absence of vestibular dysfunction may eventually help differentiate among different deafness syndromes: vestibular dysfunction is a cardinal sign of Usher's syndrome, for example, and is also frequent in postmeningitic hearing loss.

In early infancy rotating an infant and observing him for postrotational nystagmus is an inexpensive, rapid and fairly reliable test of vestibular function. The test is no longer valid after the child has developed visual fixation which overcomes labyrinthine nystagmus. Per-rotatory nystagmus, i.e., nystagmus during rotation, does not reliably intact labyrinthine function if the eyes are open, since rotation will elicit opticokinetic as well as vestibular nystagmus. In older deaf children inability to walk in tandem (one foot in front of the other) is a fairly reliable screening test for vestibular dysfunction as is inability to stand immobile with the eyes closed.

Reliable vestibular testing, like reliable hearing testing, requires specialized facilities. *Electronystagmography* consists of the recording of eye movements, vision excluded, with the head in various positions, during rotation in a torsion swing, during bicaloric stimulation of each ear with water at 30°C and 44°C and, if no response is obtained with bicaloric stimuli, after irrigation with ice water. False-positive responses may be obtained even with ice water if the child is not tested for reversal in the direction of nystagmus on being turned from supine to prone. Electronystagmography provides a permanent record of test results for later scrutiny.

Radiologic Investigation

Views of the mastoid and of the petrous bone, either through the orbit or the base of the skull, are useful for visualizing the semicircular canals, cochlea and internal auditory meatus. These structures are particularly easy to see in the skull x-rays of newborns and infants. X-rays can detect abnormal pneumatization of the mastoid in chronic mastoiditis, sclerosis of the inner ear in children deafened by purulent meningitis and lack of development of the otic capsule (Mondini malformation) in an occasional child with severe congenital sensory neural hearing loss.

Laminograms are required for identifying malformations of the ossicular chain and middle ear. Plain x-rays provide useful information in a sufficiently large number of infants and children with severe to profound hearing losses to be warranted in virtually all of them. Laminograms should be reserved for those in whom external ear malformations or tympanometric results give strong evidence for a middle ear anomaly. Since early repair of these anomalies is not indicated, laminograms can usually be deferred until the child is old enough not to require sedation, or until the time when corrective surgery (of one ear only!) is contemplated. Skull x-rays, CT scans of the base of the skull and positive contrast encephalography are used in selected children to evaluate complex anomalies of the brain and inner ear and to look for acoustic tumors.

Behavioral Tests of Hearing (Table 5)

Eliciting a specific and repeatable response to sound is the most satisfactory means for evaluating auditory function, since it implies not only that the receptors of the auditory pathway are intact but that auditory perception and discrimination have occurred and an auditory signal can be used to program behavior. Behavioral testing is the most sensitive and most economic method for assessing auditory threshold in motivated and cooperative children and adults. While responses to uncalibrated suprathreshold sound stimuli can be used as a rapid screen for hearing, they never provide definitive data.

TABLE 5   Behavioral Tests of Hearing

Nonconditioned hearing screening

Conditioned testing with complex sounds

Routine audiometry
   Pure tone (air and bone)
   Speech

Tests for anatomic localization

Nonconditioned Behavioral Screening

There is no cheap and easy method to test hearing reliably in infants and very young children. Behavioral testing at that age is indicated only for those not suspected of having hearing impairment (Gerber, 1977b). For infants with suspected or presumed abnormal hearing, behavioral tests never suffice and may in fact be falsely reassuring.

The literature is replete with arguments for and against screening hearing in newborns. Justifications are the availability of the entire population, since virtually all infants are born in hospitals, and the strong belief that early intervention (amplification and referral of the child and his mother to an infant auditory training program) is efficacious and may be crucial. Against mass screening are the cost of false-positive and false-negative results for a handicap in fewer than one per thousand newborns and the fact that not all profound hearing losses are present at birth. Automated techniques for mass screening have been developed. They permit one to set the criteria for false-positive and false-negative results after deciding whether it is costlier to overdiagnose hearing loss in a sizable number of children than to miss an occasional affected child. One of these methods is the Crib-o-gram (Simmons, 1977). It is based on the recording through a transducer of infants' movements in their crib in the seconds following a loud sound produced in the nursery several times during each 24-hour period. The computer prints out whether the infant passed or failed the screen based on the chosen criteria. This method is currently being evaluated through a pilot cooperative study involving several high-risk nurseries in the country.

Behavioral testing for suprathreshold hearing is part of well baby care. Even this rough screening requires skill. Uncalibrated noisemakers, like bells, beepers, crumpled paper and the human voice, are used more often than calibrated ones, like high-frequency warbled tones. Since infants and young children respond erratically to pure tones, tuning forks are unsuitable in this age group (Eisenberg, 1976). Hand claps, dropped metal objects and other very loud noises are equally unsuitable because their low frequency provides vibratory as well as acoustic stimulation. Reproducibility of test conditions tends to be poor in free field testing. Remember that sound intensity decreases as the square of the distance from its source and that repeated testing with the same stimulus must be avoided since habituation to sound occurs rapidly.

The state of the child during testing is critical. He must be alert but quiet, otherwise testing is futile. In one scenario the infant sits on mother's lap. One observer faces the child and attracts his attention while another presents the stimulus to one or the other ear from behind, taking care to avoid all visual clues. The only acceptable response is a repeatable turn of the head and eyes toward the stimulus (Downs and Sterritt, 1967). This type of response does not occur reliably under six months of age. Less overt responses like eye widening or change of facial expression are unreliable (Moncur, 1968). Since very loud intensity is required to elicit a blink or startle, these responses are unsuitable gauges of hearing because they do not rule out substantial hearing loss, especially if recruitment is present. (Recruitment is too rapid growth of loudness with increasing intensity, most often associated with pathology of the hair cells.)

Behavioral testing of infants in the speech and hearing center suffers from essentially the same problems as behavioral screening in the clinic except that the stimuli, usually voice music and noisemakers as well as tones, are calibrated and testing takes place in a sound-treated environment. Consequently, referral for electrophysiologic testing is essential in all infants with any question of impaired hearing.

Conditioned Behavioral Audiometry

Autonomic conditioning was advocated as a nonbehavioral means of assessing hearing in the days before electrophysiologic audiometry. Several methods were proposed: slowing of the heart rate (cardiotachometry), change in respiratory rate, high-intensity sucking and increased sweating (galvanic skin resistance). While these methods still have their place in the research laboratory (high-intensity sucking is used to study infants' ability to discriminate between speech stimuli; Morse, 1974), they are no longer acceptable for clinical audiometry.

Testing auditory sensitivity with operant methods (conditioned orienting response audiometry, COR) starts by rewarding a specific and explicit response to an easily discriminating stimulus (Sweitzer, 1977). Intensity is then decreased progressively until the child ceases to respond. For instance, the child may be taught to put a peg in a hole or to throw a bead in a bucket upon hearing a sound, being rewarded with a smile or a small piece of food for responding (play audiometry). When children are unresponsive to sound, the first step is to condition them to respond to a visual stimulus that is rewarding in itself, for example, a mechanical toy or a film strip shown briefly (peep show). If a sound regularly precedes the visual stimulus, children who can perceive the sound will learn to respond to it before the visual stimulus it announces. For example, the child will look toward the speaker that delivered the sound since he expects activation of the toy mounted above the speaker. With older children one can measure reaction time to the sound as a means for assessing threshold, since reaction time lengthens dramatically 10–20 dB above subjective threshold (Rapin and Steinherz, 1970).

Behavioral testing validates the auditory threshold obtained electrophysiologically. It also evaluates which of several hearing aids is likely to be most helpful. As the child matures and his attention and cooperation increase, the need for nonbehavioral and conditioned hearing testing lessens.

Standard Behavioral Audiometry

The ability to detect pure tones presented through earphones or by bone oscillators and to detect, or better to repeat, words with specific phonologic and acoustic characteristics is the backbone of auditory testing (Sweitzer, 1977). A higher threshold for sounds presented in air than for those presented with bone oscillators (air-bone gap) suggests a conductive loss. When hearing is much better in one ear than in the other, it is necessary to mask the function of the better ear with white noise in order to evaluate the other ear. While pure tone audiometry is the most sensitive and economic method to assess threshold in alert, cooperative persons, its reliability in childhood cannot be taken for granted (Rapin and Costa, 1969).

Tests Designed to Localize the Site
of the Auditory Impairment

This type of test tries to determine whether the cause of the hearing impairment is in the cochlea, the acoustic nerve, or the brain (Jerger and Jerger, 1975; Snow *et al.*, 1977). This is particularly important when one suspects an acoustic nerve tumor or other neoplasm compressing the acoustic nerve and/or the cochlear nuclei in the brain stem. The tests are based on the fact that nerve lesions often produce an inordinate difficulty in detecting sound in noise and in rapid adaptation to sound, whereas cochlear damage is likely to produce recruitment. Specialized tests, such as Bekesy audiometry, tone decay, small increment sensitivity index (SISI) and tests for recruitment can be employed and validated by brain stem evoked response audiometry.

There are children whose inadequate auditory perception reflects pathology in the brain stem or auditory cortex. As pointed out earlier, these children are not deaf but have difficulty perceiving the characteristics of complex sounds and localizing sound in space. To bring out these deficits speech may be degraded by filtering out the high or low end of the frequency spectrum, chopping it, accelerating it or presenting it against a background of noise (Berlin, 1977; Snow *et al.*, 1977). Differences between the ears in the ability to understand degraded speech indicates pathology in the auditory cortex contralateral to the less efficient ear.

When different competing speech stimuli (e.g., series of digits or word pairs) are presented simultaneously to both ears, stimuli presented to the ear opposite the hemisphere dominant for language (the left in right-handed persons) are reported more accurately. Conversely, nonspeech sounds, like environmental sounds or melodies, presented to the ear opposite the nondominant hemisphere are reported more reliably. This so-called ear preference has been detected in children as young as three years (Knox and Kimura, 1970; Ingram, 1975) and can be used to test for hemispheric dominance, although its reliability in ambidextrous and left-handed children is less than in strongly right-handed ones. Aberrant ear dominance and abnormality lateralized to one ear in the

TABLE 6   Electrophysiologic Tests of Hearing

Electroacoustic bridge assessment
  Compliance of middle ear transducer (drum and ossicular chain)
  Middle ear pressure
  Acoustic reflex

Evoked-response audiometry (ERA)
  Electrocochleography (ECoG)
  Brain stem-evoked response (BSER)
  Late cortical response (AER)

perception tests of the central auditory battery have been found in some children with learning disability. Their usefulness in the clinic and their correlation with asymmetries in brain stem or cortical-evoked responses remain to be evaluated.

Electrophysiologic Tests of Hearing (Table 6)

Electroacoustic Impedance Bridge

This instrument measures the mechanical properties of the middle ear transducer system (tympanic membrane, ossicles, round window membrane), the pressure in the middle ear and the contraction of the middle ear muscles in response to high-intensity sound. Impedance testing has revolutionized our knowledge of the incidence and duration of middle ear effusion in children (Feldman and Wilber, 1976). It has shown that middle ear effusion is very common and in many children very chronic. While tympanometry is not a test of hearing threshold, lack of an acoustic reflex in the face of normal middle ear and facial nerve function strongly confirms hearing loss.

The test is performed by measuring the amount of sound produced by a constant sound source that is reflected by the tympanic membrane: the tenser the membrane, the greater the amount of sound reflected. Tension of the tympanic membrane is altered by pumping air into and out of the external ear which is sealed by a rubber plug. Compliance of the membrane will be maximum at the point where the pressure on both sides of the tympanic membrane (i.e., in the plugged external ear cavity and in the middle ear) is equal. The point of maximum compliance provides an indirect reading of the pressure within the middle ear. Middle ear pressure usually is lower than atmospheric pressure in patients with eustachian tube obstruction. Fluid in the middle ear, ankylosis of the ossicles or fixation of the stapes in the round window decreases the compliance of the system, whereas dislocation of the ossicles increases compliance. Contraction of the middle ear muscles in response to loud sound decreases compliance (increases impedance).

Tympanometry enjoys several advantages: it is brief, it does not require a highly trained person for administration and it is sensitive and specific. In addition, it is inexpensive for large-scale administration, for example, screening a school population. Its disadvantages are that the initial cost of the instrumentation is high, especially for someone who will not use it daily. It does not provide data regarding hearing threshold even though threshold for the acoustic reflex is correlated with threshold for hearing. (The presence of an acoustic reflex does not indicate normal hearing since it is a suprathreshold response that may be present in the face of severe hearing loss if the ear is recruiting.) Tympanometry cannot be used in the small proportion of children whose tiny ear canals are impossible to seal and in the larger number of children who scream and squirm. The test provides no evidence regarding hearing in the presence of middle ear pathology.

Evoked-Response Audiometry (ERA)

These tests rely on the technique of averaging, that is, the repetitive presentation of a sound stimulus and the time-locked recording of the electrophysiologic response of various relays in the auditory system from electrodes on the scalp or near the ear. Averaging permits the extraction of time-locked responses of very small amplitude from background electrophysiologic activity of much larger amplitude, such as the EEG, that is not time-locked to the stimulus. Three main tests will be discussed, electrocochleography, brain stem-evoked responses and cortical responses.

Electrocochleography (ECoG) records electrical responses of hair cells (cochlear microphonic) and acoustic nerve to sound (Ruben *et al.*, 1976; Naunton and Fernandez, 1978). In many laboratories the responses are recorded through transtympanic electrodes placed on the promontory of the middle ear, although other investigators position the electrodes in the external canal or on the scalp. This technique enables one to sample the activity of the most peripheral part of the auditory pathway, the most common site of pathology responsible for deafness.

Brain stem-evoked responses (BSER) are the most useful electrophysiologic measure of hearing sensitivity in clinical use today (Naunton and Fernandez, 1978). They consist of a series of waves, the first thought to reflect activity in the vicinity of the eighth nerve, the fifth, activity in the vicinity of the inferior colliculus. The waves occur within less than 10 msec of sound stimulation. The source of each wave is still being investigated but presumably reflects activity at the various levels of the brain stem auditory pathway. The time between waves I and V measures conduction time within the auditory brain stem. The interval decreases with maturation (Salamy *et al.*, 1975; Starr, 1977) and increases in a variety of brain stem pathologies, such as multiple sclerosis (Stockard and Rossiter, 1977). There is an excellent correlation between threshold for BSER and threshold of hearing.

Because this technique does not require the child's cooperation, it is ideal for testing infants, handicapped and other hard-to-test children. BSER are not influenced by drugs and by sleep so that infants and children can be sedated for testing. Although the voltage of waves (around I μV) is so small that several thousand stimuli must be used, the response does not habituate so that rapid delivery of stimuli (10 stimuli/sec or more) is possible, making the method efficient. As mentioned earlier, detailed analysis of the waves of the response can provide information about maturation and pathology within the auditory brain stem.

This method's most important disadvantages lie in its complexity, duration and cost. One may also cite the need to use brief stimuli (clicks or filtered tone pips) and the unsuitability of the method for straightforward testing of hearing at the lower end of the frequency spectrum. (Testing responses to low tones is possible but require rather complex computer manipulations and filtering.) Small special-purpose computers have been developed for clinical testing, but the method still demands skilled interpretation and highly trained personnel. Since children must be tested asleep and thus often require sedation, safety requires medical supervision. While BSER is the method of choice for assessing auditory sensitivity in infants and children, its availability for that purpose will continue to be restricted to tertiary speech and hearing centers, usually attached to hospitals.

Cortical auditory-evoked responses (AER) can be divided into intermediate responses, with a latency between about 10 and 50 msec after sound stimulation thought to reflect activity in thalamus, white matter and auditory cortex, and late potentials (latency 50 to 500 msec or more) that reflect later cortical events (Picton *et al.,* 1974). Late potentials are widespread and appear to reflect the perception and processing of auditory information. While cortical potentials can be used to assess hearing sensitivity in infants and young children (Rapin, 1974b), there are many pitfalls in their interpretation, and the responses are affected by the alertness of the subject, the phases of sleep and the use of medication. Cortical potentials are of most service in evaluating higher order processing of auditory information (Desmedt, 1979) and for assessing low-frequency tones. They suffer from the same drawbacks as BSER in terms of the complexity and expense of the method.

In short, electrophysiologic hearing tests can assess the auditory sensitivity of any patient, however young and however handicapped. They are essential for infants at high risk for hearing impairment and for those identified by behavioral tests or by the lack of normal speech development. They are not suitable for screening because of their cost, their length and the specialized personnel they require. While they reflect the physiologic state of the peripheral auditory pathway, they cannot be taken to mean that the child can "hear," that is, interpret and utilize auditory information.

Speech and Language Evaluation —
Psychologic Evaluation

The physician himself can make many observations of the adequacy of the child's language ability as opposed to his speech, which is communication restricted to the aural-oral channel. Language is the ability to enter into a communicative interaction and transmit one's ideas or wishes to another person using any and all available channels. Eye contact, gestures, facial expression, body language and head nods all play a crucial role in communication. The child's use of toys in a way that indicates that he understands their symbolic value is a positive sign. So are the ability to recognize and enjoy pictures and to understand situations, to follow nonverbal directions and to play the examiner's "game." A child's language skills, therefore, transcend his ability to decode verbal language and produce speech.

Speech evaluation involves a more specialized and precise inventory of the child's ability to use oral language for communication. It is necessary to find out whether the child can discriminate between speech sounds (phonemes) both isolated and embedded in words and to repeat or produce them spontaneously. Additional points for assessment are the adequacy of syntax and vocabulary and how efficiently speech is used to communicate. Speech evaluation is undeniably important for planning speech therapy and evaluating and judging its efficacy. As opposed to language evaluation, however, it has limited value in the very young child, since speech production is imperfect in most children under three or four years and there are virtually no norms for the milestones of normal language acquisition. Speech comprehension is particularly difficult to assess because it is inferential and necessarily based on the child's production of a verbal or nonverbal response to a linguistic stimulus.

Besides providing an overall picture of a child's intellectual competence, psychologic evaluation helps detect nonverbal cognitive deficits that may disclose unanticipated associated handicaps (Wilson *et al.,* 1975). There are special problems, however, in interpreting psychologic test data in young children with communication disorders. Infant scales are *not* designed to yield an IQ but only to assess maturation and detect obvious lags or dysfunctions. Psychologic tests have limited predictive value even in normal preschool children. Their value is still more circumscribed in a child with a severe handicap, such as deafness or a communication disorder, because the handicap restricts the range of behaviors that can be sampled reliably and because no test has had the extensive standardization for the deaf that the Wechsler Scale or Stanford-Binet have undergone for normal children. Two batteries, the Hiskey-Nebraska Test of Learning Aptitude and the Snidjers-Domen-Nonverbal Test, were designed for school-age deaf children but have undergone only limited standardization. Nonverbal tests like the WISC Performance Scale, Leiter Scale and Raven Coloured Progressive Matrices are suitable for nonverbal administration. One should not forget, however, that nonverbal tests give a one-sided picture and that a child's overall competence depends at least as much on his verbal skills as on his ability to solve nonverbal problems. While in normal children verbal competence is acquired without special instruction, in deaf children it reflects the efficacy of their educational experience at least as much or more than their basic intelligence. Verbal competence will depend in part on whether the child has been exposed to total communication or to a strictly oral approach to language learning. It will also depend on how well his parents can communicate with him: some parents of deaf children do not learn sign language and cannot transcend their child's usually severely limited oral speech.

By mandating repeated testing of deaf children, the law recognizes that test results may be a good gauge of the child's current skills but a poor predictor of his potential. Psychologic test results are more useful for deciding on current school placement and educational strategy than for predicting educational outcome.

The physician needs to be aware that he will tend to overestimate a deaf child's communication competence and his ability to read lips and that adequate performance in a school for the deaf does not necessarily mean even marginally adequate scholastic competence by the standards used for hearing children (DiFrancesca, 1972; Conrad, 1979). Adequate nonverbal intelligence is a better predictor of social competence as an adult than of vocational achievement, because deaf adults' poor reading skills and informational deprivation limit their choice of an occupation (Schein and Delk, 1974). It is hoped that early detection of hearing loss and communication disorder—a responsibility that clearly rests on the primary physician—coupled with the introduction of total communication from infancy and with higher expectations by educators for scholastic competence of the deaf will render these pessimistic statements obsolete.

Summary and Conclusions

The differential diagnosis of a child who does not speak includes deafness, primary language disorder, mental retardation and brain damage with or without autistic behavior. Deafness is not a diagnosis but a symptom. The role of the primary physician is early detection of children at risk for hearing loss by the use of the high-risk registry, by screening of hearing as part of well baby care and by assessing the adequacy of speech development. Physical examination and appropriate laboratory tests are required to define the etiology of the hearing loss or communication disorder. The physician must be prepared to refer any young child suspected of a hearing loss or other communication disorder to a specialized speech and hearing center capable of performing sophisticated physiologic hearing tests and of comprehensively assessing the child's communicative skills. The primary physician must be able to interpret the results of auditory and psychologic testing in order to explain their meaning and limitations to the parents. The physician must also know enough about various special educational programs to evaluate the efficacy of the educational plan prescribed for the child. He must be prepared to provide genetic counseling to the family and later to the child. Finally, the physician must monitor progress throughout childhood, looking for new problems or new consequences of old problems and coordinating services provided by the speech and hearing center, the educational establishment and other professionals who will interact with the child and his family throughout the formative years.

Acknowledgments

This work was supported in part by Grant NS 3356 from the National Institute of Neurological Diseases Communication Disorders and Stroke, and by grants from the Deafness Research Foundation, the National Foundation — March of Dimes #1372 and 6-234, C.H.E.A.R., and the Manheimer Fund.

References

Altschuler, K.Z. Sexual patterns and family relationships, in Rainer, J.D., Altschuler, K.Z. and Kallmann, F.J. (eds.), *Family and Mental Health Problems in a Deaf Population,* New York: Department of Medical Genetics, New York State Psychiatric Institute, pp. 92–112 (1963).

Berlin, C.I. Hemispheric asymmetry in auditory tasks, in Harnad, S., Doty, R.W., Goldstein, L., Jaynes, J. and Krauthamer, G. (eds.), *Lateralization in the Nervous System.* New York: Academic Press, pp. 303–324 (1977).

Conrad, R. *The Deaf School Child.* London: Harper and Row (1979).

Cunningham, G. (ed.) *Conference on Newborn Hearing Screening.* Berkeley, Ca.: California State Department of Public Health, Bureau of Maternal and Child Health (1971).

Desmedt, R. (ed.) *Cognitive Components in Event-Related Cerebral Potentials.* Basel: Karger (1979).

DiFrancesca, S. *Academic Achievement Test Results of a National Testing Program for Hearing Impaired Students. United States, Spring 1971.* Washington D.C.: Office of Demographic Studies, Gallaudet College (1972).

Downs, M.P. and Sterritt, G.M. A guide to newborn and infant hearing screening programs. *Arch. Otolaryng.,* 85:37–44 (1967).

Eisenberg, R.B. *Auditory Competence in Early Life: Roots of Communication Behavior.* Baltimore, Md.: University Park Press (1976).

Eviatar, L., Miranda, S., Eviatar, A., Freeman, K. and Borkowski, M. Development of nystagmus in response to vestibular stimulation in infants. *Ann. Neurol.,* 5:508–514 (1979).

Feldman, A.S. and Wilber, L.A. (eds.) *Acoustic Impedance and Admittance: The Measurement of Middle Ear Function.* Baltimore: Williams and Wilkins (1976).

Fraser, G.R. *The Causes of Profound Deafness in Childhood.* Baltimore, Md.: Johns Hopkins University Press (1976).

Gerber, S.E. High risk registry for congenital deafness, in Jaffe, B.F. (ed.), *Hearing Loss in Children.* Baltimore: University Park Press, pp. 73–77 (1977a).

Gerber, S.E. Newborn screening and diagnostic tests, in Jaffe, B.F. (ed.), *Hearing Loss in Children*. Baltimore: University Park Press, pp. 78–88 (1977b).

Gorlin, R.J., Pindborg, J.J. and Cohen, M.M., Jr. *Syndromes of the Head and Neck,* 2nd ed. New York: McGraw-Hill (1976).

Hallgren, B. Retinitis pigmentosa combined with congenital deafness, with vestibulo-cerebellar ataxia and mental abnormality in a proportion of cases. *Acta Psychiat. Neurol. Scand.* Suppl. 138:1–101 (1959).

Ingram, D. Cerebral speech lateralization in young children. *Neuropsychologia,* 13:103–105 (1975).

Jerger, S. and Jerger, J. Extra- and intra-axial brain stem auditory disorders. *Audiology,* 14: 93–117 (1975).

Jervell, A. and Lange-Nielsen, F. Congenital deaf-mutism, functional heart disease with prolongation of the Q-T interval and sudden death. *Amer. Heart J.,* 54:59–68 (1957).

Knox, C. and Kimura, D. Cerebral processing of nonverbal sounds in boys and girls. *Neuropsychologia,* 8:227–237 (1970).

Konigsmark, B.W. and Gorlin, R.J. *Genetic and Metabolic Deafness.* Philadelphia, Pa.: W.B. Saunders (1976).

Lenneberg, E. *Biological Foundations of Language.* New York: John Wiley and Sons (1967).

Lloyd, L.L. and Reid, M.J. The incidence of hearing impairment in an institutionalized mentally retarded population. *Am. J. Ment. Def.,* 71:746–763 (1967).

Longenecker, C.G., Ryan, R.F. and Vincent, R.U. Malformations of the ear as a clue to urogenital anomalies. *Plast. Reconstr. Surg.,* 35:303–309 (1965).

Lou, H.C., Brandt, S. and Bruhn, P. Progressive aphasia and epilepsy with a self-limited course, in Penry, J.K. (ed.), *Epilepsy, the Eighth International Symposium.* New York: Raven Press, pp. 295–303 (1977).

Matkin, N.D. The child with a marked high-frequency hearing impairment. *Pediat. Clin. N. Amer.,* 15:677–690 (1968).

Moncur, J.P. Judge reliability in infant testing. *J. Speech Hear. Res.,* 11:348–357 (1968).

Morse, P.A. Infant speech perception: a preliminary model and review of the literature, in Schiefelbusch, R. and Lloyd, L.L. (eds.), *Language Perspectives – Acquisition, Retardation, and Intervention.* Baltimore: University Park Press, pp. 19–53 (1974).

Nadol, J.B., Jr. Hearing loss as a sequela of meningitis. *Laryngoscope,* 88:739–755 (1978).

Naunton, R.F. and Fernandez, C. (eds.) *Evoked Electrical Activity in the Auditory Nervous System.* New York: Academic Press (1978).

Needleman, H. Effects of hearing loss from early otitis media on speech and language development, in Jaffe, B.F. (ed.), *Hearing Loss in Children.* Baltimore: University Park Press, pp. 640–649 (1977).

Picton, T.W., Hillyard, S.A., Krausz, H.I. and Galambos, R. Human auditory evoked potentials. I. Evaluation of components. *Electroenceph. Clin. Neurophysiol.,* 36:179–190 (1974).

Rapin, I. Hypoactive labyrinths and motor development. *Clin. Pediatr.,* 13:922–937 (1974a).

Rapin, I. Testing for hearing loss with auditory evoked responses – Successes and failures. *J. Commun. Dis.,* 7:3–10 (1974b).

Rapin, I. and Costa, L.D. Test – retest reliability of serial pure-tone audiograms in children at a school for the deaf. *J. Speech Hear. Res.,* 12:402–412 (1969).

Rapin, I., Mattis, S., Rowan, A.J. and Golden, G.H. Verbal auditory agnosia in children. *Develop. Med. Child Neurol.,* 19:192–207 (1977).

Rapin, I. and Ruben, R.J. Patterns of anomalies in children with malformed ears. *Laryngoscope,* 86:1469–1502 (1976).

Rapin, I. and Steinherz, P. Reaction time for pediatric audiometry. *J. Speech Hear. Res.,* 13:203–217 (1970).

Rapin, I. and Wilson, B.C. Children with developmental language disability: Neurological aspects and assessment, in Wyke, M. (ed.), *Developmental Dysphasia*. New York: Academic Press, pp. 13–41 (1978).

Ruben, R.J. (ed.) *Workshop on Otitis Media and Child Development, Ann. Otol. Rhinol. Laryngol.* In press, 1979.

Ruben, R.J., Elberling, C. and Salomon, G. (eds.) *Electrocochleography*. Baltimore, Md.: University Park Press (1976).

Ruben, R.J. and Math, R. Serous otitis media associated with sensorineural hearing loss in children. *Laryngoscope*, 88:1139–1154 (1978).

Salamy, A., McKean, C.M. and Buda, F.B. Maturational change in auditory transmission as reflected in human brain stem potentials. *Brain Res.*, 96:361–366 (1975).

Schein, J.D. and Delk, M.T., Jr. *The Deaf Population of the United States*. Silver Spring, Md.: National Association of the Deaf (1974).

Simmons, F.B. Automated screening test for newborns: the Crib-o-gram, in Jaffe, B.F. (ed.), *Hearing Loss in Children*. Baltimore, Md.: University Park Press, pp. 89–98 (1977).

Snow, J.B., Rintelman, W.F., Miller, J.M. and Konkle, D.F. Central auditory imperception. *Laryngoscope*, 87:1450–1471 (1977).

Starr, A. Development of auditory function in newborn infants revealed by auditory brain stem potentials. *Pediatrics*, 60:831–939 (1977).

Stockard, J.J. and Rossiter, V.S. Clinical and pathologic correlates of brain stem auditory response abnormalities. *Neurology*, 27:316–325 (1977).

Sweitzer, R.S. Audiologic evaluation of the infant and young child, in Jaffe, B.F. (ed.), *Hearing Loss in Children*. Baltimore: University Park Press, pp. 101–131 (1977).

Vernon, M. *Multiply Handicapped Deaf Children: Medical, Educational, and Psychological Considerations*. Washington, D.C.: Council for Exceptional Children (1969).

Wilson, J.J., Rapin, I., Wilson, B.C. and VanDenburg, F.V. Neuropsychologic function of children with severe hearing impairment. *J. Speech Hear. Res.*, 18:634–652 (1975).

8

Behavioral Assessment of Infants' Hearing

EARL C. BUTTERFIELD

Not being able to hear denies a person sources of pleasure and inspiration. While unfortunate, it is far from the worst of the affliction of deafness. From a developmental point of view the importance of hearing is shown by the fact that practically all people who lack it fail to develop speech. Moreover, most people who cannot hear fail to develop the linguistic competence required for commerce with the world of ideas, access to which must be gained by reading if not by listening.

As we differ from other animals chiefly in the flexibility and complexity of our communication skills, so do we rank ourselves above them because of the power of our language. We even segregate ourselves from one another on the basis of our different languages. Within a tongue, too, class discrimination is often accurately manifested by mastery of the language. The sexes mate in fair measure according to the level of their speech skills. In complex societies, at least, we assess our peers by their use of language, and we designate as incompetent those who use it inadequately, particularly those who fail to speak at all. We judge the development of our young according to the age at which they first speak, ranking this with the age at which they take their first step as the earliest indicator of potential. Significant departures from the norm in either behavior, but particularly in the use of speech, are taken as cardinal signs of impaired mental status. Different kinds of delayed speech or language comprehension can by themselves lead some children to be classed as mentally retarded, deaf, autistic or aphasic and to be segregated from the normal community and even from family life. The consequent misery and cost to the impaired children, their families and society are incalculable.

Since the basics of language and social interaction are acquired early in life, it is desirable to detect correctable hearing losses as early as possible. Various diagnostic approaches exist to assess auditory functioning during the first days and weeks, including impedance audiometry and evoking brain stem potentials. Such physiologic techniques can provide important clinical information, but they do not speak to the question of whether infants can act cognitively and behaviorally upon what their ears sense. Therefore, such approaches need to be supplemented with behavioral measures. Here are some behavioral techniques that are used either to screen infants for hearing impairment or to diagnose definitively those suspected of having hearing losses:

1. An intense tone is presented near a neonate's head, and an observer notes whether the child is startled by the tone.
2. A moderately intense tone or click is produced near a sleeping infant, and an observer notes whether he opens his eyes.
3. While an infant is sucking on an instrumented, nonnutritive pacifier, an intense tone or narrow band of noise is presented to determine whether it suppresses the infant's sucking.

These procedures are thoroughly representative of present clinical approaches to assessing infants' auditory functioning. Implicit in their use are the presumptions that the infant is a passive, reflexive being incapable of processing complex signals like speech; that an infant's responses to simple, nonspeech signals can tell whether he has an auditory impairment that will impede his speech and language development; and that the source of speech and language deficits is in the sensory system rather than in the central nervous system. Recent research findings belie these presumptions and give us a new view of infants and their capabilities.

A Recently Developed View of Infants and Their Auditory Perception

Infants Participate Actively with Their Environment

Even newborn infants interact actively with their environments and quickly modify their behavior to control their experiences. Butterfield and Siperstein (1972) showed this by making complex auditory signals differentially contingent upon infants' suck duration during their first 48 hours of life. Under a *during* contingency auditory stimulation was presented to the infant only while his suck-produced negative pressure remained below a predetermined cutoff level. Under a *between* contingency auditory stimulation was presented to the infant only while his suck-produced negative pressure was above the cutoff level. The cutoff was set so that it was easily exceeded by every well-formed suck. Therefore, under the *during* contingency, increasing suck duration increased stimulation; under the *between* contingency, increasing suck duration decreased stimulation.

By comparing neonates' suck durations when vocal-instrumental music was presented according to these two contingencies, Butterfield and Siperstein showed that newborn infants sucked longer under the *during* contingency. They sucked so as to decrease their stimulation by noise, even though it had the same average frequency and spectral characteristics as the music. These results established that newborn infants learn within 20 minutes to regulate the amount of stimulation they receive. They are exceedingly active participants in their environments, provided only that they are given the opportunity to show participation with their limited response repertoire.

Other data show that young humans actively process their sensory environments. Einar Siqueland, of Brown University, has conducted an intensive research program to examine how infants under six months of age engage their environments. After various experiments he concluded "that the most striking finding of our research is that we have yet to find any stage of development in which the human infant can be characterized as a passive recipient of sensory stimulation. We have found that the infant actively seeks out stimulation, attends selectively, and, given the opportunity to control his stimulus environment, he demonstrates a vigorous appetite for stimulus change" (Siqueland, 1969).

Infants Process Complex Stimuli and They Make Sophisticated Discriminations

Infants can process and discriminate among exceedingly complex stimuli. This can be inferred from the fact that human newborns distinguish between noise and vocal-instrumental music. Better evidence comes from an experiment in which Butterfield and Siperstein (1972) separated the vocal and instrumental portions of auditory stimulation given to infants, making either *voices* alone, *instruments* alone or both contingent upon suck duration. They found that infants reacted equally strongly and positively to *voices* and *voices plus instruments* but that they had no significant reaction to *instruments* alone. This finding suggests that they were able to isolate singing voices from the compound of vocal-instrumental music and to ignore the instrumental component of the stimulation, a stimulus filtering of some sophistication.

Another line of research has used the high-amplitude suck (HAS) to show the extreme sophistication of infants' speech perception even more directly. In the HAS procedure young infants are allowed to suck on a nonnutritive pacifier. Following a brief silent baseline period, a speech stimulus is presented each time the infant emits a high-amplitude suck. When the infant's HAS rate falls below an *a priori* criterion, he is either shifted to a different contingent stimulus or left to experience the same one. *Shift* is regarded as the experimental condition and *no shift* as the control. If the infant recovers his sucking rate following *shift* but not after *no shift*, then it is inferred that he discriminated between the two shifted stimuli. Different applications of the HAS procedure have shown that two-month-old infants discriminate between stop consonants (Eimas *et al.,* 1971), between consonants that differ in place of articulation (Morse, 1972), between vowels (Trehub, 1973), between different sequences of vowels and consonants (Trehub, 1973) and between intonation cues (Morse, 1972), such as fundamental frequency contours. Some of these findings have been obtained with natural speech stimuli, and for them the precise basis for the infants' discrimination is unclear. Other HAS experiments employing synthetic speech stimuli leave no doubt that young infants are capable of discriminating a variety of subtle speech cues.

That young infants discriminate exceptionally subtle differences in speech stimuli applies even to neonates. Butterfield and Cairns (1974) used the HAS procedure to study stop consonant discrimination of children during their first 48 hours of life. They showed that these neonates discriminated stop consonants as well as did older infants like those studied by Eimas *et al.* (1971), Trehub (1973) and Morse (1972). Moreover, Butterfield and Cairns showed that the discriminative performance of their neonates depended upon the amount of prior experience they had with certain features of the speech stimuli. Without a brief period of exposure to a stimulus that contained a particular acoustic property, the neonates failed to discriminate; after a brief experience, they did discriminate. This suggests that rapid learning during the preliminary experience with speech stimuli was necessary to the neonates' discrimination, and it implicates central rather than peripheral processes in their speech perception. One can draw this same conclusion from some of Eimas's work, which disclosed that infants' discriminations are predicted by adults' categorizations of speech stimuli. Thus, young infants' perception of speech is to some extent different from their perception of other auditory stimuli. In addition, there is evidence now that speech stimuli evoke lateralized brain potentials in infants while other auditory stimuli do not (Molfese, 1972). Moreover, infants perceive identical cues differently in speech than in nonspeech contexts (Morse, 1972). These findings all implicate special central processes in young infants' speech discrimination.

Basic research into infants' processing of auditory stimuli clearly has stimulated major changes in our view of infants and their capabilities. This new view, in turn, suggests different approaches to assessing infants' auditory functioning to determine whether it is abnormal. It suggests the possibility of assessing central impairments of speech processing in the first days and months of life. It suggests that we have aimed too low with currently employed clinical audiometric techniques. It suggests that we should use the infant's readiness to involve himself with complex stimulation, and particularly his readiness to react to speech, to evaluate more thoroughly his auditory functioning.

Application of Research Techniques to Clinical Practice

Mass Screening

The major approach to identifying infants with hearing impairments has been to screen neonates for severe peripheral hearing loss while they are still in the newborn nursery. This screening typically has been done by nonprofessional volunteers who used intense pure tones in uncontrolled environments to elicit global startle responses, such as increased gross body movement and the aural-palpebral reflex. With these procedures the neonate either passes the test or he fails it.

The low incidence of severe hearing impairment presents a major problem for the mass screening of neonates. With major hearing loss probably occurring between 1 in 1,000 and 1 in 3,000 of screened infants, the screening technique must be extremely sensitive. Obviously, it is not, resulting in extremely high false-positive rates. From 3 to 5 per cent of the infants screened even in relatively well-controlled programs fail the test, prompting even the innovators of screening programs to conclude that they are not clinically useful (Conference on Newborn Hearing Screening, 1971).

Basic research techniques offer no reasonable alternative procedures for mass screening. Aside from their inherent limits, their expense eliminates them from serious consideration. Any requirement that all newborn infants be screened, combined with the low incidence of severe hearing impairment, appears to exclude a procedure that depends upon expensive instrumentation or the time of professional personnel. The issue of cost would remain even if screening techniques that identified subtle central problems as well as peripheral defects uncovered a higher incidence of children with serious problems.

Intensive Assessment of Selected Infants

Perhaps the most reasonable alternative to mass screening is to assess selected infants intensively. The problem is how to select those who are at risk for hearing impairment. In 1971 a large group of professionals concerned with the problem concluded that the vast majority of children with hearing impairments would be captured by a high-risk register that included:

1. All infants with a history of childhood deafness in some member of the immediate family, i.e., father, mother or sibling.
2. All infants whose mother had rubella documented or strongly suspected during any period of pregnancy.
3. All infants with a family history of congenital malformations of the external ear, cleft lip or palate.
4. All infants with a family history of childhood deafness in other relatives.
5. All infants found to have a structural abnormality of the external ear, cleft lip or palate, including bifid uvula.
6. All infants with bilirubin values of 20 mg./100 mg. or more, or who had exchange transfusions.
7. All infants under 1,500 grams.
8. All infants with abnormal otoscopic findings. (Conference on Newborn Hearing Screening, 1971.)

Creating a high-risk register of children who meet these criteria is feasible, since it relies upon evidence that is already collected about most infants. While some of the criteria are specific for peripheral loss, others seem likely to capture children with central problems. The question is whether basic research techniques can be applied profitably to such a circumscribed group of young infants.

I believe that most clinicians and researchers would answer "no." Both would correctly observe that basic research techniques are designed to work with groups rather than individuals, whereas clinicians need to assess individuals, not groups. The HAS procedure illustrates this point. The *shift* and *no shift* conditions have always been applied to separate groups of babies, and when the groups have differed, conclusions have been drawn about infants in general. Accordingly, the HAS procedure seems unusable to the clinician who needs to evaluate particular infants. But the fact that the procedure has been used only in groups does not mean that it cannot be adapted to individuals. Wormith (1971) has shown that two successive shifts can be made with individual children at about two months of age, and we have been able to make two stimulus shifts with neonates. There is hope, therefore, that separate *shift* and *no shift* conditions could be performed on the same infant, providing in principle at least the opportunity to determine whether he responds more strongly following *shift* than *no shift*.

Another consequence of the focus on groups of infants is that the researcher often simply excludes from his experiments infants who are uncooperative or for whom his techniques do not work. For the experimenter attrition simply limits how generally he can cast his conclusions; for the clinician attrition is nothing less than total failure. Many basic research techniques suffer from very high attrition: only a minority of those infants who enter the experiment contribute interpretable data before they leave. Consider an HAS experiment that we recently performed with neonates. We decided in advance that we needed complete data from 40 infants. We had to test 125 infants in order to obtain complete data from 40. Our rejection rate was thus 68 per cent. Such high rates are not peculiar to neonates. Comparable or even higher numbers have been reported for older infants (e.g., Morse, 1972). Such high rejection rates seem to make the HAS procedure clinically useless. However, when basic researchers have increased the number of infants to whom their techniques apply, the results have been more encouraging with respect to clinical application.

Many techniques to obtain the greatest degree of cooperation from neonates could be transferred directly to the infant clinic. Consider our methods to minimize attrition and realize maximum interpretable results from our suck duration procedures. First, we apply a simple entry criterion, namely, that it be between two and one-half and three and one-half hours since the infant was last fed. Our experience has shown that there is a critical one-hour period measured from time of feeding during which neonates will probably produce interpretable data. This is probably because prior to two and one-half hours after feeding the neonate is sleepy or drowsy. More than three and one-half hours after feeding he is hungry and agitated. Neither state is conducive to learning—which the suck duration procedure requires.

In addition to the entry criterion, the child is jiggled and moved as soon as he enters the laboratory until he opens both eyes widely and fixates directly on the experimenter's face. This is an easy response to elicit, and it ensures that each infant is alert at the beginning of our examination. Next is a sucking pretest. We simply put a nipple in the infant's mouth and observe whether he sucks regularly on it. Most neonates do. We employ a systematic cheek stroking procedure with those who do not suck spontaneously; that is, we stimulate the child's rooting reflex by moving the nipple across his cheek toward and into his mouth. We have found that this procedure fails to elicit regular sucking from only about 10 per cent of all neonates who have just passed our alertness criterion. Those infants who pass the sucking pretest are placed in our testing room and given a pacifier to suck upon. Our next precautionary measure is to secure two consecutive blocks of 100 sucks whose median duration agree to within ± .02 seconds; that is, we require stability of behavior on the response measure that we use before we introduce the contingent stimulation whose effects we wish to study.

Our final trick for securing usable information from each neonate is to allow him to pace his way through our procedure. Most basic researchers themselves control how long an infant is exposed to a particular treatment. Thus, they might allow the child three minutes under each of several conditions, regardless of how the infant behaves during those three minutes. Instead, we allow each child to remain in each condition until he has produced a predetermined number of sucking responses, say, 200.

With these various precautions fully 80 per cent of the neonates tested in our laboratory complete their testing session. Clearly, we have a way to go, but the point is valid. It is possible to make laboratory procedures more useful for clinical purposes.

Limitations of Basic Research Technology in Assessment of Auditory Impairment

The possibilities for clinical application notwithstanding, I cannot confidently recommend the use of a graded series of such research techniques described to assess infants' hearing. The fatal flaw in these procedures is that a failure to respond does not mean that the child has an auditory problem. This is because both the HAS and the suck duration procedures measure whether the infant *chooses* to discriminate rather than whether he can discriminate. The examiner can be quite confident of the discriminative and sensory capabilities of the infant who behaves differentially in both of these procedures, but he cannot be sure that the child who fails to behave differentially lacks discriminative capabilities. A variety of temporary states can lead an infant to choose not to respond. One solution would be to examine the child repeatedly with these two techniques, assuming that every additional failure decreases the probability that temporary states underlie the failure to respond and increases the chances that the infant cannot hear. A major difficulty with this proposal is monetary. These procedures require sophisticated laboratory equipment and environmental control arrangements. The cost of bringing children at risk repeatedly to the proper facilities would be outlandish.

Assessment Procedures of the Future

To solve the problem presented by infants who choose not to respond in any particular testing session, researchers have developed techniques for economically sampling a great deal of the infant's behavior, thereby increasing the chances of observing him when he will choose to behave differentially. And they have offered the child incentives over and above the reinforcing properties of the stimuli to be discriminated, which are the only incentives offered by the HAS and suck duration procedures.

Three approaches that may be useful for infant screening and assessment are:

1. Parental monitoring of infant vocalizations.
2. Friedlander's PLAYTEST technique.
3. Operant discrimination training.

Parent Monitoring of Infant Vocalizations

One potential way of identifying hearing defective infants would be for the parents to observe vocal output of their high-risk infants. We have found that parents can reliably record some simple aspects of the expressive speech of their infants (Cairns, Weaver and Wehr, 1973; Cairns and Butterfield, 1978). Moreover, beginning at six weeks of age, infants show a characteristic growth function for each of several classes of speech behavior.

Parental monitoring requires that infants under six months of age vocalize enough to allow the identification of atypical individuals. Irwin's sampling of the speech behavior of very young infants suggests that they do. He found that infants as young as one month produce approximately 62 vowels and consonants during a 30-breath observation period (Irwin, 1947). Also, our data indicate that rate of growth rather than absolute rate of sound production may be the important predictor of later performance. If an infant has any vocal behavior at all, his growth rate can be determined. This measure is not adversely affected by low rates, as are measures that depend on absolute rate.

The use of parental monitoring also presumes that hearing deficits and impairments of speech processing always or often result in expressive speech deficits. Murai (1961, 1963) has reported that normal infants' utterances do differ from those who are hearing-disordered and language-disordered. Lenneberg, Rebelsky and Nichols (1965) disagree. They found that for the first six months a deaf infant cooed during approximately the same number of six-minute observation periods during several 24-hour monitoring days as did a group of normally-hearing infants. Lenneberg (1964) concluded that "this study has revealed the following important fact. Neither deafness nor deaf parents reduce the sound activity during the first six months to any appreciable extent." This is a premature overgeneralization from weak data, as only four data points are reported for a single deaf infant. Winitz (1969) has detailed other methodological problems with this study. The bulk of the evidence seems consistent with the view that hearing-impaired infants have atypical vocalizations, and that parental monitoring of high-risk infants is called for to test the hypothesis that this is a useful way to identify hearing-impaired youngsters.

The PLAYTEST Technique

While parent monitoring depends on the relationship between vocalization and auditory dysfunction, the PLAYTEST procedure measures auditory functioning directly. It does require instruments, making it most useful if applied to a small group of infants who were identified as abnormal by parent counts of their vocalizations.

Descriptions of Friedlander's PLAYTEST procedure appear in several articles (Friedlander, 1968, 1970, 1971, 1975). I need note here only that it is a relatively inexpensive device that requires so little experimenter intervention that it can be placed in infants' homes. It has so far been used with children who were over six months of age, but it can probably be used to assess the listening preferences of younger infants by simply choosing response devices that are within their motor capacity.

Such a modified PLAYTEST would be ideally suited to determining whether infants prefer speech to nonspeech stimuli. The result from our laboratory suggests that they prefer to listen to the human voice. An older infant lacking such a preference might be expected to develop poor speech perception. If preference for speech versus nonspeech was established using the PLAYTEST, then subtle manipulations of the acoustic characteristics of the speech stimulus could be made to assess the infant's responses to acoustic dimensions that are important for speech perception. It is quite possible that infants who have auditory impairments will not reflect the same sensitivities to these manipulations as intact infants.

Operant Discrimination Training

The major difference between Friedlander's PLAYTEST and an operant discrimination procedure is the function of the auditory (or speech) stimulus. The stimulus follows the response and is a consequence in the PLAYTEST, while it precedes the response and acts as a discriminative signal in the operant discrimination procedure.

There are several methodological and theoretical advantages to making the speech stimulus function as a signal that reward is available rather than have it be as the reward itself. First, simple speech stimuli have only transient reinforcing properties. The HAS and other habituation procedures, which have been used so widely for studying the sensory processing of infants, depend on the weakness of speech as a reinforcer to achieve habituation in a reasonable time. More potent reinforcers can be used in discrimination training procedures. One effect of the more potent reinforcer is that the session may be extended for longer times. A potent reinforcer also encourages the infant to tell us what stimulus differences he *can* discriminate rather than those he *chooses* to discriminate. And, since the discriminative stimulus signals what is to follow a response, it serves one of the functions of speech for adults: it conveys a simple kind of meaning. Discrimination as reflected by differential responding in this paradigm may reflect a higher level of functioning than merely responding to obtain the beginning or end of the stimulus.

In order to show operant discrimination an infant must make a response (ideally one that is discrete and easily recorded), he must perceive the difference between a stimulus (S+) that indicates that a reward will follow his response and a stimulus (S−) that indicates that a reward will not follow, and he must be so attracted to the reward that he will work to obtain it. Each of these apparently simple requirements presents a problem for the infant examiner. Sheppard (1969) has described each of them and has shown how they can be overcome for three-month-old infants. More to the point, Wilson (1978) has shown how to use operant discrimination procedures to assess hearing thresholds of infants as young as five months of age. Using parent observations and PLAYTEST procedures to determine whether a child has a likely hearing loss could well take four or five months. Consequently, Wilson's procedures probably require no more extension than the last of the necessary behavioral assessment procedures for identifying infants with hearing losses.

My point in describing these procedures is to convey a vision of the day when modified parental observations, PLAYTEST techniques and operant conditioning procedures will be used to identify very early in infancy those who may be expected to encounter speech and language problems later on unless specific auditory processing deficits are cured or bypassed. I foresee the day when infants who are at risk will be registered at birth. Their parents will be trained to observe not only the infants' vocal productions, but also their responses to environmental sounds, particularly speech signals. Those children who are atypical according to parental observations will be provided with a PLAYTEST-like toy that will assess their preferences for different types of speech signals over extended periods. Those infants who perform atypically on this automated test will be evaluated by means of operant discrimination techniques. This might be done in specialized clinics, as is now possible, or in the infant's home with instruments that are only slight modifications of the PLAYTEST. All this vision requires for realization is a modest partnership between basic researchers and child clinicians.

Acknowledgment

The preparation of this chapter and the collection of the neonatal data reported in it were supported by U.S.P.H.S. Grants HD-00183, HD-02528, and HD-04756.

References

Butterfield, E.C. and Cairns, G.F., Jr. Whether infants perceive linguistically is uncertain, and if they did, its practical importance would be equivocal, in Schiefelbusch, R.L. and Lloyd, L.L. (eds.), *Language Perspectives—Acquisition, Retardation, and Intervention.* Baltimore, Md.: University Park Press (1974).

Butterfield, E.C. and Siperstein, G.N. Influence of contingent auditory stimulation upon non-nutritional suckle, in Bosma, J. (ed.), *Oral Sensation and Perception: The Mouth of the Infant.* Springfield, Ill.: C.C. Thomas (1972).

Cairns, G.F. and Butterfield, E.C. Assessing language-related skills of pre-linguistic children. *All. Health and Behav. Sci.,* 1:81–130 (1978).

Cairns, G.F., Jr., Weaver, S.J. and Wehr, J. Training college students to teach mothers to perform potentially useful pediatric screening functions in the home. *Newsletter of the Society of Pediatric Psychology* (1973).

Conference on Newborn Hearing Screening—Proceedings Summary and Recommendations. San Francisco, February, 1971. Maternal and Child Health Service, Health Services and Mental Health Administration, Public Health Service, Department of Health, Education and Welfare (1971).

Eimas, P.D., Siqueland, D.R., Jusczyk, P. and Vigorito, J. Speech perception in infants. *Science,* 171:303–306 (1971).

Friedlander, B.Z. The effect of speaker identity, voice inflection, vocabulary, and message redundancy on infants' selection of vocal reinforcement. *J. Exper. Child Psychol.,* 6:443–459 (1968).

Friedlander, B.Z. Receptive language development in infancy: Issues and problems. *Merrill-Palmer Quarterly of Behavior and Development,* 16:7–51 (1970).

Friedlander, B.Z. Listening, language, and the auditory environment: Automated evaluation and intervention, in Hellmuth, J. (ed.), *Exceptional Infant,* Vol. 2. New York: Brunner/Mazel (1971).

Friedlander, B.Z. Automated valuation of selective listening in language-impaired and normal infants and young children, in Friedlander, B.Z., Sterritt, G.M. and Kirk, G.E. (eds.), *The Exceptional Infant,* Vol. 3. New York: Brunner/Mazel (1975).

Irwin, O.C. Development of speech during infancy: Curve of phonemic frequencies. *J. Exper. Psychol.,* 37:187–193 (1947).

Lenneberg, E.H. Speech as a motor skill with special reference to nonaphasic disorders. *Monographs of the Society for Research in Child Development,* 29(92):115–127 (1964).

Molfese, D.L. Cerebral asymmetry in infants, children and adults: Auditory evoked responses to speech and noise stimuli. Unpublished doctoral dissertation, Pennsylvania State University (1972).

Morse, P.A. The discrimination of speech and nonspeech stimuli in early infancy. *J. Exper. Child Psychol.,* 14:477–492 (1972).

Murai, J. The sounds of infants: Their phonemicization and symbolization. *Studia Phonologica,* 3:17–33 (1963).

Murai, J. Speech development of a child suffering from a central language disorder. *Studia Phonologica,* 1:58–69 (1961).

Sheppard, W.C. Operant control of infant vocal and motor behavior. *J. Exper. Child Psychol.,* 7:36–51 (1969).

Siqueland, E.R. The development of instrumental exploratory behavior during the first year of human life. Paper presented at the Biennial Meeting of the Society for Research in Child Development, Santa Monica, California, March (1969).

Trehub, S.E. Infants' sensitivity to vowel and tonal contrasts. *Develop. Psychol.,* 9:91–96 (1973).

Wilson, W.R. Behavioral assessment of auditory function in infants, in Minifie, F.D. and Lloyd, L.L. (eds.), *Communicative and Cognitive Abilities—Early Behavioral Assessment.* Baltimore, Md.: University Park Press, pp. 37–60 (1978).

Winitz, H. *Articulatory Acquisition and Behavior.* New York: Appleton-Century-Crofts (1969).

Wormith, J.S. Pure tone discrimination in infants. Unpublished master's thesis, Carleton University (1971).

PART II

Motor Development

The knowledge of the physiology and anatomical substrates for normal motor development is far from complete. The effect of experience, sensory feedback, motivation and cognition on motor performance is presently a source of study by many researchers.

One cannot use the achievement of gross motor milestones as an assessment tool for early recognition of motor dysfunction or as a basis for estimating cognitive ability. More can be learned about the motor system if the quality (and not simply the quantity) of the motor performance is evaluated. Dyspraxic motor disability or problems in visuomotor integration may only be manifest in a difference in motor performance style and not in a significant delay in achieving a motor task.

Even in the presence of a significant motor impairment that can be classified as cerebral palsy, early recognition of the dysfunctional state is difficult. In addition, prognosis as to motor outcome and appropriate intervention strategies is complicated by the ever changing clinical picture seen in the first few years of life secondary to the maturation of the nervous system.

This section will cover aspects of normal motor development, the early recognition of a motor disability and the state of the art and science in intervention strategies that are designed to favorably impact on the motor outcome.

9

Theoretical Issues in the Development of Motor Skills

PETER H. WOLFF

Controlled movements are our only means for maintaining posture against gravity, moving in space, changing the environment and communicating by speech and gesture. The perception of controlled movement is our only source of concrete knowledge about what others are doing, thinking or feeling. Sensory motor transactions with the physical and social environment prepare the psychological structures of symbolization and operational intelligence and motor mechanisms are instrumental in organizing perception and memory. Contrary to traditional views, we might regard motor action as the essential achievement of human evolution that subordinates other psychological processes rather than as the tool that serves will, emotion and cognition.

There is considerable information about *when* children achieve the common motor milestones of postural adjustment, locomotion and object manipulation, and the various developmental motor milestones are so familiar they do not require any review here (Gesell and Amatruda, 1947; Peiper, 1963; McGraw, 1966; Illingworth, 1967; Cratty, 1976). Although there is detailed experimental information about the neurophysiology of muscle innervation and brain mechanisms of simple movements in animals (Denny-Brown, 1966; Granit, 1970; Matthews, 1972) and about the psychological mechanisms of motor performance in adults (Greenwald, 1970; Adams, 1971; Schmidt, 1975), we know very little about *how* children construct coordinated actions or what neurological, psychological and environmental conditions are essential for the development of motor skills. I submit that the investigation of motor skill acquisition raises all the essential issues in developmental theory and provides a unique opportunity for resolving problems in human development that cannot be studied productively by other means.

For example, the contributions of biology and experience to the induction of new behavioral forms (Gottlieb, 1976) have been discussed extensively in terms of motor development. Traditional explanations of motor development in infancy assume that directed movements are controlled primarily or exclusively by reflexes and that extrauterine experience makes no significant contribution to the evolution of postural and species-typical movement patterns (Wyke, 1975). Gesell (1941) characterized the maturational component in behavioral development by "its inevitableness and surety as the most impressive characteristic of early development. It is the hereditary ballast that conserves and stabilizes the growth of each individual infant." The passage implies that the maturation of behavior can be inferred from the invariability of postural reflexes and locomotor patterns. Yet, even the most common reflexes of pediatric neurology show marked individual variations in onset and inhibition (Touwen, 1978), so that the maturational factor may be represented by the *variability* rather than the *stereotypy* of motor milestones. As independent criteria of developmental age variations in neuromotor development could serve as an important corrective for contemporary studies in behavioral development. Many such studies start from the assumption that development is always mutually determined by biological ("maturational") and experiential factors but explain all normal within-age variations in terms of experiential variables, as if chronological age were the sufficient criterion of developmental state (Wohlwill, 1973).

A strong maturational hypothesis of human motor development (Gesell, 1941) is probably untenable; however, the contrary claim that conditioning and contingent reinforcement shape primitive reflexes into 'inear S-R and R-S chains is equally so. Such a formulation would have to assume that schedules of reinforcement are so uniform in content and timing as to program all normal children to achieve motor milestones in nearly the same order at nearly the same rate. Yet, the rate and sequence of gross motor development are remarkably consistent during the early years despite severe stimulus deprivation (Dennis, 1938; Dennis and Dennis, 1940), whereas experimental intervention to accelerate the development of common motor abilities has been generally disappointing (Gesell and Thompson, 1934; McGraw, 1935; Pickler, 1972; see however Peiper, 1963 and Zelazo *et al.,* 1972). Some indirect evidence for the educability of early motor skills comes from cross-cultural comparisons of child-rearing practices. The phenomenon of African infant precocity has sometimes been attributed to genetic variations in maturational rate across relatively isolated mating populations (Geber and Dean, 1957; Freedman, 1974). However, the genetic hypothesis remains essentially untested, while cultural differences in child-rearing practices can explain a significant proportion of observed group differences in developmental rate (Warren, 1972).

Neither intrinsic developmental timetables nor experience is a sufficient condition for motor skill acquisition. At every stage motor development depends not only on experience and quality of the stimulus but on the brain mechanisms that assimilate and organize information from the environment and from action in progress.

Experimental studies of adults have given us reliable methods for investigating motor skill acquisition that would, with appropriate modification, be applicable to motor development in children. Such studies have also generated theoretical models that are both relevant for and critically dependent on parallel investigations in children. Although I do not intend to propose a coherent developmental theory of motor skill acquisition on the basis of the available knowledge, I will review briefly some major theoretical models of motor skill acquisition, consider the evidence on which they are based and indicate how systematic studies in children can consolidate current theories of psychological development.

The Components of Motor Skill Acquisition

Prefunctional Contributions to Motor Performance

It is difficult to conceive of motor skill acquisition without assuming that constituent motor elements of congenital reflexes are incorporated during the construction of more complex actions (Peiper, 1963). The issue in dispute is not the existence of prefunctional motor programs but the level at which they are maintained for integration into voluntary action and the extent to which such "closed loop mechanisms" differ from fixed action patterns in lower (nonmammalian) species (Weiss, 1941, 1950; von Holst and Mittelstedt, 1950; Wilson, 1961). For example, Twitchell (1965) has concluded that observable subassemblies of congenital motor reflexes are built into voluntary motor actions. Yet it is difficult to trace the form-function relation from the neonatal traction response to directed grasping in three-month-old infants or from the stepping reflex to walking movements of one-year-old children (Peiper, 1963; Zelazo *et al.*, 1972).

On the other hand, Milani-Comparetti and Gidoni (1967) concluded that primitive motor automatisms must be "dissolved" before voluntary motor patterns can emerge, as if there were an inherent antagonism between reflexes and voluntary motor actions. The apparent contradictions in the two formulations may, however, be semantic rather than substantive. Despite the over confidence in distinguishing between motor reflexes and voluntary actions, the term "reflex" remains ambiguous. Some investigators reserve the term for movement patterns organized at a "subcortical" level, without specifying the possible involvement of cerebellar or cortical mechanisms. Others refer to "cerebral motor reflexes," which seems to contradict conventional use of the term "reflex." For any complex movement it is usually difficult to define where prefunctional motor automatisms end and acquired movement patterns begin. In humans it is also difficult to test whether movement patterns that emerge after birth result directly from continuing central nervous system maturation or from experience. Furthermore, many of the coordinated action patterns acquired by active participation of the cerebral hemispheres will, after practice and automatization, be reallocated to subcortical mechanisms, and can then be performed with greater proficiency when allowed to run their course automatically. Since the locus of movement control may shift drastically during development, neuroanatomical localization is not a reliable criterion for distinguishing between reflex and voluntary action.

Clinical evidence indicates that the abnormal persistence of primitive reflexes is associated with delayed onset of voluntary motor skills (Zapella *et al.*, 1964; Illingworth, 1967; Molnar, 1978) and that motor retardation is associated with delays of intellectual development (Neligan and Prudham, 1969; Schmitt and Erikson, 1973). However, no causal interdependence can be inferred from these associations, since all three may have a common etiology in impaired central nervous system function. Pathologic motor stereotypes may reveal the presumed antagonistic relation between congenital motor automatisms, voluntary action and intellectual development more directly. Of the many theories for motor stereotypes proposed to date, none can account for all manifestations of this widespread phenomenon, since each theory focuses on a particular clinical manifestation. Inherent in all complex motor skills is the flexibility of their serial organization (Lashley, 1951; Lenneberg, 1957; Hawles and Jenkins, 1971). One characteristic common to all motor stereotypes, whether they occur in normal infants, blind, autistic, mentally retarded, institutionalized, sensorially deprived or brain-damaged children, is the relative monotony and inflexibility of their serial organization (Wolff, 1968a). To the extent that the "closed loop" features of stereotypic motor repetitions interfere with active exploration of the physical and social environment, they may also interfere with cognitive development. A structural perspective that assumes a developmental arrest or regression in the timing for motor control (Piaget, 1951; Sollberger, 1965; Wolff, 1968b) might account for the retarding effect of pathologic stereotypes, regardless of their diagnosis. The perspective would also suggest therapeutic approaches to differentiate the timing of existing motor stereotypes rather than suppress them by negative reinforcement. Investigations on the developmental relation between congenital reflexes and voluntary motor action could contribute to the still-debated question whether severe learning disabilities can be effectively treated by re-educating early motor milestones (Kephart, 1960; Delacato, 1966; Cratty,

1978). They would provide essential background information for the rehabilitation of children with severe neuromotor disease.

Speed and Accuracy

For young children in search of novel motor solutions speed and accuracy of movement are essential for skilled performance. These parameters improve dramatically during the preschool years, but their interdependence for skill acquisition has rarely been investigated in children. Fitts (1954) and his colleagues (e.g., Fitts and Peterson, 1964) showed that adults adopt a "trade-off" strategy between speed and accuracy as they acquire a new visuomotor skill. Developmental changes in speed of movement have been examined by simple and choice reaction times (Wickens, 1974) and by finger-tapping paradigms. All such studies indicate a systematic age-dependent increase in speed of movement from age four until early or late adolescence (Bryan, 1892; Goodenough, 1935; Annett, 1970). Connolly, Brown and Bassett (1968) measured the development of accuracy as well as speed on a target-location task and found a linear age-related increase in movement speed from 6 to 10 years that was independent of practice effects. Over the same age range accuracy in target location improved with practice but not with age. Girls performed significantly faster than boys of the same age, but again there were no significant sex differences in accuracy.

The increase of movement speed is determined in part by increased nerve conduction velocity (Connolly et al., 1968). It also reflects developmental changes in speed of information processing, which can be demonstrated on tasks where rate of movement is not a critical variable (Connolly, 1975; Wickens, 1974). Developmental studies on the interaction among speed, serial order control and accuracy of spatial localization in motor performance, using younger children or more complex tasks, would provide information about how children develop trade-off strategies when one performance parameter must be sacrificed.

Knowledge of Results

Knowledge about the environmental consequences of action informs the actor whether the goal has been achieved or how movement sequences should be modified to reach the goal. Utilizing this knowledge, in turn, depends on access to a stable mental representation of the physical world, its causal properties, spatial relations and temporal characteristics (Piaget, 1951, 1952). The influence of knowledge of results on motor skill acquisition has been investigated extensively in adults by varying the quantity or quality of environmental information provided as subjects learn new motor tasks (Bilodeau, 1966; Welford, 1968;

Adams, 1971). While its effect on motor development has rarely been studied in children, the rapid differentiation of cognitive structures and increase in capacity for information processing (Farnham-Diggory, 1972; Wickens, 1974) should be reflected directly in their ability to construct new motor skills. Newell and Kennedy (1978), for example, found that preadolescent children were able to profit from very detailed and explicit knowledge of results, whereas younger children showed a deterioration of motor performance when they were given the same detailed information, as if there were an age-specific, optimum level of knowledge of results for motor learning. Elaborations on this experiment would challenge the currently popular assumption that sensory motor intelligence is of interest to cognitive psychology only as the precursor for symbolic thought. Conversely, they would provide the empirical means for investigating how cognition enhances the coordination of action (Sperry, 1952) and how young children construct plans of action, a process that usually cannot be observed directly and must be inferred once children become competent speakers.

Practice and Correction of Errors

The transformation from goal-directed movement to skilled action cannot be accomplished by knowledge about the results of action alone. The actor must also have a continuous flow of *reafferent* information about the force, speed and direction of movement contributed by sensations from the moving limbs and of *exafferent* visual information contributed by observing the limb in motion. Furthermore, the actor must be able to organize and compare such information against an internal reference criterion that tells him how closely the actual movements match the movements specified by the goal.

The theoretical models proposed by von Holst and Mittelstedt (1950) and Held (Held and Hein, 1963; Held and Bauer, 1974) deal specifically with the contributions of exafferent and reafferent feedback to skill acquisition. Experiments based on these models demonstrated that *active* movement and the resulting reafference are essential, while passive displacement of the limbs contributes relatively little to skilled performance. The experiments documented the critical importance of self-initiated action and exploration for motor development. They may also identify a major reason enrichment programs for young normal or handicapped children which attempt to short-circuit active motor participation for the sake of efficiency are doomed to failure.

Bernstein's model of motor skill acquisition (1967) retains the reafference concept. At the same time it emphasizes that practice is always a process of finding continuously new solutions to a motor problem rather than the repetition of one "correct" solution (see also Bartlett, 1932). By detailed biomechanical studies on adults Bernstein demonstrated that the motor goal is usually identified long before an efficient motor routine has been discovered, and that no goal-directed action, no matter how extensively practiced, is ever repeated in exactly the same form. He concluded that neural programs controlling co-ordinated action cannot be the direct isomorphism of any one sequence of movements but must be "prototypes" of action capable of producing a large set of functionally equivalent motor routines. He further concluded that "reduction in degrees of freedom" is essential to stabilize and automatize flexible motor skills.

Error elimination as a component of skill acquisition has occasionally been investigated in young children (e.g., White and Held, 1966; Connolly, 1975; Rosenbloom and Norton, 1975). Bruner and his colleagues (1971) used Bernstein's model to investigate how infants learn to reach for and take hold of single objects, to deal with two or more desired objects presented simultaneously, to use both hands in a means-end relation and to circumvent a physical barrier to reach the goal. Although age and task complexity introduced variations in specific aspects of performance, all children proceeded according to a similar overall strategy. First, they oriented to the goal and tried out various previously learned motor routines from which they selected an approximately suitable motor sequence. The children gradually modified the clumsy sequence by sub-stituting functionally equivalent subroutines and rearranging their sequence, while keeping the goal in mind. Finally, the elimination of extraneous move-ments automatized the appropriate solution. The children knew *what* they wanted before they realized *how* to get it, and they discovered how to get it before they had perfected the motor skill.

Thus, observing motor skill acquisition in preverbal children vividly illustrates that practice is always the elaboration of partially new solutions to an overriding problem rather than the repetition and overlearning of fixed routines. This fact alone has major implications for preschool education, because it raises serious questions about the value of programmed instructions and challenges a traditional assumption that has condemned generations of normal and handicapped children to endless hours of mindless activity.

Development of Motor Inhibition

Constructing a motor skill involves not only activating suitable motor routines but also inhibiting extraneous movements that are either not essential for per-formance or actual hindrances with achievement of the goal. Normal adults may show a latent activation of functionally related muscle groups in the contra-lateral limb when performing a unimanual action. When such activation is not apparent, it can be demonstrated by electromyography (Cernacek, 1961; Green, 1967). Even in adults the overflow may be observable during great effort or after brain damage (Konorsky, 1967; Zülch, 1975). Such overflow movements are more closely related to intentional actions than to reflex or passive movements. Similar synkineses, mirror and associated movements occur with great consistency in young children, gradually being inhibited in the course of normal development. They persist in adults who sustained cerebral damage in early childhood, occur with greater frequency in normal boys than girls of the same age and continue longer in children with minor neuropsychological impairment than in normal children (Fog and Fog, 1963; Abercrombie *et al.*, 1964; Connolly and Stratton, 1968; Woods and Teuber, 1978). After a certain age young children who still demonstrate synkineses can inhibit these when the observer calls attention to them, and the capacity for inhibition on instruction follows a predictable developmental progression (Cohen *et al.*, 1967). Since mirror movements can be inhibited by effort, and since inhibited synkineses may reappear when children or adults are required to perform a secondary nonmotor task concurrently, inhibition of extraneous movements is probably not a mechanical consequence of "brain maturation" but a process that requires effort.

Inhibition and the failure to inhibit unintended motor actions have always been of interest for clinical neurology and rehabilitation medicine. However, they have not received sufficient attention in behavioral studies of normal children, although inhibition is as essential for motor skill acquisition as activation of intended motor sequences and is an important marker of neurodevelopmental state independent of chronological age. The functional association between inhibition of unintended movements and of intended cognitive or linguistic responses has not been investigated in any detail, but the development of inhibition for unintended movements may be a more general indicator of response inhibition and, as such, a useful empirical tool for developmental studies in cognitive and perceptual development.

Motor Ideas

The feature of organized movement that most clearly distinguishes *action* from *movement* is the ability of any skilled performer to maintain an overall plan of action in the face of unforeseen obstacles by substituting functionally equivalent motor elements or modifying the order of subroutines to achieve the same end. The contribution of prefunctional *programs* to motor control can be demonstrated in lower animal species by deplantation experiments or by surgical manipulations that eliminate all sensory feedback but do not significantly interfere with quadripedal gait, coordinated swimming or flying movements (Weiss, 1941; 1950; von Holst and Mittelstedt, 1950; Marler and Hamilton, 1967). Motor programs may also control the simple reflexes and chain reflexes of postural adjustment in humans which are "subroutines" for constructing complex movement patterns, although this role can only be inferred from clinical material (Denny-Brown, 1966; Zülch, 1975). However, prefunctional motor programs are "closed loops" controlling fixed movement sequences and lack the generative properties that characterize motor ideas.

The constructive feature of motor ideas becomes apparent, for example, when a proficient violinist breaks a string during a recital but continues without interruption by reprogramming the usual fingering, playing the required notes on different strings. Similar motor ideas govern the acquisition of all complex motor skills in children and adults, although the product is usually less exalted than the performance of a trained musician. The process by which prototypes of action or motor ideas guide action without controlling specific sequences of movement remains the central problem to be explained by theories of motor skill acquisition. In principle, the same problem confronts theories of language acquisition and constructive intelligence.

The contribution of motor ideas to skilled performance of young children is illustrated by observational learning (Bandura, 1965). Several studies have reported that one-month-old infants will imitate tongue protrusions or other common facial gestures on presentation of a suitable visual model, even though they have never observed their own facial gestures and can therefore not compare their effort with the visual image (Meltzoff and Moore, 1977). An empiric definition of the boundaries within which infants will respond to suitable models by form-specific facial imitations would test the hypothesis that naive infants have implicit prefunctional knowledge about the formal similarities between movements they see and motor action they perform but cannot see (Bower, 1978).

In older preverbal infants the contribution of perceptual images to skilled performance is illustrated by the phenomenon of deferred imitations. Piaget (1951) and Werner and Kaplan (1968) have summarized data indicating that six- to eight-month-old infants will imitate the "vectorial" properties of movements or gestures which they observed hours or days before. Such deferred imitations do not produce physical identities between the model and the imitation, but they preserve the formal configuration of the observed movement. Since deferred imitations commonly occur long before children acquire language, such observations attest to the effectiveness of perceptual images as motor ideas and to the fact that perceptual motor ideas are generative in reproducing the formal properties of the model without controlling the actual movements.

Luria (1961) has reported detailed experiments on children from one and a half to five years indicating that motor ideas can also be verbally encoded. In the experiments children were required to squeeze an air-filled balloon according to increasingly complex instructions. Their performance followed a predictable progression from (a) responding directly to a simple verbal command ("squeeze the balloon"); to (b) responding when the instruction called for a delay of action ("squeeze only when the light goes on") but not being able to inhibit an inappropriate response to more complex instructions ("squeeze when the red light goes on and do not squeeze when the green light goes on"); to (c) respond-ing selectively by audibly repeating the instruction to themselves; to (d) respond-ing selectively without speaking. Luria inferred that verbal control of intended action and verbal inhibition of unintended movement are internalized progres-sively in development, beginning with appropriate responses to external commands, shifting to spoken self-instruction and ending as silent self-instruc-tion. The studies do not indicate whether verbal codes replace perceptual images as motor ideas, whether both types of motor control operate concurrently, or whether motor ideas are stored and utilized as perceptual images but decoded verbally for purposes of communication. Even proficient athletes have great difficulty communicating how they perform skilled actions without resorting to gestures; on the other hand, the athletic novice derives no benefit from verbal instruction until he has practiced the skill. The influence of verbal motor ideas may therefore be limited to controlling simple movements. Studies on the nature and formation of motor ideas would have important clinical implications for the rehabilitation of children with sensory, neuromuscular or central motor deficits. They would also provide a unique opportunity to examine how alternative strategies are constructed when the visual mechanisms of motor control are significantly impaired.

In addition to guiding coordinated actions, motor ideas facilitate the development of perception and memory (Keele, 1968). In language perception this facilitation (motor perception) is most dramatically illustrated by the fact that we can often understand more of what others intend to say than what they have actually conveyed, as if the perceiver contributed information not con-tained in the acoustic signal. From a review of the literature Liberman *et al.* (1967) concluded "though we cannot exclude the possibility that a purely auditory decoder exists, we find it more plausible to assume that speech is perceived by processes that are also involved in its production. There is typically a lack of correspondence between acoustic cues and perceived phonemes, and in all cases, it appears that perception mirrors articulation more closely than sound." Since young children are much less efficient than adults in extracting the meaning of speech sounds from the semantic context, they are probably also more dependent on "analysis by synthesis" (Halle and Stevens, 1962) or motor perception.

The Neuropsychology of Motor Skill Acquisition

Until now I have discussed the components of skilled motor performance primarily from a psychological perspective. Most of the theoretical models I have reviewed made some reference to neurological correlates of motor control, but by and large, they were not based on physiologic data. For tactical reasons most current investigations on neuromuscular mechanisms of movement control concentrate on isolated movements rather than coordinated actions (Granit, 1970; Matthews, 1972), so that their findings may be of only peripheral interest for a discussion of skill acquisition. Recent advances in the neuropsychology, however, can contribute directly to the developmental investigation of coordinated motor action.

The psychological performance of patients with surgical neocommissurotomies demonstrates that the two hemispheres can function as autonomous agencies, thereby challenging traditional philosophical speculations on the locus of consciousness and intention (Sperry, 1952). Such studies also confirm many inferences about functional specialization of the cerebral cortex that are based on pathologic data of patients with localized brain lesions (Dimond and Beaumont, 1974; Sperry, 1974; Nebes, 1974; Levy, 1977). However, impairment of function after localized brain lesions does not warrant the conclusion that the damaged region also controls the impaired function in normal subjects. Nor does the fact that surgically disconnected cerebral hemispheres *can* function as autonomous processors justify concluding that the hemispheres operate independently when the corpus callosum is intact. Furthermore, the central nervous system goes through extensive organizational changes between birth and adolescence, so that the same action may be controlled from different structures or by different mechanisms at different stages of brain development (Bronson, 1965; Lenneberg, 1967). The neurodevelopmental investigation of motor skill acquisition may therefore be on firmer ground when it starts with the phenomenology of neuromotor development in normal infants and children.

Cerebral Asymmetries in Motor Control

A convenient starting point for studying early brain correlates of motor action is the development of right-left asymmetries in self-initiated movement. Turkewitz (1977) has found that most newborns tend to keep their heads to the right under environmentally neutral conditions, although they demonstrate no consistent hand preference. Since visual monitoring of limb movements facilitates accurate reaching and object manipulation (Held and Hein, 1963; White and Held, 1966; Held and Bauer, 1974), congenital head preference may produce asymmetries of motor skill acquisition (Coryell and Michel, 1978). The demonstration that newborn infants decisively preferring a left head position also develop a left hand preference would be a strong test of the hypothesis, but until now this association has not been clearly shown. In view of persuasive evidence for the genetic control of right but not left hand preference (Annett,

1972), it is possible that congenital head preference only affects hand preference in children who are not genetically programmed to become right-handed.
An empiric test of this relation would help to clarify the role of experience in
establishing hand preference.

During the early months after birth infants grasp more with their right
hand and reach more with their left hand; after the end of the first year the right
hand gradually assumes a primary role for reaching, fine motor manipulation and
bimanual coordination as well as for grasping (Young, 1977). By tracing changes
in the direction of asymmetry for manual skills over the first two years, it should
be possible to test whether the hemispheric specialization of motor control is
fixed at birth or goes through predictable changes, and whether the cerebral
organization for motor development is more plastic than most current models
assume (Lenneberg, 1967; Levy, 1977). If consistent developmental changes
were demonstrated, cross-cultural comparisons would also permit us to assess the
relative weight of environmental and "late maturing factors" in the development
of manual asymmetry.

Hand preference is firmly established by the time children are four years
old and does not change thereafter. By most criteria of physical growth girls
mature faster between birth and late adolescence than boys. At the same time
they are developmentally advanced relative to boys on most measures of neuromotor maturation and fine motor manual skills, and they tend to demonstrate
manual asymmetries favoring the right hand earlier (Annett, 1970; Denckla,
1974; Wolff and Hurwitz, 1976). Longitudinal follow-up studies of boys and
girls comparing developmental changes in physical growth, motor performance
and manual performance asymmetries, should make it possible to test the phase
correlations between variations in physical maturation and development of
cerebral asymmetries for motor control.

However, inferences about hemispheric specialization for motor control
from manual performance asymmetries are only valid within limits. For example, motor skills that involve only finger movements are programmed primarily from the contralateral hemisphere, while motor skills involving the whole
hand or arm may be controlled from both the ipsilateral and contralateral
hemispheres (Lawrence and Kuypers, 1965; Wyke, 1971). The direction of
performance asymmetries is not consistent for all motor tasks even when they
involve only the distal musculature. Right-handed adults will perform tasks of
gestural representation, spatial localization and pattern perception more accurately with the nonpreferred left hand (Hermelin and O'Connor, 1971; Ingram,
1975), but will show a distinct right-hand advantage on fine motor manual tasks
involving precise serial order control, speed or visuomotor integration (Goodenough, 1935; Connolly *et al.*, 1968; Annett, 1970; Wolff and Hurwitz, 1976).
Such variations indicate that the functional characteristics of the motor skill
must be considered when hemispheric specialization is inferred from perform-

ance asymmetries. Furthermore, sequentially ordered, fine motor manual skills not requiring continuous feedback may not be lateralized once they have been automatized or may be lateralized only under particular experimental conditions (Flowers, 1975; Lomas and Kimura, 1976; Wolff, Hurwitz and Moss, 1977). Finally, the degree and perhaps the direction on manual asymmetry for novel fine motor sequencing tasks changes during development (Denckla, 1974; Wolff, 1977). Thus, developmental age and prior experience may influence the relation between performance asymmetries and hemispheric specialization for motor control.

Bimanual Coordination

In contrast to unimanual tasks the extent of asymmetries on bimanual tasks has rarely been investigated in normal adults (Oldfield, 1969) and almost never from a developmental perspective. Neuroanatomical studies suggest that structural maturation of the major cerebral commissures is not completed until late in childhood (Yakovkev and Lecours, 1967; Gazzaniga, 1978). At the same time experimental observations on adult patients with callosectomies indicate that an intact corpus callosum facilitates the timing control of coordinated bimanual actions (Preilowski, 1972; Kreuter *et al.*, 1972; Zaidel and Sperry, 1977). The analysis of bimanual coordination may therefore reveal brain correlates of motor development that are not apparent from unimanual motor tasks alone.

For example, Wolff and Hurwitz (1976) demonstrated a consistent age-related improvement of serial order control in children from 5 to 14 years on a task that required subjects to keep the beat of an entraining metronome by using the two hands in alternation. The most rapid improvement for bimanual co-ordination occurred between five and eight years; the right hand was consistently more stable than the left; girls were more skillful than boys at keeping a steady beat and girls showed a right-hand advantage as well as a left-hand catch-up earlier than boys. When unimanual and bimanual performance were compared, the right hand was found to lose some stability by working with the left hand, although it remained steadier than the left; whereas the left hand gained in stability by collaborating with the right hand. In other words, the preferred right hand (and, by inference, the left hemisphere) assumes an early lead for bimanual coordination as well as for sequentially ordered tasks. The leading function of the right hand for bimanual tasks is, however, not invariable and can be shown to change under experimental conditions. For example, when right-handed adults perform a secondary verbal task while tapping a rhythm in bi-manual alternation, the primary locus of timing control may shift from the right to the left hand. Such a shift does not occur either during unimanual perform-ance and concurrent verbalization or during bimanual alternation without a subsidiary interference task (Wolff and Cohen, in press). By applying the same dual task paradigm from a developmental perspective, it should be possible to investigate the ontogenesis of interhemispheric cooperation and capacity sharing when the demands on functional space within one hemisphere exceed capacity.

Kindergarten children have great difficulty maintaining the beat of an entraining metronome whether they use one or both hands, but the difficulty is most apparent during performance of bimanual alternating tasks (Wolff et al., in preparation). During unimanual performance kindergarten children, especially boys, demonstrate mirror movements of the contralateral hand that would approximate the required rhythm if the nonactive hand touched a tapping key. The mirror movements do not disrupt unimanual or bimanual simultaneous performance, but they will interfere with bimanual alternation unless they are inhibited and unless the locus of inhibition can switch smoothly and rapidly between the two hands. The relatively late inhibition of mirror movements may partly explain why fine motor manual skills that require bimanual coordination are more sensitive to variations in developmental state than unimanual tasks. In a clinical study of preadolescent boys with severe reading retardation, Badian and Wolff (1977) found that dyslexic boys did not differ from normal readers on the unimanual tapping task, but they were markedly impaired in maintaining a steady beat when alternating between the two hands. The finding suggests that many neurological functions essential for behavioral development may depend on active cooperation between the hemispheres rather than on prefunctional programs localized in either the left or right hemisphere.

Conclusions

I would like to close with excerpts from Sperry's discussion of neurology and the mind-brain problem which states the strategic advantages of studying motor behavior and development in unambiguous terms: "The layman naturally assumes the major work of the brain to be the manufacture of ideas, sensations, images, and feelings, the storage of memories, and the like, and often expects the physical correlates of these to be some kind of aural endproduct phosphorescing within the cortex or emanating from its convolutions. . . . The entire activity of the brain so far as science can determine yields nothing but motor adjust. The only significant energy outlet and the only means of expression are over the motor pathways. . . . To the neurologist, regarding the brain from an objective, analytical standpoint, it is readily apparent that the sole product of brain function is motor coordination. To repeat: *the entire output of our thinking machine consists of nothing but patterns of motor coordination*" (Sperry, 1952).

Acknowledgment

This work was supported in part by the Mental Retardation Center Core Grant #ED06276.

References

Abercrombie, M.L.J., Lindon, R.L. and Tyson, M.C. Associated movements in normal and physically handicapped children. *Dev. Med. Child Neurol.*, 6:573 (1964).
Adams, J.A. A closed-loop theory of motor learning. *J. Motor Behav.*, 3:111–150 (1971).
Annett, M. The distribution of manual asymmetry. *Br. J. Psychol.*, 63:343–358 (1972).
Annett, M. The growth of manual performance and speed. *Br. J. Psychol.*, 61:545–558 (1970).
Badian, N.A. and Wolff, P.H. Manual asymmetries of motor sequencing in boys with reading disability. *Cortex*, 8:343–349 (1977).
Bandura, A. Vicarious processes: A case of no-trial learning, in Berkowitz, L. (ed.), *Advances in Experimental Social Psychology*, Vol. 2. New York: Academic Press (1965).
Bartlett, F.C. *Remembering: A Study in Experimental and Social Psychology*. Cambridge: Cambridge University Press (1932).
Bernstein, N. *The Coordination and Regulation of Movements*. London: Pergamon Press (1967).
Bilodeau, I. McD. Information feedback, in Bilodeau, E.A. (ed.), *Acquisition of Skill*. New York: Academic Press (1966).
Bower, T.G.R. Perceptual development: object and space, in Carterette, E.C. and Friedman, M.P. (eds.) *Handbook of Perception*, Vol. 8. New York: Academic Press (1978).
Bronson, G. Hierarchical organization of the central nervous system. *Behav. Sci.*, 10:7–25 (1965).
Bruner, J.S. The growth and structure of a skill, in Connolly, K.J. (ed.), *Motor Skills of Infancy*. New York: Academic Press (1971).
Denny-Brown, D. *The Cerebral Control of Movement*. Liverpool: Liverpool University Press (1966).
Dimond, S. and Beaumont, J.G. *Hemisphere Function in the Human Brain*. New York: Wiley (1974).
Farnham-Diggory, S. *Information Processing in Children*. New York: Academic Press (1972).
Fitts, P.M. The information capacity of the human motor system in controlling the amplitude of movement. *J. Exp. Psychol.*, 47:381–391 (1954).
Fitts, P.M. and Peterson, J.R. Information capacity of discrete motor responses. *J. Exp. Psychol.*, 67:103–112 (1964).
Flowers, K. Handedness and controlled movements. *Br. J. Psychol.*, 66:39–52 (1975).
Fog, E. and Fog, M. Cerebral inhibition examined by associated movements, in Bax, M. and MacKeith, R. (eds.), *Minimal Cerebral Dysfunction*. London Spastic Society: Heinemann (1963).
Freedman, D.G. *Human Infancy*. New York: Wiley (1974).
Gazzaniga, M.S. and LeDoux, J.E. *The Integrated Mind*. New York: Plenum Press (1978).

Geber, M. and Dean, R.F.A. The state of development of newborn African children. *Lancet,* 1:1216–1219 (1957).

Gesell, A.L. The genesis of behavior forms in fetus and infant. The growth of the mind from the standpoint of developmental morphology. *Proc. Amer. Phil. Soc.,* 84:471–488 (1941).

Gesell, A.L. and Amatruda, C.S. *Developmental Diagnosis; Normal and Abnormal Child Development; Clinical Methods and Pediatric Applications,* 2nd Ed. New York: Hoeber (1947).

Goodenough, F.L. A further study of speed of tapping in early childhood. *J. Appl. Psychol.,* 19:309–315 (1935).

Gottlieb, G. The roles of experience in the development of behavior and the nervous system, in Gottlieb, G. (ed.), *Development and Neural and Behavioral Specificity.* New York: Academic Press (1976).

Granit, R. *The Basis of Motor Control.* New York: Harper (1970).

Green, J.B. An electromyographic study of mirror movements. *Neurology* (Minneap.), 17: 91–94 (1967).

Greenwald, A.G. Sensory feedback mechanisms in performance control. *Psychol. Rev.,* 70: 73–97 (1970).

Halle, M. and Stevens, K.N. Speech recognition: a model and a program for research. *IRE Transactions on Information Theory,* JT-8, 2:155–159 (1962).

Hawles, F. and Jenkins, J.J. Problem of serial order in behavior is not resolved by context-sensitive associative memory models. *Psychol. Rev.,* 78:122–129 (1971).

Held, R. and Bauer, J.A. Development of sensorially guided reaching in infant monkeys. *Brain Res.,* 71:265–278 (1974).

Held, R. and Hein, A. Movement-produced stimulation in the development of visually guided behavior. *J. Comp. Physiol. Psychol.,* 56:872–876 (1963).

Hermelin, B. and O'Connor, N. Functional asymmetry in the reading of braille. *Neuropsychologia,* 9:431–435 (1971).

Illingworth, R.S. *The Development of the Infant and Young Child,* 3rd Ed. Edinburgh and London: E. and S. Livingstone (1967).

Ingram, D. Motor asymmetries in young children. *Neuropsychologia,* 13:95–102 (1975).

Keele, S.W. Movement control in skilled motor performance. *Psychol. Bull.,* 70:387–403 (1968).

Kephart, N.C. *The Slow Learner in the Classroom.* Columbus: Charles E. Merrill (1960).

Konorski, J. *Integrative Activity of the Brain.* Chicago: University of Chicago Press (1967).

Kreuter, C., Kinsbourne, M. and Trevarthen, C. Are disconnected cerebral hemispheres independent channels? A preliminary study of the effects of unilateral loading on bilateral finger tapping. *Neuropsychologia,* 10:453–461 (1972).

Lashley, K.S. The problem of serial order in behavior, in Jeffries, L.A. (ed.), *Cerebral Mechanisms.* New York: Wiley (1951).

Lawrence, D.G. and Kuypers, H.G.J.M. Pyramidal and non-pyramidal pathways in monkeys: anatomical and functional correlations. *Science,* 148:973 (1965).

Lenneberg, E. *The Biological Foundations of Language.* New York: Wiley (1967).

Levy, J. The mammalian brain and the adaptive advantage of cerebral asymmetry, in Dimond, S.J. and Blizard, D.A. (eds.), *Evolution and Lateralization of the Brain, Ann. N.Y. Acad. Sci.,* 299:264–273 (1977).

Liberman, A.M., Cooper, F.S., Shankweiler, D.P. and Stoddert-Kennedy, M. Perceptions of the speech code. *Psychol. Rev.,* 74:431–461 (1967).

Lomas, J. and Kimura, D. Intrahemispheric interaction between speaking and sequential manual activity. *Neuropsychologia,* 14:23–33 (1976).

Luria, A.R. *The Role of Speech in the Regulation of Normal and Abnormal Behavior.* New York: Liveright (1961).

McGraw, M.B. *Growth: A Study of Johnny and Jimmy.* New York: Appleton-Century (1935).

McGraw, M.B. *The Neuromuscular Maturation of the Human Infant.* New York: Hafner (1966).

Marler, P. and Hamilton, W.J. *Mechanisms of Animal Behavior.* New York: Wiley (1967).

Matthews, P.B.C. *Mammalian Muscle Receptors and Their Central Actions.* London: Arnold (1972).

Meltzoff, A.N. and Moore, M.K. Imitation of facial and manual gestures by human neonates. *Science,* 198:75–78 (1977).

Milani-Comparetti, A. and Gidoni, E.A. Pattern analysis of motor development and its disorders. *Develop. Med. Child Neurol.,* 9:625–630 (1967).

Molnar, G.E. Analysis of motor disorder in retarded infants and young children. *Amer. J. Mental Def.,* 83:213–222 (1978).

Nebes, R.D. Hemispheric specialization in commissurotomized man. *Psychol. Bull.,* 81:1–14 (1974).

Neligan, G. and Prudham, D. Norms for four standard developmental milestones by sex, social class, and place in family. *Develop. Med. Child Neurol.,* 11:413 (1969).

Newell, K.M. and Kennedy, J.A. Knowledge of results and children's motor learning. *Develop. Psychol.,* 14:531–536 (1978).

Oldfield, R.C. Handedness in musicians. *Br. J. Psychol.,* 60:91–99 (1969).

Peiper, A. *Cerebral Function in Infancy and Childhood.* New York: Consultants Bureau (1963).

Piaget, J. *The Origins of Intelligence.* New York: Basic Books (1952).

Piaget, J. *Play, Dreams, and Imitation in Childhood.* New York: Norton (1951).

Pickler, E. Data on gross motor development of the infant. *Child Dev. and Care,* 3:297–310 (1972).

Preilowski, B.F.B. Possible contribution of the anterior forebrain commissure to bilateral motor coordination. *Neuropsychologia,* 10:267–277 (1972).

Rosenbloom, L. and Norton, M.E. Observing motor skill: a developmental approach, in Holt, K. (ed.), *Movement and Child Development.* London: Heinemann Medical Books (1975).

Schmidt, R.A. A schema theory of discrete motor skill learning. *Psychol. Rev.,* 82:225–259 (1975).

Schmitt, R. and Erikson, M.T. Early predictors of mental retardation. *Mental Retard.,* 11: 27–29 (1973).

Sollberger, A. *Biological Rhythm Research.* Amsterdam: Elsevier (1965).

Sperry, R.W. Lateral specialization in the surgically separated hemispheres, in Schmitt, F.O. and Worden, F.G. (eds.), *The Neurosciences Third Study Program.* Cambridge: MIT Press (1974).

Sperry, R.W. Neurology and the mind-brain problem. *Amer. Sci.,* 40:291–312 (1952).

Touwen, B.C.L. Variability and stereotypy in normal and deviant development, in *Clinics in Developmental Medicine,* 67:99–110. London: Spastics International Medical Publishers with Heinemann (1978).

Turkewitz, G. The development of lateral differentiation in the human infant. *Ann. N.Y. Acad. Sci.,* 299:308–318 (1977).

Twitchell, T.E. Normal motor development. *Amer. Phys. Ther. Assoc.,* 45:419–423 (1965).

von Holst, E. and Mittelstedt, A. *Das Reafferenz-prinzip Die Natureissenschaften,* 37:464–476 (1950).

Warren, N. African infant precocity. *Psychol. Bull.*, 78:353-367 (1972).

Weiss, P. Experimental analysis of coordination by the disarrangement of central-peripheral relations. *Symp. Soc. Exp. Biol.*, 4:92-111 (1950).

Weiss, P. Self-differentiation of the basic patterns of coordination. *Comp. Physiol. Monogr.*, 17:1-96 (1941).

Welford, A.T. *Fundamentals of a Skill*. London: Melliven (1968).

Werner, H. and Kaplan, B. *Symbol Formation*. New York: Wiley (1960).

White, B.L. and Held, R. Plasticity of sensorimotor development in the human infant, in Rosenblith, J.F. and Allinsmith, W. (eds.), *The Causes of Behavior*. Boston: Allin and Bacon (1966).

Wickens, C.D. Temporal limits of human information processing: a developmental study. *Psychol. Bull.*, 81:739-755 (1974).

Wilson, D.M. The central nervous control of flight in a locust. *J. Exp. Biol.*, 38:471-490 (1961).

Wohlwill, J. *The Study of Behavioral Development*. New York: Academic Press (1973).

Wolff, P.H. The development of manual asymmetries in motor sequencing skills. *Ann. N.Y. Acad. Sci.*, 299:528-538 (1977).

Wolff, P.H. Stereotypic behavior and development. *Can. Psychol.*, 9:474-484 (1968a).

Wolff, P.H. The serial organization of sucking in the young infant. *Pediatrics*, 42:943-956 (1968b).

Wolff, P.H. and Cohen, C. Dual task performance during bimanual coordination. *Cortex* (in press, 1979).

Wolff, P.H., Hurwitz, I. and Moss, H. Serial organization of motor skills in left- and right-handed adults. *Neuropsychologia*, 15:539-546 (1977).

Wolff, P.H. and Hurwitz, I. Sex differences in finger tapping: a developmental study. *Neuropsychologia*, 14:35-41 (1976).

Woods, B.I. and Teuber, H.-L. Mirror movements after childhood paresis. *Neurol.*, 28:1152-1158 (1978).

Wyke, B. The neurological basis of movement: a developmental review, in Holt, K. (ed.), *Movement and Child Development*. London: Heinemann Medical Books (1975).

Wyke, M. The effects of brain lesions on the learning performance of a bimanual coordination task. *Cortex*, 7:59-72 (1971).

Yakovlev, P.I. and Lecours, A.R. The myelinogenetic cycles of regional maturation of the brain, in Minkowski, A. (ed.), *Regional Development of the Brain in Early Life*. Oxford: Blackwell (1967).

Young, G. Manual specialization in infancy, in Segalowitz, S.J. and Gruber, F.A. (eds.), *Language Development and Neurological Theory*. New York: Academic Press (1977).

Zaidel, D. and Sperry, R.W. Long-term motor coordination problems following cerebral commissurotomy in man. *Neuropsychologia*, 15:193-204 (1977).

Zapella, M., Foley, J. and Cookson, M. The placing and supporting reaction in mental deficiency. *J. Mental Def. Res.*, 8:1-5 (1964).

Zelazo, P.R., Zelazo, N.A. and Kolb, S. Walking in the newborn. *Science*, 176:314-315 (1972).

Zülch, K.J. Pyramidal and para-pyramidal motor systems in man, in Zülch, V.J., Creutzfeldt, O. and Galbraith, G.C. (eds.), *Cerebral Localization*. New York: Springer (1975).

10

Neuromotor Assessment of Infants

LAWRENCE T. TAFT

A standard developmental screening test, such as the Denver Developmental Screening instrument (Frankenburg and Dodds), should be done routinely by the primary care physician in order to monitor whether fine and gross motor skills are being achieved at the appropriate ages. However, sole reliance on screening tests for evaluating the competence of the neuromotor system has its limitations (Stedman, 1975). These tests primarily measure the quantitative aspects of motor development. That is, if an infant achieves a motor task at the appropriate age, the tester would consider this performance normal notwithstanding that its quality or style may be abnormal. An additional limitation of screening tests for evaluating the integrity of the motor system in infants is that a young baby has so very few assessable skills in his motor repertoire. Therefore, it is essential that a neuromotor examination be added to the periodic development assessment. The addition of a few clinical tests of neurological maturity will significantly improve the success rate for the earliest detection of cerebral palsy.

In evaluating the contribution of a neuromotor exam, it is necessary to have knowledge of normal developmental motor processes. Up to the age of a few months, the neonate's motor activity is primarily on the background of simple reflex activity (Taft and Cohen, 1967). There is little, if any, voluntary control of movement. The motor cortex may be extensively damaged or, for that matter, absent and the neuromotor assessment of the neonate may be within normal limits. Hydranencephalic infants have grossly normal neurological exams. Absence of movement of an extremity noted in the newborn rarely signifies an upper motor neuron lesion, but more often represents a peripheral abnormality as seen with damage to anterior horn cells, peripheral nerve or muscles, or secondary to a fracture of a bone.

Although a lesion to the motor system might have occurred at birth and be nonprogressive in nature, the maturation of the uninvolved sensori-motor system may dramatically change the functional and neurologic manifestations as the infant grows older.

Infants and toddlers rarely are passive and cooperative enough to facilitate a careful examination of their neuromotor status. Their tendency to cry and be tense makes evaluation of tone and reflexes far from satisfactory.

Although one must be aware of the caveats inherent in a neuromotor assessment, there is a simple, rather rapidly completed clinical exam that can be performed on an active, crying infant with fairly good intra- and intertest reliability.

Neuromotor Evaluation of Infants
Under Six Months of Age
for Detection of Cerebral Palsy

Cerebral palsy is defined as a motor disability secondary to a static lesion of the brain with the insult to the brain occurring prenatally, paranatally or in early childhood (Bax, 1964). To diagnose or, at least suspect, an early motor deficit in infants requires a high index of suspicion plus periodic neuromotor assessments. However, at this early age, it is often impossible to specifically designate the clinical type of cerebral palsy or degree of functional impairment since clinical signs frequently change with maturation of the nervous system (Hanson *et al.*, 1970).

Illingworth has outlined a number of clinical observations as well as specific neuromotor assessment techniques that he believes offers the examiner a "clue" to the integrity of the infant's motor system (Illingworth, 1966). Any abnormal findings put that baby at an especially high risk for developing a diagnosable type of cerebral palsy. The following tests are recommended for the primary care physician's routine screening since the author believes that they are the most sensitive indicators of the integrity of the motor system. These routine assessments of tone, primitive reflexes, and deep tendon reflexes can be done during a routine physical examination.

Tone

A lower motor neuron abnormality results in hypotonia. In contrast, an upper motor lesion affecting an immature nervous system may be manifested as either hypotonia ("cerebral") or hypertonia. If cerebral hypotonia is present early in infancy, one can usually expect that soon after the end of the first year of life the diminished tone will gradually change to a rigid or spastic type of hypertonus (Ingram, 1964).

Decreased tone does not necessarily imply an abnormality to the neuromotor tracts. When joints are hyperextensible, pathology may exist outside the central nervous system, especially as seen in collagen disorders (e.g., Ehlers-Danlos Syndrome, congenital laxity of the ligaments and Marfan's Syndrome).

Assessing tone requires experience. Guidelines for the degree of joint mobility that can be considered normal are ill-defined. Normally, there is a wide range of tone in normal babies. To further add to the difficulties encountered in assessing tone, the examiner frequently has to cope with a crying, rigid baby.

Andre-Thomas *et al.* (1960) have attempted to develop guidelines for measuring joint mobility. The techniques for assessing shoulder and hip joint range of motion may be helpful for the examiner to judge the presence of decreased tone.

The Anterior Scarf Sign

With the baby supine and the shoulders held against a table top, the examiner draws one of the baby's hands circumferentially around the face. If that shoulder is not permitted to move from the table top, it is usually impossible in normal newborns to passively move the elbow past the chin (see figure 1). If this can be accomplished, the increased range of motion of the shoulder joint suggests the possibility of neuromotor hypotonia.

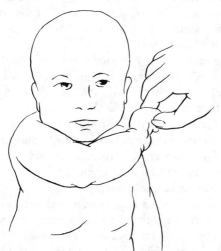

FIG. 1 Anterior Scarf Sign

The Posterior Scarf Sign

With the baby held in the sitting position and with the head in line with the trunk, the arm is pulled directly back. If the elbow is not turned outward, but kept directly parallel to the trunk, passive posterior movement of the extremity is limited and the elbow cannot go past the ear on the side. If the elbow does pass the ear, it can be considered increased range of motion of the shoulder joint, having the same significance as a "positive" anterior scarf sign.

Hip Sign

Abducting the lower extremities to 160 degrees or more with the knees extended can be considered increased range of motion of the hip joints signifying hypotonia.

Hypertonia

In a newborn infant the tone of agonists and antagonists is out of balance with flexor tone predominating. This is especially true when the infant is prone, at which time a tonic labyrinthine reflex sends more impulses to the extensors and the baby relaxes its flexor posturing, although not to the point of assuming a truly extensor pose. During the first few months of life, maturation reduces flexor posturing and results in a balance between flexion and extension. With a damaged nervous system this sequence may be altered with increased extensor posturing prevalent in the neonatal state. An extreme degree of damage results in classical opisthotonic posturing. However, minor changes in the normal relationship between flexor and extensor tone are not always obvious, but can become apparent by a number of techniques.

One technique is to suspend the baby in prone position with the examiner's hand placed under the infant's abdomen. In the first month of life the infant should have a slight convexity of the trunk with the head flexed slightly, but with possible momentary extension of the head so that it may become level with the trunk. The arms and legs should be partially flexed. As the baby approaches four months of age, the predominant flexor posture gradually changes to one of extension. A four-month-old baby in prone suspension should have the back straight and the neck extended so that the head is above the line of the trunk. The baby should be able to maintain his posture at will.

A one- to two-month-old baby with a tendency towards increased extensor tone may manifest "deceptive extensor tone" on ventral suspension and look more like a four-month-old baby in that the neck will be extended and the trunk straight (see figure 2). The mother may have proudly reported that the baby was

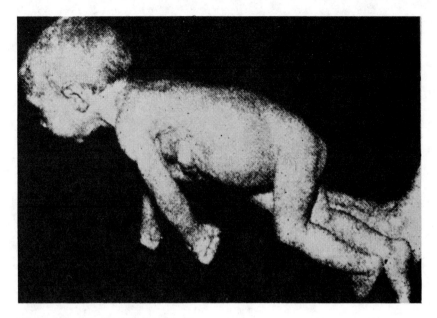

FIG. 2 Excessive Extensor Tone in Neonate

noted to roll over from prone to supine at only a few weeks of age. This may
have occurred simply because the baby had a tendency towards increased extensor tone. During crying the extensor tone was further exaggerated resulting in
opisthotonos when, by chance, the baby flipped over from back to stomach by
means of an arch created by the opisthotonos with the vertex of the skull and
the heels being the two ends of the arc.

The baby with increased extensor tone will, when picked up by the upper
extremities from the supine position, have a marked head lag as well as come
directly to a standing position because of a tendency to maintain hip and knee
extension (see figure 3).

On further testing the baby should be held in vertical suspension. If there
is increased adductor tone, scissoring will result (Forster's sign). Scissoring is
not an uncommon normal finding at one or two months after a frank breech
delivery. If seen after this time, however, it is almost always pathologic. Babies
with pyramidal tract dysfunction not infrequently will have increased tone of
the hip adductors and external rotators when supine. When quickly changed
from the supine to the erect position, a tonic labyrinthine reflex will send more
impulses to the internal rotators and adductors, which, if excessive, will be
manifested in pathologic scissoring.

Increased tone may also be demonstrated by attempting passive dorsiflexion of the ankle with the knee extended. Normally, in a baby under two months

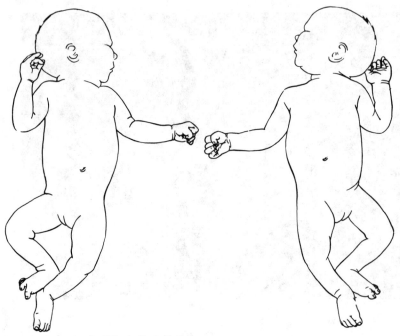

FIG. 3 Asymmetrical Tonic Neck Reflex

of age the dorsum of the foot can be passively moved so that it touches the shin. There is usually no resistance to this maneuver if the baby is quiet. If a tendency towards spasticity exists, however, a full range of movement will be difficult or impossible. The test should be done by grabbing the toes when attempting dorsiflexion. This is important since stimulating the sole of the foot may produce a positive supporting reaction that results in equinus posturing of the foot. This reflex reaction can make it appear as if there is spasticity of the gastrocs.

Primitive Reflexes

Whether or not the primitive reflexes evident in early infancy are the framework for further motor maturation or whether they must be inhibited for the development of coordinated voluntary control remains an unanswered issue. Evidence suggests that the primitive reflexes are incorporated into voluntary movement patterns with maturation of the central nervous system (Twitchell, 1965).

There are many primitive reflexes, most of which are present at birth and gradually disappear. Others become evident later in infancy. Variation in reflex responses are not uncommon as some depend on the infant's "state" (Prechtl, 1977). Many reflexes are normally not present when the baby is active or crying.

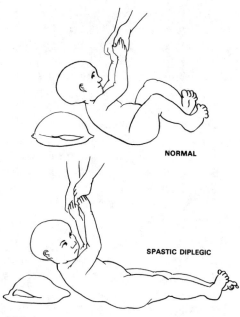

NORMAL

SPASTIC DIPLEGIC

FIG. 4

Others are not affected by changes in the baby's state and can be easily elicited and reproduced.

Two primitive reflexes are especially useful. The presence of these reflexes appear to depend on the integrity of the neuromotor system. Also, of further advantage is that the state of the baby at the time of the exam does not interfere with the interpretation of the adequacy of the response.

The asymmetric tonic neck reflex is elicited by passively turning the head of a supine baby to one side and holding it there for approximately 30 seconds. The presence of the reflex is indicated when the arm and leg on the chin side become extensor and the extremities on the occipital side flex (see figure 4). Not infrequently, the reflexes are incomplete and may only be seen by appropriate posturing of the upper or lower extremities. The asymmetric tonic neck reflex is most strongly developed around two months of age, but even at this time, it normally may not be evident. Consequently, its absence in the first few months of life is usually not considered pathologic. An "obligatory" tonic neck reflex noted before six months of age, however, is considered by many as pathologic and puts the baby at risk for cerebral palsy (Paine *et al.*, 1964). An obligatory tonic neck reflex is defined as one in which, after the head is passively turned and maintained so for 30 seconds, the extremities are maintained in the tonic neck position and remain that way while the baby is actively crying. In other words, the baby, although active and crying, is "unable to break down the reflex pattern imposed on the extremities by passive rotation of the head." A non-obligatory tonic neck reflex seen at any time after the age of six months is definitely abnormal.

A crossed extensor reflex normally disappears at four months of age (Taft and Cohen, 1967). Its persistence after that, whether unilateral or bilateral, is of concern. The crossed extensor reflex is obtained by placing the baby supine, holding one leg extended at the knee and applying a noxious stimulus to the sole. The total reflex response consists of an initial flexor withdrawal of the contralateral extremity followed by extension, abduction and then gradual adduction. This reflex is also independent of the baby's state and should be repeated two or three times to verify that it cannot be elicited.

Deep Tendon Reflexes

Exaggerated knee jerks in the first few months of life are pathologic. The responses at the ankle and biceps are not reliable since they are normally difficult to elicit during the first month or two.

To be able to judge reliably whether an exaggerated reflex is definitely pathologic, it occasionally helps to determine if there is an increase in the sensory reflexogenic zone from which the response can be obtained (Taft and Cohen, 1967). For example, in a baby more than four months old, the examiner should percuss over the shin, moving gradually toward the patellar tendon. Quadriceps contraction when the shin is percussed indicates a pathologic response. Percussion over the deltoid resulting in a reflex contraction of the biceps is similarly pathologic.

In summary, any of the following findings, positive anterior and posterior scarf signs, hip signs, increased extensor tone, hyperreflexia, obligatory tonic neck reflex or persistence of a crossed extensor reflex past four months of age, places the infant at considerable risk for having an upper motor neuron dysfunction (cerebral palsy). This obliges the physician to make a referral to an early intervention center.

Hemisyndrome

Infants born with damage to one hemisphere will not show clinical manifestations of a disability (Molnar and Taft, 1977). There will be no asymmetry in reflexes or motility. Not until approximately four months of age will abnormal signs perhaps be evident. The baby will tend to keep one hand fisted more than the other and reach out consistently only with the nonfisted hand. A history of early handedness is definitely significant since most babies are ambilateral until two to three years of age.

Formal examination of this four-month-old baby may not reveal classical neurologic signs of asymmetry. As is often the case, the baby may be crying during the exam resulting in fisting of both hands. The examiner may not be able to interest the baby in reaching out for an object in order to determine if there is a hand preference. Additionally, reflex and tone changes may not be evident at this early stage even if the baby is relaxed. The development of spasticity and hyperreflexia appears to depend on maturational factors and their presence may be delayed. For example, these changes may not be seen in the upper and lower extremities until six to eight months and ten to fourteen months of age, respectively.

Some routine functional and primitive reflex testing, however, can be done that will uncover a hemisyndrome without depending on confirmation by classical neurologic signs. For example, the examiner should routinely place a cover over the face of a five- to six-month-old baby. Most babies with normal cognitive development will attempt to pull the cover off, usually by using both hands (see figure 5). The baby with a hemisyndrome will use only one hand to pull the cover off. If this is the case, this hand should be held to see how well the baby uses the other hand. If the infant does not respond at all or, if he appears uncoordinated with one extremity, then an upper motor neuron lesion affecting that extremity must be entertained.

At six to seven months of age normal infants develop protective reactions (Andre-Thomas *et al.*, 1960). At this age babies will demonstrate lateral propping. If the infant is held in a sitting position, grasped by the trunk and suddenly tilted to one side, he will abduct and extend the extremity on the tilted side as if

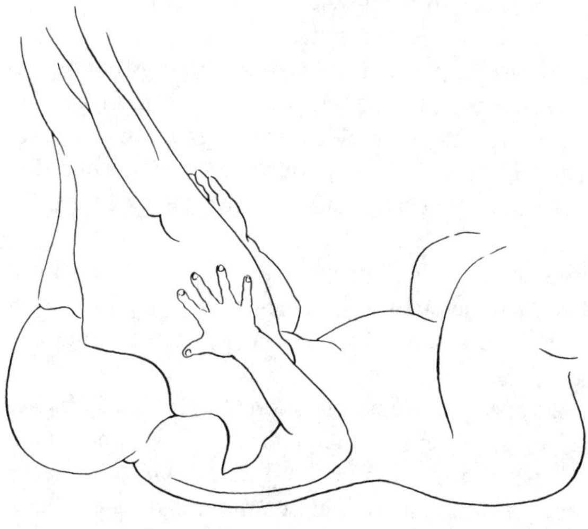

FIG. 5 Cover Test

to protect himself from falling to the side (see figure 6). The wrist will be extended and the fingers abducted. A symmetric response is expected when the baby is tilted to the opposite side. Any asymmetry in the response of the extremities can be considered abnormal.

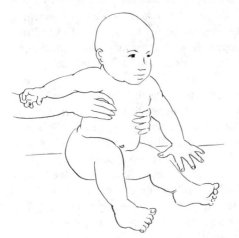

FIG. 6 Lateral Propping

    At seven to nine months, infants normally reveal anterior propping (parachute response). The baby is held by the waist with the face forward. The examiner then quickly tilts the baby's head and trunk towards the examining table. The expected response is protective extension of both extremities. An asymmetry in the response of the extremities is significant.

    At approximately ten to twelve months of age posterior propping responses are elicitable, but inconsistently obtained. If the baby is held in a sitting position and the examiner grabs the baby's shoulders from behind and quickly tilts him backwards, the infant will extend the extremities as if to prevent himself from falling backwards completely. Once again, an asymmetry in the response suggests a hemisyndrome.

    The finding of any asymmetry in these protective reactions, especially if reproducible, should alert the examiner to the presence of a hemiparetic syndrome whether or not there is confirmation by classical neurologic tone and reflex asymmetries.

    A monoparesis due to an upper motor neuron lesion is rare. Usually babies have involvement of both ipsilateral extremities. An infant with asymmetric use of the upper extremity may not manifest signs or symptoms of an abnormality in the ipsilateral lower extremity until ten to fourteen months of age. This is important to remember so that hemiplegia is not ruled out simply because no tone or reflex changes in the lower extremity could be demonstrated at the first exam. A clue to an involvement of the lower extremity would be an asymmetric crawl, in which the baby does not push off with one lower extremity, or an equino varus positioning of the foot when the baby is held erect. Additionally, a positive crossed extensor response would be significant.

Athetoid Cerebral Palsy

Continuing change in an infant's neuromaturational status during the first few years of life has best been documented in post-kernicteric babies. If bilirubin encephalopathy occurs in the neonatal period, central nervous system manifestations are evident at the third to fifth days of life. Hypertonus, occasional opisthotonic posturing, exaggerated reflexes, poor sucking, high-pitched cry and an obligatory tonic neck reflex are the classic signs of kernicterus (Pearlstein, 1957).

If the baby survives, at around two to three weeks of age the hypertonic state will gradually change to one with fairly normal tone and reflexes. Hypertonus may be evident with crying, but in the relaxed state there will be no abnormal findings except for an obligatory tonic neck reflex. This same baby, over the next couple of months, will begin to manifest the signs seen in the "floppy infant syndrome." At three months of age the baby will present with hypotonia (positive scarf and hip signs) and normal deep tendon reflexes. The tonic neck reflex will, however, be persistently obligatory.

The hypotonia will persist over the first year of life. At ten months of age a baby may have delayed motor milestones, but without evidence of dyskinetic or involuntary movements. For example, the baby will reach out for an object using a radial grasp instead of the pincer grasp expected at this age. Any finger posturing or involuntary movements would be unusual. The baby will be hypotonic with normal deep tendon reflexes and may have a persistent nonobligatory or an obligatory asymmetric tonic neck reflex. Not until the infant is one to one-and-a-half years of age can one observe a gradual change from the hypotonic state to a hypertonic or rigid state with the first evidence of slow, writhing, athetoid movements. In fact, the full degree of the hypertonus and the involuntary movement may not be manifested until age three (Molnar and Taft, 1977). The baby, at three years, may appear to have much more motor involvement than one would have expected from the clinical assessment made during early infancy.

Postkernicteric babies are frequently diagnosed as retarded because of the hypotonia, normal deep tendon reflexes and delayed language. In addition, the absence of hyperreflexia or involuntary movements early in the course makes that diagnosis a good possibility. The language delay is often secondary to a high-frequency nerve deafness due to the neonatal hyperbilirubinemia. Post-kernicteric infants, no matter how severe their motor deficit, are often normal intellectually.

Lower Motor Neuron Disease

Infants with lower motor neuron disease manifest a paucity of movements at the onset of the disease whether or not it begins in utero or during the first month or two of life (in contrast to an upper motor neuron disease). If an arm or leg does not move at birth, an upper motor neuron lesion should not be the first consideration. Rather, one should be more concerned about the possibility of a brachial or sciatic nerve palsy or trauma causing fracture of the clavicle or bones of the extremities. Babies with a more generalized hypotonia will usually be lying in a frog position with very little movement of the proximal muscles in contrast to movement of the hands and feet. The infant may have paradoxical respirations due to weakness of the intercostal muscles. This results in a negative intrathoracic pressure when the diaphragm contracts, causing the chest wall to recess while the abdomen expands. Fasciculations of the tongue would definitely prove a lower motor neuron disease.

Any baby with hypotonia, paucity of movements and diminished or absent reflexes, or one showing fasciculations or a myotonic response deserves a complete workup including serum creatinine phosphokinase, serum aldolase, electromyographic studies, nerve conduction studies and a muscle biopsy with histochemical staining and electron-microscopic studies of the tissue.

Summary

Neuromotor assessment of infants must be added to the routine developmental status exams if early recognition of a motor disorder is to be possible.

References

Andre-Thomas, Cherni, Y. and Sante-Ann Dargarsies, S. The Neurological Examination of the Infant. *Clinics Dev. Med.* No. 1. London: Spastics Society/W. Heinemann (1960).

Bax, M.C.O. Terminology and Classification of Cerebral Palsy. *Div. Med. Child Neurol.*, 6: 295 (1964).

Frankenburg, W.K. and Dodds, J.B. Denver Developmental Screening Test – LADOCA Foundation, Denver, Colorado.

Hanson, R.L., Byers, B. and Berenberg, W. Changing Motor Patterns in Cerebral Palsy. *Dev. Med. Child Neurol.*, 12:709 (1970).

Illingworth, R.S. The Diagnosis of Cerebral Palsy in the First Year of Life. *Dev. Med. Child Neurol.,* 8:178 (1966).

Ingram, T.T.S. *Pediatric Aspects of Cerebral Palsy.* Edinburgh: E.S. Livingstone (1964).

Molnar, G.E. and Taft, L.T. Pediatric Rehabilitation Part I: Cerebral Palsy and Spinal Cord Injuries, in *Current Problems in Pediatrics,* Vol. 7, No. 3. Chicago: Yearbook Med. Publisher (1977).

Paine, R.S., Brazelton, T.B., Donovan, D.E., Hubbell, J.P. and Sears, E.M. Evaluation of Postural Reflexes in Normal Infants and in the Presence of Chronic Brain Syndrome. *Neurology,* 14:1036 (1964).

Perlstein, M.A. The Clinical Syndrome of Kernicterus, in Swinyard, C.A. (ed.), *Kernicterus and Its Importance in Cerebral Palsy.* Springfield, Ill.: Charles C. Thomas (1957).

Prechtl, H.F.R. *The Neurological Examination of the Full-Term Newborn Infant,* 2nd Edition. London: Spastics International/W. Heinemann (1977).

Stedman, D.J. Review of Denver Developmental Screening Test (DDST), in Frankenburg, W.K. and Camp, B.W. (eds.) *Pediatric Screening Tests.* Springfield, Ill.: Charles C. Thomas, pp. 403–405 (1975).

Taft, L.T. and Cohen, H.J. *Neonatal and Infant Reflexology in Exceptional Infants, Volume I,* Heldmuth, J. (ed.). Seattle, Wash.: Special Child Publications, pp. 81–118 (1967).

Twitchell, T.E. Normal Motor Development. *J. Am. Phys. Therap. Assoc.,* 45:419 (1965).

11

Intervention for
Physically Handicapped Children

GABRIELLA E. MOLNAR

For the last few decades behavioral and organic structural consequences of early experience, deprivation and remedial intervention constituted a subject of intensive study (Walsh and Greenough, 1976; Tjossem, 1978). In animal models, there is evidence to indicate that behavior changes caused by various forms of sensory deprivation are reversible if rehabilitative measures are instituted within a sensitive period (Morrison and McKinney, 1976; Greenough et al., 1976) and that these functional deviations and their restitution are accompanied by demonstrable anatomic, biochemical and electrophysiologic changes if the central nervous system is otherwise intact (Stein et al., 1974; Walsh and Cummins, 1976). These experiments demonstrate that differentiation of the immature nervous system is to an extent dependent on environmental influences. More recently, there are also data suggesting that a degree of neural recovery may occur as a result of sensory experience after experimentally produced brain damage (Stein et al., 1974; Walsh and Cummins, 1976; Isaacson, 1978). In humans, early intervention studies included high risk or deprived populations and the primary focus was on cognitive and affective aspects of development (Bekwith, 1976; Hunt, 1976; Tjossem, 1978). That interference with sensory input can lead to functional loss was known for some time from clinical experience with amblyopia of disuse and defective speech development in congenital hearing deficit discussed elsewhere in this chapter.

Results of early intervention studies in humans and animals have clarified some aspects of the old controversy concerning the role of nature versus nurture, revived the previously often debated issue of critical periods and have begun to define the biological correlates of brain plasticity. While there is considerable information in support of these principles for affective, cognitive and sensory development it appears that they apply to motor function in a somewhat modified sense. It is not the purpose of this chapter to elaborate on theoretical issues related to motor development which have been discussed by Wolff earlier. Nevertheless, it seems justified to point out some considerations which have relevance to one of the topics of this discussion, namely the question of efficacy of motor training in children with neuromuscular handicap. The dependence of motor performance on sensory input is not an issue of debate. There is abundant neurophysiologic evidence that movements are elicited, monitored and modulated by sensory stimuli and feedback (Evarts *et al.*, 1971). Moreover, in the broader context of relationship between individual and surroundings, motor activity generally does not occur for its own sake but rather as an interactive response with the environment. However, current knowledge is still limited on the complex neuronal mechanisms of sensory input/motor output coupling involved in producing coordinated motion (Bizzi and Evarts, 1971). That sensorimotor integration and the learning of motor skills require active experiences is supported by many observations (Held and Hein, 1958; Held and Schlank, 1959; Held and Bossom, 1961; Held and Freedman, 1963) but most of the available evidence suggests that the chronology of gross motor development and performance on ordinary tasks are not significantly affected by motor training in early age (McGraw, 1935). On the other hand, environmental sensory enrichment was shown to advance attainment of prehension (White *et al.*, 1964; White and Held, 1967). There seems to be also some suggestion that early motor experience may have a lasting effect on refinement of agility and coordination. In McGraw's study superior motor proficiency of the trained twin on complex physical activities is quite evident in motion picture recordings taken in adulthood. This notion is in agreement with the generally held view that for outstanding athletic and other types of physical accomplishments early training is desirable. It would appear that elaboration of motor skills above a basic level of competence may be related to environmental opportunities and their timing but the neural equivalents of these differences are not known. In contrast to other areas of function the concept of critical periods with the implication of irreversibly lost functional potential does not seem to apply to motor development. Restriction of early stages of locomotion practiced in some cultures was not found to result in delay of gross motor achievements among infants who were raised in a socially appropriate milieu (Dennis, 1940). Furthermore, in non-handicapped infants environmental deprivation and intercurrent illness cause a temporary delay or setback of motor development without permanent loss of physical abilities (Dennis, 1935, 1941; Hunt, 1976). However, delayed motor accomplishments among institutionalized emotionally and socially deprived children emphasize the interactive nature of this process and demonstrate the significance of cognition, motivation and affect in utilizing a potentially available motor repertoire. These factors play a complex role in overtly manifested motor behavior and may have an important bearing on the issue of early intervention for the neurologically handicapped child.

Physical handicaps affecting the preschool child usually originate in the prenatal or perinatal period and include a variety of conditions associated with musculoskeletal deficits or neuromuscular dysfunction. Evidently, different disabilities call for different management techniques and it would not be possible to elaborate on each one. Neuromuscular dysfunction of central origin, specifically, cerebral palsy is the most common handicap among children of all ages and it represents complex problems often with profound developmental consequences (Crothers and Paine, 1959; Molnar and Taft, 1977). For the most part, this discussion will concentrate on the treatment of cerebral palsy as a model to demonstrate general principles of intervention and the role of specific treatment modalities. Reference to other handicaps will be made only occasionally to illustrate some pertinent points.

In this chapter an impressive amount of laboratory and applied clinical research data are presented on normal maturation and on intervention strategies for defective development in various areas of function. One is compelled to state that research pertaining to intervention in the physically handicapped child, particularly in those with neuromuscular dysfunction, has not been forthcoming despite the evident medical and economic significance of this question. Considering the present state of the art, one can only identify questionable issues, admit the existing hiatus between clinical experience and scientific evidence, and continue to strive to bridge that gap. Nevertheless, ideas in favor of early intervention and therapeutic sensory environment pervade current thinking about the management of young physically handicapped children and are largely responsible for a more harmonious integration of therapeutic modalities and developmental process.

Differences in the success of early or late prosthetic rehabilitation in congenital unilateral upper limb deficiency represent a good example to illustrate the significance of age at the time of intervention among children with musculoskeletal handicap (McDonald, 1958; Lambert et al., 1969; Guerrero et al., 1972; Sypniewski, 1972; Molnar and Taft, 1977). In the past, when prosthetic training was postponed as long as 3 to 5 years, a majority of the children rejected to use or even wear the device. Delayed rehabilitation was advocated for the reason that the child must understand instructions in order to learn operation of a prosthesis. On empirical basis the age of prosthetic fitting was gradually advanced. At present, the first simple device is provided in infancy, preferably around 4 to 6 months, when eye-hand coordination, reaching and bilateral hand play emerge. Most children in this group are excellent functional users. They seem to consider the prosthesis an extension of their body to the degree that some prefer to sleep with it, as indicated by observations at a summer camp (Trefler, 1972). In conjunction with this example two points merit comments. First, in the light of Piaget's (1952, 1954) concept of learning in the sensorimotor stage of development, is the evident fallacy that infants have to be taught by verbal conceptual instructions. Indeed, clinical experience shows that by trial and exploration infants soon get the idea of how to use a simple device much as they learn to manipulate toys or untie their shoelaces. The second point is that the most important reason for the failure of late training is not that the actual motor activity cannot be learned, as most children who reject the prosthesis are able to operate it skillfully. Aside from cosmetic problems, the usual complaints are that the device interferes with sensation, which emphasizes the significance of sensory feedback in motor performance. It seems that harnessing of an emerging motor behavior is the most successful method for establishing an alternative functional solution, at least in cases where neuromuscular function is unimpaired. If a therapeutically selected plan is not presented at that time the opportunity may be lost, not on account of failure to learn motor execution but rather because the sensory experience does not become sufficiently integrated if it is introduced late. In a sense, the situation appears to be analogous to a critical period with the implication of optimal but not exclusively restricted developmental stage for acquiring a compensatory motor behavior. Experience with children trained at a later age clearly illustrates the distinct differences between ability to perform a task or mastering a skill on a level which is consistent with natural use for functional advantage.

Neuromuscular dysfunction resulting from cerebral damage represents a different situation with impairment of the central executive motor system and its connections (Christensen and Melchior, 1967; Courville, 1971). Unfortunately, little is known about the various organic mechanisms underlying functional recovery in lesions affecting the motor structures and about the influence of intervention on this process in humans. Based on animal studies equipotentiality or mass action, vicarious function and redundancy, behavioral substitution, and functional reorganization, including denervation hypersensitivity, collateral sprouting and compensatory hypertrophy have been proposed as possible mechanisms (Moscona and Monroy, 1973; Jacobson, 1974; Rosner, 1974; Ellis, 1975; Greenough et al., 1976; Isaacson, 1978). Goldberger (1974), discussing recovery of movement after central nervous system lesions in monkeys, summarized the theoretical considerations and experimental evidence for these concepts. In the same review this author examined the significance of age, localization and nature of lesions, specific and non-specific pre- and post-lesion stimulation as contributory factors in promoting or limiting the degree of recovery and pointed out the methodologic shortcomings influencing the accuracy of assessing outcome. The actual mechanism and degree of recovery seems to depend on the site of lesion and other experimental variables. Furthermore, it appears that plasticity of the central nervous system is not consistently greater in young animals than in adults as it was sometimes suggested and that the extent of functional restitution may be enhanced by both pre- and post-lesion experience (Glees and Cole, 1950; Liu and Chambers, 1962; Black *et al.,* 1971, 1975).

There is a lack of controlled clinical trials on the efficacy of motor training in general and about the differential effect of early intervention, specifically, in children with cerebral palsy. This can be attributed to the virtually insurmount-able methodologic difficulties of matching a population which is not homogene-ous from the viewpoint of organic lesions and clinical signs; to the problems inherent in measuring abnormal motor function; to the fact that in humans the effect of a single therapeutic variable, particularly one which is as complex as motor training, cannot be studied in isolation; and to the uncertainties of dif-ferentiating the role of maturation when improvement occurs slowly.

Conceptually, there are three principal aims in designing an intervention plan for physically handicapped infants and young children: (1) to simulate the normal developmental sequence as closely as possible and to the extent it is feasible; (2) to create a therapeutic environment which is most conducive for nurturing optimal expected outcome with cognizance to motor and other areas of function; and (3) to prevent or minimize the secondary adverse effects of inactivity and motor deficit on the musculoskeletal system which may interfere with the realization of maximal functional potential (Denhoff and Langdon, 1966; Denhoff, 1967; Ellis, 1967; Pearson and Williams, 1972; Levitt, 1977). To formulate the practical details of intervention one should consider the current functional level of the child and anticipate future achievements in gross motor function (Molnar and Gordon, 1976), hand dexterity, activities of daily life, and whether specific skills in these areas can be accomplished with or with-out adaptive techniques or assistive devices (Molnar, 1979). Additionally, methods and goals of treatment may be influenced by associated praxic and gnosic deficits, intellectual, visual, auditory, speech or language impairment, and emotional, attentive or other behavior problems.

There are a number of treatment modalities of widely different nature which intend to improve motor performance by intervening at various levels of the dysfunction in cerebral palsy. They include conservative methods, such as therapeutic exercises and task oriented training in gross or fine motor function, the use of compensatory functional techniques and adaptive devices, drug therapy and chemical neurolysis to alleviate increased muscle tone, and surgical treatment for the musculoskeletal consequences of neurologic deficit.

Physical therapy is the most frequently used conservative treatment and its value continues to be a subject of controversy (Taft *et al.,* 1962; Mead, 1966; Bouman, 1967; Basmajian, 1971; Bax and MacKeith, 1973). From a conceptual standpoint, there are two different approaches. Attempts to alleviate the neuro-muscular dysfunction may be directed either toward specific muscle groups and joint motion or toward the abnormal tone and deranged movement components (Gillette, 1958; Halpern, 1978). In actuality, neither the pathologic features of motor disability nor the therapeutic aim are as clearly separable as this rather simplified definition suggests.

The first approach is represented by the traditional therapeutic exercises consisting of stretching, passive, active and resisted movements which are applied to maintain or increase range of motion, strength, endurance and/or coordination (Deaver, 1956; Phelps, 1958; Jones, 1967). Passive exercises may prevent musculoskeletal deformities but do not contribute to improvement of motor skills. The various types of active exercises can be applied only if there is at least some movement control. They also require cooperation which may present difficulties with infants and young children. This problem can be circumvented by incorporating treatment into play and games which are selected to include specific desired movements or skills. The traditional exercise program is complemented by practice of various gross motor activities as appropriate for the child's functional stage and with the use of assistive devices if necessary. Learning by repetition is the principle of motor training in this approach.

The second conceptual approach offers several different techniques known collectively as neuromuscular facilitation or reflex therapeutic methods (Bouman, 1967; Gillette, 1958, 1969; Pearson and Williams, 1972; Payton *et al.*, 1978). These techniques have a number of features in common (Harris, 1970; Basmajian, 1971; Harris, 1978). Treatment is concerned with movement patterns and the goal is to modify abnormal tone and posture, and to elicit desired movements. As motor output is guided by and occurs in response to sensory stimuli, the mode of intervention is a manipulation of sensory input, which is called facilitation. Tone, posture and movement abnormalities in cerebral palsy resemble the reflex behavior described in laboratory animals with transaction of the neuraxis at different levels (Illingworth, 1960; Paine *et al.*, 1964; Paine, 1964; Bobath, 1966). For this reason the concepts of reflex physiology play a significant role in these methods and various interpretations of reflex behavior are used in their technical execution (Magnus, 1926; Schaltenbrand, 1928; Weiss, 1938; Twitchell, 1958, 1959, 1965a,b,c,d; Peiper, 1963).

Among these methods the neurodevelopmental therapy proposed by the Bobaths (1966, 1972, 1975) gained the widest popularity. It is based on the view that the movement disorder of cerebral palsy is an impairment of the reflex control of postural tone and adjustment mechanism. Arrest or retardation of neuromotor development leads to persistence and preponderance of primitive reflexes (Moro, tonic neck, tonic labyrinthine, etc.) and to absence or delay of postural adjustment responses (righting, protective extension, equilibrium reactions). Tone abnormalities reflect a disturbance of reciprocal innervation. Therefore, intervention consists of inhibition of primitive reflexes, facilitation of postural reactions, and modification of tone which may be achieved by using vestibular, proprioceptive and tactile stimuli while guiding the child through various movement sequences. For example, rolling over with segmental body rotation guided from the shoulder or other key points of stabilization would inhibit tonic neck reflexes and facilitate righting reactions. Rocking in prone on a beachball may be used to decrease spastic hypertonicity and simultaneously facilitate righting and protective extension responses. Early intervention and certain techniques of handling which will be discussed later are strongly emphasized. From a clinical viewpoint the Bobaths' work reflects an intimate knowledge of normal neuromotor development and their method, regardless of its scientifically proven success or failure, is based on meticulous clinical observations of the characteristic postural and movement aberrations in cerebral palsy.

The Rood (1954, 1956, 1962) method proposes to alter tone and movement by an array of sensory modalities which include heat, cold, ice application, stretch, tactile stimuli, such as brushing, tapping and pressure, vibration, proprioceptive and vestibular stimulation. The rationale for selecting a specific sensory modality for certain therapeutic purposes is derived from the investigations of distinguished neurophysiologists which were conducted under strictly controlled experimental conditions in laboratory animals (Lindsley *et al.*, 1949; Hagbarth, 1959; Livingston, 1959; Granit, 1966; Eldred, 1967a,b; Hagbarth and Eklund, 1969). However, the liberty by which these findings are transposed to less specific and more complex clinical situations raises many questions and led to some unjustified assumptions. Nevertheless, in practical implementation the technique of sensory manipulation is carried out in conjunction with functional activities which may be beneficial by themselves.

The method of proprioceptive neuromuscular facilitation was originally outlined by Kabat (1950, 1952, 1958) and developed further by Knott and Voss (1968). Resistance is the primary sensory modality for eliciting or enhancing active motion. It is thought that movement against such modified proprioceptive input would influence the state of central excitation as described by Sherrington (1961) in his work on reciprocal innervation. Facilitation of stretch reflex, tonic neck and righting reflexes are also used as supplementary modalities to induce tone changes and to influence movement control. The exercises entail movement patterns that combine all possible motion around major joints in a prescribed manner and are performed against manual resistance provided by the therapist. The degree of cooperation required to carry out the complex movements makes this technique inapplicable to infants and most young children.

The Brunnstrom (1970) method was developed originally for the treatment of adult hemiplegic patients. It is based on the observation that following a cerebral insult motor behavior reverts to primitive undifferentiated movement patterns or reflex synergies, and that these patterns gradually break up in the course of recovery when returning volitional activity begins to exert selective control (Riddoch and Buzzard, 1921; Walshe, 1923; Twitchell, 1951; Simons, 1953). When paralysis is severe and movements are scarce, synergistic patterns are facilitated to evoke motion, for example grasp reflex to elicit finger flexion. Later, movements are practiced in the context of synergistic patterns, and finally, if the extent of recovery allows, isolated motion is carried out without synergistic support. The use of flexor synergy to activate weak or absent ankle dorsiflexion by simultaneous flexion of the hip and knee is an example of the application of this technique in cerebral palsy.

A somewhat different theory from all others is the basis for the method proposed by Fay (1948, 1954a,b) with ideas related to the phylogenetic evolution of movements. The program follows a sequence of successive stages of locomotion from amphibian homolateral crawl to the crossed reciprocal walking of vertebrates. Establishment of cerebral hemispheric dominance is considered a culmination in the evolution of central nervous system in humans. An outgrowth of this method is the Doman-Delacato (1960) system which follows a rigid routine of passive patterning several times daily. It is asserted that a child must be proficient on a lower level of motor organization before he can advance to the next. The notion is generalized from motor function to intellectual ability and hemispheric dominance is said to be a prerequisite for proper development of perceptual function and abstract thinking. The technique is recommended as a universal treatment for neuromuscular dysfunction, intellectual deficit and learning disabilities (Delacato, 1963, 1966; Doman, 1974). The Doman-Delacato method received wide publicity in the lay press and generated joint statement by several professional organizations expressing doubts about its therapeutic value (American Academy of Pediatrics, 1968). Cohen et al. (1970) discussing the theoretical foundation of this method pointed out that it is at variance with current knowledge on neurologic differentiation. In several well designed evaluations no benefit was demonstrated from patterning brain damaged or mentally retarded children (Robbins and Glass, 1962; Freeman, 1967; Robbins, 1966, 1967; Sparrow and Zigler, 1978) and the positive conclusions of one recent report (Neman et al., 1975; Neman, 1975) have been criticized by reviewers (Zigler and Seitz, 1975).

An assumption underlying the neuromuscular facilitation methods is that at some locus or loci in the central nervous system a convergence of stimuli originating from the externally applied sensory manipulation and from the internal neuronal processes would occur (Harris, 1978). It is hoped that consequent to a barrage of properly selected and timed external stimuli a set of circumstances may be created whereby the final common pathway can be influenced to act in favor of a desired movement. There has been only one experimental attempt to examine whether or not this assumption is valid. In cats and monkeys Cohen (1969, 1970) measured cortically evoked tension and its changes in the quadriceps muscle under the effect of head turning, passive leg movement and stretch, stimuli used in neuromuscular facilitation techniques. The influence of sensory manipulation was highly consistent for individual animals, but the same stimulation produced different effects in different animals. The applicability of these findings to natural conditions was criticized by Harris (1970) on the basis that the animals were anesthetized and quadriceps contraction was evoked by electrical stimulation of the motor cortex, a method not equivalent to voluntary contraction. Another consideration central to neuromuscular facilitation is to influence volitional control by modifying reflex behavior. While it is generally accepted that reflexes constitute a preprogrammed neural background for posture, tone and movement, how their integration into coordinated motion occurs is not completely understood in neurophysiologic terms (Evarts *et al.,* 1971). From the clinical literature the observations of Hellebrandt and her coworkers (1956, 1962a,b) are usually mentioned to illustrate the utilization of tonic neck reflexes in normal motor function. One observation suggesting the possibility that volitional function may be influenced by an intervention using reflex movements in the absence of neurologic abnormality is that provided by Zelazo *et al.* (1972). In a group of normal infants who were given daily practice of automatic reflex walking they reported earlier attainment of independent walking. On the other hand, it is not an unexpected finding that complete abolition of primitive reflex activity by itself does not lead to improvement of active function when the motor system is damaged. Kottke (1970) observed a number of children with cerebral palsy in whom persistent tonic neck reflex activity was eliminated by rhizotomy of the upper cervical sensory roots, afferent pathway of the reflex arc. No significant change in upper extremity function occurred in spite of intensive training.

As it was pointed out in several reviews, the neuromuscular facilitation methods evolved empirically from clinical observations of the abnormal motor behavior in cerebral palsy and in other diseases caused by central lesions (Taft *et al.,* 1962; Basmajian, 1971). A theoretical basis was formulated subsequently by seeking out supportive data from the neurophysiologic literature. Regardless of theoretical reservations the ultimate question which would have to be answered on clinical grounds is whether active motor function can be actually improved by any of the proposed techniques of physical therapy, and if so, are these changes consistent and permanent. The need for controlled clinical trials on the efficacy of therapeutic exercises in cerebral palsy had been stressed for many years (Mead, 1966) but the fact remains that very few attempts have been made to examine the results of treatment. Most papers on this subject relate the authors' clinical experience and impressions (Lipscomb and Krusen, 1943; Crossland, 1951; Zuck and Johnson, 1952; Ingram *et al.,* 1959; Karlsson *et al.,* 1960; Paine, 1962; Woods, 1964; Koeng, 1966), and only a few have tried to apply some standards of clinical investigation (Footh and Kogan, 1963; Wright and Nicholson, 1973). A brief review of three publications, selected for a number of reasons, reflects the current status of literature and should suffice to demonstrate the glaring lack of reliable data for an intervention modality which is used in virtually all cases of cerebral palsy. In 1961 Paine compared the outcome of 103 treated children with 74 who were totally untreated. Traditional types of physical therapy were used. However, treatment was not a uniformly controlled variable, as some children had only home program given by the parents and the information was obtained retrospectively, a notoriously unreliable method of data collection. This study is usually referred to as demonstrating that physical therapy is of no value. However, its conclusions are not completely negative, especially regarding early intervention. The author concluded that children with spastic types of cerebral palsy had better gait, fewer contractures and needed slightly less surgical procedures if treatment was started before two years. A contrasting, most optimistic view is presented by Koeng, who in 1966 reported that 53 out of 69 children receiving neurodevelopmental therapy before their first birthday had normal gait and minimal neurologic signs after 1 to 4 years of treatment. Since there was no control group and details of initial assessment and prognosis are not given, sample bias is a strong possibility. Yet, the unusually high incidence of mild impairment deserves some thought despite inadequate documentation and other shortcomings of the report. The latest paper published by Wright and Nicholson (1973) also employed neurodevelopmental therapy. The study included 47 children under 6 years of age. It had the basic features of a clinical trial, including independent blind assessment. Two experimental plans were used: a parallel design in which 16 children received treatment for one year and another 15 served as control subjects, and a within subject cross-over study for an additional 16 cases who were treated for one-half year and had no therapy for 6 months. The final evaluation showed no statistically significant differences between the three groups. The study resulted in a flurry of exchanges and for several faults and weaknesses in research design the validity of its negative conclusion was strongly questioned (Holt, 1973; Stern, 1973; Koeng and Aebi, 1973; Touwen, 1973; Wright, 1973a,b). The most significant objection is that some important criteria for selecting comparable groups were not considered. The subjects were matched for functional level but not for chronological age. This oversight could have led to classifying more and less severely affected children as similar subjects, thus comparing dissimilar groups. The study illustrates the inherent methodologic problems in trying to apply acceptable standards of controlled clinical trials to a population with cerebral palsy. It also explains the general reluctance of clinical investigators to embark on such studies and the difficulties with stimulating an interest for the support of similar endeavors. It may well be that clarification of some currently unanswered questions will not be forthcoming until more refined methods are available for clinical laboratory research to assess neurophysiologic aspects of motor function. The technique of cerebral evoked potentials which has been applied in experimental studies and is now used in some clinical laboratories may become a valuable tool in future investigations (Giblin, 1964; Donchin and Lindsley, 1968; Desmedt, 1973; Goff et al., 1978). Meanwhile, indications for physical therapy and the choice of technique are based on clinical experience and judgment which suggest that functional improvement is difficult to measure and may be slow to occur; that alleviation of the adverse consequence of disuse, inexperience and secondary complications may be the most significant gain; and that while progress and outcome are related to the severity of deficit early treatment seems to be more beneficial (Denhoff and Langdon, 1966; Ellis, 1967).

Drug treatment and intramuscular neurolysis provide another form of treatment by alleviating increased tone in spastic cerebral palsy. Among the drugs recommended as antispasticity agents, diazepam seems to have a non-specific tranquilizing effect rather than direct influence on muscle tone. Dantrolene sodium which acts on the muscle tissue distal to the myoneural junction has a specific effect on spastic hypertonicity. Most children report a feeling of relaxation and greater ease of movement which, in some cases, is accompanied by measurable functional improvement (Haslam et al., 1974; Denhoff et al., 1975; Molnar et al., 1978). The drug can be used under 5 years of age but liver function should be monitored. The latest antispasticity agent is baclofen which is used for cerebral palsy in Europe for some time and is now in the stage of clinical trials in this country. Personal experience with a double blind trial suggests that it is most effective in cases where volitional control is interfered by predominant extensor spasticity (Molnar and Kathirithamby, 1979). Unlike the generalized tone reducing effect mediated by pharmacologic agents, chemical neurolysis can produce selective localized decrease of hypertonicity. Phenol solution, which has neurolytic properties, injected around a motor nerve or into the motor points of a muscle temporarily alleviates spasticity by producing transient partial denervation weakness (Halpern and Meelhuysen, 1967; Easton et al., 1979). Most frequently, it is used to decrease excessive spastic contraction of ankle plantar flexors and hip adductors.

An integral part of any program is to encourage functional accomplishments, including gross motor and manual skills and their use in different situations of daily life. Play and interactive games are a natural method for fostering development of eye-hand coordination, active manual exploration, and hand use (Denhoff and Langdon, 1966; Denhoff, 1967). As usual, toys should be chosen to provide a variety of experiences; however, their selection must be adjusted to the child's abilities and difficulties (Rogers and Thomas, 1949; Logan, 1957; Finnie, 1975). In therapeutic training, as in any other learning situation, the mutually reinforcing role of success and motivation is an important consideration. Children naturally select the less impaired or unaffected hand as the dominant extremity. Continuous verbal reminders to use both hands tend to provoke resistance and frustration, and are not advisable. However, assistive function of the affected extremity can be improved by more subtle and acceptable means such as using a large ball or toy, pushing a doll carriage, and other similar play activities requiring bimanual function. They are suggested, particularly, for children with hemiplegia to decrease the often striking neglect of the affected upper extremity associated with cortical sensory deficit. Barrett and Jones (1967) reported significantly increased spontaneous function of the hemiparetic arm and hand in young children following repeated presentation of multi-sensory stories during which the verbal narrative was accompanied by placing the actual object near the unaffected hand and then close to the affected one. Progress in adaptive skills and independence in activities of daily life is related to both gross motor development and fine manipulatory skills. Feeding, dressing and other self-care activities are the tasks in which training is initiated first but it may be extended to any other area of physical function where the child has difficulties (Brown, 1950). The choice of activities is guided by general developmental norms which are adapted to physical potential and mental age. If necessitated by the extent of upper extremity dysfunction the child can be taught to use compensatory techniques. Some examples of this approach are the one-handed method of tying shoelaces, substitution of Velcro closure for buttons, donning garment sleeves first on the affected arm and using the opposite sequence on removing (Ward, 1958; Bare *et al.*, 1962; Wagner *et al.*, 1963; Brown, 1966). Simple assistive devices are sometimes useful, such as a built-up handle for spoon and other feeding or writing utensils when prehension is ineffectual (Lowman and Rusk, 1963; Hopkins, 1966). Hand and upper extremity braces are generally not helpful for functional purposes in cerebral palsy and are rarely accepted by children. Splinting may be used in selected cases to prevent progressive contractures.

Independent walking may not be an attainable goal in all cases but active mobility which gives access to the environment should be encouraged in any form from prone to erect progression. There are a number of assistive devices that help in gross functional activities which otherwise could not be performed (Deaver, 1956). Lower extremity braces provide passive support, help to prevent deformities and by controlling abnormal joint positions result in a more efficient gait. However, for movement external force is required which at the present state of technology must be provided by muscle action of the legs or of the torso and arms in case of crutch walking. Therefore, it is important to bear in mind that braces cannot make a child walk unless these prerequisites are met, a fact that some parents may find difficult to understand or accept. Orthotic management of children with cerebral palsy has changed considerably over the years (Molnar, 1979). The past trend of bracing to include all lower extremity joints has been replaced by less extensive and selective action orthoses, particularly in ambulatory children (Garrett *et al.*, 1966; Guess, 1967). Ankle foot orthosis which prevents plantar flexion attitude in stance and provides dorsiflexion substitute in the swing phase of gait is the most frequently used device. Orthoses extending above the knees and hips are less often indicated and, generally, serve as preventive measures rather than as ambulatory aids. In which case and at what time braces should be prescribed depends on the purpose for which they are intended and on the child's functional level, not chronological age. If the goal is to provide means for passive standing the minimal motor functional requirement is head control. In these cases, parapodium (Motlock, 1971) and similar new designs (Taylor and Pemberton, 1972; Taylor and Sand, 1975) which are simple to apply may be more appropriate than the cumbersome conventional leg and trunk braces. If the outlook for some level of ambulation is good, the decision about bracing is usually made when the child pulls to stand and begins to cruise. The new plastic orthoses are lighter and cosmetically more acceptable than conventional metal braces but some disadvantages, particularly lack of adjustability for growth, do not make them universally applicable to children. When balance is not developed and arm function is adequate the child can be trained to walk with walkerette or crutches (Deaver, 1966; Hoberman, 1978). A mental age of about 2 years is needed to learn the principles of crutch walking; however, the actual acquisition of this compensatory skill is also related to the degree of overall motor control, motivation and other factors. A walkerette is easier to maneuver but crutches provide greater functional versatility on various terrains. When ambulation is limited or not feasible wheelchair mobility is a functional substitute (Kamenetz, 1966). It is not a mere replacement for a stroller which the child has outgrown. Training in maneuvering and transferring in different situations is a step toward independence. In addition to conventional wheelchairs, there are new models with modular design that fulfill better the requirements of support and postural relaxation for severely affected children.

A brief but nonetheless emphatic mention should be made of the need to prevent complications which arise as a result of inactivity and abnormal muscle action, especially in spastic types. By definition cerebral palsy is a non-progressive neurologic lesion; however, its musculoskeletal manifestations are not static. Biomechanically, spasticity creates an imbalance of opposing forces as muscle groups with preponderant hypertonicity are virtually in a continuous uncontrolled state of contraction. At first, this is a reversible process and when spasticity is diminished the abnormal postures subside as, indeed, it happens at this stage during sleep. However, in a longstanding dysfunction muscles with predominant hypertonia become tight and eventually shortened due to changes in their viscoelastic properties. On the other hand, opposing muscles are overstretched and develop weakness from disuse. Next, ligamentous and capsular joint contractures occur with deformities which are consistent with the habitual spastic postures. Finally, unbalanced muscle forces affect the configuration of the growing skeleton, articular surfaces and epiphyses. The sequence of events constitutes a cycle from neurologic abnormality to skeletal deformities and, eventually, neuromuscular dysfunction may be compounded by mechanical limitations of mobility with consequent functional decline. The incidence of deformities is directly related to the degree of spasticity and increases with age. The usual abnormal postural attitudes or deformities in the upper extremity are the well known adducted shoulder, flexed and pronated elbow, wrist flexion and fisted hand; in the lower extremity equinus attitude of the ankle with heel-cord contracture, scissoring with hip adduction deformity and, especially in non-ambulatory children, hip and knee flexion contractures. The most serious musculoskeletal complications of spasticity, usually occurring in children who cannot walk, are coxa valga and/or femoral anteversion with subluxation and eventual dislocation of the hip leading to or aggravating already existing spinal deformities. Physical therapy and bracing have an important role in preventing or decreasing joint deformities. Well selected and properly timed orthopedic surgical procedures are also effective to alleviate spastic muscle imbalance and its sequelae (Samilson, 1975; Bleck, 1979). The purpose of surgical treatment may be cosmetic and functional, as in the case of heelcord lengthening for better gait; preventive, e.g., release of hip flexion and adduction contractures to avert deterioration of hip joint in a non-ambulatory child; or any combination of these goals. In general, surgery is rarely considered or needed before 3 years as prior to this age the clinical manifestations of motor dysfunction may still be in a state of flux and conservative treatment is usually sufficient to prevent deformities.

Children with cerebral palsy require modified handling in many aspects of daily physical care and function. Ideas for this most valuable mode of intervention evolved from the neurodevelopmental therapy. They are based on observations made by the Bobaths (1966, 1972, 1975) demonstrating that the stereotyped abnormal postures can be either enhanced or alleviated by the manner in which a child is moved, placed or held. Utilizing these observations, Finnie (1975) described various simple practical methods that are more appropriate for passive handling and are helpful in promoting active function. In most children with spastic cerebral palsy, supine, semi-reclining and vertical positions cause an increase of extensor tone. When the infant is pulled to sit by the arms, as one would do with a non-handicapped youngster, this posture becomes more pronounced. Parents will note that instead of coming to sitting the child gets stiffer. If one's hands are placed over the occiput and back, the hips can be slowly flexed. As the trunk is pushed gently forward resistance will gradually subside. When held in sitting the infant should be astride over the thigh, or straddle the hip while being carried, to prevent scissoring and to relax extensor spasticity in the legs. Many infants and young children with cerebral palsy have difficulties with sucking, swallowing and chewing. They are often fed in semi-reclining position with neck extended which helps the food to trickle into the pharynx by gravity. This type of "bird feeding" should be discouraged because it does not promote active swallowing. Food is not propelled by tongue movements and the opisthotonic posture makes it more difficult to initiate contraction of palatopharyngeal muscles. However, when the trunk and neck are supported in slight flexion during bottle or spoon feeding, active swallowing is easier to perform. Mueller (1972) developed further refinement of feeding techniques for controlling lip closure and jaw movements and for activating oropharyngeal automatisms necessary for swallowing and chewing. An additional importance of proper feeding is that the same anatomic structures participate in speech production and early swallowing difficulties are often followed by other signs of suprabulbar palsy, such as drooling and dysarthria. These are only a few examples of modified handling techniques which parents are advised to use and which should be utilized consistently by all professionals and caretakers involved in the management of children with cerebral palsy.

When motor dysfunction is a leading symptom a great deal of professional attention is directed at problems arising from this deficit. Similarly, parental concern tends to revolve around the child's physical disability, particularly at an early age. However, intervention for the young physically handicapped child has many implications which extend beyond the goal of improving gross or fine motor achievements. From a broader perspective, a well conceived treatment program in the motor functional mode can serve as a vehicle to encompass other aspects of developmental stimulation (Denhoff and Langdon, 1966). Piaget's (1952, 1954) concept of intellectual development proposes that the practical knowledge which infants acquire in active physical encounters with their environment is the basis for learning the rules of object permanence, space, self and surrounding world, cause and effect. It does not seem unjustifiable to assume that when a physical handicap limits the opportunities for active exploration a degree of deprivation occurs and that lack of experience may interfere with the process of early cognitive development.

In this context, practicing sitting, crawling and other gross motor milestones or providing play activities to encourage reaching, prehension and manipulation have other purposes than the originally apparent intention of enhancing motor skills. Functional training implies that the child is expected to perform certain activities not only in the course of therapy sessions but also in other situations of daily life. If complete self-sufficiency is not feasible the child should learn and carry out any part of the task that he is able to. The goal is not solely to improve motor function but also to foster self-reliance. Dependent passive personality is frequently observed among handicapped children. The psychiatric view of personality development emphasizes that the ability to separate physically when crawling and walking are achieved precedes and contributes to the loosening and eventual dissolution of early emotional symbiosis between infant and mother (Mahler, 1963). Encouragement and provision for alternative and substitutive physical means to accomplish locomotion may be regarded as a way to promote this process. One would hope to achieve such additional benefits with greater success if a pattern is established by early intervention.

An elementary need in developmental stimulation programs for youngsters with motor handicap is the creation of access to active encounters. In addition to promoting self initiated or assisted mobility, environmental adjustments may be needed to place interactive opportunities within the sphere of physical reach and ability of the children. An interesting clinical experiment by Barrett *et al.* (1967) and Jones *et al.* (1969) was designed to enhance sensory and social experiences by simple environmental manipulations. A number of 2 to 3 year-old children with cerebral palsy were placed in a confined space which provided a 2½ square foot area per occupant. The behavior of each child was recorded in the regular nursery school setting and inside the "little play house" of confined space. Observations indicated that spontaneous exploratory behavior and play, non-verbal communication and social interaction increased while the children were in the confined space. The question of optimal quality, quantity and intensity of sensory stimulation has been raised in discussions concerning environmental enrichment programs (Wolff, 1969).

These issues are highly pertinent to intervention for children with cerebral palsy who exhibit attentional difficulties, who may not tolerate apparently nonexcessive stimuli and who may have abnormal postural responses to certain types of sensory input; for example, clapping or other loud auditory stimulation could elicit a startle response. To provide a well rounded developmental enrichment program which would duplicate, or at least approximate, the heterogeneous experiences of non-handicapped children requires a great deal of thought (Wolff and MacKeith, 1964; Haynes, 1974; Hayden *et al.*, 1976). The previously discussed handling techniques and other special considerations highlight the necessity of individually designed curricula for youngsters with motor disability of central origin (Safford and Arbitman, 1975).

A crucial phase of intervention is that which is implemented through the family. Early treatment offers support in the stage of initial anguish and depression which parents experience after learning that their child is handicapped. It can be a valuable supportive measure in helping the family toward reaching constructive adjustment and coping. Parental education and the expected benefits of this intervention have many aspects which can only be touched upon briefly in the context of this paper. The range of concerns includes guidance to overcome the problems which stem from differences in both practical transactions of daily life and in more subtle forms of interaction when mobility and responsiveness of the child are curtailed by a handicap. Modifications in the usual methods of physical handling have been discussed earlier (Finnie, 1975). As these techniques mitigate non-functional abnormal postures the child will be more available for active exploration and interaction. In a recent review Beckwith (1976) summarized extensive research data on the intricacies of infant-caregiver interaction, the mutually reinforcing nature of this relationship and its influence on early development. Since differences in the infant's responsiveness can significantly alter the caregiver's style of rearing the question has been raised whether this could further aggravate developmental deviations in infants at risk. While some families show a resourceful natural ability for adjusting their child-rearing practices to the need of their handicapped youngster others have considerable difficulties in this respect. Based on observations of children with cerebral palsy and their mothers at home Shere and Kastenbaum (1966) and Shere (1971) provided many examples of the altered interaction and other environmental obstacles which may hinder the overall development of these youngsters. Lack of cuddling and talking to a child who seemed unresponsive or was unable to engage in reciprocal interaction, inappropriate and inaccessible toys, and physical set-up which interfered with functional activities were among the problems reported. Guidance in growth fostering management is a logical extension of treatment to the child's natural milieu. It is a necessity for successful environmental therapy to achieve an optimal overall functional outcome which constitutes the most ambitious and far-reaching aim of intervention. Application of developmental stimulation and proper handling techniques or practicing functional skills which the child learned in therapeutic training can be part of daily routine and usually do not make excessive demands on a family which may be already stressed. However, in recommending formal therapeutic exercises which would place the parents in the role of a therapist one should carefully consider the dynamics of the child-family unit. When the family is overly anxious and the issue of home exercises is an area of potential conflict this decision should be made by weighing both physical needs and emotional aspects of the situation.

As a final point, one should raise some questions which have to be faced by all professional providers of long-term rehabilitation but are seldom discussed, perhaps, because they have no easy or categorical solutions. A complex decision to make and implement is the transition between intensive as opposed to maintenance treatment when progress is minimal or the expected goals have been achieved, at least temporarily, for the child's current developmental stage (Ellis, 1967). Parental reactions of depression, confusion, disappointment, and even anger are inevitable and the emotional impact can be dampened only partly by stressing the progress already achieved and by emphasizing the dynamic nature of development which may be utilized therapeutically at some future time again. The second and somewhat related issue is that of excessive dependence on a professional team, which has been observed among handicapped of all ages and their families and which may conceivably occur more frequently in the case of early intensive and long lasting treatment. Are we, perhaps, encouraging and perpetuating a feeling of helplessness and incompetence in the families of handicapped children by our unspoken but unmistakably conveyed attitude of authority and self-assured knowledge? We must view our contribution with humility to avoid this pitfall of paradoxic outcome, for a well implemented successful intervention should instill a strong feeling of self confidence in the child and family.

In the treatment of motor disability many different therapeutic modalities are utilized. Each modality has to be applied with a clear purpose and understanding as to its potential benefits and limitations. The effectiveness of some treatment methods has not been properly tested and adherence to any one approach by exclusion of others is not justifiable. In a well conceived program, treatment of the physical dysfunction should be blended with provisions for stimulating progress in other functional areas. Early intervention is favored on the basis of clinical experience and for its implications concerning overall development. The keystone of success is a therapeutic alliance between the family and the professional team.

References

American Academy of Pediatrics. Statement on the Doman-Delacato treatment of neurologically handicapped children. *J. Pediatr.*, 72:750 (1968).

Bare, C., Boettke, E.M. and Waggoner, N. *Self-Help Clothing for Handicapped Children.* Chicago: National Society for Crippled Children and Adults (1962).

Barrett, M.L., Hunt, V.V. and Jones, M.H. Behavioral growth of cerebral palsied children from group experience in a confined space. *Develop. Med. Child Neurol.,* 9:50 (1967).

Barrett, M.L. and Jones, M.H. The "sensory story": a multisensory training procedure for toddler. I. Effect on motor function of hemiplegic hand in cerebral palsied children. *Develop. Med. Child Neurol.,* 9:448 (1967).

Basmajian, J.V. Neuromuscular facilitation techniques. *Arch. Phys. Med. Rehabil.,* 52:40 (1971).

Bax, M.C.O. and MacKeith, R.C. Treatment of cerebral palsy. Editorial. *Develop. Med. Child Neurol.,* 15:1 (1973).

Beckwith, L. Caregiver-Infant Interaction as a Focus for Therapeutic Intervention with Human Infants, in Walsh, R.N. and Greenough, W.T. (eds.), *Environments as Therapy for Brain Dysfunction.* Advances in Behavioral Biology, Vol. 17. New York: Plenum Press, p. 276 (1976).

Bizzi, E. and Evarts, E.V. Translational mechanisms between input and output, in Evarts, E.V. *et al.* (eds.), *Central Control of Movement.* Neurosciences Research Program Bulletin, 9:31 (1971).

Black, P., Cianci, S.N. and Markowitz, R.S. Differential recovery of proximal and distal motor power after cortical lesions. *Trans. Am. Neurol. Assoc.,* 96:173 (1971).

Black, P., Markowitz, R.S. and Cianci, S.N. Recovery of Motor Function after Lesions in Motor Cortex of Monkey, in *Outcome of Severe Damage in the Central Nervous System.* Ciba Foundation Symposium. Amsterdam: Elsevier (1975).

Bleck, E.E. *Orthopedic Management of Cerebral Palsy.* Philadelphia: Saunders (1979).

Bobath, K. *The Motor Deficit in Patients with Cerebral Palsy.* Clinics Develop. Med. No. 23. London: Heinemann (1966).

Bobath, K. and Bobath, B. Cerebral Palsy, in Pearson, P.M. and Williams, C.E. (eds.), *Physical Therapy Services in the Developmental Disabilities.* Springfield, Ill.: C.C. Thomas (1972).

Bobath, B. and Bobath, K. *Motor Development in the Different Types of Cerebral Palsy.* London: Heinemann (1975).

Bouman, H.D. Delineating the dilemma. *Am. J. Phys. Med.,* 46:26 (1976a).

Bouman, H.D. (ed.), An exploratory and analytical survey of therapeutic exercise. *Am. J. Phys. Med.,* 46:1 (1976b).

Brunnstrom, S. *Movement Therapy in Hemiplegia.* New York: Harper and Row (1970).

Brown, M.E. Daily activity inventories of cerebral palsied children in experimental classes. *Phys. Ther. Rev.,* 30:415 (1950).

Brown, M.E. Self-Help Clothing, in Licht, S. (ed.), *Orthotics.* New Haven: E. Licht (1966).

Christensen, E. and Melchior, J. *Cerebral Palsy – A Clinical and Neuropathological Study.* Clinics Develop. Med. No. 25. London: Heinemann (1967).

Cohen, J.H., Birch, H.G. and Taft, L.T. Some considerations for evaluating the Doman-Delacato "patterning" method. *Pediatr.,* 45:302 (1970).

Cohen, L.A. Manipulation of cortical motor responses by peripheral sensory stimulation. *Arch. Phys. Med. Rehabil.,* 50:495 (1969).

Cohen, L.A. Response to Letter to the Editor. *Arch. Phys. Med. Rehab.,* 51:442 (1970).

Courville, C.B. *Birth Anoxia and Brain Damage.* Los Angeles: San Lucas Press (1971).

Crossland, J.H. The assessment of results in the conservative treatment of cerebral palsy. *Arch. Diseas. Child.,* 26:92 (1951).

Crothers, B. and Paine, R.S. *The Natural History of Cerebral Palsy.* Cambridge, Mass.: Harvard University Press (1959).

Deaver, G.G. Cerebral palsy, methods of treating the neuromuscular disabilities. *Arch. Phys. Med. Rehabil.,* 37:363 (1956).

Deaver, G.G. Crutches, Canes and Walkers, in S. Licht (ed.), *Orthotics.* New Haven: E. Licht (1966).

Delacato, C.H. *Diagnosis and Treatment of Speech and Reading Problems.* Springfield, Ill.: C.C. Thomas (1963).

Delacato, C.H. *Neurologic Organization and Reading.* Springfield, Ill.: C.C. Thomas (1966).

Denhoff, E. and Langdon, M. Cerebral dysfunction. A treatment programme for young children. *Clin. Pediatr.,* 5:332 (1966).

Denhoff, E. *Cerebral Palsy – The Preschool Years: Diagnosis, Treatment and Planning.* Springfield, Ill.: C.C. Thomas (1967).

Denhoff, E., Feldman, S., Smith, M.G., Litchman, H. and Holden, W. Treatment of spastic cerebral palsied children with sodium dantrolene. *Develop. Med. Child Neurol.,* 17: 736 (1975).

Dennis, W. The effect of restrictive practices on walking, sitting and standing in 2 infants. *J. Genet. Psychol.,* 47:17 (1935).

Dennis, W. The effect of cradling practices upon the onset of walking in Hopi children. *J. Genet. Psychol.,* 56:77 (1940).

Dennis, W. Infant development under conditions of restricted practice and of minimal social stimulation. *J. Genet. Psychol.,* 23:143 (1941).

Dennis, W. Causes of retardation among institutionalized children in Iran. *J. Genet. Psychol.,* 96:47 (1960).

Desmedt, J.E. (ed.) *New Developments in Electromyography and Clinical Neurophysiology.* Vol. 2. Basel: Karger (1973).

Doman, R.J., Spitz, E.B., Zucman, E., Delacato, C.H. and Doman, G. Children with severe brain injuries. *JAMA,* 174:257 (1960).

Doman, G. *What To Do About Your Brain Injured Child.* New York: Doubleday (1974).

Donchin, E. and Lindsley, D.B. (eds.) Average evoked potentials: methods, results and evaluations. National Aeronautics and Space Administration. NASA SP-91. Washington, D.C., p. 45 (1968).

Easton, J.K.M., Ozel, T. and Halpern, D. Intramuscular neurolysis for spasticity in children. *Arch. Phys. Med. Rehabil.,* 60:155 (1979).

Eldred, E. Peripheral receptors: their elicitation and relation to reflex patterns. *Am. J. Phys. Med.,* 46:69 (1967a).

Eldred, E. Functional implications of dynamic and static components of the spindle response to stretch. *Am. J. Phys. Med.,* 46:129 (1967b).

Ellis, E. *The Physical Management of Developmental Disorders.* Clinics Develop. Med. No. 26. London: Heinemann (1967a).

Ellis, E. How long should treatment be continued. *Develop. Med. Child Neurol.,* 9:47 (1967b).

Ellis, N.R. (ed.) *Aberrant Development in Infancy: Human and Animal Studies.* Hillsdale, New Jersey: Erlbaum Assoc. (1975).

Evarts, E.V., Bizzi, E. *et al.* (eds.) Central Control of Movement. Neurosciences Research Program Bulletin 9:1 (1971).

Fay, T. The neurophysiologic aspects of therapy in cerebral palsy. *Arch. Phys. Med. Rehabil.,* 29:327 (1948).

Fay, T. The use of pathological and unlocking reflexes in the rehabilitation of spastics. *Am. J. Phys. Med.,* 33:347 (1954a).

Fay, T. Rehabilitation of patients with spastic paralysis. *J. Internat. College Surg.,* 22:220 (1954b).

Finnie, N.R. *Handling The Young Cerebral Palsied Child At Home.* New York: E.P. Dutton and Co. (1975).

Footh, V.K. and Logan, K.L. Measuring the effectiveness of physical therapy in the treatment of cerebral palsy. *J. Am. Phys. Ther. Assoc.,* 43:867 (1963).

Freeman, R.S. Controversy over "patterning" as a treatment for brain damage in children. *JAMA,* 202:385 (1967).

Garrett, A., Lister, M. and Bressnan, G. New concepts in cerebral palsy bracing. *J. Phys. Ther. Assoc.,* 46:728 (1966).

Giblin, R.S. Somatosensory evoked potentials in healthy subjects and in patients with lesions of the nervous system. *Ann. NY Acad. Sci.,* 112:93 (1964).

Gillette, H.E. Exercises for Cerebral Palsy, in Licht, S. (ed.), *Therapeutic Exercise.* New Haven: E. Licht, p. 692 (1958).

Gilette, H.E. *Systems of Therapy in Cerebral Palsy.* Springfield, Ill.: C.C. Thomas (1969).

Glees, P. and Cole, J. Recovery of skilled motor function after small repeated lesions of motor cortex in macaque. *J. Neurophysiol.,* 13:137 (1950).

Goff, W.R., Allison, T. and Vaughan, H.G. The Functional Anatomy of Event Related Potentials, in Callaway, E. and Koslow, S.H. (eds.), *Event Related Brain Potentials in Man.* New York: Academic Press (1978).

Goldberger, M.E. Recovery of Movement after CNS Lesions in Monkeys, in Stein, D.G., Rosen, J.J. and Butter, N. (eds.), *Plasticity and Recovery of Function in the Central Nervous System.* New York: Academic Press, p. 265 (1974).

Granit, R. (ed.), *Muscular Afferents and Motor Control.* Nobel Symposium. Stockholm: Almquist and Wiksell (1966).

Greenough, W.T., Fass, B. and De Voogd, T.J. The Influence of Experience on Recovery Following Brain Damage in Rodents: Hypothesis Based on Developmental Research, in Walsh, R.N. and Greenough, W.T. (eds.), *Environments as Therapy for Brain Dysfunction. Advances in Behavioral Biology.* Vol. 17. New York: Plenum Press, p. 10 (1976).

Guerrero, V. and Epps, C.H. Early prosthetic rehabilitation of the child with unilateral below elbow congenital deficiency. *Interclinic Information Bull.*, 12:9 (1972).

Guess, V.S. Control of Lower Extremity Movement in Cerebral Palsy, in Perry, J. and Hislop, H.J. (eds.), *Principles of Lower Extremity Bracing.* New York: Am. Phys. Ther. Assoc. (1967).

Hagbarth, K.E. Excitatory and inhibitory skin areas for flexor and extensor motorneurons. *Acta Physiol. Scand.* Suppl 94. 26:1 (1952).

Hagbarth, K.E. and Eklund, G. The muscle vibrator – a useful tool in neurologic therapeutic work. *Scand. J. Rehab. Med.*, 1:26 (1969).

Halpern, D. and Meelhuysen, F.E. Duration of relaxation after intramuscular neurolysis with phenol. *JAMA*, 200:1152 (1967).

Halpern, D. Therapeutic Exercises for Cerebral Palsy, in Basmajian, J.V. (ed.), *Therapeutic Exercise.* Baltimore: Williams and Wilkins, p. 281 (1978).

Harris, F.A. In defense of facilitation techniques. *Arch. Phys. Med. Rehabil.*, 51:438 (1970).

Harris, F.A. Facilitation Techniques in Therapeutic Exercise, in Basmajian, J.V. (ed.), *Therapeutic Exercise.* Baltimore: Williams and Wilkins, p. 93 (1978).

Haslam, R.H.A. Dantrolene sodium in children with spasticity. *Arch. Phys. Med. Rehabil.*, 55:384 (1974).

Haynes, V. *Programming for Atypical Infants and Their Families.* New York: United Cerebral Palsy Association (1974).

Hayden, A.H. *et al.* Early and Continuous Intervention Strategies for Severely Handicapped Infants and Very Young Children, in Haring, N.G. and Brown, L.J. (eds.), *Teaching the Severely Handicapped.* New York: Grune and Stratton, p. 239 (1976).

Held, R. and Hein, A. Adaptation of disarranged hand-eye coordination contingent upon reafferent stimulation. *Percept. Motor Skills*, 8:87 (1958).

Held, R. and Schlank, M. Adaptation to disarranged eye-hand coordination in the distance dimension. *Am. J. Psychol.*, 72:603 (1959).

Held, R. and Bossom, J. Neonatal deprivation and adult rearrangements: complementary techniques for analyzing plastic sensory-motor coordination. *J. Comp. Physiol. Psychol.*, 54:33 (1961).

Held, R. and Freedman, S.J. Plasticity in human sensorimotor control. *Science*, 142:455 (1963).

Hellebrandt, F.A., Schade, M. and Carns, M.D. Methods of evoking the tonic neck reflexes in normal human subjects. *Am. J. Phys. Med.*, 41:90 (1962).

Hellebrandt, F.A., Houtz, S.J., Partridge, M.Y. and Walters, E.E. Tonic neck reflexes in exercises of stress in man. *Am. J. Phys. Med.*, 35:144 (1956).

Hellebrandt, F.A. and Waterland, J.C. Expression of motor patterning under exercise stress. *Am. J. Phys. Med.*, 41:50 (1962).

Hoberman, M. Crutch and Cane Exercises and Use, in Basmajian, J.V. (ed.), *Therapeutic Exercise.* Baltimore: Williams and Wilkins, p. 228 (1978).

Holt, K.S. Letter to the Editor. *Develop. Med. Child Neurol.*, 15:537 (1973).

Hopkins, H.L. Self-Help Aids, in Licht, S. (ed.), *Orthotics.* New Haven: E. Licht, p. 646 (1966).

Hunt, J. McV. Environmental Programming to Foster Competence and Prevent Mental Retardation in Infancy, in Walsh, R.N. and Greenough, W.T. (eds.), *Environments as Therapy for Brain Dysfunction.* Advances in Behavioral Biology, Vol. 17. New York: Plenum Press, p. 201 (1976).

Illingworth, R.R. *The Development of Infant and Young Child. Normal and Abnormal.* Edinburgh: Livingstone (1960).

Ingram, A.J., Withers, E. and Speltz, E. Role of intensive physical and occupational therapy in the treatment of cerebral palsy. Testing and results. *Arch. Phys. Med. Rehabil.,* 40:429 (1959).

Isaacson, R.L. Recovery from Early Brain Damage, in Tjossem, T.D. (ed.), *Intervention Strategies for High Risk Infants and Young Children.* Baltimore: University Park Press, p. 37 (1978).

Jacobson, M. Neuronal Plasticity: Concepts in Pursuit of Cellular Mechanisms, in Stein, D.J., Rosen, J.J. and Butters, N. (eds.), *Plasticity and Recovery of Function in the Central Nervous System.* New York: Academic Press, p. 31 (1974).

Jones, A.M. The traditional method of treatment of the cerebral palsied child. *Am. J. Phys. Med.,* 46:1024 (1967).

Jones, M.H., Barrett, M.L., Olonoff, C. and Andersen, E. Two Experiments in Training Handicapped Children at Nursery School, in Wolff, P.H. and MacKeith, R. (eds.), *Planning for Better Learning.* Clinics Develop. Med. No. 33. London: Heinemann, p. 108 (1969).

Kabat, H. Central mechanisms for recovery of neuromuscular function. *Science,* 112:23 (1950).

Kabat, H. The role of central facilitation in restoration of motor function paralysis. *Arch. Phys. Med. Rehabil.,* 33:521 (1952).

Kabat, H. Facilitation in Therapeutic Exercise, in Licht, S. (ed.), *Therapeutic Exercise.* New Haven: E. Licht (1958).

Kamenetz, H.L. Wheelchairs, in S. Licht (ed.), *Orthotics.* New Haven: E. Licht (1966).

Karlsson, B., Neumann, B. and Gardestroem, L. Results of physical treatment in cerebral palsy. *Cerebral Palsy Bull.,* 2:278 (1960).

Koeng, E. Very early treatment of cerebral palsy. *Develop. Med. Child Neurol.,* 8:198 (1966).

Koeng, E. and Aebi, U. Letter to the Editor. *Develop. Med. Child Neurol.,* 15:538 (1973).

Kottke, F.J. Modification of athetosis by denervation of the tonic neck reflexes. *Develop. Med. Child Neurol.,* 12:236 (1970).

Lambert, C.N., Hamilton, R.C. and Pellicore, R.J. The juvenile amputee program. Its social and economic value — a follow-up after the age of twenty one. *J. Bone Joint Surg.,* 51:1135 (1969).

Levitt, S. *The Treatment of Cerebral Palsy and Motor Delay.* Oxford: Blackwell Scientific Publ. (1977).

Lindsley, D.B., Schreiner, L.H. and Magoun, H.W. An electromyographic study of spasticity. *J. Neurophysiol.,* 12:197 (1949).

Lipscomb, P.R. and Krusen, F.H. Cerebral birth palsy with special reference to physical therapy. *Arch. Phys. Med. Rehabil.,* 24:342 (1943).

Liu, C.N. and Chambers, W.W. Conditioned tactual responses and discrete movements in monkeys with pyromidal lesions. *Fed. Proc.,* 21:367 (1962).

Livingston, R.B. Central Control of Receptors and Sensory Transmission Systems, in Field, J., Magoun, H.W. and Hall, V.E. (eds.), *Handbook of Physiology.* Section I. Neurophysiology. Washington, D.C.: Am. Physiol. Society, Vol. I, p. 741 (1959).

Logan, J.A. *There Is More to Toys Than Meets the Eye, as Seen by the Physical Therapist.* Chicago: National Society for Crippled Children and Adults (1957).

Magnus, R. Physiology of posture. *Lancet,* 2:531, 585 (1926).

McDonald, J. The age of fitting upper extremity prostheses in children. *J. Bone Joint Surg.,* 40:655 (1958).

McGraw, M. *Growth: A Study of Johnny and Jimmy.* New York: Appleton Century Co. (1935).

Mahler, M. *Thoughts about Development and Inviduation. The Psychoanalytic Study of the Child.* Vol. 18. New York: International Universities Press, p. 307 (1963).

Mead, S. The treatment of cerebral palsy. *Develop. Med. Child Neurol.,* 10:423 (1968).

Molnar, G.E. and Gordon, S.U. Cerebral palsy: predictive value of selected clinical signs for early prognostication of motor function. *Arch. Phys. Med. Rehabil.,* 57:153 (1976).

Molnar, G.E. and Taft, L.T. Pediatric Rehabilitation. Part I. Cerebral Palsy and Spinal Cord Injuries. *Current Problems in Pediatrics,* VII:3 (1977a).

Molnar, G.E. and Taft, L.T. Pediatric Rehabilitation. Part II. Spina Bifida and Limb Deficiencies. *Current Problems in Pediatrics,* VII:4 (1977b).

Molnar, G.E., Evangelista, L.A. and Kathirithamby, R. Dantrolene sodium in spasticity. Long term administration in children. *NY State J. Med.,* 78:1233 (1978).

Molnar, G.E. Cerebral palsy: prognosis and how to judge it. *Pediat. Ann.,* 8:596 (1979a).

Molnar, G.E. Orthotic Management of Children, in Redford, J. (ed.), *Orthotics.* Baltimore: Williams and Wilkins (1979b).

Molnar, G.E. and Kathirithamby, R. Lioresal in the treatment of children with cerebral palsy: report of a double blind study. *Arch. Phys. Med. Rehabil.,* in press (1979).

Morrison, H.L. and McKinney, E.T. Environments of Dysfunction: the Relevance of Private Animal Models, in Walsh, R.N. and Greenough, W.T. (eds.), *Environments as Therapy for Brain Dysfunction.* New York: Plenum Press, p. 132 (1976).

Moscona, A.A. and Monroy, A. (eds.) *Current Topics In Developmental Biology.* New York: Academic Press (1973).

Motlock, W. The parapodium: an orthotic device for neuromuscular disorders. *Artif. Limbs,* 15:36 (1971).

Mueller, H.A. Facilitating Feeding and Prespeech, in Pearson, P.H. and Williams, C.E. (eds.), *Physical Therapy Services in the Developmental Disabilities.* Springfield, Ill.: C.C. Thomas (1972).

Neman, R., Roos, P., McCann, B., Menolascino, F.J. and Heal, L.W. Experimental evaluation of sensorimotor patterning used with mentally retarded children. *Am. J. Mental Defic.,* 79:372 (1975).

Neman, R. A reply to Zigler and Seitz. *Am. J. Mental Defic.,* 79:493 (1975).

Paine, R.S. On the treatment of cerebral palsy. The outcome of 177 patients, 74 totally untreated. *Pediatr.,* 29:605 (1962).

Paine, R.S. The evolution of infantile postural reflexes in the presence of chronic brain syndromes. *Develop. Med. Child Neurol.,* 6:4 (1964).

Paine, R.S., Brazelton, T.B., Donovan, D.E., Drorbaugh, J.E., Hubbell, J.F. and Sears, E.M. The evolution of postural reflexes in normal infants and in the presence of chronic brain syndromes. *Neurol.,* 14:1036 (1964).

Payton, O.D., Hirt, S. and Newton, R.A. *Neurophysiologic Approaches to Therapeutic Exercise.* Philadelphia: F.A. Davis (1978).

Piaget, J. *The Origins of Intelligence in Children.* New York: International Universities Press (1952).

Piaget, J. *The Construction of Reality in the Child.* New York: Basic Books (1954).

Pearson, P.H. and Williams, C.E. (eds.), *Physical Therapy Services in the Developmental Disabilities.* Springfield, Ill.: C.C. Thomas (1972).

Peiper, A. *Cerebral Function in Infancy and Childhood.* New York: Consultants Bureau (1963).

Phelps, W.M. The Role of Physical Therapy in Cerebral Palsy, in Illingworth, R.S. (ed.), *Recent Advances in Cerebral Palsy.* London: Churchill (1958).

Riddoch, G. and Buzzard, E.F. Reflex movements and postural reactions in quadriplegia and hemiplegia with special reference to those of the upper extremities. *Brain*, 44:397 (1921).

Robbins, M.P. and Glass, G.V. The Doman-Delacato Rationale: a Critical Analysis, in Hellmuth, J. (ed.), *Educational Therapy.* Seattle: Special Child Publications, p. 321 (1962).

Robbins, M.P. A study of the validity of Doman-Delacato's theory of neurological organization. *Exceptional Children*, 32:517 (1966).

Robbins, M.P. Test of the Doman-Delacato rationale with retarded readers. *JAMA*, 202: 389 (1967).

Rogers, G.G. and Thomas, L. Toys, games and apparatus for children with cerebral palsy. *Phys. Ther. Rev.*, 29:1 (1949).

Rood, M.S. Neurophysiologic reactions as a basis for physical therapy. *Phys. Ther. Rev.*, 34:444 (1954).

Rood, M.S. Neurophysiologic mechanisms in the treatment of neuromuscular dysfunction. *Am. J. Occup. Ther.*, 10:220 (1956).

Rood, M.S. The Use of Sensory Receptors to Activate, Facilitate and Inhibit Motor Response, Autonomic and Somatic Developmental Sequence, in Slattely, C. (ed.), *Approaches to Treatment of Patients with Neuromuscular Dysfunction.* Dubuque, Iowa: W.C. Brown (1962).

Rosner, B.S. Recovery of Function and Localization of Function in Historical Perspective, in Stein, D.G., Rosen, J.Y. and Butters, N. (eds.), *Plasticity and Recovery of Function in the Central Nervous System.* New York: Academic Press, p. 1 (1974).

Safford, P.L. and Arbitman, D.C. *Developmental Intervention with Young Physically Handicapped Children.* Springfield, Ill.: C.C. Thomas (1975).

Samilson, R.L. (ed.) *Orthopedic Aspects of Cerebral Palsy.* Clinics Develop. Med. No. 52/53. Philadelphia: Lippincott (1975).

Schaltenbrand, G. The development of human mobility and motor disturbances. *Arch. Neurol. Psychiat.*, 20:270 (1928).

Shere, E.S. and Kastenbaum, R. Mother-child interaction in cerebral palsy, environmental psychosocial obstacles to cognitive development. *Genet. Psychol. Monogr.*, 73:255 (1966).

Shere, E.S. Patterns of child rearing in cerebral palsy, effect upon the child's cognitive development. *Pediatr. Digest*, 23:28 (1971).

Sherrington, C.S. *The Integrative Action of the Nervous System.* New Haven: Yale University Press (1961).

Simons, A. Head posture and muscle tone. *Phys. Ther. Rev.*, 32:409 (1953).

Sparrow, S. and Zigler, E. Evaluation of a patterning treatment for retarded children. *Pediatr.*, 62:137 (1978).

Stein, G., Rosen, J.J. and Butters, N. (eds.), *Plasticity and Recovery of Function in the Central Nervous System.* New York: Academic Press (1974).

Stern, F.M. Letter to the Editor. *Develop. Med. Child Neurol.*, 15:539 (1973).

Sypniewski, L. Questionnaire survey concerning the age of initial fitting. *Interclinic Information Bull.*, 6:1 (1972).

Taft, L.T., Delagi, E.F., Wilkie, O.L. and Abramson, A.S. Critique of rehabilitative techniques in treatment of cerebral palsy. *Arch. Phys. Med. Rehabil.*, 43:238 (1962).

Taylor, N. and Pemberton, D.R. The Verlo: an orthosis for children with severe motor handicap. *Arch. Phys. Med. Rehabil.*, 53:534 (1972).

Taylor, N. and Sand, P. Verlo orthosis: experience with different developmental levels in normal children. *Arch. Phys. Med. Rehabil.*, 56:120 (1975).

Tjossem, T.D. (ed.) *Intervention Strategies for High Risk Infants and Young Children.* Baltimore: University Park Press (1978a).

Tjossem, T.D. Early Intervention: Issues and Approaches, in Tjossem, T.D. (ed.), *Intervention Strategies for High Risk Infants and Young Children.* Baltimore: University Park Press, p. 3 (1978b).

Touwen, B.C.L. Letter to the Editor. *Develop. Med. Child Neurol.*, 15:693 (1973).

Trefler, E. An evaluation of 1970 summer training program for children with upper extremity amputations. *Interclinic Information Bull.* XI. 4:10 (1972).

Twitchell, T.E. The restoration of motor function following hemiplegia in man. *Brain*, 74: 443 (1951).

Twitchell, T.E. On the motor deficit in congenital bilateral athetosis. *J. Nerv. Ment. Dis.*, 129:105 (1959).

Twitchell, T.E. The grasping deficit in infantile spastic hemiparesis. *Neurol.*, 8:13 (1965a).

Twitchell, T.E. Normal motor development. *J. Am. Phys. Ther. Assoc.*, 45:419 (1965b).

Twitchell, T.E. Attitudinal reflexes. *J. Am. Phys. Ther. Assoc.*, 45:411 (1965c).

Twitchell, T.E. Variations and abnormalities of motor development. *J. Am. Phys. Ther. Assoc.*, 45:424 (1965d).

Ward, M. Self-help fashions for the physically disabled child. *Am. J. Nursing*, 58:14 (1958).

Wagner, E.M., Kunstadter, R.H. and Shover, J. Self-help clothing for handicapped children. *Clin. Pediatr.*, 2:122 (1963).

Walsh, R.N. and Greenough, W.T. (eds.), *Environments as Therapy for Brain Dysfunction. Advances in Behavioral Biology.* Vol. 17. New York: Plenum Press (1976).

Walsh, R.N. and Cummins, R.A. Neural Responses to Therapeutic Sensory Environments, in Walsh, R.N. and Greenough, W.T. (eds.), *Environments as Therapy for Brain Dysfunction. Advances in Behavioral Biology.* Vol. 17. New York: Plenum Press, p. 171 (1976).

Walshe, F.M.R. On certain tonic or postural reflexes in hemiplegia with special reference to the so-called "associated movements." *Brain*, 46:2 (1923).

Weisz, S. Studies in equilibrium reactions. *J. Nerv. Ment. Dis.*, 88:150 (1938).

White, B.L., Castle, P. and Held, R. Observations on the Development of Visually Directed Reaching, in Hellmuth, J. (ed.), *Exceptional Infant.* Vol. I. New York: Brunner/ Mazel (1964).

White, B.L. and Held, R. Plasticity of sensorimotor development in the human infant. *Child Develop.*, 35:349 (1967).

Wolff, P.H. and MacKeith, R. (eds.), *Planning for Better Learning.* Clinics Develop. Med. No. 33. London: Heinemann (1969).

Wolff, P.H. What We Must and Must Not Teach Our Children from What We Know about Early Cognitive Development, in Wolff, P.H. and MacKeith, R. (eds.), *Planning for Better Learning.* Clinics Develop Med. No. 33. London: Heinemann, p. 7 (1969).

Woods, G.E. The outcome of physical treatment in cerebral palsy. *Cerebral Palsy Rev.*, 25: 3 (1964).

Wright, T. and Nicholson, J. Physiotherapy for the spastic child: an evaluation. *Develop. Med. Child Neurol.*, 15:146 (1973).

Wright, T. Reply to letter to the Editor. *Develop. Med. Child Neurol.*, 15:539 (1973a).

Wright, T. Reply to letter to the Editor. *Develop. Med. Child Neurol.,* 15:694 (1973b).

Zelazo, P.R., Zelazo, N.A. and Kolb, S. "Walking" in the newborn. *Science,* 176:314 (1972).

Zigler, E. and Seitz, V. On "An experimental evaluation of sensorimotor patterning": a critique. *Am. J. Mental Defic.,* 79:483 (1975).

Zuck, F.N. and Johnson, K. The progress of cerebral palsy patients under inpatient circumstances. *Amer. Acad. Orthop. Surg.* Instructional Course Lectures 9:112 (1952).

PART III

Cognitive Development

While the study of cognitive development has received considerable emphasis and a large body of data on the preschool child's intellectual growth has been collected, there is only a small portion of this vast research that has made its way into the dysfunctional literature. Besides the use of IQ testing, at best a rather gross estimate of the child's ability and competence, relatively little information on the various cognitive capacities uncovered by researchers in the last 25 years has been utilized in the assessment and intervention fields. The task of any interdisciplinary effort is to apply this knowledge of the study of individual differences in a clinical setting. Not all aspects of cognitive abilities can be covered in one section; however, those covered provide an example of how information on cognitive processes and individual differences can be transferred into a clinical setting.

Intervention in cognitive dysfunction has received the most attention and in some ways represents both positive and negative results. From one perspective it is clear that intervention in cognitive dysfunction results in improvement; however, especially clear is the current limitation, even after considerable effort, in eliminating these forms of dysfunction.

12

Issues in the Early Development of Intelligence and Its Assessment

ROBERT B. McCALL

"The child is father to the man." Despite the sexism of its phraseology this aphorism conveys a certain axiomatic truth. It belies a faith most of us have in the inherent consistency in the individual from one year to the next: we are not born again *de novo* at each stage of development. Perhaps, then, it is not surprising that pediatricians and psychologists have spent nearly a half-century attempting to assess the intelligence of infants and to predict IQ in childhood or adulthood.

Many reasons justify this pursuit:

1. Parents are curious about whether their child will be bright or not. "Intelligence," rightly or wrongly, is viewed as the key to educational and occupational success in America, and parents are anxious to know how their offspring will fare.
2. When it was common to match children with prospective adoptive parents, there was a desire to determine an infant's intelligence in order to find an appropriate family.
3. Assessing mental performance in infancy might tell scientists about the nature of early mental growth and how to promote its development.
4. If we are able to detect future abnormalities and mental deficiencies, perhaps treatment can be initiated early enough to prevent such retardation. This is at the heart of the government's Early and Periodic Screening, Detection and Treatment Program, now called Child Health Assessment Program (CHAP).

Numerous tests of infant development have been constructed during the last decades. The best known include the Gesell, Bayley, Cattell, Griffiths and the Denver Developmental Screening Test which is composed of selected items from the other tests. More recently, tests based upon Piaget's conception of sensory motor development have appeared.

Predictions to Later IQ

Normal Samples

Much of the research on infant tests has focused on their ability to predict IQ in childhood or adulthood using essentially normal samples. How well have they fared? Not very. The correlation between an infant test administered during the first six months of life and childhood IQ between 5 and 18 years of age is between .00 and .09—essentially nothing (McCall *et al.*, 1972). If the infant test is given between 7 and 12 months of age, these correlations rise to approximately .20 to .25; a test administered between 13 and 18 months yields correlations of approximately .33; and between 19 and 30 months the correlations are between .39 and .49. In short, from a practical standpoint, infant tests administered before 18 months of age are useless in predicting later childhood IQ for normal samples. In fact, the parent's level of education or IQ (which correlates approximately .50 with childhood IQ) is the best single predictor we have during infancy of a child's later IQ.

While infant tests do not predict later IQ with clinical utility for normal samples, this is probably less the fault of the test than of nature. The reliability of the infant test is surprisingly good after three months of age (McCall *et al.*, 1972), and few people have questioned its validity in measuring mental capability at the time of administration. It lacks predictive validity, not contemporary validity.

Some clinicians have suggested therefore that infant tests are worthless. But contemporary without predictive validity is not a totally damning indictment. For example, birth weight does not predict adult weight, but it is a valid index of general health state at the moment. Apparently, the determinants of weight before birth are different from the determinants of weight after birth.

Perhaps this is also true of early versus later mental ability. Perhaps our intelligence does not simply get bigger, while remaining essentially the same commodity across the years. Rather, it is more like building a brick wall with rows of different kinds of bricks. Each row is qualitatively different from the previous row, but each nevertheless depends on previous rows to hold it up. And each row is built by a different workman so that the rate of construction may vary from row to row. Therefore, the infant who is first to reach a stage may not be first to leave it. The determinants of one stage may not be the same as those of the next stage.

Clinic Samples

Generally, the predictions of later IQ for clinic samples are considerably better than for normal samples, although the actual correlations depend greatly on the nature of the abnormal cases in the sample (McCall *et al.,* 1972). For example, some reports from large samples indicate that only 1 of 20 infants who scored in the top 5 per cent on an infant test at eight months still scored in the top 5 per cent on an IQ test at age seven. That is exactly chance, which means that a child's likelihood of being in the top 5 per cent at seven years is about as great if he scored low, average or superior at eight months of age. One of four infants who scored in the lowest 5 per cent at eight months, however, were still in the lowest 5 per cent at seven years. On the one hand, this says that predicting mental subnormality is five times more accurate than predicting mental superiority. On the other hand, it says that predicting later mental subnormality, while better than predicting superiority, nevertheless is not very good, because you will be wrong three times as often as you will be correct (given these procedures and samples).

On the hopeful side, a low score on an infant test *or* a prognosis of risk made by a pediatrician at 20 months of age can predict low levels of mental test performance well into childhood (Werner, Honzik and Smith, 1968). This means that the infant tests have the potential to detect future abnormality even among infants appearing normal to pediatricians. The tests may have some latent power that should be exploited in this regard.

The Use of Infant Tests in Screening for Mental Retardation

The fact that the tests may predict mental subnormality has encouraged their use as a screening device. Indeed, literally millions of children have been seen as part of the Early and Periodic Screening, Detection and Treatment program now called the Child Health Assessment Program (CHAP). The purpose of this program is to screen children beginning in infancy for possible medical, mental and personality dysfunctions and to provide treatment where indicated. While the main thrust of this effort is medical, the detection and treatment of "developmental dysfunction"—read "potential mental subnormality"—is also a stated goal. The Denver Developmental Screening Test is one of several instruments being used in this program for assessing infants and toddlers.

Test Accuracy

Given what we know about infant tests, is this a good idea? The answer rests on how the test is used and interpreted. For example, the utility of the test depends on what abnormalities one wishes to detect. Obviously, we don't need a test to tell us that Down's syndrome infants and those with other obvious medical syndromes have a poor prognosis. Much of the apparent success of infant tests to detect abnormality in clinic samples may be due to "detecting the obvious." What we do need is a test that can detect, in a group of "normally appearing" babies, infants who will suffer later developmental delay and retardation.

We also need to know what other assessment techniques are being used in addition to the infant test to weed out truly normal individuals before the test is administered. The more normal individuals who can be eliminated, the more useful the infant test as a screening device.

Good research studies on these issues are lacking, so a definite status report on how infant tests perform as a screening device is not possible. We can, however, emphasize the importance of certain issues when using a test as a screening device. Table 1 shows the importance of the test's detection accuracy, the base rate of the abnormal characteristic in the screening population and the test's ultimate hit rate or utility. For the moment, we are only concerned with people which the test calls "abnormal." (Of course, the test may call "normal" those who are in fact not normal, but this seems less dangerous than labeling a child abnormal who is actually not.)

The detection accuracy is simply the percentage of abnormal individuals that the test correctly calls abnormal and the percentage of normal individuals it falsely calls abnormal. Obviously, these percentages will depend on the composition of the sample, the nature of the infant test and the cut-off scores used. Table 1 presents several possible levels of detection accuracy.

Base rate refers to the percentage of actually abnormal individuals in the screening sample. In the American population severe retardation is under 5 per cent (3.27 per cent have IQ's below 70; Dingman and Tarjan, 1960). Sample selection, other screening devices and examinations by pediatricians, however, may eliminate a great many normals so that the test is administered to a group primarily composed of "suspect" or "at-risk" infants. Since the actual base rate is unknown for most screening populations, Table 1 displays base rates for abnormality that range between 5 per cent and 80 per cent.

For each level of detection accuracy and base rate, Table 1 presents the number of individuals per 1,000 screened that the test would call abnormal— either correctly (the number of true abnormals so labeled) or falsely (the number of true normals incorrectly called abnormal). It also gives the test's *hit rate* in the screening population, that is, the percentage of those the test calls abnormal who are indeed so.

TABLE 1 Detection Accuracy, Base Rate, and Hit Rate in Screening Population

Detection Accuracy		Base Rate	Number Per 1000 Called Abnormal		Hit Rate
Percent Correct Abnormals	Percent Normals Falsely Called Abnormal	Percent Abnormals in Screening Population	Correctly	Falsely	Correct Calls in Screening Population
60%	20%	5%	30	190	13%
		20%	120	160	43%
		40%	240	120	67%
		60%	360	80	82%
		80%	480	40	92%
70%	15%	5%	35	142	20%
		20%	140	120	54%
		40%	280	90	76%
		60%	420	60	88%
		80%	560	30	95%
80%	10%	5%	40	95	30%
		20%	160	80	67%
		40%	320	60	84%
		60%	480	40	92%
		80%	640	20	97%
90%	5%	5%	45	95	33%
		20%	180	40	82%
		40%	360	30	92%
		60%	540	20	96%
		80%	720	10	99%

For example, consider the first row of Table 1. This hypothetical test correctly identifies 60 per cent of the abnormals and only falsely labels 20 per cent of the normals as deficient. If such a test were routinely applied to the unselected population of infants containing about 5 per cent abnormals, only 13 per cent of the infants called abnormal by the test would actually be abnormal. That is, *for every child correctly identified as abnormal, almost seven normal children would be falsely labeled.* It is not until 80 per cent of the children screened with the instrument are indeed abnormal that the test's hit rate would be over 90 per cent.

The true figures for the detection accuracy of The Denver Developmental Screening Test and for the base rate of the CHAP screening population are not known. I am aware of only one study that has made normal/abnormal classifications during the first two years of life and reassessed the same subjects years later to check on the accuracy of the predictions (van Doorninck *et al.*, 1976). Only 54 infants under two years of age were involved. Twenty per cent of the 10 infants called abnormal by the test had difficulty later in school, and only

13 per cent of the nonproblem youngsters were incorrectly diagnosed as abnormal when infants. But given these figures and a 5 per cent incidence of abnormality, almost four infants would be wrongly diagnosed for every correctly diagnosed problem child. The hit rate would not reach 90 per cent until two of every three infants screened were indeed abnormal. (Incidentally, the infant test identified only one-third of those who eventually developed school problems, but that is another issue.)

The crucial point here is not the particular figures for the Denver or any other test but that the ability of a test to detect abnormality is not the only consideration for a screening device. The false-positive rate—the percentage of normals that the test incorrectly calls abnormal—is more important than the percentage of correct detections if the base rate of abnormality in the screening population is lower than 50 per cent. Moreover, the base rate is also important, because the more true normals who can be eliminated, the higher will be the test's hit rate and the fewer errors will be made. This fact explains why screening devices are used in combination with other diagnostic techniques that help to eliminate normals and confirm suspected abnormals. But we have no solid information about the predictive accuracy of the Denver test (especially among "normal-appearing" infants), no solid information on the base rate of abnormality in the screening population and no solid information on the accuracy of the total set of screening and diagnostic procedures used in EPSDT/CHAP.

We should not be totally gloomy about using infant tests as part of a screening battery, but we must be cautious. On the positive side there is evidence that the tests can identify some infants as being at risk who would go undetected by pediatric exams. Therefore, a low score should encourage the physician to take a second look. If further examination identifies a treatable condition, the test has paid its way.

On the other hand, I am particularly concerned about those infants who score very poorly on the test but who have no obvious medical indication of a problem. These are the infants placed in the nonspecific, redundant category of "developmental delay." These are the "normally appearing" babies, the ones for which a good infant test—one that can detect future mental problems not obvious to a pediatrician—is sorely needed. But this is precisely the group that the test serves poorly. This group is essentially comparable to normal samples, and we know the test does not predict well for such individuals. For these cases the rate of false-positives will be especially high.

Not only is the likelihood great for this group to be inflicted with an incorrect diagnosis of potential mental subnormality, but such an error is perhaps more serious than being incorrect about predicting certain other medical conditions. For one thing, it is more serious if physicians make the diagnosis than if psychologists do so. Physicians enjoy much more credibility than any other group in society. Parents will believe this diagnosis, it may be accepted as inevitable, and it turns out to be a self-fulfilling prophecy.

It may have yet another effect. Many people still accept certain diseases as a matter of chance or God's will. The public has a fatalistic outlook about medical problems ("I try to stay healthy, but when your number's up, it's up"). They are not nearly so resigned about their intelligence, personality and social behavior. The past decade of emphasis on the environmental contribution to intelligence has made the public reject the idea of "destiny" when it comes to intelligence. Allergies, cerebral palsy and hyperactivity are no one's fault, but mental subnormality, if not the result of disease or identifiable medical disability, is somebody's fault.

Lawsuits have been prosecuted over similar labeling and treatment of poorly achieving students in public schools where the evidence of a correct diagnosis is much clearer. Labeling a child "at risk," "special," or whatever euphemism for mental inferiority or retardation we can come up with, is a serious decision, and to be wrong in that prognosis is at least humanly, if not legally, criminal.

Even if a test accurately identifies "developmental delay," it offers no diagnostic information. The test will not specify the problem or the treatment; and psychologists and educators do not have a ready arsenal of techniques that professionals or parents can implement at a reasonable cost with a reasonable chance of improving the prognosis of large numbers of children. Research on enrichment programs is encouraging, but for the most part they are still too costly for large-scale implementation with acceptable effectiveness and cost efficiency. A program like Head Start helps. It may even be a cost-effective approach to minimizing the need for special remedial educational programs. But it cannot make every child bright.

Effective therapies, when available, are likely to be complex and long-term. Mental development is not like a simple immune system: there is no vaccination at eight months that will prevent mental inferiority thereafter. We would not expect nutritional supplements given only during the first year to prevent malnutrition five years later. One-shot treatments do not work much magic for mental development either, especially when children are returned to homes and schools that fail to support intellectual achievement. Intelligence is a dynamic, changing set of abilities that requires similarly dynamic, changing and continuing nurture.

Although my presentation has been more negative than positive, I believe we must consider the issue of screening in its practical, political and social contexts. The government, with good intentions, has decided during the last few years that screening should be done, and legislation is pending that would expand the program. Our task is not to despair of success with respect to mental and personal/social behaviors. Rather, we must do the best job we can— accurately, cautiously, responsibly, sensitively and compassionately.

References

Dingman, H.F. and Tarjan, G. Mental retardation and the normal distribution curve. *Am. J. Ment. Deficiency*, 64:991–994 (1960).

McCall, R.B., Hogarty, P.S. and Hurlburt, N. Transitions in infant sensorimotor development and the prediction of childhood IQ. *Am. Psychol.*, 27:728–748 (1972).

Van Doorninck, W.J., Dick, N.P., Frankenburg, W.K., Liddell, T.N. and Lampe, J.M. Infant and preschool developmental screening and later school performance. Paper presented at The Society for Pediatric Research, St. Louis, April (1976).

Werner, E.E., Honzik, M.P. and Smith, R.S. Prediction of intelligence and achievement at 10 years from 20 months pediatric and psychologic examinations. *Child Devel.*, 39:1063–1075 (1968).

13

Attention as a Measure of Cognitive Integrity

MICHAEL LEWIS

Introduction

Within the last 10 years, there has been an increasing interest in the area of neo-natal distress and birth trauma. Because new and improved medical equipment and techniques are now available and in use, the survival rate of infants who have suffered some kind of perinatal insult has greatly increased. It has been clear for some time to clinicians that the continuing use of the traditional criteria of mortality/morbidity is no longer appropriate when used in conjunction with the sophisticated technology at their disposal. Standard neurological techniques are poor and identify only the most obvious pathology. More sensitive criteria must be found.

Within the same decade, interest in the neonate and young child concurrently stirred the psychological community. Behavioral research psychologists have been at work creating a technology that would enable them to test the very young and, through these means, answer crucial questions about the development of both intelligence and personality. Psychologists such as Fantz (1964), Lewis (1971), Kagan (1970), and Lipsitt (1963), have made significant contributions in the study of infant behavior and have shown that there are significant individual differences in attention and perception early in life. They have argued that these processes represent in the infant the basis of higher functions such as cognition and memory and have created a particular technology for measuring them. It is time that the advances made in assessing neonatal development by behavioral psychologists be applied to the field of neonatology and pediatrics.

The Attention Paradigm

One of the most prominent traits of the young infant is his ability to attend. Psychologists have observed that young infants are capable of sustained attention to a variety of stimuli. They have used this ability to observe and explore the infant's internal processes. A widely studied phenomenon in the field of infancy, it has been postulated that attention is an information-processing operation and therefore can be viewed as a core process crucial to subsequent intellectual growth. CNS involvement in attention is suggested by the fact that state differences in subjects affect attending behavior (Lewis *et al.*, 1967). A large body of the experimental literature both with animal and human subjects has demonstrated that abnormal cortical involvement produces wide variations in attending behavior (Thompson and Spencer, 1966).

Thompson and Spencer (1966), reviewing the literature on attention, cited numerous studies showing that attention distribution differs markedly as a function of cortical involvement in animals. The Russians have demonstrated similar findings using human subjects—brain-damaged children, prematures and hydrocephalics (Bronstein *et al.*, 1958). Brackbill (1971) found no decrease in attending in an anencephalic infant even after 200 trials. Thus, the attention technique can be seen to be sensitive to CNS dysfunction and can be used as a diagnostic tool in deviant populations. Moreover, the technique is particularly appropriate when testing deviant infant populations because of its non-motor nature. As opposed to most infant tests of cognition, the attention task minimally requires the infant to motorically perform in order to demonstrate his knowledge. This unique feature is particularly appropriate when testing premature or small-for-date infants who may be motorically deficient but cognitively intact.

Figure 1 illustrates the attention paradigm. Trials $1 - N$ repeatedly present the original stimulus, S_1, over time. The model predicts that response will be large during the first presentations but, with repetitions, will decrease. Trial $N + 1$ presents S_2 which is a novel stimulus, discrepant from S_1. The model predicts that not only will response increase in intensity on trial $N + 1$ but will increase as a function of the interest of the organism in the particular discrepant element (S_{2a}, S_{2b}, etc.). The attentional model provides us with two measures of cognitive integrity—response decrement $\dfrac{(\text{trial 1 minus trial } N)}{\text{Trial 1}}$ and response recovery (trial $N + 1$ minus trial N). Response decrement is defined as the decrease in attending or the habituation of the organism to the original stimulus as it is repeated. Response recovery is the increase in attending behavior when the dis-

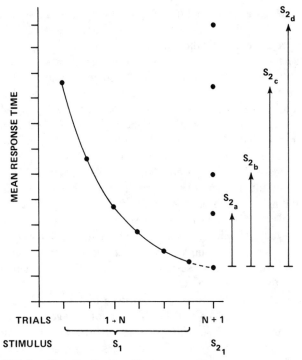

FIG. 1. The attention paradigm.

crepant stimulus is presented—indicating that the organism was not attending to the original stimulus, not because it was fatigued, but because of boredom.

Through the use of a repeated-stimulus presentation, attention can be measured within several modalities. Fantz (1964) was one of the first psychologists to study visual attention by measuring the amount of fixation on varying stimuli. Others have used auditory stimulation, using the sucking response of the infant as a measure of attention (Sameroff, 1968). Data using both modalities will be presented here as well as case histories.

Study 1

Method

Seventy-one sick infants who were enrolled in the high-risk follow-up project at Babies Hospital, Columbia-Presbyterian Medical Center, New York, were given the visual attention task. Infants were accepted into the follow-up if they met the criteria of having respiratory distress syndrome, birth asphyxia or a combination of the two, or if they necessitated total intravenous alimentation. Although these difficulties are not exclusively experienced by premature infants, our sample can be characterized as being overwhelmingly premature.

The data presented today represent a cross-sectional analysis of attention over a two year period. Three groups were studied—22 subjects between 3–6 months of age, 19 subjects between 9–12 months of age, and 30 subjects between 18–24 months of age. The data of a comparatively aged, normal group of infants using the same technique and stimuli will be presented in order to compare the risk infants to children without CNS insult. These subjects were seen at the Infant Laboratory, Educational Testing Service, Princeton, New Jersey. The risk infants consisted of two groups, RDS and BA infants. Respiratory Distress Syndrome, for the most part, is the result of premature birth—an event which leaves what may have been a normal *intrauterine* organism unequipped for extrauterine life. The RDS infant, therefore, is in a pathological state because of external factors and *not* because of any inherent deficiency. When placed in an environment which mimics his natural one—i.e., the isolette with respirator, CPAP, etc.—he is able to survive. Moreover, the physician is able to control his therapy to aid in the survival.

The asphyxiated infant, on the other hand, arrives in the world as a damaged organism, having experienced an insult—lack of oxygen and/or acidemia—at some point during labor and delivery. There is little the physician can do to mediate the effects of the trauma. For this reason, physicians have intuitively felt that the BA subjects would be more likely to show behavioral deficit.

To date, our infants have been followed for three years. Well-baby care such as immunization, prescriptions, examinations, etc., are administered to them in our private clinic. Although our sample is equally distributed across ethnic groups (one-third Caucasian, one-third Black, and one-third Hispanic), it is decidedly skewed toward the lower half of the SES scale (Hollingshead, 1957). Eighty per cent of our subjects were born into lower class families most of whom have more than one child at the time of our subject's birth and many of whom have only one parent, the mother. The behavioral follow-up consisted of visits to our laboratory in the hospital at three month intervals beginning at 3 months of age. The infant was tested at both his chronological (actual age calculated from date of birth) and corrected (chronological age adjusted for number of weeks premature) age points.

Procedure

Visual attention is measured by presenting three series of slides to the infant who is sitting in an infant seat or in a high chair. Each series consists of six redundant slides and a seventh discrepant slide. The stimuli consist of lines which vary in number, color and form, and a picture of a family—father, mother and little girl. The slides are automatically presented on a screen which is adjusted to the individual infant's eye level. The infant's mother sits beside him and is free to touch and/or comfort her child. An observer who is hidden from the child records the amount of visual fixation for each slide by pressing a device which is connected to an event recorder. The recorder pens mark the amount of looking in intervals of 1/2 second. Fixation behavior can then be examined by reading the pen and paper record produced by the event recorder. Each slide is presented for 30 seconds and each intertrial interval is 30 seconds. The total procedure takes 21 minutes.

Results

Two measures of attention will be discussed: (1) the mean amount of fixation and (2) response decrement.

Mean Data

The mean amount of fixation over all 6 trials is the first measure to be explored. No significant differences were found between the diagnostic categories. Both the RDS and BA *S*s looked a similar amount of time at the stimuli at each age. Comparison between age groups with RDS and BA collapsed into one group revealed that the youngest infants looked at the stimuli more than the older infants ($F = 4.61$, $p < .10$). This finding has been reported in studies of normative samples (Lewis and Scott, 1972), and is indicative of the fact that the youngest infants do not habituate to the repeated stimulus as quickly as do the older infants.

Response Decrement

Figure 2 shows the mean amount of fixation for each trial for the three age groups by diagnostic category. No significant differences in response decrement were evidenced between the RDS or BA *S*s. The differences in the nature of these clinical conditions did not produce significantly different attending behavior.

Figure 3 shows response decrement for the total sample of risk infants at each age. As can be seen, the 3-6-month-old *S*s evidenced no decrement as did the 9–12 month olds. The 18–24 month old infants do show response decrement. The oldest risk infants decreased their looking behavior as the original stimulus was repeated over the 6 trials. When the discrepant stimulus was presented, looking increased to a level approximately equal to trial one of the original stimulus.

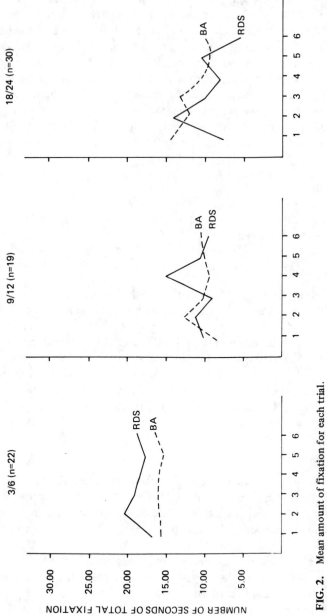

FIG. 2.   Mean amount of fixation for each trial.

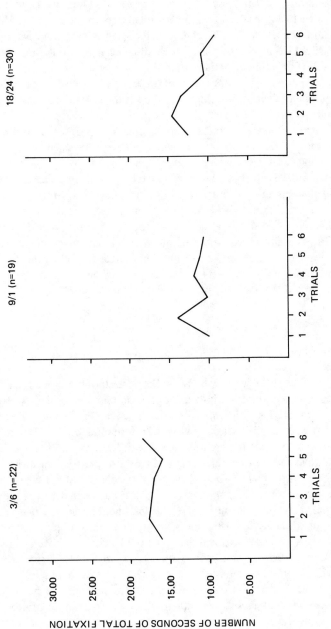

FIG. 3. Response decrement for the total sample at each age.

The attention data for these risk infants reveal several interesting findings. First, although we had hypothesized more severe deficit appearing in the asphyxiated *S*s, no differences in their attending behavior was evidenced when compared to the RDS *S*s. Second, the risk *S*s' attending behavior was age-related—the oldest infants showing more decrement than the younger infants.

Let us now turn to a comparison between risk and normal *S*s. Figure 4 shows the amount of decrement evidenced by both the risk subjects and a group of normal subjects at three age points. The measure of response decrement is the difference in fixation between the 1st and 6th trial as a proportion of the total looking time on trial 1. A positive value indicates response decrement while a negative value indicates response increment over the 6 trials of the redundant stimulus. The normal subjects show an age-related pattern—response decrement monotonically increasing as a function of age. The risk *S*s, on the other hand, evidence no decrement until the 18-24 month period. In fact, there is a slight response increase to the redundant stimulus for the infants younger than 18 months. A test of significance between the risk and normal groups indicated that both show little decrement at 3-6 months of age. By 9-12 months, however, the normal *S*s do show response decrement while the risk *S*s do not. Interestingly, by 18-24 months of age, both groups show similar patterns of attending.

A Case Study

Nancy is a follow-up baby who was 37 weeks of gestation and weighed 2760 grams at birth. She was admitted into the follow-up because of birth asphyxia. Nancy is the third and last child in a family of three daughters. Nancy's mother, Mrs. J., graduated from high school and was 34 years old when she gave birth to Nancy. Her older two daughters were healthy and suffered no perinatal difficulties. Mrs. J. had received prenatal care and was always attentive to her doctor's suggestions. Although suffering herself from sarcoidosis, Mrs. J. was reliable and consistent in keeping her appointments. She always came to the hospital herself, however, and always brought all three girls—who during the first year of testing were approximately 3½, 18 months, and the newborn subject.

Nancy was a pleasant, relaxed baby who did not exhibit any obvious motor disabilities during her first year. Several times within the first year, however, she failed to complete the attentional task and had to be re-scheduled for another visit. It was difficult to know what the problem was for her in completing the task—whether it was aversion to the light from the projector, persistent wariness in the laboratory situation, or a real inability to focus on the stimuli. These difficulties are either non-existent or easily overcome in time in a normal population and just the fact that she consistently could not complete the task alerted us to possible deviancy. Our suspicions are confirmed when we

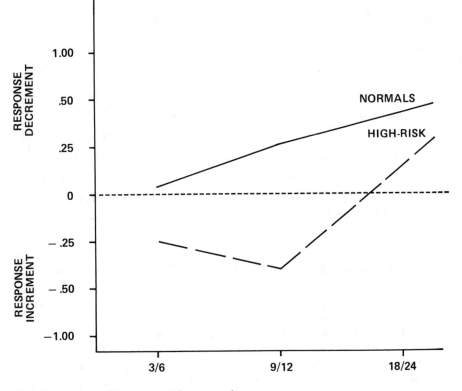

FIG. 4. Amount of decrement at three age points.

compare Nancy's fixation data to that of a normal infant of the same age. Striking differences can be observed.

Figure 5 presents the percentage of response decrement (trial 1–trial 6/ trial 1) for a normal, full-term infant and our asphyxia premature infant. The ordinate of the graph represents the percentage of response decrement and the abscissa, age in months. A "0" value represents no change in attending from trial 1 to trial 6. A positive value represents a decrease of response from trial 1 to trial 6 and a negative value an increase in response over trials. The asphyxiated infant's graph charts both chronological age (solid bars) and corrected age data (striped bars).

It can be seen that the normal-term infant decreases his attention to a repeated stimulus very little at 3 months. However, following a linear trend, response decrement gradually increases with age until, by 12 months, the infant shows marked response decrement. This pattern has been observed to be the norm when testing full-term well infants—increasing response decrement as

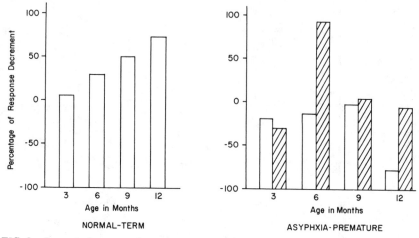

FIG. 5. Percent of response decrement.

a function of age (Lewis, 1975). That this is not the case for the asphyxia-premature infant is more than apparent. First, it is striking to note that, out of eight completed testing sessions (four for chronological and four for corrected age), response decrement was strongly exhibited only once—at 6 months corrected age, when she exhibited a large decrement in attending. (This performance is so deviant, however, from her other attending behavior as well as from a normally expected behavior that we have attributed it to chance.) All other tests, including every one given at her chronological age, indicate an increase in attending rather than a decrease. The general lack of response decrement leads us to conclude that Nancy is having difficulty processing information presented to her.

Figure 6 presents percentage of response recovery (trial 7 minus trial 6) for the same normal-term and asphyxia-premature infant. The ordinate of the graph represents percentage of response recovery and the abscissa, age in months. Both chronological age (solid) and corrected age data (striped bars) are reported for the asphyxia-term infant.

A negative value on response recovery means there was less looking on the presentation of the discrepant stimulus than on the last presentation of the original stimulus. The normal infant shows increasing response recovery with age, from 3 to 12 months. It is to be expected that little recovery would be demonstrated at 3 months; however, as age and experience in the world increase, response recovery increases as well. Once again, the differences between the two infants are striking. For the asphyxia-premature infant, response recovery actually decreases with age—peaking at 3 months and falling to its lowest point

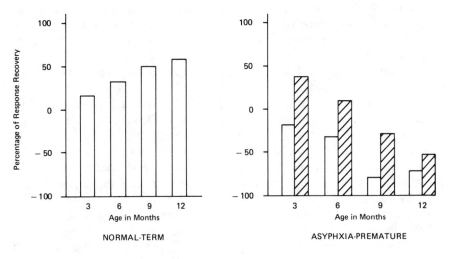

FIG. 6. Percent of response recovery.

at 12 months. This indicates that she looks *less* when a discrepant stimulus is presented rather than looking more. Discrepant information seems to become aversive for her as she gets older instead of more intriguing. She clearly recognizes that trial 7 is different from trials 1–6, since she has increased her looking through trial 6 and should increase her looking through trial 7. The fact that looking drops for trial 7 shows that she recognizes a change but isn't interested in it.

Taken into consideration along with the response decrement data, the pattern occurring here seems to be one where the information processing system is either malfunctioning and not storing and coding information at all, or functioning so slowly that much more time is needed to deal with the information presented on trial 1 through 6. The presentation of new information on trial 7 is useless or premature since the original stimulus has not been assimilated and processed and therefore cannot provide adequate contrast to the discrepant stimulus. It is interesting to note, however, that response recovery is negatively, monotonic age function which would indicate that new information presented in trial 7 becomes less and less desirable to the subject with growing maturity rather than, as we would expect of maturing organisms, more and more interesting (Lewis and Scott, 1972). The meaning of this is unclear to us at this time. We do know that pre- and perinatal insults do not always totally express themselves at the time of insult but may grow gradually in effect along with the organism. Perhaps Nancy's response to novel stimuli is an example of this process. However, since we do not know the effects of birth asphyxia on a child's cognitive capacity, we are limited at this time to non-causal, descriptive statements.

Although we have presented both chronological and corrected data, we have not yet discussed the results and value of testing at both age points. The rationale behind corrected-for-gestational-age testing is that we can compensate for the infant's prematurity by administering the tasks at the time he had arrived at his proper maturational age rather than at his age based on date of birth. We predicted that the corrected-gestational-age testing would yield better predictive data than the chronological-age testing because we had adjusted for prematurity and would therefore get a more accurate fit between the organism and the age-assigned task norms which have been established for most standardized tests. Although it is difficult to assess the results from looking at only one subject, we have presented Nancy's fixation data broken down into periods of testing.

Figure 7 presents individual graphs which represent the four periods of testing in the first year—3, 6, 9, and 12 months of age. The ordinate of the graph represents number of seconds of looking while the abscissa represents trials 1, 6, and 7 of the stimulus presentation. Both the chronological and corrected-for-age data across trials are shown.

It is interesting to note that it is in the early months (through 6 months) that corrected testing is yielding significantly different results from the chronological testing whereas, in the later two testing periods, chronological and corrected patterns are almost identical. Further, it is significant that while the corrected and chronological patterns differ at 3 and 6 months, it is the corrected-for-gestational-age testing which yield normative fixation patterns which would be predicted from the attention paradigm. At ages 9 and 12 months, chronological and corrected testing produce very similar looking patterns to one another. Needless to say, our next step is to examine fixation patterns for Nancy in her second year at 18 and 24 months, to see if this negative, age-related relationship continues to express itself.

Overall, even a cursory comparison between a normal and high-risk infant has revealed significant differences in the pattern of response to visually presented stimuli in the first year of life. Neither response decrement nor response recovery have been strongly evidenced. Most significantly, it is crucial to note that neurological assessment of Nancy from ages 2 months to 12 months consistently placed her in a "normal" category, rather than in a possible "suspect" or "abnormal" category. Although displaying no gross pathology, Nancy apparently has suffered some type of CNS dysfunction. Whether this dysfunction will continue into her second year or not, serious consequences for later cog-

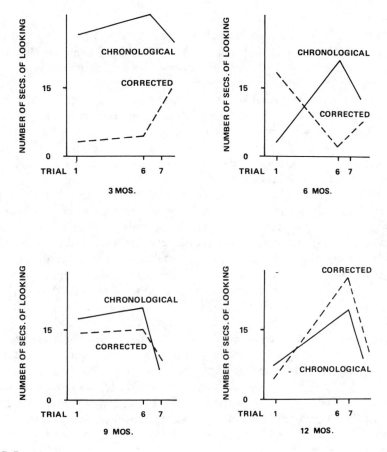

FIG. 7.

nitive and intellectual development may already have taken place. Hopefully, further analyses will help clarify the exact nature of this situation.

Study 2

The second study presented here was a project that investigated the attending response in neonates using the auditory, rather than the visual, mode of stimulus presentation. Attending was measured by recording the infants' sucking response.

Method

Forty-five infants were randomly selected from two nurseries of the Pediatric Clinic at Babies Hospital, Columbia-Presbyterian Medical Center in New York City. Although most of the infants showed records of some degree of birth problem resulting from toxic medication (phenobarbitol, demerol), maternal complications (dysfunctional labor), prematurity and resuscitation at birth, two types of infants were identified. Thirty subjects were considered to be at "high" risk because they were chosen from an intensive care unit of the clinic to which they were transferred immediately after delivery. The remaining 15 subjects were selected from a nursery without special treatment procedures and were classified to be at "low" risk.

Within the "high" risk group, infants received scores from 3 to 10 on the Apgar scale at 5 minutes. Apgar scores have appeared useful in discriminating homogeneous groups such as the "normal" on various behavioral and medical measures (Apgar and James, 1962; Drage and Berendes, 1966; Lewis *et al.*, 1967). Accordingly, the "high" risk group was dichotomized at the median of its Apgar scores to refine the assessment of their conditions at birth. Two equal subgroups ($N = 15$) were formed, one with Apgar scores of 9–10, the other with Apgar scores of 8 and below. Thus, three groups were tested as follows: Low Risk (LR), High Risk–High Apgar Scores (HRHA), and High Risk–Low Apgar Scores (HRLA). It was predicted that a hierarchical order would exist among the LR, HRHA, and HRLA groups with the LR group showing the most efficient response decrement and recovery behavior and the HRLA, the least.

Table 1 presents the sample characteristics of the infants and the results of the Kruskal-Wallis one-way analysis of variance (Siegel, 1956) that tested whether there were any group differences for those variables. There were no group differences in sucking frequencies either when there was no stimulus presented or when stimulation was applied. Age at testing represents the number of days from birth until the time of testing. This time was different for the three groups as tested by a Kruskal-Wallis Test (Siegel, 1956). Age at testing was different for the three groups, and a Mann-Whitney U Test was used to test pairwise differences. The LR group was younger than both the HRHA ($p < .10$) and the HRLA groups ($p < .01$). Moreover, the HRHA group was younger than the HRLA group ($p < .05$). This age of testing difference was due to the fact that these groups differed in the degree of severity of their birth condition. The HRLA and HRHA infants could not be tested until it was thought that they were no longer at risk in terms of mortality. In addition, there was a significant difference between the groups for their gestational ages. The LR group was significantly older than both the HRHA and HRLA groups ($p < .001$). However,

TABLE 1 Means of Age at Testing, Gestational Age Plus Age at Testing,
Sucking Frequencies During Stimulus Off and Stimulus On for Three Groups of Infants

Item	Low Risk	High Risk–High Apgar	High Risk–Low Apgar	H*	p
Sucking Frequency† Stimulus Off	117.4	97.4	96.5	2.58	N.S.
Sucking Frequency† Stimulus On	89.9	91.7	89.9	1.86	N.S.
Age at Testing (in days)	3.00	6.33	15.33	15.21	.001
Gestational Age (in days)	276.73	256.2	250.13	10.12	.01

*Test statistic for the Kruskal–Wallis one-way analysis of variance, two-tail (15)
†These mean data represent total sucking frequency across all eleven trials

there were no differences in gestational age between the HRHA and HRLA groups, indicating these groups were similar in the degree of prematurity. In short, while the groups are not totally comparable in terms of their ages, their overall sucking capacity was not different.

Procedure

Subjects were usually tested within the first week of life. With ill infants, testing was administered as soon as permission was granted by the clinic's physicians. Test sessions were conducted during the half hour before the regularly scheduled afternoon feeding time. At the start of each session, the experimenter (E) brought an infant into the testing room. The infant was awakened, placed at the midline of a reclining crib or isolette and was allowed a few minutes to adjust to the surroundings. A sterile nipple, attached to a polyethylene tube, was positioned in the infant's mouth. The E sat to the side of the subject and touched him only in cases of crying or obvious discomfort. The auditory stimuli were then presented by a tape recorder, placed about four inches in back of the infant's head. Each newborn was exposed to ten 15-second presentations of a human voice reciting a paragraph (65 decibels) followed by a single 15-second presentation of a musical score at the approximate decibel level as the former stimuli. Each stimulus period was followed by a 30-second rest period of no sound. At the conclusion of the session, the E returned the infant to the nursery and recorded data such as Apgar scores from his hospital record.

Measures of Attention

The infant's mouthing behavior during the testing session was continually recorded on a polygraph. A suck was defined as an alternating process of creating a vacuum in the oral cavity and the compression of the tongue against the nipple which generated a distinct wave on the polygraph record. Sucking rate was assessed by subtracting sucking frequency during stimulation from the frequency during the 15 seconds immediately preceding each stimulation. The difference score was regarded as the index of attention; positive scores indicated sucking suppression and attentiveness whereas negative scores indicated sucking activation and nonattentiveness. The rationale behind counting only sucks during the latter half of the rest period was based on the desire to (1) disregard sucking that resulted from stimulation and continued after stimulus offset, and (2) generate a baseline of an equal time interval with which to compare sucking during stimulation. Two raters independently scored sucking rate on a sample of subjects ($N = 8$). The interrater product-moment coefficients for total sucking frequency before and during stimulation were .966 and .955 respectively; the median coefficient for the individual trials was .982.

Results

Figure 8 shows the mean sucking rate for each of the three groups over the 11 trials. A "0" score indicates that there was no change in sucking frequency between the intertrial interval and the stimulus presentation; a positive value indicates sucking suppression while a negative value indicates sucking activation. In the figure, the solid lines indicate the observed points with trial 11 (S_2) shown as an isolated dot. The dotted line represents the points predicted by the regression equations for trials 1–10.

The data indicate marked differences in the infants' attentional behavior. The LR group showed both sucking suppression and response decrement of this response over trials. The HRHA group showed little sucking suppression and while there was response decrement over trials it was due in general to increases in sucking activation. Finally, the HRLA group showed some sucking suppression but no indication of response decrement over trials.

In order to determine the significance of these results, best-fit linear regression equations were computed over the first ten trials for each group; the slopes indicate both the rate and direction of responding. F-tests were calculated which tested the hypothesis of zero linear regression (Hays, 1963). Alpha level was set at .05, one-tail.

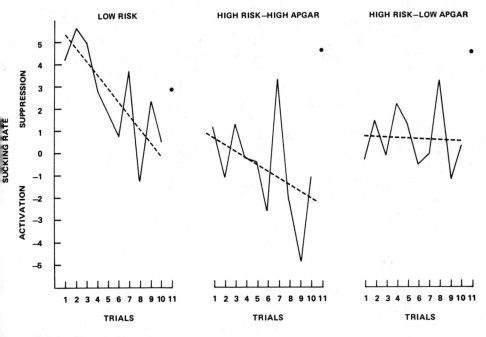

FIG. 8. Mean sucking rate.

Regression analysis revealed that a negative linear rule was significant for scores of the LR group, $Y' = -.625 (X - 5.5) + 2.54 (F = 10.40, p < .01)$; the rule for the HRHA group was in the predicted direction, $Y' = -.312 (X - 5.5) - .746 (F = 3.42, .05 > p < .10)$; and the slope of the HRLA group did not differ from .00, $Y' = -.025 (X - 5.5) + .546 (F < 1)$. Thus the regression analyses support the differential rates of response decrement as a function of "risk" groups.

It was predicted that response recovery on trial 11 should occur due to the stimulus change. In order to test whether response recovery occurred, the individual difference scores between trials 10 and 11 for each group were subjected to a Wilcoxon matched-pairs signed-ranks test (Siegel, 1956). The data indicate that both the LR ($p < .05$) and HRHA ($p < .01$) groups, but not the HRLA group, showed response recovery to the stimulus change. Thus, for both response decrement and recovery, the LR group showed the most effect of perceptual-cognitive behavior while the HRLA group showed the least.

Apgar and James (1962) have associated the following intervals of the Apgar scores with various conditions at birth: 0-3, poor; 4-6, fair; 7-10, good. Since our HRLA group contained infants with scores of 8 and below, we wanted to see whether infants within this group, who were differentiated on the basis of their Apgar scores, would differ in their response decrement and recovery scores. A secondary analysis was conducted with the HRLA group. Of these 15 subjects, 7 had Apgar scores of 8 whereas the remainder had scores of 6 or below. (None had scores of 7.) The data indicate that the two subgroups neither showed response decrement to the redundant stimulus according to the best-fit regression analysis—Apgar 8, $Y' = -.051 (X - 5.5) - .63 (F < 1, p = NS)$ and Apgar 6 and below, $Y' = -.046 (X - 5.5) + .546 (F < 1, p = NS)$—nor showed response recovery to the discrepant stimulus. These data suggest that at least for the perceptual-cognitive tasks, infants with Apgar scores of 8 or less should be considered at risk.

A Case Study

The sucking responses of two subjects from the neonatal sample are presented here for comparison. Subject 22 was a normal, well infant. Subject 63 was an infant who was born to a methadone-addicted mother and was therefore addicted himself. Figure 9 presents the pattern of sucking suppression over trials. Sucking suppression is represented on the top half of the ordinate while sucking activation, or an increase in sucking, is represented on the lower half of the ordinate. When normal and methadone-addicted subjects' patterns are compared, wide differences can be seen. The normal subject shows a general decrease in sucking suppression over repeated trials of the original stimulus with a clear increase in suppression, i.e., attending, upon presentation of the discrepant stimulus. The methadone-addicted infant, however, shows little suppression of sucking during the first few presentations, indicating little attention being paid to the original stimulus and very little recovery of response upon presentation of the discrepant stimulus. It is apparent that CNS disturbance has taken place which may very well be exclusive from the gross motor disturbances of withdrawal symptoms.

Discussion

We have presented evidence which indicates that infants can come to know or represent events perceptually, rather than strictly motorically. The infant has a

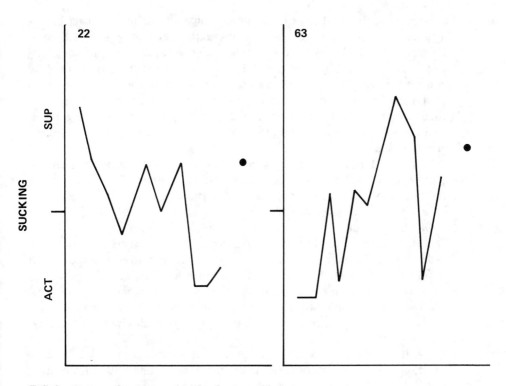

FIG. 9. Pattern of sucking suppression for two subjects.

sophisticated sensory system capable of very complex sensory acts, while at the same time being an immature output system in terms of its motor or response behavior. A meaningful conception of the infant's manner of representing the world must include more than motoric responses; that it is biologically advantageous for an organism, at birth, to be able to experience the world around it and form cognitive structures from that experience, without being required to engage in sophisticated actions in that world. Support for this view comes from the work on habituation that demonstrates perceptual learning even during the newborn period, when physical interaction with stimuli in the environment is minimal (Friedman, 1975). In addition, data on handicapped infants suggests that physical inability to act does not necessarily prevent the organism from forming cognitive structures and from developing normally (Decarie, 1969). Thus, at least for some cognitive structures, a sensory interaction may be all that is necessary. Granted, the development of certain schemata clearly requires a motoric component, and the interaction between sensory and motor systems in the child's cognitive and social development needs further consideration. It is our contention that motor activity has received too prominent a role in theory, especially in the sensori-motor stage of development. A consequence of this has been the strong tendency to focus on motoric behavior by those attempting to assess the intellectual ability of the newborn and young infant, as evidenced by the importance placed on motor functions in our standardized infant intelligence tests.

For all the work that has been and continues to be generated, attention is not easily definable. In a general sense, attention involves those processes by which organisms direct their sensory and cognitive systems. The direction of these systems is in the service of all subsequent action, thought, or affect. James (1890) has said that attention is the first and fundamental aspect of volition. That is, it is intentional and central to all cognition. Researchers have attempted to define attention more specifically through the indices used to measure it, such as (a) receptor orientation; (b) decreases in such activities as moving, talking, vocalizing, and sucking; (c) autonomic nervous system changes such as heart rate decreases, galvanic skin resistance change, vaso-dilation in the head, vaso-constriction in the extremities, and changes in breathing rate; and finally, (d) cortical changes.

Although there is a variety of parameters which may be used to assess attention, in order for these measurements to have meaning within the context of the developing organism, they need to be incorporated in a model of attention as it relates to cognitive processing. William James (1890) described two types of attending processes, "passive, immediate attention" by which the organism is drawn to attend to stimuli that are of interest in themselves, and "associational ("derived") voluntary attending" which is active attending to stimuli whose interest value is derived from their association with past experience.

A review of the research investigations bearing on these two types of attention reveals that a major distinction between them is the role of the infant's previous involvement with the stimuli. Whereas research on the first type of attention has to do with effects of such factors as stimulus complexity and intensity, research on the second involves effects of stimulus novelty and familiarity. One must take the developmental characteristics of the infant into consideration prior to defining scaling dimensions for constructs such as novelty or familiarity. Unlike intensity or complexity, novelty and amount of familiarity are completely dependent on the past experience of the organism. Hence, the features of the environment which elicit associational attending are designated by the organism rather than being inherent in the stimuli; their effect is determined by the interaction between one's current cognitive set and past experiences or learning.

Research on associational attention and related memory processes can be further divided into two categories. The first category deals with the study of attention as a reflection of the organism's mental structures, these including not only schema acquisition but also such basic processes as memory capacity. The second category focuses on attention as a measure of central nervous system functioning. This latter research rests on the assumption that attention and the memory processes upon which it depends are vital for the infant's intellectual development. Specifically, it is assumed that the rate of change in the organism's attention to an external stimulus is directly proportional to the rate at which an internal model of the stimulus is constructed. Based on this assumption, the reduction in attention which accompanies the repeated presentation of a stimulus, or habituation, can be viewed as a measure of cognitive functioning. Consequently, individual differences in the rate of habituation can be viewed as indicative of important differences in intellectual growth and capacity. Also, the degree of response recovery or novelty can be used as a measure of memory or cognitive functioning.

Distinctions involving other aspects of attention are also important. Fagan (1977), McCall (1971), and others have reviewed the research on visual information-processing during infancy. They note that researchers have made great advances beyond early attempts to identify the infant's perceptual abilities. They have proposed a conceptualization of information processing in terms of two stages of perception which underlie the distribution of visual attention in infancy: attention getting and attention holding.

It then follows that if response decrement is a measure of the speed of model acquisition, then the amount or rate of this decrement should be associated with a more efficient system of forming representations such that those infants who show more rapid response decrement are those who build internal representations faster. Consequently, the infant is conceptualized as an active organism capable of building up an internal representation of an event, and of using this internal representation or memory trace to influence ongoing processing. In agreement with these assumptions, most of the models of infant memory development are based on the notion that reduction in attention to a repeated stimulus reflects the formation of internal representations. In our study of attention, we have chosen to follow the model proposed first by Pavlov and then Sokolov in looking at dysfunction.

Clinical Applications of Individual Differences in Habituation

We maintain that a habituation task can be a valuable clinical assessment tool for use in detecting central nervous system (CNS) dysfunction in infancy. Two lines of evidence for this position are those just discussed, showing that rate of habituation changes with developmental status; and performance on a habituation task discriminates between individuals who differ on standardized measures of intellectual functioning (Lewis *et al.*, 1969). A third line of evidence is that derived from research on attention and habituation of attention as a function of variables assumed to be associated with mental impairment.

Several investigators (Bowes *et al.*, 1970; Brackbill, 1971; Brackbill *et al.*, 1974; Conway and Brackbill, 1969; Stechler, 1964) have found that habituation of attention in the newborn was directly related (negatively) to the amount and type of medication given to the infant's mother during labor. For example, Bowes *et al.* (1970) presented auditory stimuli and measured heart rate deceleration in infants 2 days, 5 days, and 1 month after birth. The highly medicated infants required 3 to 4 times as many trials to habituate as did the lightly or nonmedicated infants. Since the drugs themselves could not have been present in the infant's bloodstream at 1 month, yet effects of the drugs on responsivity to stimulation were still observed at this time, these results suggest that cortical structure may have been affected. These investigators concluded that the influence of the medication on the CNS of the infant was revealed in the differential attention behavior, even though no clinical signs of dysfunction had been observed at the time of birth.

Lewis *et al.* (1967) explored the relationship between an infant's Apgar score at birth (a standard index of neonatal condition) and subsequent performance on a habituation task. Infants were presented with a redundant visual stimulus at 3, 9, and 13 months of age. The infants were divided into a group with perfect Apgar scores and a group with less than perfect scores (all infants were within the normal range). The results showed that at 3 months the two groups differed significantly in amount of habituation, with greater response decrement shown by the perfect scoring group.

In a review of the literature on individual differences in information processing, Lewis *et al.* (1969) and Lewis (1971, 1975) stressed that a relationship between habituation and cortical functioning has been observed in research on animals (Thompson and Spencer, 1966). He also noted that infants' habituation rate has been related to incidence of birth injury (Bronstein *et al.*, 1958), and prematurity (Polikania and Probatova, 1958). Research on infants' preference for novelty also bears an infant's ability to encode and remember a repeatedly presented stimulus. And like the work on habituation, this research indicates marked differences as a function of factors associated with cognitive dysfunction. Sigman (1973) found that full-term infants preferred novelty more than did premature infants even when both groups were equated for conceptual age, or estimated age from conception. Werner and Siqueland (1978), also working with premature infants, found that visual exploration and responsiveness to novelty were positively correlated with maturational level, while they were negatively correlated with perinatal complications. Fagan, Fantz and Miranda (1971) looked at full-term and preterm infants' responses to paired familiar and novel stimuli and examined effects of both conceptual and postnatal age. Both full-term and preterm infants showed a developmental trend toward increased preference for novelty. The term infants' developmental curve was a full month more advanced than that of the preterm group, when postnatal age was the independent variable. However, there was little difference between groups when performance was plotted as a function of gestational or conceptual age, as both groups began showing a preference for novelty at about 51 weeks of conceptual age. In contrast, Sigman (1973) and Sigman and Parmalee (1974) found that even by 59 weeks full-term infants showed a greater preference for a novel stimulus than did premature infants. In fact, the premature infants failed to demonstrate a reliable preference for the novel stimulus.

In general, these investigations demonstrate a relationship between CNS function and either rate of habituation to repeatedly presented stimulation or preference for novelty. These data would allow us to conclude that the effect of stimulus familiarization may be an important indicator of CNS integrity, and that individual differences in habituation to environmental stimulation should have important implications for predicting subsequent intellectual development. Several recent studies in our laboratory have been designed to further explore the notion that factors associated with cognitive dysfunction in infancy are related to habituation rate and response recovery.

One area of study relevant to assessment of CNS dysfunction is the work with infants who have various types of intellectual handicaps. One such type of handicap is Down's syndrome, a condition that has recently received considerable study. Miranda (1970) investigated differential responsiveness to novelty in normal and Down's syndrome infants. He reported that at 8 months of age, both groups of infants demonstrated a reliable preference for a novel design after familiarization to abstract black and white patterns. In a similar investigation, Fagan (1971) tested Down's syndrome and normal infants at 22 weeks of age. Again, the results indicated that both groups showed a preference for a novel display, both immediately and after a delay of several minutes. These two subject populations, therefore, did not appear to differ in recognition memory, as assessed by their response to novelty. These researchers suggested that their findings do not necessarily indicate identical cognitive functioning in normal and Down's syndrome infants, but may have been due to a ceiling effect. It is possible that their stimuli were not sufficiently complex to differentiate between the two groups.

Miranda and Fantz (1974) conducted an investigation to test this possibility. They used younger infants, shorter familiarization exposures and memory problems that were more difficult, in that the novel stimulus in each recognition test was minimally discrepant from the familiarized stimulus. Three tasks which represented different levels of difficulty were used to assess the formation of a memory trace in normal and Down's syndrome infants. Infants were tested at 12, 24, and 36 weeks of age with a presentation exposure of only 30–60 seconds, followed by a two-choice test of recognition memory. For each age level three tasks were given: in one, the subjects were shown abstract patterns varying along a number of dimensions; in the second the stimuli varied in arrangement of the pattern elements only; and in the third the stimuli were face photos. The fixation data from each task revealed a marked superiority in recognition memory on the part of the normal infants over those with Down's syndrome. Consistent with earlier data, the results indicated that by 5 months of age, Down's syndrome infants preferred a novel design after this short term familiarization period, when the stimuli in the recognition test differed in several dimensions. This novelty preference was observed immediately and after a delay of several minutes. By 8 months of age, these infants were capable of discriminating face photographs, clearly demonstrating the ability to acquire, store, and retrieve visual information.

Of particular significance, however, is the fact that the abovementioned abilities appeared at a later age in Down's syndrome than in normal infants, indicating a developmental delay in the former group. The delay across all three tasks was about 2 months. The patterns which most clearly revealed a difference between the two groups were the ones that were equated in area of black and white, shape of elements, and number of elements—patterns whose recognition required analysis of the relations among elements in the configuration. Also, the Down's syndrome infants had considerably more difficulty than normal infants with the face stimuli. Miranda and Fantz (1974) suggest that this reflects the need for a longer period of neural maturation and/or long-term exposure to faces. They concluded that both age and type of stimulus difference are central factors underlying the difference in recognition memory between normal and abnormal groups of infants.

A study of developmental changes in habituation from 3 to 36 months in normal and Down's syndrome infants was conducted by Hawryluk and Lewis (1978). Using a fixed trial approach, in which six trials of a redundant visual stimulus were presented, followed by a seventh trial with a novel stimulus (each 20 seconds in duration with a 20 second intertrial interval) they obtained several interesting results. First, while normal infants showed an increase in amount of habituation as a function of age, Down's syndrome infants failed to show this pattern. Of particular theoretical importance is the observation that differences between these groups become apparent around 3 months. From studies using a variety of techniques, there is converging evidence for the belief that around 2 to 3 months there is a significant change in attentional and information processing ability in normal infants. Before this time, infants show relatively little habituation and little preference for novelty, whereas after this time, both habituation and novelty preference are in evidence. While this pattern has been found for the normal infants, it has not been observed for Down's syndrome children. For these children, it was not until 2 or 3 months later that they showed a comparable developmental change (Miranda and Fantz, 1974). That even Down's syndrome children advance to a higher level of cognitive functioning, albeit later than normals, argues that their problem lies not so much in lack of ability to show normal functioning as in their delay in developing this ability. Individual differences obtainable at so early an age ultimately may have value for predicting later social and intellectual achievement.

One other area of research bearing on attention and CNS dysfunction is that on the effects of malnutrition, a condition often assumed to be associated with cognitive impairment. Lester (1975) used a habituation paradigm in studying infants suffering from malnutrition, hypothesizing that the basis for the poor intellectual performance of these infants is their general lack of responsiveness to stimulation. Well-nourished and malnourished infants, 12 months of age, were presented with 20 trials of a 90-decibel pure tone. As predicted, the normal infants showed a marked orienting response followed by rapid habituation to the repeatedly presented tone; however, the malnourished infants showed no orienting response to the tone and no evidence of habituation throughout the 20 presentations. Lester interpreted these results as indicating a substantial attention deficit attributable to nutritional insult to CNS development. Similar findings have been obtained in a nutritional study conducted in Bogota, Colombia (Herrera, 1978).

Attention and Later Development

Lewis *et al.* (1969) explored this issue in a normal population of infants; they reported a .50 correlation between the amount of habituation before 12 months of age and Stanford Binet IQ scores at 44 months of age. In addition, the amount of habituation has been shown to be related to other mental operations at concurrent stages of development; e.g., concept formation and discrimination learning (Lewis, 1971, 1975). Gelber (1972) reported that the degree of habituation in 4-month-old females predicted their later performance on a two-choice discrimination problem. In general, the infants who showed the greatest habituation were the same infants who later demonstrated faster learning.

Lewis and Brooks (1981) attempted to extend these findings. They examined the relationship between (a) different measures of cognitive functioning at 3 months of age including a habituation task, and (b) intellectual ability at 24 months as measured by the Bayley Mental Development Index (MDI). Correlations between habituation and intelligence measures suggested that perceptual-cognitive ability at 3 months is related to later performance on intelligence tasks. Specifically, rate of habituation at 3 months was significantly related to 24-month MDI scores in part of the sample and degree of response recovery was related to 24-month MDI scores in the entire sample.

Summary

We have sought to present a new methodology for behavioral assessment. We have argued that, when used in a clinical population, the attention task is a sophisticated measure which can alert us to subclinical dysfunction previously left undetected by more traditional neurological procedures. It is time to update our criteria of success with traumatized infants from one of survival/mortality to a more refined scale that would take subtle CNS dysfunction into account. Ultimately, our goal is to be able to predict the expression of dysfunction in the hopes of creating and applying specific preventative intervention.

References

Apgar, V. and James, L.S. Further observations on the newborn scaling system. *Am. J. Dis. of Child.,* 104:419–428 (1962).

Bowes, W.A., Brackbill, Y., Conway, E. and Steinschneider, A. The effects of obstetrical medication on fetus and infant. *Monographs of the Society for Research in Child Development,* 35(4, Serial No. 137) (1970).

Brackbill, Y. The role of the cortex in orienting: Orienting reflex in an anencephalic human infant. *Devel. Psychol.,* 5:195–201 (1971).

Brackbill, Y., Kane, J., Manniello, R.L. and Abramson, D. Obstetric premedication and infant outcome. *Am. J. Obstet. and Gynecol.,* 118(3):377–384 (1974).

Bronstein, A.I., Itina, N.A., Kamenetskaia, A.G. and Sytova, V.A. The orienting reactions in newborn children, in Voronin, L.G., Leontiev, A.N., Luria, A.R., Sokolov, E.N. and Vinogradova, O.S. (eds.), *Orienting Reflex and Exploratory Behavior.* Moscow: Academy of Pedagogical Sciences of RFGSR (1958).

Conway, E. and Brackbill, Y. Effects of obstetrical medication on infant sensorimotor behavior. Paper presented at a meeting of the Society for Research in Child Development, Santa Monica, March (1969).

Decarie, T.G. A study of the mental and emotional development of the thalidomide child, in Foss, B.M. (ed.), *Determinants of Infant Behavior IV.* London: Methuen, pp. 167–188 (1969).

Drage, M.S. and Berendes, H. Apgar scores and outcome of the newborn. *Pediat. Clin. N. Amer.*, 13:635–643 (1966).

Fagan, J.F. Infants' recognition memory for a series of visual stimuli. *J. Exper. Child Psychol.*, 11:244–250 (1971).

Fagan, J.F. An attention model of infant recognition. *Child Devel.*, 48:345–359 (1977).

Fagan, J.F., Fantz, R.L. and Miranda, S.B. Infants' attention to novel stimuli as a function of postnatal and conceptional age. Paper presented at a meeting of the Society for Research in Child Development, Minneapolis, April (1971).

Fantz, R.L. Visual experience in infants: Decreased attention to familiar patterns relative to novel ones. *Science*, 146:668–670 (1964).

Friedman, S. Infant habituation: Process, problems and possibilities, in Ellis, N.R. (ed.), *Aberrant Development in Infancy*. Hillsdale, N.J.: Lawrence Erlbaum, pp. 217–237 (1975).

Gelber, E.R. Habituation, discrimination learning, and visual information processing in infants. Unpublished doctoral dissertation. University of Illinois (1972). (Cited in Cohen and Gelber, 1975.)

Haup, W.L. Statistics. New York: Holt, Rinehart and Winston, 1963.

Hawryluk, M.K. and Lewis, M. Attentional patterns in infants with Down's syndrome: A preliminary investigation. Paper presented at the Eastern Psychological Association meetings, Washington, D.C., March (1978).

Herrara, M.G. Personal communication (1978).

Hollingshead, A.B. Two-factor index of social position. New Haven, Conn.: Author (1957).

James, W. *The Principle of Psychology*. New York: Holt (1890).

Kagan, J. The determinants of attention in the infant. *Amer. Scient.*, 58:298–306 (1970).

Lester, B.M. Cardiac habituation of the orienting response to an auditory signal in infants of varying nutritional status. *Devel. Psychol.*, 11:432–442 (1975).

Lewis, M. Individual differences in the measurement of early cognitive growth, in Hellmuth, J. (ed.), *Exceptional Infant, Vol. 2. Studies in Abnormalities*. New York: Brunner/Mazel, pp. 172–210 (1971).

Lewis, M. The development of attention and perception in the infant and young child, in Cruickshank, W.M. and Hallahan, D.P. (eds.), *Perceptual and Learning Disabilities in Children* (Vol. 2). Syracuse University Press (1975).

Lewis, M. and Brooks, J. Visual attention at three months as a predictor of cognitive functioning at two years of age. *Intelligence* (1981).

Lewis, M., Bartels, B., Campbell, H. and Goldberg, S. Individual differences in attention: The relationship between infants' condition at birth and attention distribution within the first year. *Am. J. Dis. of Child.*, 113:461–465 (1967).

Lewis, M., Bartels, B. and Goldberg, S. State as a determinant of infants' heart rate response to stimulation. *Science*, 155(3761):486–488 (1967). Article reviewed in *Cardiology Digest*, September (1967).

Lewis, M., Goldberg, S. and Campbell, H. A developmental study of learning within the first three years of life: Response decrement to a redundant signal. *Monographs of the Society for Research in Child Development*, 34(Serial No. 133) (1969).

Lewis, M. and Scott, E. A developmental study of infant attentional distribution within the first two years of life. Paper presented at the Twentieth International Congress of Psychology, Symposium on Learning in Early Infancy, Tokyo, Japan, August (1972).

Lipsitt, L.P. Learning in the first year of life, in Lipsitt, L.P. and Spiker, C.C. (eds.), *Advances in Child Development and Behavior*, 1:147–195 (1963).

McCall, R.B. Attention in the infant: Avenue to the study of cognitive development, in Walcher, D. and Peters, D.L. (eds.), *Early Childhood: The Development of Self-Regulatory Mechanisms.* New York: Academic Press, pp. 107–140 (1971).

Miranda, S.B. Response to novel visual stimuli by Down's syndrome and normal infants. *Proceedings of the 78th Annual Convention of the American Psychological Association,* 5:275–276 (1970).

Miranda, S.B. and Fantz, R.L. Recognition memory in Down's syndrome and normal infants. *Child Devel.,* 45:651–660 (1974).

Polikania, R.I. and Probatova, I.E. On the problem of formation of the orienting reflex in prematurely born children, in Voronin, I.C., Leontiev, A.N., Luria, A.R., Sokolov, E.N. and Vinogradova, O.S. (eds.), *Orienting Reflex and Exploratory Behavior.* Moscow: Academy of Pedagogical Sciences of RSFSR (1958).

Sameroff, A.J. The components of sucking in the human newborn. *J. Exper. Child Psychol.,* 6:607–623 (1968).

Siegel, S. *Nonparametric Statistics for the Behavioral Sciences.* New York: McGraw-Hill (1956).

Sigman, M. Visual preferences of premature and full-term infants. Paper presented at meeting of the Society for Research in Child Development, Philadelphia, Pa., March (1973).

Sigman, M. and Parmalee, A.H. Visual preference of four-month-old premature and full-term infants. *Child Devel.,* 45:959–965 (1974).

Stechler, G. Newborn attention as affected by medication during labor. *Science,* 144:315–317 (1964).

Thompson, R.F. and Spencer, W.A. Habituation: A model phenomenon for the study of neuronal substrates of behavior. *Psychol. Rev.,* 173(1):16–43 (1966).

Werner, J.S. and Siqueland, E.R. Visual recognition memory in preterm infants. *Infant Behav. and Devel.,* 1:79–84 (1978).

14

Early Description and Prediction of Developmental Dysfunction in Preschool Children

MELVIN D. LEVINE
FRANK OBERKLAID

Low-severity handicaps, uneven patterns of development or discordant cognitive styles are being recognized as possible harbingers of disordered learning, difficulties with social interaction and affective disorders during the school years. A range of such subtle dysfunctions have been observed to impair the performance of school-age children. Their effects go beyond the classroom, pervading behavior at home and in the neighborhood, often extending into adolescence and adult life (Poremba, 1975).

Pediatricians throughout the United States report increasingly that school-age learning problems, difficulties with selective attention or activity regulation, and behavioral disorders occupy an expanding segment of their professional time (Haggerty *et al.*, 1975). In many cases these patterns of childhood failure represent the convergence of strong constitutional propensities that have transacted with suboptimal environmental factors, mismatched patterns of nurture and traumatic life events (Sameroff, 1975). Health care personnel have become more aware of the need to monitor and support the milieu in which young children are reared. Concurrently, there is also a growing awareness of the importance of identifying early those endogenous or constitutional characteristics of a child that may result in maladaptation and early humiliation during the school years.

Some of the likely constitutional antecedents of dysfunction one might watch for are summarized in Table 1.

Selective attention entails a child's propensity to choose from among multiple stimuli. Pediatricians commonly are asked to help youngsters with attention deficits and their parents. Weak concentration is likely to be embedded

TABLE 1 Some Elements of Function

1. Selective attention
2. Visual processing
3. Temporal–sequential organization
4. Language
5. Gross motor function
6. Fine motor function
7. Memory
8. Behavioral adaptation
9. Neuromaturational status

in a matrix of symptoms, including distractibility, impulsivity, insatiability, impersistence at tasks and difficulty regulating activity levels (Cantwell, 1975; Ross, 1976). Those affected may struggle to attend to tasks at school, to retain skills or information and to gain control over their own behavior. Some children with attention deficits are overactive, others hypoactive. Their common problem is difficulty selecting or reducing stimuli for focus. As one child noted: "My head is just like a television set, but it's got no channel selector. All the programs keep coming on my screen at the same time!"

Developmentally inclined pediatricians can survey information processing at two basic "inlets" in young children. These involve the "fielding" of *simultaneous* or *successive* stimuli by a child, perhaps best illustrated by considering the following examples: If you were to present your face to a child one feature at a time, it would be difficult for him to recognize you during a subsequent encounter. It is certainly preferable to offer an overall view of the face, a configuration that can be appreciated as a simultaneous pattern rather than a chain of events. On the other hand, a child given verbal directions in a classroom collects information in a succession of bits of data rather than as a message that can be delivered simultaneously as a verbal utterance or configuration. Optimally, a child needs to utilize information delivered in both ways.

Simultaneously interconnected stimuli commonly gain entry as visual-spatial data. The whole and the parts offer themselves in one field as one scrutinizes a painting in a museum, surveys a pastoral scene or attempts to recognize symbols such as letters or words. Children who have difficulty with such processing may experience considerable anguish in attempting to master skills such as reading, spelling or writing. They may become confused over directionality proportion or figure-ground interactions. Symbol reversals may occur, and they may have difficulty recognizing or retrieving the visual configurations of words for spelling.

Children who experience problems fielding successive stimuli may have deficits in temporal-sequential organization. Time is the *sine qua non* of sequences; in early life affected children may become confused about temporal prepositions such as "before" and "after." Later they may have difficulty assimilating the days of the week or the months of the year. They may lag in learning to tell time. They may become confused when presented with multi-step directions, appearing to have problems with short-term memory. They may be secondarily inattentive as they tune out because of the futility of trying to process and retain the daily barrage of sequentially packaged data. Difficulties may ensue with spelling, mathematical operations and eventually with organizing narrative in an appropriate order for oral or written communication (Rudel and Denckla, 1975; Bryden, 1972).

Language acquisition is another critical element of developmental health. Some children may have difficulties with receptive language, with accurate and efficient comprehension, with the storage and retrieval of verbal data or with the expression and utilization of words. Language disabilities may masquerade in the physician's office as "pure" behavioral problems (Oberklaid *et al.,* 1979). Subtle disorders of language may lead to chronic inattention in school, poor mastery of academic skills, social frustration, learning inhibition and precipitous reductions in self-esteem.

Effective motor function in the school-age child often contributes to self-esteem and social competence (Levine *et al.,* 1980a). Children with poor gross motor function may feel ineffective. Judging themselves harshly in comparison to their peers, they may become passive and withdrawn. Such nonathletes may have underlying weaknesses in one or more areas. There may be problems with "outer space," with the judgment of trajectories and other external visual-spatial phenomena upon which to program a motor response. Alternatively, there may be difficulties with proprioceptive-kinesthetic feedback, resulting in poor body position sense, inappropriate integration of muscle groups and general clumsiness. Some children have trouble with motor sequence, others with motor planning (manifesting a gross motor apraxia) and still others with memory for motor skills.

Fine motor function constitutes another complex developmental process. The capacity to coordinate eyes and fingers, to receive and respond to kinesthetic feedback from the digits and to perform manual tasks efficiently and with appropriate speed contribute to competence in this area. Increasing numbers of children are being seen clinically with writing disorders. Such problems tend to reach their apogee in late elementary and junior high school, when children harbor the greatest concerns about humiliation before peers. Many such youngsters deteriorate when more and faster work must be produced (often in fourth or fifth grade), necessitating good, comfortable pencil control, rapid grapho-motor output and the ability to stave off fatigue. We have described these youngsters as having "developmental high-output failure." They present clinically with a diminished working capacity, becoming increasingly nonproductive as the school year proceeds. In many cases they acquire learning inhibitions and undergo social alienation.

The multiple components of memory clearly play a central role in the learning process (Levine *et al.*, 1980a). Clinical disorders of memory in childhood have not been well defined. Nevertheless, there appear to be youngsters who have difficulty with the effective storage and retrieval of information and skills. Some appear not to retain because of weak attention. Still others cannot recognize or recall information because what is registered is not meaningful enough or sufficiently relevant. Some children appear to have modality-specific memory problems, that is to say, trouble retaining specifically visual-sequential or verbal data. In observing and evaluating a child's memory, therefore, one must always ask: memory for what?

A child's behavioral style and social competence may represent both precursors and end points of failure (Thomas and Chess, 1977). Dealing with stress, interacting meaningfully with peers and adults, understanding and nurturing relationships and using human resources effectively are likely to be critical elements of adjustment during the school years. Yet these parameters are hazardous to measure and poorly understood. No doubt they are affected by numerous variables deriving from a youngster's constitutional profile, environmental context and early experience.

Most clinicians are familiar with so-called soft signs. Minor neurological findings, including associated movements, choreiform twitches, dysdiodochokinetic phenomena, tendencies toward stimulus extinction and finger agnosia, have all been studied extensively and have been frequently associated with developmental dysfunctions and learning problems in older children (Peters *et al.*, 1975; Touwen and Prechtl, 1970). These indicators can sometimes suggest central nervous system immaturity or inefficiency, especially in older children. Their significance in preschool youngsters has not been studied extensively. Other elements of development in the school-age child might include higher order conceptual ability, intersensory integrative capacity, coping style, inferential skills and personality development. These are particularly difficult to measure clinically, especially in preschool children.

If it is true that these briefly described elements of development constitute some precursors of academic success or failure, then it is natural to account for them as early as possible in the life of a child. Critical questions arise: can we describe such functions prior to entry into kindergarten? How predictive are strengths and weaknesses in these areas? If specific deficits are uncovered, are they remediable? If a youngster demonstrates a relative weakness in one or two areas, is he likely to bypass these by utilizing other developmental strengths? Is there in fact any value to the early description of developmental profiles? A great deal of research and many years have and will be consumed in grappling with these questions.

Stimulated by federal legislation, professionals from several disciplines have devised a large number of preschool screening and readiness tests to assess facets of a child's development relevant to later school achievement (Dixon, 1974). Most of these tests have had problems with reliability and validity (North, 1974). The risks of screening in this area have been clearly stated (Solnit, 1976). The hazards of labelling (Hobbs, 1975), self-fulfilling phophecies (Rosenthal and Jacobson, 1968), and the unavailability and questionable efficacy of intervention have all been raised as issues. Unlike most traditional medical assessments that attempt to detect an already existing condition, preschool assessments yield hypotheses about school failure, a problem that has yet to develop (Oberklaid and Levine, 1980). Nevertheless, the growing demand for pediatricians to provide assessments of the preschool child—a request emanating from both parents and schools—does not allow clinicians to await perfection of the state of the art.

One early identification effort is the Brookline Early Education Project (BEEP) in which approximately 300 children from Boston and Brookline were enrolled in a public school system three months before birth. The project has consisted of periodic diagnostic assessments which have included evaluations of health, development, neurological status, sensory intactness and family function. A strong educational component has included home visits, center-based parent activities and an active preschool program (Levine et al., 1977).

Part of BEEP has been a continuing effort to develop appropriate tools for the pediatric contribution to early life assessment. One outgrowth of the Pediatric Examination of Educational Readiness (The PEER) is an attempt to integrate a standardized description of some measurable elements of development with a health and behavioral assessment (Levine et al., 1980b). Intended for youngsters between the ages of four and six the examination is meant to be integrated with a thorough preschool physical examination and a parent inventory of behavior, health and development. The PEER was designed to enable pediatricians to observe preschool children performing developmentally appropriate tasks. It was intended to generate a narrative description rather than a score or a diagnostic label while evoking a child's strengths as well as concerns regarding development. It was anticipated that the PEER would help physicians uncover specific service needs and routes for further evaluation. For example, a physician observing a poorly functioning child might recognize a possible language disorder and refer the youngster for a speech and language evaluation instead of or in addition to psychological testing. The PEER was also thought to have the potential for training pediatricians to observe children as they function.

The PEER is set up so that for any individual task several performance variables are observed to expose such dimensions as efficiency in carrying out tasks, the existence of neuromaturational indicators and the child's own adaptation to the test-taking situation. A sample item is illustrated in Table 2. At three points during the PEER attention and behavioral adaptation to the procedure

TABLE 2   Rhythm Tapping (Imitation)

Developmental Attainment:	1 = One or more correct	
	2 = None correct	☐
Neuromaturation:	1 = None, or slight associated head movements	
	2 = Marked associated movements of head	☐
Processing Efficiency:	1 = None, or occasional sequencing error	
	2 = Consistent sequencing errors	☐

are rated according to a standardized checklist, permitting the physician to detect youngsters who are "slow to warm up" or those whose selective attention is uneven or deteriorates with time. Component measures are summarized in Table 3. The PEER also includes a rating system for dressing and undressing, a naturalistic observation that can be made during the physical examination. The contents are summarized in Table 4. The neurodevelopmental section of the PEER requires 20-30 minutes to administer, depending on the observer's experience and the child's cooperation. In addition, 10-15 minutes generally is needed for the physical and sensory examinations.

To establish the reliability and validity of the PEER, a community field testing program was carried out during three successive summers from 1976 through 1978. The sample included 386 children, of whom 88 had been enrolled in BEEP. The remainder were nonBEEP children who also served as a comparison group for the overall evaluation of the project. Youngsters were all registered to enter kindergarten in September. Their mean age was 61 months, with a range of 53-70 months. Fifty-three per cent were males. Approximately 90 per cent had had some preschool or day care experience.

TABLE 3   Attention–Activity Parameters

Impulsivity–reflectivity
Fidgetiness
Distractibility
Perseveration
Attention–attractability
Attention–continuance
Attention–absences
Motor overactivity
Motor underactivity
Fatigability

Behavioral Adaptation Parameters

Adaptability
Responsiveness
Reinforceability
Cooperativeness

TABLE 4 Stand On Right Foot (Imitation)

Developmental Attainment:	1 = Ten seconds or more	
	2 = Less than ten seconds	☐
Neuromaturation:	1 = Falters once or less	
	2 = Falters more than once	☐
Processing Efficiency:	1 = Demonstration need not be repeated	
	2 = Demonstration had to be repeated	☐
Indicate all applicable	Asks for help ☐	Changes task ☐
	Completes partially ☐	Refuses ☐

Behavioral and health history questionnaires were completed by all of the parents (Levine, 1980a). Partly to establish some concurrent validity for the PEER, each child was given the McCarthy Scales of Children's Abilities, a standardized intelligence test. The PEER was performed by a staff pediatrician, nurse or ambulatory pediatrics fellow from The Children's Hospital Medical Center. Two physicians or a physician and a nurse were present, recording their observations simultaneously in order to establish inter-rater reliability.

There were 10 categories of developmental concern that might be elicited by the PEER. For each of these, criteria were developed to determine if there were "no concerns," "possible concerns" or "definite concerns." Through task analyses certain items were selected as major criteria in an area. To qualify as having a "definite concern" in an area, a child had to fail two or more of the major items. "Possible concerns" was indicated when a child failed three or more minor items in the absence of any major failure (Table 5).

Table 6 shows the prevalence of specific concerns in the 10 areas. These cover the elements shown earlier with the exception of neuromaturation which is considered separately. Two other measures, spatial-body awareness and basic information, have been added and have multiple developmental underpinnings. It can be seen that the highest occurrences of "definite concerns" were in the areas of sequential organization, attention-activity, language and behavioral adaptation with short-term memory and visual processing close behind. Diffi-

TABLE 5 Peer Contents Summary

Physical Examination
Dressing/Undressing Inventory*
Neurodevelopmental Assessment
    Spatial–body awareness
    Gross motor
    Fine motor*
    Visual processing
    Auditory–Language
    Experiential–information*

*Attention–behavior rating point

TABLE 6 Prevalence of Specific Concerns (N = 386)

Area	% Definite	% Possible
Sequential organization	13	8
Language	13	2
Attention/activity	13	–
Short term memory	12	6
Visual processing	11	20
Behavioral adaptation	11	–
Spatial body awareness	7	6
Basic information	7	0
Gross motor function	4	14
Fine motor function	4	32

culties with spatial-body awareness, gross motor function, fine motor function and basic information were less common.

Did "definite concerns" cluster within the same children? As the distribution on Fig. 1 shows, 56 per cent of children had no "definite concerns," while 14 per cent had three or more "definite concerns." The 51 youngsters with three or more "definite concerns" included 61 per cent males and 39 per cent females, a significant difference in distribution from the group with no developmental concerns.

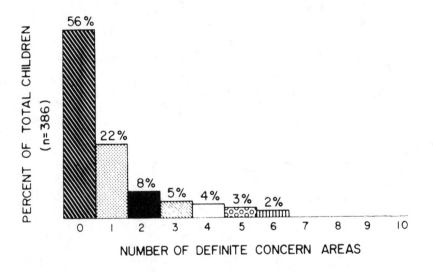

FIG. 1. Histogram showing the distribution of major concerns of the PEER.

An effort was made to determine whether any findings were particularly common in the group with three or more "definite concerns" (Table 7). Problems with sequential organization, short-term memory, language and selective attention most commonly clustered in this group (see Table 7). Less prevalent were difficulties with behavioral adaptation and motor function.

TABLE 7   Children With 3 or More Concerns–
Distribution of Individual Concerns (N = 51)

Area	% With Definite Concern
Short term memory	67
Sequential organization	65
Language	55
Attention/activity	53
Basic information	43
Spatial body awareness	41
Behavioral adaptation	29
Visual processing	26
Fine motor function	22
Gross motor function	14

A subgroup of 187 youngsters was studied further to examine the predictive validity of the PEER. The Kindergarten Performance Profile (Walker *et al.,* 1978) was used as an outcome instrument. This criterion-referenced teacher rating scale assesses five areas (see Table 8). Teachers were asked to rate the children in the fall and again in the spring. They were unaware of performances on the PEER. It can be seen in Table 9 and Figure 1 that with regard to mastery skills, having three or more "definite concerns" on the PEER was highly correlated with relatively low teacher ratings in comparison with those youngsters who had "no concerns." Interestingly, minor differences in the groups with "possible concerns" and those with one to two "definite concerns" tended to wash out during the year. This suggested that youngsters with one or two areas of concern might in fact have bypassed these, utilizing appropriate compensatory strengths.

A similar trend for the group with three or more definite concerns was seen in social skills (see Table 10). This suggests a not very surprising association between developmental attainment and kindergarten social adjustment. Predictive validity also was observed in the academic skill area (see Table 11). Having no concerns on the PEER was closely associated with the capacity to acquire basic skills easily in kindergarten. Similarly, there were high correlations between PEER results and gross and fine motor skills as rated by kindergarten teachers.

TABLE 8 Kindergarten Performance Profile

1. Mastery	Task persistence; Use of time
	Class routine; Follows directions
2. Social	Leadership; Peer interaction
	Classroom participation; Communication skills
3. Academic	Reading level
	Use of numbers
4. Gross Motor	Catching a ball
	Skipping
5. Fine Motor	Use of pencil
	Use of scissors

TABLE 9 Peer Concerns vs KPP Mastery Skills

	KPP Mastery	
Concern Groups	Fall	Spring
None	14.1	15.2
Possible, no definite	12.3*	14.4
1–2 definite	11.6**	13.9
3 or more definite	8.6**	10.3**

*p ≤ .01 Significantly below no concern group
**p ≤ .001

TABLE 10 Peer Concerns vs KPP Social Skills

	KPP Social	
Concern Groups	Fall	Spring
None	13.7	14.8
Possible, no definite	11.9	13.3
1–2 definite	11.9	13.5
3 or more definite	8.6*	11.0*

*p ≤ .001 Significantly below no concern group

TABLE 11 Peer Concerns vs KPP Academic Skills

	KPP Academic	
Concern Groups	Fall	Spring
None	7.5	9.7
Possible, no definite	7.0	9.0
1–2 definite	6.7	8.9
3 or more definite	4.4*	6.9*

*p ≤ .001 Significantly below no concern group

As part of this study of the PEER, neuromaturational indicators in this age group were analyzed. It is generally accepted that many such soft signs are common and probably normal in preschool children, becoming increasingly less prevalent in older elementary school populations. If this were so, one would anticipate that such findings as associated movements, dysdiodochokinesis, choreiform movements, delays in assimilating laterality and poorly established hand preference would not be correlated closely with developmental signs of dysfunction; nor would such signs predict performance problems in kindergarten.

Table 12 lists neuromaturational indicators and their prevalence within the PEER sample. Several of these, such as the associated movements, were elicited on multiple items; a composite rating was derived as part of the analysis. No signs were universal or even nearly so in this age group. On the other hand, only 38 per cent had *none* of these indicators. One may then ask in what ways, if any, do the presence or absence of these signs distinguish between groups of pre-school children?

TABLE 12   Prevalence of Neuromaturational
Indicators

Associated movements	10%
Dysdiodochokinesis	32%
Choreiform movements	8%
Delayed laterality	14%
Poorly established hand preference	20%
No neuromaturational indicators	38%

The PEER analysis clearly indicated some tendency for neuromaturational signs to diminish in the older segment of the age group studied. For example, there were one or more neuromaturational indicators present in nearly 70 per cent of children who were between 53–57 months old; this declined to 53 per cent between 64–70 months. No significant sex differences were noted between children with a heavy loading of these indicators and those without.

Were children with specific neuromaturational indicators more likely to have problems in discrete areas of developmental attainment on the PEER? It is evident from Table 13 that 36 children had a significant array of associated movements. Of these, 30.6 per cent had three or more definite developmental concerns compared to only 12.3 per cent of children with no associated movements. Similarly, of the 122 children with dysdiodochokinesis, 19.7 per cent had three or more definite developmental concerns compared to only 10.8 per cent of children without dysdiodochokinesis.

Similar significant associations are shown for other neuromaturational categories with the exception of poorly established hand preference. Thus, there was evidence that if a child has a high loading of neuromaturational signs he is

TABLE 13 Neuromaturational Indicators vs Developmental Concerns
(N = 386)

NM Category		Percent With Definite Developmental Concern
Associated movements	–Absent (N = 349)	12.3
	–Present (N = 36)	30.6
Dysdiodochokinesis	–Absent (N = 260)	10.8
	–Present (N = 122)	19.7
Choreiform movements	–Absent (N = 347)	12.7
	–Present (N = 30)	26.7
Delayed laterality	–Absent (N = 325)	10.2
	–Present (N = 54)	35.2

significantly more likely to have a cluster of definite developmental concerns. There remain groups of youngsters with developmental concerns but no significant neuromaturational findings and another with neuromaturational flags unaccompanied by observable developmental problems.

An attempt was made to discern additive effects of developmental concerns and neuromaturational findings to determine if children with both significant neuromaturational indicators and three or more developmental concerns were more disabled than those who had the developmental concerns without neuromaturational finding. Table 14 shows a comparison of McCarthy Test Scores. The results were unanticipated. Those children who had three or more "definite concerns" and many neuromaturational signs were significantly *higher* on the cognitive and memory subtests of the McCarthy than those who had three or more developmental concerns *without* significant neuromaturational findings. The group with multiple developmental concerns and neuromaturational indicators scored lowest in the McCarthy Scales Assessment of Motor Abilities. It was striking that within the group with multiple developmental concerns and neuromaturational signs there were higher overall cognitive, verbal and memory scores, suggesting possibly that such findings in the group with multiple developmental concerns may actually be a *positive* sign. One might hypothesize that the neuromaturational indicators suggest a different patho-

TABLE 14 Combined Developmental Concerns–Neuromaturational Indicators
vs McCarthy Scores

	General Cognitive	Verbal	Memory	Motor
Dev. Concerns With NM Flag (N = 8)	96.8	48.2	47.8	41.2
Dev. Concerns No NM Flag (N = 15)	90.0	43.0	40.8	44.2
Low Dev. Concerns With NM Flag (N = 24)	110.9	58.0	55.0	47.3
Low Dev. Concerns No NM Flag (N = 141)	111.4	56.2	53.7	50.7

genetic mechanism for dysfunction, one that may in fact have a better prognosis and less impact on overall intelligence. Further studies of larger samples will be necessary to establish this.

Of interest was the fact that the group with three or more developmental concerns *with* neuromaturational flags obtained somewhat higher spring kindergarten academic ratings than the group with the same degree of developmental concerns without neuromaturational findings. However, the numbers were too small to achieve statistical significance on a T-test. Once again, further studies on large and deviant samples may continue to demonstrate that the group with multiple neurological indicators includes many children whose developmental concerns arise from neuromaturational lags or other less stable phenomena rather than from fixed disabilities or handicaps. This is a tempting hypothesis but one which we have not confirmed because of the relatively small numbers in this study. At any rate, it suggests that the further investigation of these signs in this age group may be worthwhile.

Considerable disagreement exists with regard to the extent to which pediatricians should offer their own direct observations of function. Some might argue that health professionals should focus exclusively on traditional medical findings and on compiling a history and interpreting tests performed by other professions. Others would maintain that physicians cannot partake of the care of children by remote control, that functional stethoscopes in the form of direct assessments are as relevant as those applied in cardiac auscultation! Most would agree that physicians should not rely exclusively on any *one set of observations*. Their own culled data need to be blended with observations by parents, teachers and other professionals. The Pediatric Examination of Educational Readiness represents one attempt to allow pediatricians an opportunity to observe children performing developmentally appropriate tasks. It sets the stage for a range of empirical findings, covering such diverse issues as developmental attainment, selective attention, coping ability, reinforceability, reaction to stress and even alliance formation with the examiner. Such material must be combined with an evaluation of health and with a careful assessment of psychosocial, environmental and temperamental issues to assemble a more complete picture of a child.

The potential prescriptive value of this kind of assessment is clear. It is likely to play a part in the medical evaluation of children qualifying for services under Public Law 94-142. The PEER has been utilized within The Children's Hospital Medical Center as a pediatric component of an interdisciplinary evaluation for preschool children with behavioral and learning problems (Oberklaid *et al.*, 1979). It may have a role in similar consultative settings.

Our studies of the PEER suggest strongly that a child with multiple developmental concerns is more susceptible to a slower start in school than one with an isolated deficit. This is consistent with a multivariate model of development and with the recognition that children are able to bypass deficits if appropriate compensatory strengths are available and utilized. This view justifies a broad empirical scanning of functional elements, one that subsumes the direct assessment of multiple behavioral and cognitive areas with an eye toward describing both strengths and weaknesses. Moreover, it would suggest that oversimplified, narrow, rapid screening tests may be misleading and susceptible to both false-negative findings and overidentification.

It was of interest in the data analysis from the PEER that a high predictive weight of dysfunctions involved sequential organization, attention, short-term memory and language. The first three frequently are excluded from routine pediatric screening tests of preschool development. Although they actually may be intrinsic to certain tasks, they may not be rated as influential readiness components. The results from the PEER field testing program would suggest that these elements are likely to affect initial school adjustment. Motor and visual-motor aspects of the PEER were not nearly as predictive as these areas. Yet, traditionally, visual perceptual and motor assessments have comprised the largest portion of developmental screening tests. There has been little or no systematic attempt to evaluate temporal-sequential organization, selective attention and short-term memory. Preschool language assessments have in fact been receiving increasing emphasis.

At this point we cannot justify recommending universal application of the PEER. Further analyses and studies are ongoing. In view of the predictive value of this type of assessment, physicians need to be aware of a broader range of developmental issues than has been traditionally pursued. The PEER is intended not as an instrument but as an evolving system of observations that can be modified to reflect current knowledge and contemporary service options. It is hoped that some such system will be sought by child health providers who will seek to monitor its development and supervise revisions.

Further studies of the PEER will examine its predictive validity in more detail. In addition, there will be efforts to study associations between the PEER and parent reports of function. Children who have received the PEER are being evaluated at the end of the second grade. Such studies, it is hoped, will continue to elucidate the antecedents of early failure. If our observations acquire increasing predictive and prescriptive value, the pediatric contribution to developmental health maintenance may in time minimize the labelling of children and the misunderstanding, misattribution and mismanagement of the symptoms of developmental dysfunction.

Acknowledgments

This work was supported by The Robert Wood Johnson Foundation, Princeton, New Jersey and The Carnegie Corporation of New York.

References

Bryden, M. Auditory-visual sequential-spatial matching in relation to reading ability. *Child Dev.*, 43:824 (1972).

Cantwell, D.P. *The Hyperactive Child.* New York: Spectrum Publications (1975).

Cantwell, D.P. and Baker, L. Psychiatric disorder in children with speech and language retardation. *Arch. Gen. Psychiat.*, 34:583 (1977).

Dixon, M.S. EPSDT (Early and Periodic Screening, Diagnosis and Treatment Programs). *Pediatrics*, 54:84 (1974).

The Education for All Handicapped Children Act of 1975, Public Law 94-142, November 29 (1975).

Haggerty, R.J., Pless, I.B. and Roughman, K.J. *Child Health and the Community.* New York: John Wiley and Sons, p. 94 (1975).

Hobbs, N. *The Futures of Children.* San Francisco: Jossey-Bass (1975).

Levine, M.D., Brooks, R. and Shonkoff, J.P. *A Pediatric Approach to Learning Disorders.* New York: John Wiley and Sons (1980a).

Levine, M.D., Oberklaid, F., Ferb, T.E., Hanson, M.A., Palfrey, J.S. and Aufseeser, C.I. The Pediatric Examination of Educational Readiness: Validation of an extended observation procedure. *Pediatrics*, 66:341 (1980b).

Levine, M.D. *The Answer System: Questionnaires for the Assessment of Learning and Behavior Problems in Children.* Cambridge, Mass.: Educators Publishing Service (1980).

Levine, M.D., Palfrey, J.S., Lamb, G.A., Weisberg, H.I. and Bryk, A.S. Infants in a Public School System: The indicators of early health and educational need. *Pediatrics*, 60: 579 (1977).

North, A.F. Screening in child health care: Where we are now and where are we going? *Pediatrics*, 54:631 (1974).

Oberklaid, F., Dworkin, P.H. and Levine, M.D. Developmental-behavioral dysfunction in preschool children. *Am. J. Dis. Child*, 133:1126 (1979).

Oberklaid, F., Levine, M.D., Ferb, T.E. and Hanson, M.A. The Pediatric Examination of Educational Readiness: An integrated health and neurodevelopmental assessment instrument. Paper presented to American Educational Research Association, Annual Meeting, Toronto, Canada, March (1978).

Oberklaid, F. and Levine, M.D. Precursors of school failure. *Pediatrics in Review*, 2:5 (1980).

Peters, J.E., Romine, J.S. and Dykeman, R.A. A special neurological examination of children with learning disabilities. *Dev. Med. Child Neurol.*, 17:63 (1975).

Poremba, C.D. Learning disabilities, Youth and Delinquency, in Myklebust, H.R. (ed.), *Progress in Learning Disabilities.* Vol. III. New York: Grune and Stratton (1975).

Rosenthal, R. and Jacobson, L. *Pygmalion in the Classroom.* New York: Holt, Rinehart, and Winston (1968).

Ross, A.O. *Psychological Aspects of Learning Disabilities and Reading Disorders.* New York: McGraw-Hill (1976).

Rudel, R. and Denckla, M. Relationships of I.Q. and reading score to visual, spatial, and temporal matching tests. *J. Learn. Disabil.*, 9:169 (1975).

Sameroff, A.J. Early influences on development; fact or fancy? *Merrill-Palmer Quarterly*, 21:267 (1975).

Solnit, A.J. The risks of screening. *Pediatrics*, 57:646 (1976).

Thomas, A. and Chess, S. *Temperament and Development*. New York: Brunner/Mazel (1977).

Touwen, B.C.L. and Prechtl, H.F.R. The Neurological Examination of the Child with Minor Nervous Dysfunction. *Clinics in Developmental Medicine,* n. 38. London: Spastics International Medical Publications (1970).

Walker, D.K., Ferb, T.E. and Swartz, J.P. Kindergarten teacher ratings of school competence. Brookline, Mass.: The Brookline Early Education Project (1978).

15

An Information Processing Approach to Infant Cognitive Assessment

PHILIP R. ZELAZO

There is a revolution in mental assessment under foot and it is not likely that this upheaval will be turned back. It is equally unlikely that there will be much fervor for turning back following this most recent round of scrutiny. It has been demonstrated repeatedly that tests of infant development have little or no predictive validity (e.g., Bayley, 1966; Brooks and Weinraub, 1976; Lewis, 1976; Lewis and McGurk, 1972; McCall, this volume; McCall *et al.*, 1973; Miranda *et al.*, 1977; Stott and Ball, 1965; Willerman and Fiedler, 1974). These researchers have argued that a child's score on a traditional test of infant development does not predict his or her performance during adulthood or even later childhood. Because we have known about the limitations of infant tests of development since the mid-1960's when Stott and Ball and Bayley published their often quoted critiques of infant tests, it might be asked what makes this recent clamoring any different? One answer is that since the mid-1960's, developmental psychology has produced a methodology for the study of attention in infancy that provides the potential for a rigorous alternative to the conventional format.

A number of researchers (e.g., Fagan, 1978; Fantz and Nevis, 1967; Lewis, 1971; McCall, 1971; Miranda and Fantz, 1974; Zelazo, 1976a) have seen this potential and have worked toward either creating or urging the creation of an alternative. Much work remains to be done, but there appears to be a sufficient corpus of data to indicate that a viable, clinically applicable alternative can be generated from the research on visual and auditory processing during infancy (Fagan, 1979; Fantz and Nevis, 1967; Kearsley, 1979; Lewis, 1971 and this volume; Miranda *et al.*, 1977; McDonough and Cohen, 1980; Zelazo, 1979).

Not only do these studies demonstrate that the child's capacity to process visual and auditory information may be a more direct and valid avenue for the assessment of later intellectual functioning than conventional procedures, but they bear potential for seriously altering our view of cognitive development during infancy. A perceptual-cognitive approach to infant assessment has major theoretical implication.

Should the Assumption of Sensori-Motor Intelligence Be Modified?

One factor that stands in the way of the acceptance of new procedures for the assessment of intellectual functioning in infants is the widely held assumption that infant intelligence is strictly sensori-motor in origin. We have been bound theoretically and practically by the belief, held with varying degrees of aware-ness and commitment, that the child's intelligence is directly and necessarily tied to his sensori-motor development. However, many findings are at variance with this assumption and a relaxation of our commitment to a sensori-motor view of cognition during infancy appears to be in order. Yet, the traditional tests of infant development, virtually without exception, rest on the assumption of sensori-motor intelligence either directly or indirectly. As the data to challenge this pervasive assumption come into focus, the foundation upon which tradi-tional tests rest is likely to be shaken, perhaps irreparably.

Can we continue to assume that the assessment of a child's neuromotor status is a valid indication of his/her cognitive ability? Many data imply that mental and motor development, although mutually facilitative, may proceed independently. For example, approximately one-third of the children who display cerebral palsy during development eventually reveal normal intelligence (Crothers and Paine, 1957; Holman and Freedheim, 1959). Other children who have experienced thalidomide poisoning have displayed normal intellectual development when assessments were modified to accommodate their specific malformation (Decarie, 1969; Kopp and Shaperman, 1973). In addition, the closely related assumption of an invariant cephalo-caudal sequence in neuro-motor development appears to be more variant and influenced by child rearing practices than expected (Konner, 1973, 1977; Super, 1973; Rovee and Rovee, 1969; Solomons and Solomons, 1975; Zelazo et al., 1972a,b; Zelazo, 1976b).

In clinical terms, relinquishing the assumption of sensori-motor intelli-gence means that we cannot rely solely on measures of neuromotor status or speech to make inferences about a child's intellectual development. Much of the discussion in this paper will examine the methodological limitations of con-ventional tests and the contrasting implications derived from the research on the determinants of attention during infancy. One of a number of possible approaches to assess the child's capacity to process information—a position that appears inherently at variance with the assumption of sensori-motor intelligence—will be presented. A case study to illustrate the nature of this cognitive-developmental approach using both information processing and play procedures will be discussed.

Limitations of Conventional Tests

It has been stated frequently that tests of infant development have poor predictive validity. Why is it that psychologists have not been troubled sufficiently with this fact in the past to produce an alternative? One reason is that viable competing interpretations were generated. Some researchers argued that the low correlations between infant performances on conventional tests and later IQ scores were produced by the genetic blueprint which includes differing spurts and lags in development (Wilson, 1972; Wilson and Harpring, 1972). Other researchers suggested that the child's abilities vary across ages during the early years of life. This view implies that the manifestations of intelligence differ as the child matures (Bayley, 1966; Stott and Ball, 1965). Others (e.g., McCall, 1971; Zelazo, 1976a, 1979) suggested that traditional tests of infant development may display poor predictive validity because the items used to measure infant mental development may be poor indicators of cognitive ability. Moreover, it was argued that the fallible indices of development not only raise doubt about the tests themselves, but question the assumption of sensori-motor intelligence upon which these tests are based (Zelazo, 1976a, 1979).

An examination of the items used in conventional tests indicates that there are few measures of cognitive ability that are free from reliance on gross and fine motor performance. An objective re-examination of the demands placed on the infant in a conventional test format reveals that three classes of behavior—gross and fine motor skills, imitation and speech—require at least minimal motor competence. A fourth factor—compliance with the examiner indicating the child's testability—is a behavioral condition that may seriously interfere with test results.

Consider each of these classes in turn. First, gross and fine motor items are measured directly, particularly in the motor scales of traditional infant tests where they often are included separately. The following examples from the motor portion of the Bayley Scales of Infant Development (Bayley, 1969) appear to be representative. At 7.4 months of age, credit is given for early stepping movements occurring when the child is supported under the arms in an upright position; at 8.9 months of age if the child picks up a pellet precisely with his thumb and forefinger demonstrating a pincer grasp; and at 11.7 months of age if he or she walks alone, taking three steps without support.

The second class of behaviors include gross and fine motor responses measured indirectly, usually in the form of imitation items on the Mental portion of the infant schedules. For example, at 9.4 months of age, a child is given credit on the Mental portion of the Bayley Scales of Infant Development if he/she puts a cube in a cup on command. At 11.3 months of age, the child is given credit if he/she pushes a toy car along the table top and at 13.8 months of age, for building a tower of two cubes. In each instance, the examiner demonstrates and coaxes the child using both gestures and words to encourage imitation.

The third class of behaviors, those involving language items, also require motor facility for successful performance although the motor demands are more subtle and difficult to discern than those of the first two classes. The language items scattered throughout the mental scale fall under two categories, those indicating comprehension and others demanding expression. In practice, the child's comprehension of spoken language is indicated primarily by pointing and/or reasonably explicit gestures and both require facility of the upper extremities. For example, at 9.1 months of age, the child is given credit on the Mental portion of the Bayley Scales if he or she responds to a verbal request appropriately such as clapping his/her hands when asked to do so, but without any gestures from the examiner to elicit imitation. At 15.3 months of age, comprehension of the examiner's speech is credited if the child points, touches, or looks at the item named. If the child is asked, "Where are your shoes?", he/she is expected to point to his/her shoes.

The child's language production as indicated by his/her speech is a motor based component of language. At 12.5 months of age, the child is given credit if he/she verbally imitates words such as "mama" or "dada" and at 14.2 months of age if he/she uses two words appropriately to a specific object or situation. The child's speech can be elicited through verbal imitation or it may be spontaneous. Speech items appear with increasing frequency during the second and third years on the Bayley Scales and other tests as McCall, Appelbaum and Hogarty (1973) have shown. Beyond age three, both language comprehension and production play dominant roles in most tests of intellectual development. This reliance on language items places children with language delays at considerable risk for intellectual impairment.

The fourth condition, the necessity to comply with the examiner's requests, is inherent in the conventional test format and is common across the various infant tests, but is a behavioral disposition that has not received sufficient recognition. Resistance to the examiner's requests is not a trivial problem when trying to assess a group of children who are either approaching, well into or just coming out of the "terrible twos." This description of the toddler is well founded and reflects a dominant characteristic of the age group that is not suspended when the child enters the room with the examiner. Indeed, children vary greatly in their willingness to comply with the demands of a stranger, but they are often less compliant than with familiar persons. However, in conventional tests even though disclaimers are offered, unwillingness is often subtle and too frequently equated with incompetence.

Unfortunately, difficulties in any one of these modalities—neuromotor problems, speech delays or behavioral problems—automatically reduce the child's score on traditional tests and imply intellectual impairment. In methodological terms, the measures of the child's mental ability are confounded with the child's handicapping condition. In other words, the conventional tests were developed with and standardized on normal children and assume facility in areas that may be deficient among handicapped children. It is important to keep in mind that the use of normal samples of children for standardization is not the same as having a statistically normal distribution. A statistically normal distribution would include children with handicapping conditions and delayed development. Moreover, the tests are constructed in a way that leaves little allowance for the possibility that cognitive and motor development may proceed independently and there is too little recognition that the child's failure to comply with the examiner's requests may indicate unwillingness and not inability.

Most tests of infant development have been influenced by the pioneering work of Gesell (1925, 1928) either directly or indirectly (Honzik, 1976). Gesell created a "Developmental Schedule" that was explicitly maturational and heavily based on motor performance. Many subsequent tests have relinquished the explicit adherence to a maturational view, but nevertheless, retained many of the items that are bound to motor facility. In practice, conventional tests rely on similar motor items to infer intellectual development and are, therefore, limited by the same constraints that limit an explicit sensori-motor view of intelligence. Moreover, the tests are designed to provide unitary scores, an IQ or DQ, and departures from this practice often lead to confusion. For example, if items are deleted because of a child's handicap, a unitary score is generally not given. The absence of the IQ score often renders the result uninterpretable by individuals in other disciplines who may be unaccustomed to this justifiable, but idiosyncratic use of the conventional test schedules.

Difficulties for Children
with Developmental Disabilities

It can be argued that conventional tests of infant development are often ill suited for the very children who display the greatest need for assessment: children with developmental disabilities. It is understandable that conventional tests were standardized on normal children with intact neuromotor abilities who displayed reasonably normal speech and who were not excessively non-compliant with the demands of the examiner. But these are not the children for whom the need for assessment is greatest. Indeed, unless normal children participate in projects evaluating conventional tests of infant development or using these tests for research means, normally developing infants and toddlers are not likely to receive conventional test evaluations. Tests of infant development are typically administered to children with developmental disabilities whose intellect has come under question. Frequently, these are children who have experienced neuromotor insults, display delays in motor development, lack speech or have marked behavioral or emotional problems. Unfortunately, a difficulty in any one of these areas of development is likely to reduce the child's test score and imply an intellectual delay. It is understandable that conventional tests would be developed with normal children, but our understanding does not erase the logical contradiction created by applying the tests to developmentally disabled children. The measures used to infer intellectual ability among children with developmental disabilities are confounded with the childrens' handicapping conditions. In many instances, it is not possible to distinguish whether a child's poor performance on a conventional test is peripheral and limited to his/her handicapping condition or whether it is central in origin and indicative of an intellectual deficit.

The confounding relation between childrens' handicapping conditions and conventional test items can be seen clearly by examining specific disabilities. It is necessary to ask whether assessment schedules containing age appropriate speech items should be used as valid indicators of cognitive development among a sample of speech delayed children? A 30-month-old child who does not speak is likely to fail most of the speech items, earn a Mental Age score that is below his/her chronological age and be placed at risk for delayed intellectual functioning. Similarly, it is necessary to ask whether the traditional tests of infant development should be used as valid indicators of intellectual development among a neuromotor impaired sample of children? A 20-month-old child with cerebral palsy and impairment of the upper and lower extremities is not likely to be able to manipulate objects with enough facility to pass many of the imitation items on the traditional mental scales. Additionally, it is necessary to ask whether the traditional tests should be used as valid indicators of cognitive development among a sample of children with moderate to severe behavior problems? A 25-month-old child with a severe behavior problem is less likely than a normal child to comply with the examiner's requests on any class of items. Conventional tests simply are not designed to accurately identify children with limited or peripheral instances of speech delay, neuromotor impairment, or behavioral non-compliance from those with centrally mediated intellectual deficits.

Difficulties in each of these areas may, in themselves, contribute to additional delays. In one instance, a child with a temporary medical handicap experienced restricted environmental opportunities that contributed to delays in object manipulations (Zelazo and Kearsley, 1980a). Similarly, children with moderately to severely resistant behavior may develop speech delays as Zelazo *et al.* (1980) have argued. The identification of delays with speech and object manipulations as peripheral, rather than centrally mediated difficulties in some instances, is strengthened by the sharp reduction of those delays with treatment.

Some researchers have suggested that the infant tests have their greatest predictive validity for low-scoring children (e.g., Honzik, 1976). The logical analysis suggested here as well as data from our own research (Zelazo, 1976b, 1979; Kearsley, 1979) imply that the tests themselves may contribute to lower expectations which, in turn, may increase the child's delays in development. Indeed, Hunt (1976) has shown that conventional tests are likely to err in the direction of estimating an intellectual deficit for children who later go on to achieve normal development. Tests that are biased against children with developmental disabilities often yield depressed scores that confirm the doubts of both professionals and parents and themselves contribute to reduced parental expectations, albeit inadvertently. Lowered expectations may depress the quality and appropriateness of parental demands and instruction. Thus, given the current construction of infant-toddler tests, a child with a developmental disability is not only immediately at risk for intellectual impairment, but the assessment is likely to confirm that suspicion. It has been argued that this conclusion is unwarranted in many instances on methodological grounds alone.

Once the disabled child has received a formal evaluation and earned a depressed score on tests biased against him or her, the onus is on the child and the parents to prove that he/she may have normal intellect. We should ask what percentage of children with depressed conventional test scores and normal intellect do not go on to pass into the normal category? If one-third of the children who displayed cerebral palsy during their early development eventually display normal intelligence as adults (c.f., Crothers and Paine, 1975; Holman and Freedheim, 1959), what percentage possess intact intellect trapped in impaired bodies, who are unable to display their intelligence?

It might be asked for whom are the conventional infant-toddler tests useful if they are inappropriate for developmentally disabled children? Because of the logical and methodological difficulties, it appears that tests of infant development are most appropriate for children with normal development. This point is neither facetious nor without merit. If a child scores at an age appropriate level on a traditional test of infant-toddler development it is a good indication of normal development and normal intelligence at that point in time. Indeed, Bayley (1969) explicitly states this to be the primary function of the Bayley Scales. A great deal of uncertainty can be reduced for the parents of a child whose intellect is in doubt and who scores at an age-appropriate level. It appears that achieving an age appropriate or better score may announce intact intellectual ability, but a depressed score may simply reflect a depressed estimate due to a peripheral rather than centrally mediated problem. The analogy to assessment in the educational setting is appropriate. The goal is not to fail the child in the course, but to assess what he/she knows. Similarly, we should seek the child's best performance as an indication of his/her highest level of functioning.

Since conventional tests, as they are presently constructed, are more likely to lead to a depressed rather than inflated estimate of the developmentally disabled child's intellectual ability, practicing professionals should be alert for this possibility. Pediatricians, psychologists and early educators should leave open the possibility that the developmentally delayed child will display his/her intellectual ability in areas other than those affected by the disability. In this instance, uncertainty in the diagnosis is preferable to a firm proclamation based on fallible indices. The weight of negative expectation in the form of erroneously depressed scores can bring its own self-fulfilling nightmare. The uncertainty, although often difficult to bear, at least offers the parents and the child an opportunity to display the child's intelligence at a later date and perhaps with different skills. For example, a speech delayed child responding to an intensive effort to promote speech is not only more likely to achieve an improved conventional test score, but can dismiss considerable doubt about his/her intellectual ability through informal conversation (c.f., Zelazo, Kearsley, and Ungerer, 1980).

What Can be Done to Limit
the Potential Negative Impact
of Infant Assessment?

Rather than ask how this state of assessment could develop, it is more productive to ask what can be done to minimize the possibility of placing children in the circular bind. There are at least three courses of action for the professional. First, practitioners, including physicians, psychologists, and early educators, can make allowances for a child's handicap in the administration and interpretation of conventional test scores. For example, Decarie (1969) modified the Griffiths Mental Developmental Scale (Griffiths, 1954) for a sample of 22 infants who had severe malformations associated with thalidomide. It was found that when the test was modified to accommodate the child's specific area of impairment, 44% of the sample scored from average to superior. Second, it is possible to look at the child's highest performances on a test as a means for mitigating a potential negative impact on developmentally disabled children. Often, the child's highest performance implies prerequisite abilities. For example, a capacity for pretend play implies the ability for a less mature functional use of toys (c.f., Fenson *et al.*, 1976; Nicolich, 1977; Ungerer *et al.*, 1979;

Watson and Fischer, 1978; Zelazo and Kearsley, 1980). The capacity for functional play could be inferred from the appearance of pretend play even if functional play were not displayed directly in the test situation. Among disabled children, it makes sense that their disability may mask their intellectual ability under some circumstances. Thus, one corrective is to look at the highest related ability that the child can display, rather than to adhere strictly to the requirement for prerequisite abilities.

Psychologists would argue that allowances are made in the administration and interpretation of conventional tests and they are, indeed. Unfortunately, allowances occur too infrequently particularly outside psychology, in medicine and education, for example. It is the psychologist's responsibility to make other professionals aware of the limitations inherent in conventional testing procedures. The practicing pediatrician is in the best position to convey the testing limitations to the parents and to keep the door open for possible improved performance in a standardized test situation. For example, the pediatrician can indicate that the infant with cerebral palsy who may score poorly on conventional tests during the first year of life may receive a more accurate assessment if and when he/she develops speech. Keeping the question open with respect to diagnosis, although often in opposition to the physician's training and inclination, may permit a sufficiently favorable environment with positive expectations for improved development to occur. This strategy reflects a cautious and humane approach that may prevent a negative bias based on circular logic and fallible indices for evaluation.

A third course of action that can be pursued to alter the current state of assessment during infancy is more directly in the hands of the infant researcher— principally the developmental psychologist. It is incumbent upon developmental psychologists who have participated in the basic research on infant attention to refine their procedures into clinically useful instruments if they wish them to be used. It is possible to exploit the recent methodological advances in the study of infancy to create assessment procedures that do not rely on speech, gross and fine motor facility and compliance with the examiner. Measures of infant attention offer promise. For example, if an infant's attention to the repeated brief presentation of the vertical array of X's and Y's shown in Figure 1a were followed by a decrement of looking time, called habituation, it would imply that the infant had at least a partial memory for that event. If the infant smiled to the presentation of the vertical array before habituation occurred, recognition could be inferred and it would be even more certain that the infant formed an internal representation for the event.

It is a straightforward task to test an infant's capacity to form a memory for an event and to measure his/her reactions to departures from that stimulus. Lewis and Goldberg (1969) described a paradigm that permitted the formation and violation of expectancies to be studied experimentally in 3½ year old

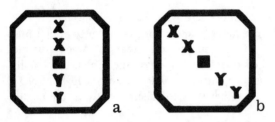

FIG. 1. Stimuli presented as a standard (a) and discrepancy (b) in a study of habituation and dishabituation. (From R. B. McCall & W. H. Melson, Attention in Infants as a function of magnitude of discrepancy and habituation rate. *Psychonomic Science* 17:317–319 (1969).

children. McCall and Melson (1969) used a similar paradigm with 4-to-5-month-old infants. They demonstrated that a vertical array of X's and Y's shown in Figure 1a led to habituation of first visual fixations to the stimulus and cardiac decelerations. Moreover, the introduction of the same array in the oblique orientation shown in Figure 1b resulted in increased cardiac deceleration, called dishabituation. Not only is a memory for the standard inferred from the habituation of first fixations and cardiac deceleration, but dishabituation to the differing orientation diminished the likelihood that fatigue accounted for the initial decrement in responding. This simple demonstration implies that the child is capable of processing and storing information and of assimilating moderate changes from an experimentally produced standard.

The child's behavior in this standardized situation implies a capacity for processing and solving elementary perceptual-cognitive problems. Moreover, infant information processing capacity, demonstrable with different paradigms from the early weeks of life (e.g., Adkinson and Berg, 1976; Ungerer *et al.*, 1978) and throughout much of infancy (Cohen, 1972, 1973; Fagan, 1978; Kagan, 1971; Kagan *et al.*, 1978; Lewis and Goldberg, 1969), is at odds with the assumption of sensori-motor intelligence. Although differences exist among the basic researchers participating in the study of infant attention, there appears to be agreement that habituation and dishabituation imply the capacity to form memories for specific events and to process changes from these experimentally formed expectancies.

Traditional tests can indicate delayed performance and impaired development adequately. The difficulty is that they do not distinguish peripheral difficulties from centrally mediated delays. However, if a child's ability to process information can be measured without reliance on speech, gross and fine motor performances and compliance with the examiner, the nature of the child's disability can be determined with greater precision than previously. The need for alternative procedures for children with developmental disabilities is great. The implication derived from the basic research on attention in infancy that central processing delays can be distinguished from peripheral delays is a testable hypothesis and research on this problem is well underway.

Reactivity to Sequential Visual
and Auditory Events:
An Alternative Approach

One of several possible approaches to the assessment of the child's capacity to process information has been adapted for clinical use (Zelazo, 1979). This approach using sequential visual and auditory events (Zelazo, 1972; Zelazo *et al.,* 1975) is based on procedures developed with a large cross-sectional sample of children between the ages of 3½ and 11½ months. Five events, two visual and three auditory sequences, were selected from this initial investigation to be used with approximately 100 children examined longitudinally in a long-term investigation of day care and home reared children (Kagan, Kearsley, and Zelazo, 1978). These studies yielded a procedure that successfully captures childrens' attention between the ages of about 3½ through 36 months—an age range during which children undergo major developmental changes. Many of the results of this longitudinal investigation were presented in the form of changes over age to the same sequential stimuli (Kagan *et al.,* 1978). A major advantage derived from repeating the same stimuli at different ages was that changes in reactivity were more likely to be a function of changes within the child. The usual confounds between changes of items with age occurring in conventional tests was avoided.

Despite the cross-sectional and longitudinal studies, major modifications were necessary before the information processing procedures could be applied and examined in a clinical setting. In 1974 Richard Kearsley, a pediatrician and psychologist, and I began to examine the utility of the information processing procedures in a clinical setting within the Department of Pediatrics at Tufts-New England Medical Center. Their application with a relatively large sample of developmentally disabled patients yielded many insights. Moreover, a crucial change in the procedure for scoring childrens' responses to these events was also developed (Zelazo, 1979; Zelazo and Kearsley, 1980b). Nevertheless, much work, particularly in the form of data analysis, remains. However, the presentation of this procedure and a description of the technique for assessing a child's reaction to these events, can be offered as an illustration of one alternative approach.

Paradigm

The primary objective is to present an engaging visual or auditory event and to repeat that event until the child creates an expectancy for it. After a fixed number of presentations, and generally before the child has lost all interest in the event, a moderately discrepant variation of the standard is introduced and that too is repeated. Following three presentations of the discrepancy, the standard is re-introduced for three presentations. Not only is the child's capacity for creating an expectancy for the standard assessed, but whether the child recognizes the reappearance of the standard following the discrepancy, and lastly whether the child can assimilate the discrepant variation itself is measured. This paradigm remains constant for each of five events: six presentations of the standards is followed by three presentations of a moderate discrepancy from the standard, followed in turn by three presentations of the reappearance of the standard. The engaging sequential visual and auditory events function as relatively simple, perceptual-cognitive problems for children to solve. Generally, but not always, solutions are announced by the children when they create a memory for the standard, recognize the reappearance of the standard following the discrepancy, and/or create a memory for the discrepancy itself.

Stimuli

One example of a visual event called the car-doll sequence is illustrated in Figure 2. A toy car rests on a ramp that is approximately 22 inches in length. The presenter, concealed behind a black curtain holds the car at the top of the ramp for approximately 4 seconds and releases the car to roll down the ramp to tap over a styrofoam object. It takes 3 seconds for the car to roll down the ramp and the styrofoam object is left down for an additional 4 seconds. The presenter returns the styrofoam object to its upright position and pushes the car up the

FIG. 2.   Sequential car-doll stimulus.

ramp to the starting position to begin the second trial. This event is repeated for six trials followed by a discrepant variation on the seventh presentation. After remaining at the top of the ramp for 4 seconds, the car is released and rolls down the ramp to tap the styrofoam object, but without knocking it over. This moderate discrepancy from the child's expectancy is repeated for three trials, followed by the return of the standard sequence which is also presented for three trials. Without warning, the toy car taps over the styrofoam object upon contact once again on the fourth trial. Thus, the child has an opportunity to create an expectancy for the object to fall, to recognize the reappearance of this standard sequence following the discrepant variation and finally to assimilate the discrepant variation itself.

In the second of three auditory sequences, a meaningful phrase, "Hello baby. How are you today?" serves as the standard. The discrepant variation involves a grammatically incorrect variation of the standard presented with the same rhythm and intonation: "Are today. How baby you hello?" The discrepancy is followed by three reappearances of the standard, just as it is in the visual sequences.

Usually three auditory and two visual events are presented to each child requiring a total of about 40–45 minutes. One auditory and one visual event are usually paired followed by a short break of about 5 minutes to refresh the child. Following the break, a second pair of auditory and visual events is presented which in turn is followed by a short break and the third auditory sequence.

FIG. 3.   Laboratory setting.

Setting

The stimuli are presented on a three foot high stage in a room and setting that resembles a puppet theater. The bottom of the stage is draped with yellow curtains and the back of the stage is covered with black curtains to conceal the presenter. Four, 100 watt light bulbs projecting down on the stage serve as the sole illumination in the room during testing. The overhead bulbs, concealed in part by a yellow curtain, help focus the child's attention towards the activity on the stage. The stage itself, depicted in Figure 3, has large wings extending outward approximately 5 feet wide by 7 feet high and covered with black curtains. The child is seated on his/her mother's lap directly in front of the stage. Small plexi-glass windows are embedded in the curtains on both sides of the stage to permit coders to record the occurrence and duration of the infant's behaviors using button boxes.

Measures

Two observers are used to record selected behaviors during each event. One observer records the duration of visual fixation to the stimulus, smiling, vocalization and fretting. A second observer, positioned behind the opposite wing, codes a second set of dependent measures. During an auditory sequence, pointing to the speaker and baffle, clapping, waving of the arms through an arc greater than 60 degrees and twisting or extreme bending (an effort to get out of the situation) are coded. In addition, searching, a conservative and reliable indication of the child's attention, is coded when the child maintains eyes widened at a plane parallel to the ground or above. Visual searching to the auditory information may be accompanied by head movement and/or a reduction in movement of the extremities. This definition is aided by positioning a speaker and two white baffles above and behind the infant on either side of the stage.

During one visual event, the car-doll sequence, the second observer records anticipatory fixation, defined by the darting of the eyes ahead of the action in the sequence, rather than searching. Aside from pointing to the visual stimuli, all other measures are similar to those coded for the auditory sequences. The combined depression of the searching and twisting buttons is used to record the act of turning to mother to share the event, generally a mature reaction.

The child's heart rate is also monitored in order to provide a record of sustained cardiac accelerations and decelerations to the stimulus information. Small surface electrodes are attached to the child's sternum to permit recording of an electrocardiogram (EKG). A cardiotachometer is used to convert the EKG signal to a beat-by-beat recording of heart rate on a polygraph tracing. A detailed record of each stimulus event for each trial is also made. For example, a series of circuits are closed at various points in the car-doll sequence to indicate its progression. Thus, a signal is made on the polygraph paper when the car is resting on the top of the ramp, a different signal when it reaches the bottom and still another when the styrofoam object is horizontal. This analogue of the stimulus event, both sets of behavioral measures, and the child's heart rate are integrated and recorded on a polygraph tracing to provide a time-locked picture of selected variables during the entire sequence. Two video cameras—one focused on the child and the other on the stage—are used to make videotaped recordings of the testing. The videotaped records serve as a fail-safe system and permit access to idiosyncratic or omitted behaviors that might otherwise be lost. The polygraph and video recording unit and monitor are contained in an adjacent room.

Scoring of Behavioral Clusters

A major modification in the use of this procedure involves the scoring of clusters of behaviors. The child's formation of a firm memory for the event is inferred from a cluster of behaviors, portions of which were first reported by Lewis and Goldberg (1969). The child must display visual fixation, cardiac deceleration of six beats or more, and one or more other behaviors that include smiling, vocalizing, pointing, clapping, and/or turning to mother. There is opportunity for a cluster of behaviors to be somewhat unique to each child while still sharing common features across children. For example, a typical result observed with a 20-month-old child during the third presentation of the standard for the car sequence may include a 12 beat cardiac deceleration, smiling, vocalizing, and pointing when the car taps the styrofoam object. This cluster of behaviors may wane on the fourth, fifth, and sixth presentations of the standard and stop abruptly with the introduction and repetition of the discrepancy. Typically, the first reappearance of the standard elicits renewed smiling, vocalizing, pointing, and cardiac deceleration while attending vigilently. These clusters of behaviors in this controlled context permit the inference of recognition of the standard following the discrepant trials. It appears that the child announces nonverbally that "he's got it."

These clusters of behaviors do not appear reliably until the end of the first year of life. At about 12 months, relatively weak clusters of behaviors occur late during the standards and late during the return trials. Reactivity during the first year is less unified although a steady increase in visual fixation and searching occurs. Nevertheless, some measures such as vocalization are relatively high at 5½ and 7½ months, constricted at about 9½ months and reappear at about 11½ months apparently in the service of recognition (c.f., Zelazo, Kagan and Hartmann, 1975; Zelazo, 1975, 1979). Reactivity to these events at about 20 months of age is characterized by rapid evidence of recognition during the standard trials and almost immediate recognition during the first reappearance of the standard following the discrepancy. Clusters implying recognition and memory formation during the discrepancy trials typically do not occur reliably until about 30 months of age. At that point, recognition of the standard sequences is usually prompt and recognition of the return of the standards is immediate. It is the appearance of clusters during the transformation trials that distinguish the most mature children, generally about 30 months of age or older, using these procedures. By about 36 months of age, clusters implying assimilation occur almost immediately to the discrepant information. Thus, these procedures appear to be measuring the child's increasing speed of information processing over the first three years of life.

Results: Illustrations From a Case Study

The presentation of a case study in which the perceptual-cognitive procedures and observations of play were used longitudinally, is probably the simplest way to illustrate the utility of this approach. Observations of play, including the child's response to instruction with object manipulations and a therapeutic trial period during which behavioral treatment procedures were introduced, offered a relatively quick validation of the information-processing findings.

Subject's History

J. was 14 months, 9 days of age when administered his first testing with the perceptual-cognitive procedures. He was a child with a diaphramatic hernia, agenesis of the left diaphragm and glottic stenosis requiring repeated surgery and intensive care during the first 380 days of his life. He required a tracheostomy and gastrostomy during most of that time. An extraordinary effort was made to provide J. with as nearly normal an environment as possible given the constraints of ventilatory assistance and the need to be in the intensive care unit for the first critical year of his life. Obviously, severe restrictions were placed on the gross and fine motor stimulation that he could experience. Moreover, although his mother visited nearly every day and the nursing staff developed a fond relationship with J., his confinement to the intensive care unit for such a prolonged period is unusual.

Procedures

Dr. Kearsley and I shared in the repeated evaluations of J. who was tested on three occasions using the perceptual-cognitive procedures; at 14.25, 20.25 and

36.5 months. He was also administered a standard 15-minute free play sequence (Zelazo and Kearsley, 1980a) at these three ages and again at 17.25 months.

Changes in the quality of play involving stereotypical, relational, functional and symbolic activity were observed. Stereotypical play included indiscriminate mouthing, waving, banging and fingering of the various toys. Functional play included the display of appropriate, adult-defined uses for the toys such as bringing the telephone receiver to one's ear. Relational play, apparently a transitional behavior between the stereotypical and functional use of objects, involved the inappropriate manipulation of two or more objects. Putting the telephone receiver to the wheel of a truck is an instance of relational play. Symbolic play, referred to the pretend use of toys such as placing the receiver to a doll's ear. For the purposes of this presentation, symbolic or pretend play is subsumed under functional play.

In the 15-minute free play sequence, J.'s mother was asked to remain seated and to avoid initiation of interaction. An array of six sets of toys with 36 conservatively defined appropriate uses were arranged in a semi-circle within J.'s reach. All six sets of toys including a teaset, telephone, large doll with a hair brush and bottle, a small doll with furniture, a truck with garage, and a baseball set had clearly defined functional and symbolic uses. The three play measures—stereotypical, relational and functional—were recorded on checklists using 10 second blocks.

It was considered inappropriate to administer a traditional test of infant development when J. was first examined and those scores are not available. However, observations of his behavior at 14.25 months indicated that he had no words, could not walk, and could sit well with support only. When left to his own means, securely propped during the free play sequence and with toys brought well within his reach, he did not display any appropriate uses for the toys. Only 64.4% of the 15 minute session was spent in active manipulation of objects and 97% of this play was spent in immature waving, fingering, banging and mouthing of objects. There were only two relational acts. Thus, observations of his behavior indicated marked delays in motor development, object manipulation and the absence of words.

Results for the Perceptual-Cognitive Procedures

In contrast to the profile presented by J.'s grossly observable behaviors, his performance on the perceptual-cognitive tasks was clearly age-appropriate. The results for the car-doll sequence at each of the three ages are presented in Table 1 to illustrate this point. The first assimilative cluster of behaviors occurred on the fourth presentation of the standard. This cluster of behaviors, including a 17 beat cardiac deceleration and laughter involving smiling and vocalization while

TABLE 1 First Behavioral Cluster Implying Recognition Scored
for Each Portion of the Car–Doll Sequence at Three Ages of Testing

Age of Testing (Months)	Standards	Returns	Transformations
14.25	$\bar{S}_4*$	$R_{1-3}*$	None (Reduction of laughter; Mechanical difficulty)
20.25	S_2*	R_2*	None (First break in fixation)
36.50	S_1*	R_1*	T_1*

attending vigilently, imply that J. formed a clear expectation for the event. The introduction of the discrepancy during which the styrofoam object did not tap over upon contact with the car elicited a reduction in laughter and stimulus-related cardiac decelerations, although attention remained high. However, when the standard sequence reappeared, a cluster of behaviors implying recognition of the event re-occurred. There was renewed cardiac deceleration and laughter accompanied by intent watching. This result was confirmed in the other sequences implying near age-appropriate information processing ability at 14.25 months.

J.'s performance on the perceptual-cognitive procedures revealed continued age appropriate information processing at 20.25 and 36.25 months of age. Scoring of first assimilative clusters for the car-doll sequence, displayed in Table 1, revealed that recognition was announced on the second presentation of the standard at 20.25 months in contrast to the fourth presentation at 14.25 months. The reappearance of the standard elicited recognition clusters at approximately equal points during the first and second testings, occurring most clearly on the second reappearance of the standard. It should be pointed out that a mechanical failure with the presentation of one discrepant trial during the first testing disrupted the sequencing of standards and transformations. This problem did not appear to affect the reaction to the discrepancy, but may have produced more rapid recognition of the return sequence than may have occurred otherwise. Despite this problem, recognition clusters were not produced during the discrepancy trials in either case. In fact, the first break in visual fixation to the car-doll sequence occurred to the discrepant event during the second testing. By 36½ months, not only were the standard and its reappearance recognized on first presentation, but the discrepancy itself elicited a recognition cluster immediately. It was not until the third testing that J. displayed a recognition cluster to the discrepant portion of the sequence. It is expected that he would have done so around 30 months, although with less speed, had he been retested at that time. These changes in recognition clusters to the various portions of the car-doll event are similar to those observed with normal children in our samples.

Results for the Play Sequences

J.'s behavior during the play sessions presents a somewhat different picture than indicated by the perceptual-cognitive procedures during the first two testings. The relative percentages of stereotypical, relational and functional play for each of J.'s four testings are presented in Figure 4. At 14.25 months, 97% of J.'s play was of an immature, stereotypical form, more like a 9-month-old or younger child than a normal 14-month-old.

In order to clarify the disparity between the quality of J.'s play and his performance on the perceptual-cognitive procedures, a 12 minute teaching session was introduced. It was reasoned that the display of functional uses

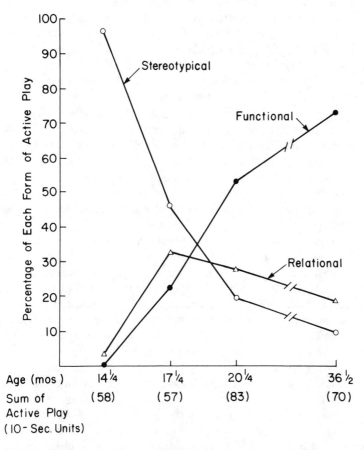

FIG. 4. Percentages of Stereotypical, Relational, and Functional Play at each of four ages for a single child. The incidences of three forms of play combined are also listed. From Zelazo, R.R., & Kearsley, R.B. The emergence of functional play in infants: Evidence for a major cognitive transition. *Journal of Applied Developmental Psychology* 1:95–117 (1980).

following 4 minutes of instruction with each of three toys would support the finding of age-appropriate information processing ability. The absence of functional play when given instruction would be consistent with less mature cognitive ability. Therefore, J.'s mother was asked to use her own style of interaction to demonstrate the appropriate uses for a telephone, xylophone, and four part puzzle, immediately after the free play session. The incidence of functional play for each 10 second unit and the number of different appropriate uses were recorded.

J. displayed 8 10-second units of simple functional play in response to brief instruction, implying that his immaturity during the free play sequence was probably the result of inexperience rather than inability. Based on the results derived from the perceptual-cognitive assessment and the supportive evidence from the teaching session, J.'s parents were urged to begin a treatment program to encourage the functional manipulation of objects and the production of speech (c.f., Zelazo *et al.*, 1980) on a daily basis.

The second evaluation of J.'s play occurring at 17.25 months, three months after the first testing, revealed the initial fruits of the treatment program. It can be seen in Figure 4 that stereotypical play decreased to 46%, relational play increased to 32% and, more importantly, functional play rose from 0 to 22% of the active play occurring during the 15 minute session. This distribution is an approximation of the distribution seen in a normal sample of children at 11½ months of age. The display of results for a cross-sectional sample of normal children at 9½, 11½, 13½ and 15½ months of age, reported by Zelazo and Kearsley (1980a), is shown in Figure 5. The normal distribution at 11½ months contained approximately 47% stereotypical, 39% relational and 15% functional activity.

The parent implemented efforts to foster play and speech were continued and a re-evaluation of J.'s play 3 months later at 20.25 months of age revealed sharp improvement. Functional play rose from 22 to 53%, whereas relational and stereotypical play declined to 27 and 19%, respectively. The distribution of J.'s play at 20.25 months of age was comparable to the results for normal children at 15.5 months where approximately 53% of the play was functional, 28% relational, and 21% stereotypical. In fact, the distribution of J.'s active play over the six month period from the beginning of treatment to his third evaluation is similar to the results for the cross-sectional sample tested between 9½ and 15½ months of age. J.'s performance, 16 months later at 36.25 months revealed that 73%, the vast majority of his play, was functional and symbolic, 18% was relational and only 9% involved the stereotypical manipulation of objects. Moreover, the number of appropriate uses for the 36 toys in the array rose steadily from 0 to 3 to 8 to 15 over the four testings, indicating that not only the frequency of appropriate uses increased, but the diversity of applications expanded as well.

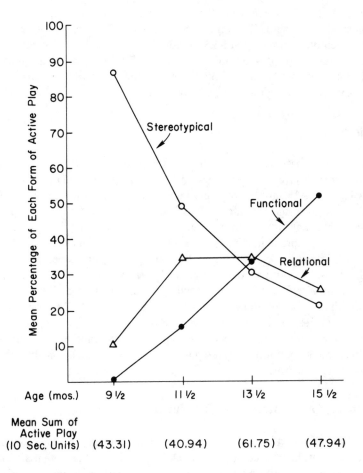

FIG. 5.   Mean percentages of Stereotypical, Relational, and Functional Play at each of four ages. The means for the incidences of the three forms of play combined are also listed. From Zelano, P.R. and Kearsley, R.B. The emergence of functional play in infants: Evidence for a major cognitive transition. *Journal of Applied Developmental Psychology* 1:95–117 (1980).

Conventional Testing

At 37 months of age, J. was administered the Form L-M of the Stanford-Binet Intelligence Scale (Terman and Merrill, 1973). He earned a Mental Age of 38 months, corresponding to a low-average score. However, the examiner reported that J.'s performance was "definitely a minimal estimate of his intellectual abilities." He was highly distractable and not fully cooperative during testing.

The examiner's overall impression was that J. was "developing normally in terms of his intellectual attainments." Informal observations of J. revealed that he not only spoke in complex sentences at 36.5 months as normal children do, but was reading such words as "stop" and "open." In general, by three years of age most signs of development were within normal limits despite his restricted gross and fine motor experience during the first 380 days of life.

Implications

There are several implications from these results that should be articulated. First, the perceptual-cognitive procedures appeared to detect age-appropriate information processing at 14.25 months of age when J.'s overall appearance reflected marked delays in gross and fine motor development and object manipulations. Second, qualitative changes in J.'s play occurred coincidental with direct efforts to encourage the appropriate manipulation of objects. Third, evaluation with the Stanford-Binet Scales at 37 months revealing an age appropriate performance lends validity to the perceptual-cognitive assessment procedures in this instance. Fourth, J.'s history and development showing reasonably normal intellectual ability despite the absence of normal gross and fine motor stimulation during the first year, contributes to the doubts raised earlier about the assumption of sensori-motor intelligence. This specific case appears to be another illustration that cognitive and sensori-motor development, although mutually facilitative, may proceed independently.

Summary, Observations and Conclusions

It has been argued that the limitations of conventional tests of infant and toddler development have become unacceptable in light of the potential for assessment inherent in the research on information processing during the early years of life. The demonstration that infants can create expectancies for visual and auditory events and process discrepant variations of these expectancies raises doubt about the validity of the sensori-motor assumption as it is generally viewed and particularly as it is applied in conventional assessment schedules. One alternative approach to infant-toddler assessment derived from the perceptual-cognitive research in infancy offers distinct advantages, but requires further validation. The case study presented to illustrate reliable changes in speed of information processing over age (c.f., Zelazo and Kearsley, 1980b) also illustrates how changes in the quality of play can be used to validate information processing assessments in individual cases.

Research on information processing among infants implies that one aspect of the infant's central processing capability that appears to be measurable over the first three years is the speed with which memories are formed (Lewis, 1971;

Zelazo, 1979; Zelazo and Kearsley, 1980b). Moreover, the documentation of reliable changes in the speed of information processing to sequential visual and auditory events can alter our view of the infant's cognitive development substantially if validated by subsequent research.

The assumption that the child has a central processing capability, based on the repeated findings of habituation and dishabituation to both visual and auditory events and visual preferences in a choice situation, can allow assessment to occur with fewer demands on the child and fewer confounds between the child's disability and his central processing capability. The problems involved with requiring gross and fine motor ability, speech and compliance with the examiner in traditional tests in order to make inferences about intelligence can account for some of the recurrent errors in traditional assessments. Dependence on these measures may indicate why the error in assessment with traditional tests is usually unidirectional. Why have traditional tests underestimated the intellectual abilities of children with cerebral palsy (Holman and Freedheim, 1959)? Why has a similar result been reported with developmentally delayed children who have not experienced neuromotor impairment (Hunt, 1976)? Similarly, why has McCall (this volume) found that the error rate is more likely to be in the direction of calling children delayed when they are intact? A portion of the error in prediction using conventional assessments may be due to fallible indices that reflect delays in peripheral or output measures such as speech and object manipulations rather than central processing ability during early childhood. In contrast, the information processing procedures described here attempt to measure one aspect of central processing, namely the speed of memory formation, using measures that are more subtle than traditional indices.

For many reasons, it is necessary to validate the predictions based on the assessment of central processing ability. How do you know that a child with a normal 20-month-old profile with the perceptual-cognitive procedures has normal intellect if he/she also has seriously immature play and speech? This gnawing question compels the use of a therapeutic trial—a technique designed to achieve an empirical answer—as in J.'s case (c.f., Zelazo, 1979). This intervention approach is based on the assumption that a child with delayed intellect could not acquire age appropriate play or speech readily despite treatment efforts.

It would be reasonable to speculate that the underlying cognitive competence—referred to here as central processing capacity—may be part of the biological program of normally developing children in a normal, intellectually supportive environment. In other words, this central processing ability that appears to develop even in children with cerebral palsy, children with known brain damage and limited means for expression, is a reasonable candidate for a maturing biological capacity. Nevertheless, it is clear that the ways children display this central ability appear to be highly influenced by environmental factors. For instance, a child may have the cognitive capacity to support functional play, but may have neither the appropriate toys, models or opportunities (as in J.'s case) for functional play to develop. The manifestations of the central processing capacity—object manipulations and language, for example—appear to be highly dependent upon environmental factors for their expression.

At present, the perceptual-cognitive procedures described here do not lend themselves to tight age discriminations, but it may be that the monthly distinctions made in the traditional assessment schedules are primarily statistical conveniences that do not reflect accurately the course of development. Rather than the steady linear progression implied by conventional schedules, development may be characterized by regressions and accelerations. Transitions in development are suggested by a number of authors (Bever *et al.*, 1980, in press; Fenson *et al.*, 1976; Fischer and Corrigan, 1980, in press; Kagan *et al.*, 1978; McCall *et al.*, 1977; Piaget, 1952, 1962; Zelazo, 1975, 1979; Zelazo and Kearsley, 1980a). For example, McCall *et al.* (1977) suggest that during the first two months of life, the infant is "primarily responsive to selective stimulus dimensions that match the structural dispositions of the sensori-perceptual systems." Between 3 and 7 months, the infant explores the environment more actively, but the view of the world is subjective. Between 8 and 13 months, another transition occurs during which the child begins to differentiate means from ends. These authors argue that the means-end distinction is completed between about 14 and 18 months "permitting the infant to associate two environmental entities without acting on either one." They suggest that between 21 and about 36 months, the capacity for symbolic relations appear to emerge. These transitions based on a re-analysis of the Fels and Berkeley Growth Study data correspond roughly to the changes that appear to occur using the perceptual-cognitive procedures. This approximate correspondence implies that it may be possible to refine the information processing procedures to monitor the central processing correlates of these transitions.

A Final Comment

If there is a contribution that developmental psychology can share with pediatrics, it is that infants can process visual and auditory events without reliance on gross and fine motor performance almost from birth. This information not only challenges some assumptions within pediatrics, but questions the very bedrock of infant assessment practiced by psychologists, namely the assumption of sensori-motor intelligence. This assumption, like any valued belief that has served well in the past, is not likely to be relinquished easily. The observations and experiments that are at odds with this belief are derived from nearly 20 years of sound basic research in the area of infancy. Although many questions still remain, there is a relatively solid foundation upon which to launch this challenge. However, it is necessary to keep in mind, not the unanswered questions that lie ahead, but the relatively immature empirical foundations upon which the conventional procedures rest. Foremost in our minds for both psychologists, pediatricians, and early educators is the welfare and development of young children. It follows that the combined concern for young children and the recent research on perceptual-cognitive development offers sound justification for questioning our assumptions, creating new testing procedures and keeping options open with respect to the identification of mental retardation among disabled infants and toddlers. There is reason to believe that questioning our assumptions and seeking alternative measures may lead to a reduction in human suffering for developmentally disabled children and their parents.

References

Adkinson, C.D. and Berg, W.K. Cardiac deceleration in newborns: Habituation, dishabituation, and offset responses. *J. Exper. Child Psychol.,* 21:46–60 (1976).

Bayley, N. Psychological Development of the Child, Part III: Mental Measurement, in Faulkner, F. (ed.), *Human Development.* Philadelphia: Saunders, p. 397–467 (1977).

Bayley, N. *Manual for the Bayley Scales of infant development.* New York: The Psychological Corporation (1969).

Bever, T. (ed.) *Regressions in development: Basic phenomena and theoretical alternatives.* Hillsdale, N.J.: L. Erlbaum Associates, Inc. (1981).

Brooks, J. and Weinraub, M. A history of infant intelligence testing, in Lewis, M. (ed.), *Origins of intelligence.* New York: Plenum Press, p. 19–58 (1976).

Cohen, L.B. Attention-getting and attention-holding processes of infant visual preferences. *Child Devel.,* 43:869–879 (1972).

Cohen, L.B. A two process model of infant visual attention. *Merrill-Palmer Quarterly,* 19: 157–180 (1973).

Crothers, B. and Paine, R.S. *The natural history of cerebral palsy.* Cambridge, Mass.: Harvard University Press (1957).

Decarie, T.G. A study of the mental and emotional development of the thalidomide child, in Foss, B.M. (ed.), *Determinants of infant behavior* (Vol. IV). London: Methuen and Co. (1969).

Fagan, J.F. Infant recognition memory and early cognitive ability: Empirical, theoretical, and remedial considerations, in Minifie, F.D. and Lloyd, L.L. (eds.), *Communicative and cognitive abilities—early behavioral assessment.* Baltimore: University Park Press (1978).

Fagan, J.F. Infant recognition memory and later intelligence. Paper presented at the *Society for Research in Child Development.* San Francisco, March (1979).

Fantz, R.L. Pattern vision in young infants. *The Psychological Record,* 8:43–47 (1958).

Fantz, R.L. and Nevis, S. The predictive value of changes in visual preferences in early infancy, in Hellmuth, J. (ed.), *The exceptional infant.* Volume 1. Seattle: Special Child Publications (1967).

Fenson, L., Kagan, J., Kearsley, R.B. and Zelazo, P.R. The developmental progression of manipulative play in the first two years. *Child Devel.,* 47:232–236 (1976).

Fischer, K. and Corrigan, R. A skill approach to language development, in Stark, R. (ed.), *Language behavior in infancy and early childhood* (1981).

Gesell, A. *The Mental Growth of the Pre-School Child.* New York: Macmillan (1925).

Gesell, A. *Infancy and human growth.* New York: Macmillan (1928).

Griffiths, R. *The Abilities of Babies.* London: University of London Press (1954).

Holman, L.B. and Freedheim, D.K. A study of I.Q. retest evaluation of 370 cases of cerebral palsy. *Am. J. Phys. Med.,* 38:180–187 (1959).

Honzik, M.P. Value and limitations of infant tests: An overview, in Lewis, M. (ed.), *Origins of Intelligence.* New York: Plenum Press, p. 59–95 (1976).

Hunt, J. Environmental risk in fetal and neonatal life and measured intelligence, in Lewis, M. (ed.), *Origins of Intelligence: Infancy and early childhood.* New York: Plenum Press, p. 223–258 (1976).

Kagan, J. *Change and continuity in infancy.* New York: Wiley (1971).

Kagan, J., Kearsley, R. and Zelazo, P. *Infancy: Its place in human development.* Cambridge, Mass.: Harvard University Press (1978).

Kearsley, R. Iatrogenic retardation: A syndrome of learned incompetence, in Kearsley, R. and Sigel, I. (eds.), *Infants at risk: Assessment of cognitive functioning.* Hillsdale, N.J.: L. Erlbaum Associates, Inc., p. 153–180 (1979).

Konner, M. Newborn walking: Additional data. *Science,* 178:307 (1973).

Konner, M. Maternal care, infant behavior, and development among the Kalahari Desert San, in Lee, R.B. and DeVore, I. (eds.), *Kalahari hunter-gatherers.* Cambridge, Mass.: Harvard University Press (1977).

Kopp, C.D. and Shaperman, J. Cognitive development in the absence of object manipulation during infancy. *Develop. Psychol.,* 9:430 (1973).

Lewis, M. Individual differences in the measurement of early cognitive growth, in Hellmuth, J. (ed.), *Exceptional Infant,* Vol. 2. Bainbridge Island, Washington: Bruner, Mazel, Inc. (1971).

Lewis, M. (ed) *Origins of Intelligence.* New York: Plenum Press (1976).

Lewis, M. and Goldberg, S. The acquisition and violation of expectancy: An experimental paradigm. *J. Exper. Child Psychol.,* 7:70–80 (1969).

Lewis, M. and McGurk, H. Evaluation of infant intelligence. *Science,* 178:1174–1177 (1972).

McCall, R.B. New directions in the psychological assessment of infants. *Proceedings of the Royal Society of Medicine,* 64:465–467 (1971).

McCall, R.B., Appelbaum, M.L. and Hogarty, P.S. Developmental changes in mental performance. *Monographs of the Society for Research in Child Development,* 38:3, Whole No. 150 (1973).

McCall, R.B., Eichorn, D.H. and Hogarty, P.S. Transitions in early mental development. *Monographs of the Society for Research in Child Development,* 42:Serial No. 171 (1977).

McCall, R.B. and Melson, W.H. Attention in infants as a function of magnitude of discrepancy and habituation rate. *Psychonomic Science,* 17:317–319 (1969).

McDonough, S.C. and Cohen, L.B. Habituation and perceptual-cognitive development in cerebral palsy infants. Paper presented at the Second Meeting of the International Conference for Infant Studies, New Haven, Connecticut, April (1980).

Miranda, S.B. and Fantz, R.L. Recognition memory in Down's Syndrome and normal infants. *Child Devel.,* 45:651–660 (1974).

Miranda, S., Hack, M., Fantz, R., Fanaroff, A. and Klaus, M. Neonatal pattern vision: A predictor of future mental performance? *Pediatrics,* 91:642–647 (1977).

Nicolich, L. Beyond sensorimotor intelligence: Assessment of symbolic maturity through analysis of pretend play. *Merrill-Palmer Quarterly,* 23:89–99 (1977).

Piaget, J. *The origins of intelligence in children.* New York: International University Press (1952). (French edition, 1936.)

Piaget, J. *Play, dreams, and imitation in childhood.* New York: Norton (1962).

Rovee, C.D. and Rovee, A.T. Conjugate reinforcement of infant exploratory behavior. *J. Exper. Child Psychol.,* 8:33–39 (1969).

Solomons, G. and Solomons, H. Motor development in Yucatecan infants. *Develop. Med. and Child Neurol.,* 17:41–46 (1975).

Stott, L.H. and Ball, R.S. Infant and preschool mental tests: Review and evaluation. *Monographs of the Society for Research in Child Development,* 30:Serial No. 101 (1965).

Super, C. Environmental effects on motor development: The case of African infant precocity. *Develop. Med. and Child Neurol.,* 18:561–567 (1976).

Terman, L.M. and Merrill, M.A. *Stanford-Binet Intelligence Scale: Manual for the third revision Form L-M.* Boston: Houghton, Mifflin Co. (1973).

Ungerer, J., Brody, L. and Zelazo, P. Long-term memory for speech in the newborn. *Infant Behav. and Devel.,* 1:177–186 (1978).

Ungerer, J., Zelazo, P., Kearsley, R. and O'Leary, K. Developmental changes in the use of representational mediums by 18 to 34-month-old children during play. Paper presented at the Biennial Meetings of the Society for Research in Child Development, San Francisco, March 16 (1979).

Watson, M.W. and Fischer, K.W. A developmental sequence of agent use in late infancy. *Child Devel.,* 48:828–835 (1977).

Willerman, L. and Fiedler, M.F. Infant performance and intellectual precocity. *Child Devel.,* 45:483–486 (1974).

Wilson, R.S. Twins: Early mental development. *Science,* 175:914–917 (1972).

Wilson, R.S. and Harpring, E.B. Mental and motor development in infant twins. *Develop. Psychol.,* 7:277–287 (1972).

Zelazo, P.R. Smiling and vocalizing: A cognitive emphasis. *Merrill-Palmer Quarterly,* 18: 349–365 (1972).

Zelazo, P.R. The year-old infant: a period of major cognitive change. Paper presented at the Conference on Dips in Learning and Development Curves, St. Paul de Vence, France, March 24–28 (1975).

Zelazo, P.R. Comments on genetic determinants of infant development: An overstated case, in Lipsitt, L. (ed.), *Developmental psychobiology: The significance of infancy.* Hillsdale, N.J.: L. Erlbaum Associates, Inc. (1976a).

Zelazo, P.R. From reflexive to instrumental behavior, in Lipsitt, L. (ed.), *Developmental psychobiology: The significance of infancy.* Hillsdale, N.J.: L. Erlbaum Associates, Inc. (1976b).

Zelazo, P.R. Reactivity to perceptual-cognitive events: Application for infant assessment, in Kearsley, R.B. and Sigel, I. (eds.), *Infants at risk: The assessment of cognitive functioning.* Hillsdale, N.J.: L. Erlbaum Associates, Inc., p. 49–83 (1979).

Zelazo, P.R., Kagan, J. and Hartmann, R. Excitement and boredom as determinants of vocalization in infants. *J. Genet. Psychol.,* 126:107–117 (1975).

Zelazo, P.R. and Kearsley, R.B. The emergence of functional play in infants: Evidence for a major cognitive transition. *J. Appl. Devel. Psychol.,* 1:95–117 (1980).

Zelazo, P.R. and Kearsley, R.B. Recognition changes to visual sequences in 2 and 3 year-olds: Evidence for increasing speed of processing. In preparation (1980b).

Zelazo, P.R., Kearsley, R.B. and Ungerer, J. *Learning to Speak: A Manual to Aid the Acquisition of Speech.* Boston: Center for Behavioral Pediatrics and Infant Development (1979).

Zelazo, P.R., Zelazo, N.A. and Kolb, S. Walking in the newborn. *Science,* p. 314–315 (1972).

Zelazo, P.R., Zelazo, N.A. and Kolb, S. Newborn walking. *Science,* p. 1058–1059 (1972).

16

Effects of Educational Intervention Programs on the Cognitive Development of Young Children

DONALD J. STEDMAN

Nearly 50 years after the first systematic studies of the effects of educational programs on the intellectual development of young children there is still debate on whether such programs are useful. For the most part, the argument has narrowed to the preschool population, especially the toddler group, and to children known to be developmentally disabled.

Early stimulation programs to *prevent* borderline mental retardation and school failure are based on the assumption that infant development, particularly intellectual development, is subject to environmental influences. The potential efficacy of such programs is not jeopardized by the fact that intellectual development, like most human traits, is also the subject of substantial genetic influences. Indeed, a fundamental principle of modern genetics holds that human traits are influenced by both environmental and genetic factors. Even the most radical estimates of heritability for human intelligence leave some room for environmental variation, thus suggesting that intelligence can be changed to some degree by environmental manipulation.

That intelligence can be influenced by carefully planned environmental manipulation seems strongly supported by studies reported thus far. This finding is of particular importance for children believed to be at risk for subnormal development and school failure. Children from home environments unsuited to the type of intellectual development measured by IQ tests and school achievement tests may fail to develop adequately. Viewed from this perspective, infant stimulation programs do not attempt to stimulate intellectual growth beyond some expected mean level of performance; rather, they attempt to *prevent declines* in intellectual growth during infancy and the preschool period. A key and frequently stated assumption of stimulation programs is that early intervention is necessary to *prevent the decline* in intellectual growth attributable to environments that fail to support development adequately.

The Concept of Risk

The logic of stimulation programs depends on the ability to predict which children are likely to fall victim to subnormal intellectual development. Even accepting the notion that genes specify a fairly broad range of phenotypic outcomes, for a large group of children in our society the natural environment will not adequately support the development of intelligence. Stimulation programs attempt to identify these children early and intervene to modify their deleterious environments. To do this it is necessary to identify variables that will allow prediction of which children will manifest such declines in IQ.

In general, risk is a probabilistic concept referring to an empirically established relationship between two variables such that knowledge about one variable improves predictions about the other. Thus, a mother carrying the gene for Huntington's chorea is "at risk" for producing a baby with the symptoms of this condition; pregnant women over 40 are at risk for delivering a baby with Down's syndrome. Similarly, a mother living in poverty, and particularly with an IQ less than 80, may rear children at risk for subnormal mental development and school failure. Children identified for this type of risk are variously labeled as sociocultural or cultural-familial mentally retarded.

Risk, then, is essentially a statistical concept. Further, the particular family history, economic, psychological or demographic variables used to determine who is at risk and for what condition should not be interpreted etiologically. This is particularly true with regard to predicting retardation associated with poverty. Poverty provides information useful for predicting behavior but in itself is far too general to explain the behavior. Rather, as we shall see, it is more likely that poverty is correlated with other variables, such as maternal child-rearing practices, that are more helpful in explaining the predicted developmental outcome.

Regardless of academic perspective research concerning the effects of poverty on infants and children has produced a fundamental point of agreement—that infants from poverty environments are at a disadvantage from the beginning, and that this disadvantage is associated with social factors in the family that begin their impact on the infant's intellectual development very early in life.

During the 1960s the relationship between poverty and intellectual development prompted a number of investigators to design and implement two general types of programs intended to ameliorate the effects of poverty environments. The first type was variously referred to as day care, center care, preschool or preprimary education. Though these programs varied widely in philosophy, objectives, materials, curriculum and teacher behavior, they were similar in that children were removed from their homes and brought to a central location to receive the types of stimulation thought to promote intellectual growth. Typically, children began these programs at age three or four. Removal from the home was more than an incidental feature of such programs since their basic assumption was that poverty children were not adequately stimulated at home.

The second type of program attempted to influence directly the relationship between lower SES mothers and their children. These programs either brought mothers to a central location for training or went directly into the home to teach mothers techniques for interacting with their child.

Before reviewing selected examples of these programs, we need to make two points. First, there has seldom been an absolute separation between day care programs and home programs that attempt to use mothers as the primary instrument of stimulation. Most day care programs, including those for normal children and nearly all those supported by federal funds, require or encourage parental involvement. Parents serve as members of advisory committees, participate in curriculum decisions, visit the classrooms, act as teacher aides or implement part of the curriculum in their homes. The current view seems to be that parents, including parents living in poverty, are an essential part of the intervention program, and program planners miss an important opportunity if they fail to involve parents in the child's education. Nonetheless, it is useful to distinguish between those programs that administer their curriculum primarily outside the home with a trained staff of teachers and those that train mothers to administer the curriculum at home.

Second, the objectives of early stimulation programs are not confined to the intellectual domain. Edward Zigler has argued this point quite forcefully regarding Head Start, saying,

> "... this preschool program was not mounted in hopes of dramatically raising IQ scores. ... Rather, the creators of Head Start hoped to bring about greater social competence in disadvantaged children."

Zigler is probably correct. Indeed, his distinction between intelligence and social competence is similar to that of the American Association on Mental Deficiency between intelligence and adaptive behavior. The point of this distinction is that human development consists of more than intellectual growth. Human traits and behaviors such as sharing, flexibility, cooperation, honesty, persistence and creativity are worthy goals for intervention programs in their own right. Further, these traits, no less than intelligence, can and do have a substantial effect on a child's progress in the public schools and his ability to lead a productive and satisfying life as an adult. Zigler is also correct in his claim that nurturing these traits and behaviors has always been an objective of stimulation programs. The problem has been that such traits and behaviors are extremely difficult to measure. Nevertheless, since recent work has demonstrated that evaluating these traits is possible, we can probably expect further refinements in this measurement.

Summary of IQ Data from Stimulation Programs

In a recent issue of *Pediatric Annals,* Haskins, Finkelstein and I described the effects of day care and home stimulation programs on intellectual development as well as the effect of such programs on nonintellectual development and health.

The data from programs reviewed in the article can be summarized in the following four points:

First, there appears to be a relationship between poverty and borderline mental retardation and school failure. This relationship is probably stronger for children of poverty if their mother's IQ is less than 80. Although poverty is certainly no explanation for delayed intellectual growth, it probably correlates with a number of factors present in, or absent from, the child's environment during infancy and the preschool period. One of these seems to be the absence of appropriate stimulation from the mother during preschool years. Whatever may be responsible for the relationship between poverty and subnormal intellectual growth, prediction of IQ growth may be based on information about socioeconomic status and maternal IQ. As a result, infants born into these environments may be considered at risk for borderline mental retardation and subsequent school failure.

Second, carefully designed and implemented infancy and preschool stimulation programs, whether conducted primarily in day care centers or in the home by mothers, do maintain normal or near-normal intellectual growth in children of poverty. These programs are more effective if initiated early in the infant's life, perhaps during the first or second year, though this conclusion is not yet certain.

Third, there is some evidence that training mothers to implement the curriculum produces longer lasting IQ gains in children. The pioneering work by Gordon, the early work of Levenstein and current studies by Ramey and others at the University of North Carolina support this conclusion, with recent modifications reported from Levenstein's program. To the extent that this type of program produces IQ gains, the critical activity seems to be verbal interaction between mother and child in the context of a challenging task.

Fourth, all types of early stimulation programs have difficulty producing gains in IQ that last after children enter the public schools. However, extensive school achievement data have not yet been reported by the Milwaukee and Carolina projects, both of which have enrolled their children in stimulation programs since shortly after birth.

In general, then, early stimulation programs can sustain normal intellectual development during the preschool years but appear to have greater difficulty insuring adequate intellectual development and academic achievement once children reach the public schools. On the other hand, the objectives of stimulation programs include the nurturing of traits other than intelligence. Let us turn our attention to these nonintellectual objectives, especially to the process of motivation and its relation to the social environment and the continuing capacity to learn.

A Summary of the Results
of Educational Intervention Programs

A close examination of more than 40 longitudinal intervention research programs for high-risk children included the following major findings:

(1) It has been demonstrated without much doubt that *how a child is raised* and *the environment into which he is born* have a major impact on what he will become.

(2) Factors such as race and sex do *not* appear to be related to the child's ability to profit from intervention programs.

(3) The family's methods of establishing *social roles* leave little doubt that early family environment (parental language styles, attitudes toward achievement, parental involvement and concern for the child) have a significant impact on the child's development before he reaches his second birthday.

(4) Where families are so disorganized that they cannot supply a supportive environment, an intensive *external* supportive environment may contribute to the child's development.

(5) The effects of a stimulating or depriving environment appear to be most powerful in the early years of childhood when the most rapid growth and development take place. As the primary locus of the child during this time is the home, *home-based* intervention programs or one-to-one teacher-child stimulation activities appear to be the most appropriate and effective.

(6) There is evidence that the effects of early intervention programs for children are strengthened by the involvement of the child's *parents*.

(7) It is only possible to describe in *general* terms the training conditions that handicap a child or lead to a child's success.

(8) The child's socioeconomic status and entry IQ level bear an *uncertain* relationship to his ability to profit from intervention. Design problems and the current state of the art in measurement render the effect of these factors difficult to determine.

(9) Where access to children can be gained in the early years, preferably during the language emergent years (one to two years of age), intervention programs will be *more* effective than those begun later.

(10) Between the ages of four and six a *systematic organized* program can contribute significantly to a child's social and intellectual development.

(11) The primary effects of intervention programs appear to last only so long as the child *remains* in the intervention program. They appear to last longer in home training studies and "wash out" sooner in school programs.

(12) Follow-up studies of children in intervention programs suggest that initial gains are no longer measurable. This is partially so because we cannot determine at this point whether it is due to program failure, to problems of measurement, to inadequate criterion measures or to the later interfering effects of other competing environments such as the home and school.

(13) The quality and motivation of the staff are *directly* related to the program's success and therefore are prime factors in determining the extent to which a program is exportable or replicable.

Some findings are worthy of special note since they address frequently asked but seldom answered questions of importance to researchers and educational practitioners:

(1) **In the successful programs gains occur regardless of age of entry.** The starting age of children placed in intervention programs ranged from a few months of age to five or six years. At least one study reported that children who enter learning-to-learn programs at age four make gains of nearly 20 IQ points which are maintained during the following two years. Children who enter at age five make smaller gains for each of the two years (nine points the first year and seven points the second year). Although these results suggest differential gains as a function of age of entry, they do not answer whether gains would be sustained after the first year in the absence of such a program.

However, data from another project indicate that children who made gains in the project when they entered did not lose them as long as they remained in the program. The data do not strongly support any one year as more preferred to realize gains in intellectual growth. Hence, the general conclusion must be that programs have been effective with all ages, and one cannot specifically support the advantages for work at any one year versus another. None of the studies reviewed supports a well-defined critical period as a preference for preschool or early childhood intervention. Essentially, programs can be designed that will work effectively with a wide age range. A comprehensive review of intervention programs in 1970 suggested that vulnerability to adverse influences at certain ages does not necessarily imply a time when children are especially sensitive to treatment. This study supported the contention that, based on current knowledge, intervention can be justified throughout the period of early development and possibly beyond.

(2) **In successful programs gains occur regardless of sex.** Studies have reported that girls have higher initial IQs than boys, while also observing that the sex of child was not related to gain scores. These findings are supported in general by other investigators, many of whom do not separate IQ scores by sex when reporting gains because of the lack of differences.

(3) **In successful programs gains occur regardless of race.** Studies again report that although whites enter with higher initial IQ scores race is not a significant variable in considering gain scores.

(4) **Differential gains in IQ scores occur as a function of the entering or initial IQ score, the program intensity and the length of time a child is in the program.** In general, the lower the initial IQ, the greater the gain in IQ in the intervention program; the more intense the program, the greater gain; the longer a child is in a program, the more likely he is to have a higher IQ gain. Finally, the interaction between program intensity and duration contributes to differential gains. Some researchers, for example, Bronfenbrenner, attribute the high initial gains to the phenomenon of regression to the mean and characterize them as being inflated for that reason.

(5) **In successful programs gains occur regardless of approach but some programs appear to be better than others.** The success of programs is apparently due to a higher degree of *structure*. The more structure, the greater the gain in IQ of participating children. A large-scale comparison among programs has been conducted using four groups (regular nursery school, children from low-income families in middle-class nursery groups, Montessori or perceptual motor skill groups and an experimental group with a highly structured format). When scores on the Stanford-Binet were compared, the experimental group (the structured program) was seen to have the largest gains.

Critical Review

There are a number of cautions which emerge from any review of research and development activity in this area.

(1) Many projects use samples too small to use the results in massive intervention programs.

(2) There is insufficient research in the area to date. After 20 years the number of well-designed and well-executed studies is still less than 50.

(3) Most studies do not involve the children in the intervention program for a time sufficient to permit long-term change or an adequate assessment of the program.

(4) Insufficient attention is being paid to the effects of combinations of children, handicapped and nonhandicapped, to improve the learning environment in which the intervention program is taking place.

(5) The current measures available to assess change in children as a result of intervention programs are inadequate in number and quality.

(6) The low utility and low reliability of pretest scores from high-risk children, caused by meager experience with testing or inadequate evaluation, may lead us to infer greater gains from posttest scores than are warranted.

(7) There is increasing doubt as to the value of certain critical periods; therefore, the extent to which we can continue to emphasize only one period during which we can expect positive outcomes of early intervention activities is questionable.

(8) Programs do not meet individual needs. There is instead a homogeneity of treatment across heterogeneous groups with little regard for social class, IQ level, sex, minority group or other critical feature.

(9) There are often significant cultural differences among minority and ethnic groups that may elicit exaggerated responses from the children in either direction. Also, in many cases extreme value differences between subjects and their families and the project staff may lead to inadequate or inappropriate intervention program components and results.

(10) Program goals are often too narrow and constricted. There is more to development than IQ.

(11) Certain gains or responses to the intervention activities are related to the motivation of the parents to encourage and assist their child's participation in the program. This factor is not often considered as a part of what accounts for intervention programs' success.

(12) There are several logistical problems in connection with both the conduct of longitudinal studies and the development of exportable components of intervention programs.

(13) There are insufficient replications of special studies which show positive results.

(14) The cost of longitudinal research has resulted in too few comprehensive studies, including health, education, social and parent program aspects.

A number of obstacles and special problems in conducting studies appears to add to the difficulty of making definitive statements, based on research, about what determines a program's effectiveness and credibility.

(1) **Inadequate control groups**: Given the problem of adequately describing the population, it is seldom possible to determine the adequacy of the control group. Rarely are children selected from the same population pool and randomly assigned to treatment groups.

(2) **Treatment drift**: Once an evaluation model is adopted, decisions are made to change the program according to information gathered. This is a highly acceptable practice in the remediation of children's deficiencies. However, as this occurs, the intervention program is no longer conducted as originally described. The refinements of longitudinal study call forth new strategies, thus markedly changing the original procedures. Frequently, the change is not described in the write-up.

(3) **Press to do well**: Most innovators are funded to demonstrate the effectiveness of a given idea or program. They are expected to succeed, and the program is constantly revised and modified based on the child's performance.

(4) **Educator effect**: Evidence indicates that the educator, not the program, may be the crucial variable in creating change and that the method or program adopted interacts with the stylistic treatment of the educator. The factors relative to the change are highly idiosyncratic and difficult to control. One researcher has identified four major clusters based on control and expressions of warmth. Another researcher has pursued other personality factors of the teacher that influence pupil change. Yet another has identified planning and supervision as more important to the program than the curriculum components themselves. In essence, how you do something may be more important than what you do.

(5) **Teachers reach criterion performance**: Frequently, a program is developed by an innovator who then hires a staff to conduct it. In the author's experience it frequently takes as long as two to three years before the staff can conduct the program as originally conceived. Massive in-service efforts are needed in all intervention programs with frequent supervision and evaluation of teacher performance with replacement of those unable to reach criterion performance.

(6) **Ethics with human subjects**: In dealing with human subjects the innovator cannot manipulate the research environment unless he is sure he will not damage the child in any way. This ethical "restriction" is necessary and limits the degree of manipulation the innovator can apply. For example, does one remove children from their mothers in order to work intensively with them?

(7) **Continuity of staffing**: As with life-span research projects, it is difficult for a principal investigator to commit himself over his own life span. If he leaves the project, there may be a shift in focus or interest when a new investi-

gator takes over. Also to be considered are staff turnover and changes in staff training or staff development activities, especially in university-based programs where graduate students are used extensively.

(8) **Testing procedures**: As with life-span research projects, testing schedules, instrument revision and discontinuity and low correlation between tests contribute problems in conducting the project as well as in interpreting data.

(9) **Data processing**: The masses of data that can accumulate in longitudinal studies present problems both of data processing and difficulties in deciding which data to process. This is especially true for the new researcher.

(10) **Environmental changes**: Children in longitudinal studies are often influenced by major shifts in the community or neighborhood environment which may directly influence the outcome of the intervention activities. Shifts in cultural mores, social attitudes and values may have similar effects.

(11) **Attrition**: While techniques are available to deal with subject attrition, the process is expensive and often requires resources not provided in the intervention programs. It is essential that large subject samples be acquired and maintained over a long period of time.

Often, interpreting the results of well-designed and conducted studies constitutes a major task in itself.

(1) **Nature of the population**: In working with high-risk youngsters the set of variables associated is multiple and often incomparable. For example, the concept of being "culturally deprived," used by different research workers, includes: income level, racial differences, inadequate diet, protein deficiency, punitive child-rearing practices, low language stimulation, isolation, oppression, high disease rates and alcoholism, among others. It often is assumed that all of these factors contribute the same degree of influence. Clearly, dealing effectively with high-risk populations is not developed to the point at which the children can be described with the precision needed to replicate a study. In addition, children who live in poverty are still found in markedly different environments. For example, the migrant worker's child and the children of the inner city dweller or the sharecropper all have markedly different life experiences.

(2) **Problems of program description**: One of the major problems in interpreting intervention programs is that often the program descriptions are not sufficiently detailed to understand what the innovator did. Global terms are frequently used that make it difficult either to replicate or to isolate the variables that were related to the treatment. For example, a study of adopted versus nonadopted children may not adequately define the nature of the treatment; i.e., what happened in the homes that did not happen in the orphanages

to cause the results? Longitudinal intervention studies rarely describe all of the procedures undertaken in a program. To be fair, however, it is frequently impossible to describe exactly what was done. A major intervention program may have components that deal with classroom experiences, parent training, improved nutrition, medical screening and vision and hearing tests. Ascribing treatment success to any one variable is a tenuous practice.

(3) **Failure to develop appropriate instruments**: One of the major difficulties in conducting studies with children is specifying exactly what evaluation the innovator will be able to perform following the intervention. Many programs specify IQ scores as their objective. However, not only are IQ scores unreliable and invalid for most minority-group children, but they reflect traits related to school performance more than cognitive functioning. The appeal of the behaviorally oriented programs is their tendency to limit goals to observable behaviors. However, with this approach one is still left with the problem of defining the "internal processes" of the child and frequently minor and sometimes irrelevant behaviors.

Global measures of intelligence and achievement are inappropriate measures of program impact. Intelligence measures assume common cultural experiences, equal opportunity to learn and equal motivation to do well on the tests. For most minority-group children these assumptions cannot be met.

Achievement tests contain many items aimed at assessing reasoning ability rather than the skill under treatment. For example, as much as 50 per cent of the items on elementary school reading tests are inference problems rather than reading problems. Reading is learning a set of abstract arbitrary symbols and relating them to another set of spoken symbols. Children can relate words to print and learn that the printed word stands for the spoken word or for objects, but unless long trials of memorization, drill and practice are used, children do not understand the abstraction of graphemics until 10 to 12 years of age. Thus, many reading tests are misnamed; they would be more appropriately titled "reasoning from reading" tests.

(4) **Intuitive appeal of gains scores**: In spite of the work of Cronback, Thorndike and others demonstrating that gain scores are unrealiable, statistically indefensible and subject to great misinterpretation for individuals or groups, there still exists great pressure for programs to demonstrate effectiveness by measuring gains on the same instrument.

Measurement should not be concerned with change as reflected in gain scores but by performance of the desired behavior that defines the criterion performance. Criterion-referenced tests are difficult to construct unless the behaviors are readily observable. For example, it is easier to specify that as a result of the program children will be able to count to 10 or identify six primary colors than to specify that they will develop a positive self-concept and attitude toward others.

(5) **Inadequate or naive theory of human behavior**: Many longitudinal studies fail to conceptualize human learning and the processes of development. The results of these studies can easily be misinterpreted and attributed to dubious reasoning. Recent findings in developmental theory and learning have furnished massive evidence that the human organism is an impressive information processor from the moment of birth. However, many researchers still fail to recognize the infant's capacity to process information and continue to perceive him as a passive recipient, thereby attributing to their training procedures more power than is likely to be present. Equally, the innovator who works with the handicapped child frequently views all the child's lacks in terms of this handicap without taking into account his age and the normal stages of growth and development.

(6) **Retrospective data, time and cost**: Most retrospective data collected from teachers and parents bear little resemblance to the child's actual functioning. Their unreliability makes longitudinal studies all the more necessary. However, longitudinal studies require time and careful record-keeping. It may be 20 years before the effects of the intervention program can be fully measured. Longitudinal studies are costly ventures, although they may be the only means by which some questions can be answered.

(7) **Delayed effects**: Rarely do longitudinal studies measure delayed effects of treatment. For example, does the program introduced in kindergarten have any measurable effects on adolescent behavior? Rarely do school programs measure adult attitudes, voting and reading habits or other goals which were part of the school curriculum.

(8) **Narrow focus of the program**: Some longitudinal studies are so specialized and deal with such a narrow population that they cannot be replicated. For example, a program that provides a one-to-one teacher/pupil ratio for six hours a day, six days a week, with supporting psychological, medical and speech staff would be difficult to find in a regular school.

(9) **Sample problems**: The size and representativeness of the sample must be taken more seriously into account. Samples have generally been too small to allow for much generalization. The results of a program that also limits itself to a unique population have little applicability to other high-risk populations. Further, shrinkage of already small samples occurs over time and contributes to the lack of follow-up of results or effects.

(10) **The effect of continued assessment or observation**: The effects of continuous testing in long-term studies, including observer effects, can have an equal or perhaps greater effect on performance than some or all of the program components. In many programs the continuous assessment and the intervention

curriculum are confounded so as to prevent identification of which contributed to change. In some cases continuous assessment of control groups may contribute to equal change as compared with the experimental group, leading to an inability to measure the effect of the intervention program itself. In some cases researchers suggest that continuous assessment is equivalent to minimal intervention. Intervention studies are no less immune to the Hawthorne effect than any other study.

Summary

In the final analysis, even given the cautions, design problems and difficulties with data interpretation, we already know a great deal about the effectiveness of educational intervention. Generally, the effects are positive. A host of factors make education more or less effective for the individual child, including child variables, the choice of variables and the characteristics of the intervention program and the people delivering it.

More research is required in the field with carefully described curriculum components and the best child variable control possible, within the bounds of natural groupings of children. If there is a prime obstacle, it is lack of measurement tools for social, affective and interpersonal change as well as for academic gain. These measures will need to include observational techniques. Methods for coding and analyzing observational data lag far behind other methods in the social sciences.

Finally, the expensive, long-term, longitudinal study of development in children is still the best strategy for discovering environmental effects—either on cognitive or affective development. The major difficulty here is getting public or private resources to support these operations and having the patience to pursue this course while the short-term pressures for improving education persist.

Effects of Repeated Testing
on the Results of Intervention Programs

For a number of years investigators have been faced with explaining why their positive results—that is, experimental group gains over control group—were not due to "all that testing" that the experimental group subjects experienced. This was a criticism of my own comparative study of home-reared versus institution-reared infants with Down's syndrome conducted at Sonoma State Hospital nearly 20 years ago (Stedman and Eichorn, 1964).

Studies in which no post-test differences are noted between experimental and control groups are not sufficient to assert that the effects of continuous testing are not a factor in experimental group gains *or* a "booster" for control groups. A well-designed study was required to evaluate whether it was the continuous testing effects or the experimental program that provided the experience and stimulation. Such a design would also account for, or at least examine, the effect during testing of the presence of the mother or a surrogate.

I designed such a study and in 1976 conducted it with Ramey and Haskins at the Frank Porter Graham Child Development Center at the University of North Carolina at Chapel Hill. The design and results were as follows (Haskins *et al.*, 1978):

Infant intervention programs that evaluate their effectiveness by repeatedly testing infants with standardized tests may confound intervention effects with repeated-testing effects. Further, maternal participation in testing may increase infants' test scores, either directly, by giving infants practice with test-like items at home between test administrations, or indirectly, by helping infants adapt to the test setting. Thirty-five infants were tested at three-month intervals between four and 28 months of age with the Bayley Scales of Infant Development and at 31 months of age with the Stanford-Binet; 25 infants were tested with the Bayley at four months and the Stanford-Binet at 31 months. Mothers of some infants in each group participated in the testing process. Between-subjects analysis on the Stanford-Binet revealed no effects for repeated testing or maternal participation. Within-subjects analyses for repeatedly tested groups demonstrated that maternal presence during testing, but not repeated testing, was associated with significantly higher Bayley scores. It was concluded that maternal presence is a potent influence on Bayley performance, that repeated experience with the Bayley biased neither performance on another standardized test of development nor subsequent Bayley performance, and that infant intervention programs are not likely to confound their evaluation designs by testing infants repeatedly.

The primary question pursued in this experiment was whether infants tested repeatedly with a developmental test acquire test-taking skills that generalize to another test of development. Within the restraints imposed by the design of this experiment, the answer seems clear. For infants tested at three-month intervals between four and 28 months with the Bayley, there is no significant generalization to the Stanford-Binet. Thus, the Stanford-Binet will yield an estimate of children's intellectual development that is not biased by extensive previous experience with the Bayley. Stated more broadly, we found no evidence for general test sophistication in infants. In addition, we found that involving mothers in Bayley administration resulted in significantly better performance on the MDI.

This study was also designed to yield information about narrow test sophistication, i.e., about the effect of repeated experience with the Bayley on subsequent Bayley scores. A repeated-measures effect would have produced a positively sloped linear trend between four and 28 months. This trend, however, was not observed. For the MDI there were significant linear and quadratic changes with repeated testing, but these changes left infants in the two repeatedly tested groups with MDI scores at 28 months that were nearly equal to their scores at four months. Averaged across the two repeatedly tested groups, the four-month and 28-month MDI scores were 109.1 and 108.6. It appears that the Bayley MDI is quite resistant to the effects of repeated testing. Therefore, when used to assess intervention effects, the Bayley should yield scores that are unbiased by the effects of previous experience with it.

For the Bayley PDI, on the other hand, there was a significant and orderly decline of about 10 points between four and 28 months. This decline brought the average of both groups toward the mean of the standardization sample, leaving Group 1 with a mean of 105.6 and Group 3 with a mean of 101.7 at 28 months. The decline, then, may have constituted a regression toward the mean from initially inflated scores at four months of age. In any case, there was not an increase in PDI scores associated with repeated assessment and, thus, no evidence supporting narrow test sophistication.

The above findings seem somewhat at odds with results from previous studies of repeated-testing effects in older children. Researchers have long known that a single repeated test induces gains of four to six points (Cattell, 1931; Rugg and Colloton, 1921). Further, several studies have shown that repeated practice produces even more substantial gains in children (e.g., Vernon, 1952a, 1952b; Wiseman and Wrigley, 1953; Yates, 1953). The order of test score increases for practice effects is about 6 to 12 points, and most investigators have attributed these increases to "test sophistication."

If experiments with older children have consistently shown increases with repeated testing, why did the present experiment fail to find increased scores for repeatedly tested infants? Though a persuasive reason is not at hand, two tentative explanations are offered. First, items on the Bayley change substantially across the first three years of life. Because infants encounter many completely new items with each test administration, the effects of practice are minimized. Second, studies with older children imply that test score gains are attributable not simply to experience with specific items on a test but to experience with the general aspects of the test situation: familiarity with the test organization and procedure, listening to instructions, responding appropriately to the tester's demands. Older children may be better than infants at attending to and profiting from these aspects of experience.

Two practical conclusions pertinent to intervention programs can be drawn from this experiment. First, since repeated experience with the Bayley does not produce test-sophisticated infants in either the general or narrow sense, it follows that (a) previous experience with the Bayley should not bias intervention effects revealed by subsequent use of other standardized tests, and (b) use of the Bayley in within-subjects designs should indicate intervention effects unbiased by repeated testing effects. Second, since infants tested with their mothers present received significantly higher Bayley MDIs, intervention programs must carefully control this factor in both between- and within-subjects evaluations.

Early Identification Strategies

There are basically two approaches to tagging infants or preschoolers for special educational programs. The first is epidemiologic in style. The second is more individualized and predictive. Both approaches should be used when this nation ever gets around to screening its infants and toddlers for possible casualties of life.

Most researchers agree that educational intervention during the preschool years can result in improved intellectual performance for children who have received systematic educational programs when compared to those who have not. A major unresolved issue, however, is who needs these compensatory educational programs? Essentially, this is an issue of the epidemiology of school failure in the mildest form and of socioculturally determined mental retardation in the extreme case. Unfortunately, epidemiologic data reported in the literature have been insufficient to identify those individuals who without special assistance will become classified during the early school years as developmentally delayed.

Past approaches to the early prediction of intellectual and school performance have tended to fall into two major classes: predicting later performance from previous performance measures and predicting performance from demographic data and other characteristics known at birth.

The literature on the prediction of later developmental status, including school performance, from standardized tests of intellectual functioning administered during infancy has not, in general, been very encouraging. Bayley (1970) has summarized this point succinctly by stating:

> The findings of these early studies of mental growth in infants have been repeated sufficiently often so that it is now well established that test scores earned in the first year or two of life have relatively little predictive validity (in contrast to tests at school age or later), although they may have high validity as measures of children's cognitive ability at the time. (p1174)

The demographic approach to predicting school-age performance may represent a viable alternative to child-assessment procedures for early screening programs. Although socioeconomic status as a molar variable has been linked to mental development generally (e.g., Jensen, 1969), very few researchers have identified specific demographic or perinatal characteristics at birth that have been associated with mild mental retardation as measured during the school years using representative samples of the general population. For example, Smith *et al.* (1972) reported data from the Collaborative Child Development Study showing that prenatal, perinatal and postnatal information predicted developmental status at seven years of age; however, their sample was unrepresentative of the general population in that it contained only urban black children of low SES. Where specific predictive variables have been identified, the process of obtaining the data has prohibited their routine inclusion into screening programs. Heber *et al.* (1968), for example, have identified maternal IQ below 80 as important in predicting subaverage intellectual functioning in biologically "normal" children. This level of information, however, is not generally available for mothers and is expensive to collect on large samples.

If preschool compensatory education programs are to be implemented on a large scale, then relatively inexpensive, routinely collected and analyzed data will be necessary to determine the ongoing need for such services. A study designed by Dr. Ted Scurletis and me in 1975 and conducted in 1976-77 attempted to identify those children who were most likely to need special educational services at school age by using information that was routinely and systematically collected at birth (Ramey, Stedman, Borders-Patterson and Mengel, 1978). Every state now routinely collects information for birth certificates that meets minimum standards set by the federal government. Thus, if the information contained in these public records proves to be predictive of later school performance, a relatively simple and cost-effective system already exists to serve as a first-line monitoring and screening mechanism for intellectual and social development.

The study had two main purposes: (a) to ascertain the power of routinely collected birth information to predict developmental status of a representative sample of first-grade children who varied widely in ability, and (b) to determine which birth and demographic variables, if any, discriminate between children who are either "normal" or developmentally delayed at first grade.

Information available from birth certificates was used to predict the psychological and educational status of approximately 1,000 randomly sampled first-grade children. The purpose of the research was to explore the feasibility of using birth certificate information as a cost-effective mechanism to identify children who were likely to need special educational services at public school entry. Multiple-regression and discriminant-function analyses revealed the following factors to be important in predicting psychoeducational status: birth order, race, educational status of the mother, month prenatal care began, survivorship of older siblings and the child's legitimacy.

Several implications from this study are apparent. We found that information available on birth certificates can be used to predict educational and psychological status of first-grade children. For all of the first-graders taken as a whole in this sample, the most predictive characteristics of educational and psychological status were race and mother's educational level. These factors, for the group as a whole, seemed to be more important than the mother's biological history for predicting intelligence, achievement, visual-motor integration and teachers' ratings of classroom performance.

The results of comparing children who are at moderate risk for educational difficulty with those who are not at risk clearly implicate the importance of birth certificate information as an early screening and detection mechanism. If we restrict our generalization to those variables that significantly discriminate between the moderate- and low-risk children on each of the four variables, then the following variables seem particularly important as potential screening criteria: birth order, education of mother, birth weight, month prenatal care began, race and legitimacy.

On the average, the children who appeared to be most severely at risk for retarded development were third or later born siblings whose mother had a tenth grade or lower educational level, who herself had had a previous live birth now dead and who began care for the target child in the third month or later of pregnancy. The most severely at-risk children also tended to be black and illegitimate. That such obvious characteristics currently foretell children's educational and psychological status tells us nothing about the causal pathways whereby such molar variables are translated into direct influences upon children's development. Indeed, the kinds of analyses reported here cannot even demonstrate that the identified variables are *causally* related to child performance. They may merely be correlates of interactions among much more subtle and complex variables. Nevertheless, these analyses do demonstrate that it is possible to identify children at birth who, presumably for sociocultural reasons, are likely to need special services before or during grade school.

It would be inaccurate and unscientific to claim at this point that we have all the proof required to know exactly who is at risk, who is likely to profit from intervention programs, or who is not likely to gain from such programs.

However, there is overwhelming evidence, far surpassing the circumstantial, that educational intervention programs and environmental manipulation do prevent developmental retardation caused by environmental deprivations, do maintain initial skills over substantial periods of time and can reverse the injurious effects of social deprivation in terms of adaptive and academic objectives and expectations in our culture. To abandon pursuit of further study, to dampen application of the validated results of many programs, or to forestall educational intervention as a major tool in the prevention of mental retardation would be tantamount to immorality.

References

Bayley, N. Development of mental abilities, in Mussen, P.H. (ed.), *Carmichael's Manual of Child Psychology* (3d ed.). New York: John Wiley and Sons (1970).

Haskins, R., Finkelstein, N. and Stedman, D. Infant-stimulation programs and their effects. *Ped. Ann.*, 7:123–144 (1978).

Haskins, R., Ramey, C., Stedman, D., Blacher-Dixon, J. and Pierce, J. Effects of repeated assessment on standardized test performance by infants. *Am. J. Ment. Defic.*, Vol. 83, No. 3:233–239 (1978).

Heber, R., Dever, R. and Conry, J. The influence of environmental and genetic variables on intellectual development, in Prehm, H., Homerlynck, L. and Crosson, J. (eds.), *Behavioral Research in Mental Retardation*. Eugene: University of Oregon Press (1968).

Jensen, A.R. How much can we boost IQ and scholastic achievement? *Harvard Educational Review*, 39:1–123 (1969).

Ramey, C., Stedman, D., Borders-Patterson, A. and Mengel, W. Predicting school failure from information available at birth. *Am. J. Ment. Def.*, Vol. 82, No. 6:525–534 (1978).

Ramey, C., Farran, D. and Campbell, F. Predicting IQ from mother-child interactions. *Child Devel.*, 50:804–814 (1979).

Ramey, C. and Campbell, F. Educational intervention for children at risk for mild retardation: A longitudinal analysis, in P. Mittler (ed.), *Frontiers of Knowledge in Mental Retardation* (vol. 1). Baltimore: University Park Press (1981).

Ramey, C. and Haskins, R. The modification of intelligence through early experience. *Intelligence*, 5:5–19 (1981).

Smith, A.C., Flick, G.L., Ferriss, G.S. and Sellmann, A.H. Prediction of developmental outcome at seven years from prenatal, perinatal and postnatal events. *Child Devel.*, 43: 495–507 (1972).

Stedman, D. and Eichorn, D. A comparative study of growth and development trends of institutionalized and noninstitutionalized mongoloid infants. *Am. J. Ment. Defic.*, 69:391–400 (1964).

Stedman, D., Anastasiow, N., Dokecki, P., Gordon, I. and Parker, R. *How can effective early intervention programs be delivered to potentially retarded children?* DHEW Report OS-72-205, USGPO, October (1972).

Stedman, D. Important considerations in the review and evaluation of educational intervention programs. *Viewpoints*, Bulletin of the School of Education, Indiana University, Vol. 52, No. 4, July (1976).

17

The Effects of Educational Intervention on Cognitive Development

ALICE H. HAYDEN

On the premise that there is no more natural association than that between pediatricians and early childhood educators, this chapter will address several issues that have special relevance for both. First, with emphasis on the role of the pediatrician, we will discuss the children we believe such early education programs should serve and consider how to find them more reliably and work together to help them. Second, we will consider the essential components of the programs devised for our target population and touch on some of the interdisciplinary collaboration that is not only possible but beneficial in these programs. Third, with the above considerations in mind, we will review the experience of one student in our program, emphasizing what is best in classroom-based management and the pediatrician's role. Finally, after this discussion of what we might call "ideal" strategies, we will suggest some measures to ensure that we provide services to many more children who need but at present do not receive them.

Who Should be Served in Early Intervention Programs?

If intervention is to be effective, it should be undertaken as early in life as possible. Therefore services may have to be provided for children who are only suspected of having impairments as well as for those who have been definitively diagnosed (Haskins, Finkelstein and Stedman, 1978).

One of the admissions we must make is that our assessment procedures, while getting better, are not infallible. We need to establish a bias toward inclusiveness and agree that we will tolerate a fair proportion of false-positives in order to accommodate all infants and young children who do in fact warrant our attention.

Clearly, some children can be identified at birth or even before as being "at risk" and needing special services, possibly for a lifetime. Children with the more subtle handicaps, some of which can be "definitively diagnosed" only at a later age (often because they are expressed as difficulties in school) frequently slip through the net. What is necessary in these cases is the kind of systematic, careful observation *over time* that the concerted efforts of clinicians, parents and teachers can provide as they follow the child's developmental progress, in the context of normal development. Such ongoing observation also permits us to see important changes. For example, Parmelee and colleagues have developed a "cumulative risk" scoring procedure for infants that calls for evaluations in the neonatal period, at three and four months and then at eight and nine months. They reported (1976) that of 39 infants followed, "22 would have been considered as high risk on the basis of their newborn score and 17 considered at low risk. However, at 9 months, on the basis of the cumulative risk score on all 14 tests, only 11 were still at high risk and 28 were at low risk. This is consistent with these authors' previous clinical experience and with reported observations of others that infants often improve during the first year of life." Only through careful observation can we reliably sort and identify the children who need special services. Further, what we learn from such observation will structure the services provided. For the benefit of the children and their families, early childhood educators urge pediatricians and other clinicians to over-refer, to make sure that *any* infant or child whose biological or environmental conditions suggest "risk" for impaired development is referred to an intervention program.

The Advantages of Over-Referral

The premature infant who survives idiopathic respiratory distress syndrome and other complications, the small-for-dates infant, the infant whose physical examination fits a recognizable syndrome, the infant who recovers from meningitis, the infant born with CNS malformations—all of these very young children pose a similar problem today in the practice of comprehensive pediatrics. First, there is no single assessment tool to predict the developmental potential of any of them. Second, these children will remain in their communities year after year, with or without individual intervention programs. Recognizing the need for early referral and identifying the classroom as a resource for these infants and parents has the following implications for the pediatrician:

(1) Diagnosis of developmental delay is often not possible prior to referral; identifying the child as being at risk is sufficient. This allows the physician to tell parents that the developmental prognosis for their infant is not known but that a continuous intervention program is the place to discover how the child learns and to find out more about that prognosis.

(2) Early referral emphasizes the importance of the local community-based intervention, which provides the continuity as well as specific diagnosis and intervention so essential for successful management.

(3) The classroom provides the base from which remote referral can be most judiciously utilized—for example, birth defects clinics and regional child development centers.

(4) Since teaching parents to observe, record and intervene at home is a critical component of most early intervention programs, even if the infant "graduates" or develops normally, the secondary gain by parents is extremely rewarding. In fact, greater attention to needs of parents is a major responsibility of intervention programs. It is sobering to realize that without their expressions of concern and their demands for services and programs over the years we would not have made the advances in educational programs now available.

Are There Dangers In Such an Approach?

Two concerns that warrant mention are the dangers of inappropriate labelling and the possibility of causing distress to parents. Historically, labels have always had some usefulness as a means of organizing services for certain children. Funding has often been built around the needs of specific populations and through the efforts of parents and other advocates (for example, the March of Dimes or the Cystic Fibrosis Foundation). Labels have also been used to organize classes in schools (classes for the hearing impaired, the deaf, the blind or visually impaired, for example). But we are moving away from the use of inappropriate labels these days, and with the mandate of P.L. 94-142 to include *all* handicapped children in a free, appropriate education, there is even less "organizational" need for labels.

Some labels do more harm than good because they tend to put children into boxes without suggesting treatment possibilities. Some labels, such as Trainable Mentally Retarded and even Educable Mentally Retarded, seem out of tune with the intent of P.L. 94-142 and frequently convey notions of what a child can or cannot do as reflected by earlier textbook definitions. A label may not reflect secondary or "associated" handicapping conditions that may affect a child's behavior and learning.

There is no substitute for ongoing, systematic observation of a child's developmental progress with what it can suggest in terms of intervention. If a child is severely handicapped, the clinician and teachers have an obligation to explain the condition to parents or other guardians. If the child is less handicapped but is being referred because of "risk" factors or other reasons, those reasons must also be explained, and they can be discussed in the context of developmental progress, without labels. Another side of the coin is that parents sometimes are comforted by having a name to attach to the child's condition; "explaining" a handicapped child by saying that he has one syndrome or another is often easier than having to answer distressing questions from friends or relatives. Using the name of the condition is one thing; using a label ("severely emotionally disturbed") is another.

The other potential danger, alarming or distressing parents, is almost a nondanger. For many years, some handicapped children were almost automatically referred to institutions by pediatricians, teachers and other experts precisely to avoid distressing their families. Fortunately, we have come a long way from those dark ages. Our experience tells us now that parents are already alarmed and under extreme stress as they try to care for their handicapped children. Referring families to programs that can alleviate that stress by helping them teach their children more effectively, by augmenting their parenting skills, and by working *with* them to promote the child's development is better than offering kind words and no help. Also, parents of children with the more subtle handicaps are often the first to suspect that something is wrong. Through their immediate contact with the child—and their opportunities for seeing him in situations that pediatricians and teachers rarely see—they often detect warning signals that cause alarm. For example, Shah and Wong recently (1979) published an article on failures to detect hearing impairment in preschool children, citing example after example of parents' first noticing a problem and being falsely reassured by clinicians that nothing was wrong. We must respond to these concerns. Taking a "wait and see" approach or dismissing parents' concerns does nothing to reduce anxiety and can often delay needed intervention. Referrals for specialized diagnosis should be made immediately. In addition, referral to a program where the child's progress can be monitored by trained, experienced observers *can* reduce parents' anxiety: if such monitoring detects a condition warranting treatment, the treatment can begin; if the warning signals turn out to be a false alarm, so much the better.

Diagnostic Considerations

Given our bias for inclusiveness, how should the pediatrician proceed? We know that there may be literally thousands of conditions that can be considered "risk" factors in a child's development. For example, there are over 500 isolated anomalies associated with mental retardation (Bergsma, 1973) and at least 220 recognizable patterns of malformation (Smith, 1976). Not all of these are compatible with survival beyond the newborn period; some are more impairing than others. Most occur so rarely that it is unlikely for a clinician outside a tertiary care facility to see more than a small percentage of them in a career. Some of the risk factors much more likely to be seen are those less well-defined but recognized factors associated with socioeconomic circumstances: poverty, parents' limited education, malnutrition. Conditions of major concern because of their outcome are caused by assaults to the fetus, by agents such as alcohol, tobacco, drugs, or by premature birth, or by demographic factors such as the mother's age (Smith, 1979).

Faced with the enormous array of possible diagnostic indicators, we have tried to sort and organize our response to them. The late David Smith, a noted pediatrician at the University of Washington, suggested a useful strategy for diagnosing the child with mental deficiency (Smith, 1975). The diagnosis begins with a careful history (including family genetic and other factors, sociocultural, prenatal, perinatal and postnatal information), and a thorough physical examination, particularly for major and minor nonCNS malformations. Afterward, the clinician can categorize the child's condition based on the probable timing of insult.

Under those disorders in the prenatal category (accounting for 44 per cent of the target population, according to Kaveggia, 1973) are single defects in brain morphogenesis (one-third) and multiple major and minor nonCNS malformations (two-thirds), of which 40 per cent are chromosomal abnormalities, 20 per cent are recognized syndromes and 40 per cent unknown patterns of malformation. In the perinatal category are birth-related insults to the brain through complications at birth or immediately after, e.g., hypoxemia, infections, disturbances of electrolyte balance. In the postnatal category are those conditions that are either expressions of an inborn metabolic error (e.g., PKU) or "slowing or deterioration of developmental progress with signs of CNS dysfunction." These can be caused by trauma, infection and other environmental factors. Smith also has a category of "unknowns" and a special group for disorders which fit several categories (such as hypothyroidism). He suggests that only after the history and physical examination are complete and the child's disorder defined should further laboratory or other tests be undertaken, though for many severely impaired children with more obvious diagnoses that is not necessary. Coleman provides a superb discussion of the rationale and elements of a history and thorough, systematic diagnostic examination of a neurologically handicapped infant (1979).

From the educator's point of view, and possibly the pediatrician's, we can make two general statements about the diagnostic information. First, knowing the etiology of a child's disorder is most useful when that diagnosis can tell us something about educational implications. To say *only* that a child has Down's syndrome, for instance, is to tell us primarily that there was a chromosomal accident at some point in his prenatal development. We would like to know more about the child's condition in the neonatal period, information about his health generally, about any "associated" handicaps, about his development up to the time of referral and any other data that would help us plan an appropriate program. Then, together we can begin to fill in the gaps about the child's capabilities and problems by a fine-focus review of his performance over time.

Second, etiologic information is useful when it can tell us about the array of insults the child is likely to have sustained, because these findings are important for educational programming. Syndromes by definition involve clusters of impairments, some more and some less likely to have educational impact. Knowing what these possibilities are (even though not all aspects of a syndrome have all the impairments or the same degree of impairment) is useful in planning an educational program, in setting priorities for the child based on the different problems, and in gathering the resources required to provide the necessary services.

The Need for Information Sharing

The educator looks to the pediatrician for a willingness to refer all "at-risk" and identifiably handicapped children to early intervention programs and for diagnostic information to help plan and evaluate an educational program. Further, pediatricians and early childhood educators need to exchange information as a means of *preventing* problems in the children they care for. Interestingly, a major foundation has recognized the need for pediatricians to receive more information on behavioral and developmental pediatrics and now funds several such residency programs (Sapir, 1977).

Ideally, an educational program for handicapped children must have the *ongoing* expertise of specialists from many disciplines. Educators rely on pediatricians for their critical skills as well as for specific information. For example, if a child is receiving medication, the teachers will need to know what it is, when it must be given, what effects it is likely to produce, and what its impact will be on the child's attentiveness in the classroom. Teachers in turn can share with the pediatrician their own observations about the child's response to the medication and its effects on his classroom behavior. Reviewing such data together, the teacher and pediatrician can decide about dosages and timing that will have *educational* impact. It may be a new concept for pediatricians to consider themselves as early childhood educators, but that is an important role for them.

The two disciplines must also communicate with parents, who can contribute much to their children's development in all areas. Professionals are often viewed as lacking compassion and understanding of parents' feelings and needs. We frequently assume that parents understand more than they do, that they are ready for the information when we are ready to share it and that all we have to do is "tell" the parents rather than sharing information with them and attempting to respond to their concerns and questions. With greater participation being required of parents in child placements and in developing short- and long-range educational objectives, and with parents increasingly aware of their rights and the rights of their handicapped children, we must talk more effectively with parents and with representatives from different disciplines. This may diminish instances of parents seeking court testimony from some of us against administrators or other professionals within our own disciplines.

What to Look For in an Early Intervention Program

Let us assume that the purposes of an early intervention program for high-risk or handicapped young children are (1) to promote development of each child's skills in order to lessen the impairing effects of the handicap(s) and, whenever possible, to prevent secondary or associated handicaps; (2) to assist parents in acquiring or sharpening the skills needed to teach their children effectively; and (3) to seek and coordinate services from community agencies. Within this framework we must consider a number of organizational and program components—and an enormous financial problem.

This discussion will draw on our experiences in the Model Preschool Center for Handicapped Children at the University of Washington's interdisciplinary Child Development and Mental Retardation Center. In some respects our program is atypical. We are associated with a major university, with its tertiary care capabilities; our training requirements, largely for graduate students, are more extensive than in a nonuniversity program; we serve a very large population from birth to six, approximately 200 children each year. But our experience with every variety of intervention program for young handicapped children and families is extensive: two model programs at our center were approved for "adoption/adaptation" by the U.S. Office of Education's Joint Dissemination and Review Panel, so that part of our mission is to assist other programs in developing their services to this population. We have found that the essential components of our models "travel" very well and can be replicated or adapted in diverse settings, many of which lack the rich resources of a demonstration/ training/technical assistance center such as ours (Hayden and Haring, 1978).

Ours is a center-based model to which infants and children are referred by physicians, nurses, clinics, school districts, maternal and infant care centers and parents. Some children remain in the center for diagnostic work-ups only and then are referred to community agencies. Other children spend from one academic quarter to two years at the center. Those pupils in the program for Down's syndrome and other developmental delays may be served from birth to age five or six at the center, if approved by the local school district, and then "graduate" to public school-based primary classes replicating our models. Our goal is to help each child achieve as nearly normal development as possible and to prepare the child for an orderly transition to a program in his home community.

Organizational Considerations

Kinds of Programs Now Available

Until P.L. 94-142 is extended to include children from birth to three—thus covering *all* handicapped children to age 21—and programs are operated under the auspices of public education systems, it is not likely that services for some children in the 0–3 or even in the 0–5 categories will be provided, except as diverse programs made available through parent groups, preschools associated with university training centers, hospital-affiliated classes, or programs operated by such organizations as associations for retarded citizens, cerebral palsy associations and developmental disabilities centers, to name a few. Such programs may serve particular populations with specific handicaps. Other limitations related to the geographic location—urban, suburban or rural—may impose problems in service delivery. Thus, there may be center- or home-based programs or a combination of both.

Any study of the effectiveness and cost-efficiency of such programs must take into account the needs of specific children and families as well as the geographic location in which service is to be delivered. A very important consideration is the training of paid staff or volunteers (including parents) to work in such programs. Some home-based programs, for example, employ trained paraprofessionals to make weekly home visits to the families. In addition to the personnel qualifications other factors, such as weather conditions, can interrupt the steady provision of services.

Another factor that has received little attention is that in some remote or rural programs the home visitor may feel overwhelmed by the wide variety of problems encountered with the children and families to be served. In addition, some of these people report feeling isolated, frustrated and lonely. They lack stimulation and opportunities to exchange information, which could be arranged through a combined center- and home-based program.

The problems associated with providing service to infants and children at risk in rural areas are of great concern to pediatricians and educators alike.

Working together, we must make use of technologies available to us, such as the telephone. We could also use videotapes that could be shared with professionals to determine if the concerns of the parents and the home visitor are indeed valid and suggest the need for further monitoring or treatment. With tape recorders the home visitors could record language samples for review by specialists in communication disorders at the center.

Access to Networks

Some services to young handicapped children are provided through national or regional networks. Under the administrative auspices of our Model Preschool Center programs are associated with the following networks: university-affiliated programs; handicapped children's early education assistance programs; National Diffusion Network; developmental disabilities centers; regional technical assistance centers (operated by the Washington State Superintendent of Public Instruction); Western States Technical Assistance Resource consortium; Administration for Children, Youth and Families RAP (regional Resource Access Projects); and parent-child services centers. These differ in funding sources and program emphasis, but all exist to extend and improve services to young handicapped children and their families. Still other local, state, regional and national networks and task forces are committed to furthering interagency coordination and collaboration.

Clinicians wishing to work with such agencies or to refer children to their programs have several avenues for obtaining information about local resources. For instance, HEW and ACYF regional offices can provide information about activities in their catchment areas. The regional Resource Access Projects integrate handicapped children in Head Start and then find or provide the required services. In many communities the Easter Seal Society can furnish a comprehensive list of resources and persons who can help to locate specific types of services. State departments of education, educational service districts and local school districts are usually pleased to share their knowledge about resources; so, too, are developmental disabilities centers, state departments of social and health services, and local and regional chapters of the Association for Retarded Citizens. Many organizations have lists of programs and resources for potential service users. Closer Look (a project of the Parents' Campaign for Handicapped Children and Youth) can also provide information about resources and programs in communities throughout the country.*

Closer Look has also prepared a book entitled One Step at a Time designed for parents "of a baby or young child whose growth is slow, unusual or affected by a disability."

---

*Closer Look, P.O. Box 1492, Washington, D.C. 20013

Staffing and Resources

Within the limitations of a program's funding, another major consideration is the staffing pattern employed and the access to ancillary resources (Hayden and Gotts, 1977). If the program is concerned with one specific disability, it may be easier to gather resources and coordinate service delivery. Most centers, however, serve children with a wide variety of handicaps—which essentially is the public school model—and therefore need teachers who are generalists but who have ready access to specialists. Given the concern for promoting children's development in all skills—cognitive, motor, communication, self-help and social—and given the interdependence of skill development, it is necessary to have the services of medical and nursing clinicians, communication disorders specialists and occupational and physical therapists, at the very least. How these professionals elect to deploy their resources is probably less important than that they actively participate in the program.

In one of our model programs, the communication program for children with communication delay or impairment, teachers and communication disorders specialists work together as a classroom team. This is quite different from the usual model where a child is referred to a CDS who offers therapy away from the classroom. Our model is based on the idea that the classroom is one obvious natural setting where children can practice and generalize the skills they acquire. Here, the teacher and CDS share responsibility for assessing each child and planning programs to help remediate delays or deficits in communication, language and other skills. Assistance is available from specialists in other disciplines.

The Down's syndrome program uses a different staffing pattern. Each class in this large program, which serves children from birth to six with a very wide variety of handicaps, is staffed by a head teacher, a teaching assistant and parent volunteers who receive intensive training in working with their own and other children. The program aims to accelerate and maintain developmental gains in the children and to train parents to be effective teachers. Precisely because of the high incidence of associated handicaps in Down's syndrome, physicians, nurses, CDS and physical therapists are used extensively in planning and evaluating each child's program.

The staff in all of our programs has ready access to many specialists at our interdisciplinary center, which is a university-affiliated program. Although responsibility for overall management in each separate program is shared, the teacher maintains all data collection and management, working with other staff to establish goals and to monitor the children's progress. The particular management strategy and the staff involved in any given session will depend on the child's need and, to some extent, on his age. For instance, the CDS might work only briefly with parents of a very young infant, helping them learn to give feedback for the infant's sounds. As the child develops, the CDS will spend more time with this family, working with them to elicit communication from the older infant and to promote such communication by their own behavior.

All staff members work closely with parents, offering considerable support to the families, referring them to other sources and ensuring that needed services are obtained.

Finding the Children

Many early intervention programs begin because some group, often parents, wishes to provide or locate services for unserved children. Once the initial population is identified, word spreads fast and a program grows. But the sad fact is that not all children who need services are identified and referred. The reasons are numerous. Among those cited by the editors of *Closer Look* in their December 1978 issue are the insufficient numbers of trained specialists to identify all children in need and the fact that parents, "among the best sources of information about the whereabouts of handicapped children," are often not invited to participate in child identification efforts. According to the Council for Exceptional Children (1977), only 25 per cent of preschool-age handicapped children receive appropriate specialized educational services (p. 93). One encouraging note, however, is that "the number of preschool children, age 3 to 5, receiving services nationwide has increased by 20,000 in the past three years, a growth rate of 10 per cent" (Stimson, 1979). An aggressive search for eligible children must be a responsibility of any intervention program. This means that the staff must make the program known to potential referral sources and must work with them to ensure the widest possible coverage. Here again is a natural opportunity for educators and clinicians to collaborate.

Program Considerations

Data-based Programs

Any program designed to promote children's development and monitor their progress must have some means of assessing its own impact. Through careful review of children's performance, the staff and parents can make *data-based* decisions about services and instruction they will provide or arrange for, and they can evaluate their own effectiveness in assisting the children. This focuses staff and parent efforts exactly where they belong: on developing the best possible program for each child. In using such a system it is never appropriate to ask "What is wrong with this child?" or "What is wrong with me?" Instead, the orientation is on a constructive and positive inquiry into what can be done to improve the child's program. Especially in view of the extreme stress parents experience in caring for their children, and the sometimes discouraging work of teachers, it seems appropriate to provide a setting that is as nurturing and stress-free for the adults involved as for the children. We must take the approach that if a child is not making progress it is not the fault of the child, the parent or the staff. Rather, it is the fault of the program—and that can and should be changed based on careful shared observations and data recorded over time.

What are some of the elements of a data-based program? The first is the need for a framework in which to review progress. In our programs and most early childhood intervention centers, the sequences of normal development in the various skill areas provide a background for assessing and programming each child. Such a system also permits individualization of both activities; no two children are alike or have the same developmental history or needs. Further, by measuring progress in terms of normal milestones and "schedules," one never needs to compare one child to any other—the child is his own "control." We know that development is not necessarily linear and that a child may show considerable "scatter" across the different developmental areas. Depending on his history and other factors, he may show better than normal performance in one skill and be quite deficient in others. By examining all of his capabilities and problems in terms of expectations for normal development, everyone involved in his care can set reasonable short- and long-term educational objectives and design a program accordingly. His progress in achieving these objectives can then be measured and the program changed when assessment data so indicate.

The second element in data-based programs is the kinds of data to collect and how often to collect them. Common sense dictates that the system be manageable enough to leave teachers time to further the children's learning. In our programs the staff collect ongoing performance data each day, using various checklists and other simple formats they have devised, and administers standardized measures regularly (e.g., quarterly). The combination of periodic and ongoing measures fills two needs: daily monitoring permits teachers and parents to check progress so closely that any potential problems can be dealt with before they become serious or intractable. In addition, it allows teachers and other staff to make plans for the next day or week that immediately respond to needs and can take advantage of unexpected developments in the child's progress. Periodic measures are a more global reflection of progress and act as a kind of check against daily progress notes. They also provide a means of determining the overall effectiveness of the program, since most standardized measures are different from the daily ratings.

Selecting the best assessment instruments is not easy. DuBose *et al.* (1979) have commented that "selection of formal assessment instruments for use with the severely handicapped has been a frustrating task for professionals in this field. No single assessment instrument exists that can adequately tap the potential of all severely handicapped children or that serves all examiners' purposes." These authors list the following characteristics for an instrument:

1. They should be easily obtained and simply scored.
2. They should possess adequate validity and reliability.
3. The items should be primarily manipulative in nature.
4. Scoring should be minimally dependent upon the child's speed of performance.
5. The items should be acceptable across all handicapping conditions.
6. The instrument should yield data immediately transferrable into sequentially planned and developmental activities for educational programming (p. 83).

Investigators throughout the country are trying to assess handicapped young children more effectively, to identify developmental "pinpoints" fine enough to measure children with substantial delay or dysfunction.

One such effort is underway at the University of Washington, where the Uniform Performance Assessment System (UPAS) is being developed. A curriculum-referenced instrument based on normal sequences of child development, UPAS data help teachers and parents develop IEP objectives. The Birth-6 Year Level has been published, and the 6–12 Year Level is now in its third revision. A consortium of investigators from several universities and colleges, CAPE (the Consortium on Adaptive Performance Evaluation) is developing another instrument under the auspices of The Association for the Severely Handicapped and funded by the Bureau of Education for the Handicapped. CAPE's instrument will allow individual items to be adapted to accommodate an infant's particular handicap(s) without altering the basic assessment *intent* of the items, for example, by substituting appropriate tasks for the handicapped infant to assess functional level. The original list of items, covering all common developmental areas from birth to age two, has been completed along with the basic adaptation parameters. Specific suggested adaptations to account for various handicapping conditions are still being developed. The instrument will be field tested and the revised version disseminated to selected sites in the coming academic year (Hayden, 1979a).

The kinds of daily observation should reflect the needs for information by the staff and others. As long ago as 1972 staff at the Model Preschool Center published an article on systematic observation as a tool for recognizing potential handicaps in young children addressed primarily to teachers in preschool centers and Head Start who might need to refer children for special services (Allen, Rieke, Dmitriev and Hayden). A similar article was incorporated into a manual we produced for Head Start programs when Congress mandated in 1972 that Head Start make at least 10 per cent of its enrollment opportunities available for handicapped youngsters. The basic message then, as now, is that only by carefully observing all facets of a child's behavior and development can we detect acute problems and possible warning signs whose significance must be determined over time.

In developing our categories of observational data we were helped by professionals from several disciplines. The checklist, which is now widely used, is entitled: "Teacher Observation Form for Identifying Children Who May Require Additional Services" (Model Preschool, 1975). The form is useful because: (1) it gives teachers a basis for systematically observing all aspects of a child's functioning and development, and (2) it conveys specific referral information to professionals in clinics. The checklist has been used in the eight manuals on different handicaps encountered in Head Start (Project Head Start: Mainstreaming Preschoolers, 1978). Information gained through use of these checklists helps practitioners from the different disciplines review the children's progress and make instructional plans before the next staff meeting. While teachers confer daily, their meetings with other professionals are less frequent. Having structured and individual information to discuss about each child makes these sessions as fruitful as possible.

Concern for Developmental Continuity

Early childhood educators must recognize that their work with a given child is not confined to the time he spends in their program. Concern for his next placement should be an ongoing consideration with some follow-up when the child "graduates." Promoting developmental continuity also involves two other considerations: arranging for and coordinating with community services and working with parents to ensure that strategies used in the school are continued at home.

Referral and Follow-up

Whether graduates of an early intervention program are referred to public school classes or other centers (and this depends on local legislation regarding mandated or discretionary services to young handicapped children), the staff's responsibility is the same: working with parents and school districts to identify an appropriate placement (especially if none is available through the public school); exchanging information with the new staff; making recommendations regarding the child's continuing need for community-based ancillary services; knowing the expectations for "entry" behaviors and ensuring that the child has acquired them and, as time and budget permit, periodically checking the child's progress in the new setting.

One reason for the follow-up, of course, is to evaluate the early program's effectiveness in preparing the child for his new "school." Another is to ensure that the critical elements of the preschool program are being continued. If the receiving programs cannot provide the needed services, the child's gains from the earlier program may well wash out, as several investigators have reported. Very recently, Dr. J. McVicker Hunt, whose book, *Intelligence and Experience*, changed many people's thinking about the educability of intelligence, commented on this problem in connection with children in Head Start. Although these children were "disadvantaged" rather than handicapped, the message is the same: "There's no question that it [Head Start] failed to achieve the hopes for it, but the hopes were naive. It was crazy to think that a summer or a year of nursery schooling would enable children of poverty to catch up and to compete on equal terms with children from educated families of the middle class" (Pines, 1979). Hunt in his interview with Pines went on to point out that it is "much easier to foster development early . . . there's so much malleability in the first year. In fact, there is no time in life when intelligence isn't somewhat malleable. Those functions that are used, develop; that never stops, at any age. It's the *rate* of development that changes. And the highest rate of development is from birth to age two." Thus it is important to focus on the maintenance of developmental skills as well as on their acceleration in our early education programs. Fortunately, the Administration for Children, Youth and Families has requested that the Resource Access Projects work with parent-child services centers across the country. These 34 centers serve the infants, siblings and extended families in their areas.

Ensuring the best placement for graduates from preschool programs involves working with the staff in the receiving school—not only exchanging information but exchanging visits whenever possible. Another strategy is to transport replicable and tested models whose components can be used or adapted in the receiving school. In such cases the receiving program must be willing to request assistance in implementing the model, which may involve more formal training and information exchange. It is precisely this kind of strategy that is being fostered by the National Diffusion Network: state facilitators arrange for school districts to receive assistance from centers which have developed models approved for adoption/adaptation by the U.S. Office of Education's Joint Dissemination and Review Panel.

Community Services

Working through the maze of public and private agencies offering potentially useful services can be frustrating for anyone. This is especially true for the families of handicapped children. We believe that an early intervention program is responsible for helping families to locate and exploit the community resources they need. Children may need medical or social services or arrangement for prostheses; their families may need respite care. Not all communities can offer everything needed by every child, and finding elusive services is often quite challenging. In some cases the task becomes one of *developing* the resources—

even presenting a case to a state legislature or a city council for funding. Some of the parents in our Down's syndrome program organized an informal parent-to-parent service at a local hospital in order to help parents of newborn Down's children. Our parents are on call at the hospital to talk to, counsel and suggest resources to the newborns' parents, who are usually in emotional disarray and welcome this empathic assistance.

Working with public and private agencies and developing or locating resources are best performed in collaboration with other professionals. Using the observational data collected by educators and the clinical data provided by pediatricians or others is more likely to pinpoint the need for services correctly and to carry more weight than using one set of findings. Pediatricians and others who have been frustrated in finding appropriate educational placements for their patients certainly understand the frustrations of educators who have trouble finding ancillary services for their pupils. Together, we should be able to do a better job—finding exactly the right services, ending duplication of effort and even creating resources where none existed before.

Working with Parents

The literature on early intervention states the case so clearly it is no longer arguable: parents are indeed the primary educators of their young children. Bronfenbrenner has even gone so far as to suggest that when parents are not involved in an intervention, whatever child gains are achieved will be lost when the intervention ends (1975). Drs. Stedman and colleagues, in their review of early stimulation programs (1978), comment that when mothers are trained to implement the curriculum, "to the extent that this type of program produces IQ gains, it appears that the critical activity is verbal interaction between mother and child in the context of a challenging task." The literature is also replete with reports concerning the stress endured by parents of handicapped children, and how they feel about the child's impact on their caretaking styles, which in turn affect the child's development. Gath (1977) has attempted to measure some of the stress. In her study of matched families she found that the significant difference between the two groups was the marital breakdown or "severe disharmony" in almost one-third of the families with a handicapped child and in none of the control families.

Clearly, early childhood educators are not marriage counselors or psychiatrists or social workers. We cannot attempt to "fix" all the problems associated with having a handicapped child. But we do have an enormous role to perform—and it helps if others join us—in trying to reduce parental stress as much as we can. Our part of the task is to help the parents exploit their incredible natural advantage as educators of their children, by training them as teachers, observers, data-takers, and by working with them to become advocates for their children as they move through the school system and the community's service agencies. We believe that by helping parents to understand that "they have something critically important to do, work that can alter the course of their child's development" (Hayden and Pious, 1979), we can benefit parents and child.

One concern about parent involvement, however, must be addressed: most programs focus exclusively on training mothers to work with their children. Although in some families there are obvious reasons for this—in "traditional" families where the father works and the mother stays at home—there are equally obvious reasons why such practices should be changed. First, these traditional families are going out of style so fast that it is almost meaningless to consider them the norm anymore. Mothers work. Fathers who do or do not work are increasingly taking a more significant share of the care-giving role, a development we should do everything we can to promote. Second, to exclude fathers in any case is a dreadful waste of resources and neglects their needs, which may be as compelling as the mothers'.

The Fathers and Infants Program, developed by Sam Delaney at the Model Preschool Center, recognizes that fathers share the stress of parenting a handicapped infant and that the infant's handicap may interfere with the attachment between infant and father. The program seeks to increase attachment through building the fathers' skills as educators, increasing their knowledge of child development and encouraging joyous interaction between them and their babies. The program meets on Saturday mornings for two hours. It is loosely structured and includes opportunities for play, talk, review of developmental progress and plans for the week at home, talks by invited speakers (on topics selected by the fathers), music and exercises. To our knowledge, this popular program is the only one of its kind in the United States, and voluminous requests we have received for information about it suggest that it will be a widely used model (Hayden and Pious, 1979).

Case Studies From the Model Preschool Center

To illustrate the collaborative role of educators and pediatricians in serving young handicapped children, here are two brief case studies from our center.

W.P. was born to an alcoholic mother who placed him for adoption at birth. He was born with multiple physical abnormalities, now recognized as the fetal alcohol syndrome (Jones et al., 1973). Besides demonstrating intrauterine growth failure, he had microcephaly, microphthalmia with visual acuity problems and severe developmental delay. He was placed in a foster home and received routine medical care in a general pediatrics clinic. In the second year of life he was intellectually performing at the six- to nine-month level and was beginning to become a major behavior problem in the foster home, with complaints voiced about his destructive behavior, self-stimulation and sleeplessness. These problems were severe enough for the foster mother to consider giving up W.P. At this point the pediatrician referred him to the infant program at the Model Preschool Center. There W.P. was seen by the teacher, physical therapist, occupational therapist and psychologist. He was scheduled to be seen in the classroom once weekly for a preacademic skills program. The foster mother was included in this program and was trained to perform the developmental exercises and tasks prescribed.

In the class W.P.'s appropriate and inappropriate behaviors were observed. When behavior modification tactics failed to reduce the number of inappropriate behaviors which interfered with his acquisition of preacademic skills, the staff raised the question of using medication. The pediatrician met with the teacher, and a double-blind treatment of medication was begun, during which the teacher continued to measure both appropriate preacademic and inappropriate behaviors. Two different medications were evaluated, phenobarbital and methylphenidate. While W.P. increased appropriate preacademic skills and decreased inappropriate behaviors on both medications, the teacher recorded new self-stimulating behaviors on methylphenidate which were incompatible with home and classroom expectations. The child was placed on phenobarbital and continued in the early intervention program.

Most important, the pediatrician had objective measurement of both behaviors that were expected to increase (preacademic skills) and to decrease (inappropriate behaviors). Also, during the subsequent years in the program, W.P. has been tried off all medications and re-evaluated periodically on the two drugs, finally being taken off all medication. Without data from the teacher it would have been impossible to decide which, if any, medication to use and when and if medication was still required.

R.R.'s case was reported in the literature (Haring *et al.,* 1977). She is an older child with holoporencephaly and multiple other anomalies including cleft lip and palate and talipes equinovarus. Her lip and palate had been repaired; however, her partial diabetes insipidus was treated only for about one year before medication was stopped.

For approximately four years, being cared for at home, she was hospitalized every three to four months with dehydration. It was unclear to her physician whether or not her mother was able to get R.R. to take sufficient fluids to meet her daily needs. She was severely delayed as well as nonambulatory. Her mother was having increasing difficulties caring for her, lifting her and getting her to take fluids.

At this point she was started in our class for severely handicapped young children. Part of the teachers' daily objectives was to get her to take required fluids and to measure urine specific gravity. The data showed clearly that R.R.

still had partial diabetes insipidus (treatable by oral medication). Once she was medicated, she had no further admissions to the hospital for dehydration. Further, as her classroom program included the teaching of partial weight-bearing, for transfers from wheelchair to toilet, for example, it became necessary to have her feet repaired. After this was accomplished, R.R. could assist herself in transfers, remaining at home in the care of her family. This multiply handicapped young person is now bused to school daily. She still lives at home rather than in an institution and has not been hospitalized in over three years. She receives regular health care at her school.

The financial savings for the community realized by classroom management of R.R. have been substantial. More important, this child has the chance to develop whatever potential she has in the least restrictive setting.

Summary and Conclusions

> In the past ten years, a virtual knowledge explosion has occurred in all areas of infant research. Innovative study and technological advances have enabled us to enormously broaden our understanding of the amazing capabilities of babies. Such advances have permitted a remarkably different view of the infant to emerge (Kaiser and Hayden, 1977, p. 4).

In a conference held at the University of Wisconsin in Milwaukee in 1977, I attempted to examine the "Implications of Infant Intervention Research" (Hayden, 1978) and pointed out that two overall categories emerged: implications concerning the voluminous literature being amassed about infants, and implications about specific developmental areas and environmental conditions that should be explored more fully.

Efforts to bring together different disciplines have created a new and exciting approach to providing services for handicapped children and their families. We have a new sense of humility and a recognition that no one discipline can manage the extensive problems we face.

We realize that many children and families are unserved or underserved and that we have at least some of the knowledge and expertise that could help them. We have found that the infants and toddlers are much more interactive and responsive than we thought just a few years ago and that parents are remarkably interested in how they can learn and carry over into the home some of the procedures we have developed. We know how effective early intervention programs can be in furthering the coordination of resources from different disciplines. We realize most acutely that the public and those who can provide funds must be made aware of our work. However, all of our efforts to develop curricula, programs and services are of little or no value unless we have a delivery system that will reach those in need. We cannot afford to be apathetic or let the public be apathetic and short-sighted if we really have confidence in our programs and services. We cannot permit the public, or our state and federal governments, to make excuses and ignore children's needs because the cost is too high. We cannot afford piecemeal, too-little, too-late, penny-wise and pound foolish, exclude-rather-than-include approaches if we are to meet the needs of our people. Our failure to provide good services and programs for the birth to three population simply compounds our problems. The 21-year-olds in the year 2000 will be born in 1979. What are we doing now and what will we do in those years before that group reaches the age of 21 to ensure that the quality of life for the handicapped in the twenty-first century will be an improvement over the quality of life this population has experienced in the twentieth century? (Hayden, 1979b)

References

Allen, K.E., Rieke, J., Dmitriev, V. and Hayden, A.H. Early warning: Observation as a tool for recognizing potential handicaps in young children. *Educational Horizons,* Winter, pp. 43–55 (1971-72).

Bergsma, D. *Birth Defects: An Atlas and Compendium.* Baltimore: Williams and Wilkins (1973).

Bronfenbrenner, U. Is early intervention effective? in Friedlander, B.Z., Sterritt, G.M. and Kirk, G.E. (eds.), *Exceptional Infant, Vol. 3: Assessment and Intervention.* New York: Brunner/Mazel, pp. 449–475 (1975).

Coleman, M. Neonatal diagnosis of neurologically handicapped infants. Paper presented at WESTAR Topical Conference on Infant Assessment and Intervention, May 31–June 2, 1978, Seattle, Wa., in *Proceedings of Topical Conference on Infant Assessment and Intervention.* Seattle: WESTAR (Western States Technical Assistance Resource) (1979), in press.

Dubose, R., Langley, M.B. and Stagg, V. Assessing severely handicapped children, in Meyen, E.L., Vergason, G.A. and Whelan, R. (eds.), *Instructional Planning for Exceptional Children.* Denver, London: Love Publishing Co., pp. 73–91 (1979).

Full educational opportunities for handicapped individuals, in Jordan, J.B. (ed.), *Exceptional Child Education at the Bicentennial: A Parade of Progress.* Reston, Va.: The Council for Exceptional Children (1977). (Chapter originally presented by The Council for Exceptional Children at the White House Conference on Handicapped Individuals.)

Gath, A. The impact of an abnormal child upon the parents. *Brit. J. Psychiat.,* 130:405–410 (1977).

Haring, N.G., Hayden, A.H. and Beck, G.R. General principles and guidelines in "programming" for severely handicapped children and young adults, in Meyen, E.L., Vergason, G.A. and Whelan, R.J. (eds.), *Instructional Planning for Exceptional Children.* Denver, London: Love Publishing Co., pp. 216–235 (1979).

Haskins, R., Finkelstein, N.W. and Stedman, D.J. Infant stimulation programs and their effects. *Pediat. Ann.,* 7:123–144, Feb. (1978).

Hayden, A.H. The implications of infant intervention research. *All. Health and Behav. Sci.,* 1:4, 583–595 (1978).

Hayden, A.H. Curriculum evaluation designs for infant learning, in Wilson, J. (ed.), *Planning and Evaluating Developmental Programs*. Chapel Hill, N.C.: Dept. of Medical Allied Health Professions, School of Medicine, University of North Carolina (1976). Revised edition (1979a), in press.

Hayden, A.H. Handicapped children, birth to age 3. *Exceptional Children* (special issue: The Yet To Be Served), 45:7, 510–517, April (1979b).

Hayden, A.H. and Gotts, E.A. Multiple staffing patterns, in Jordan, J.B., Hayden, A.H., Karnes, M.B. and Wood, M.M. (eds.), *Early Childhood Education for Exceptional Children: A Handbook of Ideas and Exemplary Practices*. Reston, Va.: The Council for Exceptional Children, pp. 236–253 (1977).

Hayden, A.H. and Haring, N.G. Increasing service delivery to handicapped children by replicating a basic model: "Transporting" the University of Washington's Down's Syndrome Program, in Fink, A.H. (ed.), *International Perspectives on Future Special Education*. (Proceedings of the CEC World Congress, June 25–30, 1978, Stirling, Scotland) Reston, Va.: The Council for Exceptional Children, pp. 122–126 (1978).

Hayden, A.H. and Pious, C.G. Parents as educators of risk infants. Proceedings of the International Workshop on the "At Risk" Infant, Tel Aviv, July 25–27, 30–31, 1979. *Excerpta Medica*, in Harel, S. (ed.), *The at risk infant*. Amsterdam: Excerpta Medica, 1980.

Jones, K.L., Smith, D.W. and Ulleland, C.N. Pattern of malformation in offspring of chronic alcoholic mothers. *Lancet*, 1267–1271 (1973).

Kaiser, C. and Hayden, A.H. The education of the very, very young, or: But what can you teach an infant? *Educational Horizons*, 56:1, 4–15, Fall (1977).

Kaveggia, E.G. *et al.* Diagnostic genetic studies on 1,224 patients with severe mental retardation. Proceedings of the Third Congress of the International Association for the Scientific Study of Mental Deficiency. The Hague, Netherlands, September 4–12 (1973).

Mainstreaming preschoolers. (Series) Washington, D.C.: Project Head Start, Administration for Children, Youth, and Families, Office of Human Development Services, Department of Health, Education, and Welfare (1978).

Parmelee, A.H., Sigman, M., Kopp, C.B. and Haber, A. Diagnosis of the infant at high risk for mental, motor, and sensory handicaps, in Tjossem, T. (ed.), *Intervention Strategies for High Risk and Handicapped Young Children*. Baltimore: University Park Press, pp. 289–297 (1976).

Pines, M. A head start in the nursery (Interview with J. McVicker Hunt). *Psychology Today*, 13:4, 56–68, September (1979).

Sapir. P. President's statement, in *William T. Grant Foundation Annual Report*. New York: William T. Grant Foundation (1977).

Shah, C.P. and Wong, D. Failures in early detection of hearing impairment in preschool children. *Journal of the Division of Early Childhood*, Council for Exceptional Children, 1:1, 33–40 (1979).

Smith, D.W. Rational diagnostic evaluation of the child with mental deficiency. *Am. J. Dis. Child*, 129:1285–1290 (1975).

Smith, D.W. *Recognizable Patterns of Human Malformation*. (2nd ed.) Philadelphia: W.B. Saunders Co. (1976).

Smith, D.W. *Mothering Your Unborn Baby*. Philadelphia: W.B. Saunders Co. (1979).

Stimson, J. Handicap child count, federal support slowly increasing. *Education Funding News*, IX:32, 4 (August 14, 1979).

Teacher observation form for identifying children who may need additional services. *Identification, assessment, referral, follow-up model*. Seattle, Wa.: Model Preschool Center for Handicapped Children, University of Washington (1975).

Where are the children? Closer Look, 7–9, December (1978).

PART IV

Language Development

Language development represents one important aspect of cognitive development. Its central role in development has not been overlooked by researchers and clinicians. No clinical assessment fails to observe language development. However, more recently, the role of the communicative functions of language and its relationship to early social interactions have become more obvious. The recent studies of communicative skills in the very young infant and preschool child have not found their way into specific assessment strategies in clinical settings, nor has the use of non-verbal forms of communication which are important to the sensory impaired child. This is especially important since these other forms of communication may serve as a prototype for later language development, or in some dysfunctions as a replacement. In this section a review of language and communication literature in the preschool child is presented and is followed by a practical clinical assessment procedure. Perhaps nowhere else is there greater effort in intervention than in language development and communication skills.

18

Theoretical Bases of Language and Communication Development in Preschool Children

LOUISE CHERRY WILKINSON
KAREN SAYWITZ

Introduction: The Cases of Paul and Allen

Parents rarely bring preschool children to pediatricians with the presenting complaint of a language problem or language disorder. More typically, preschool children are brought in for a routine checkup or for a variety of other complaints. Language problems are more often noticed with older, school-aged children; however, these problems are rooted in the developmental process of early language acquisition, which takes place to a large extent during the preschool years. This chapter is an attempt to acquaint you with an understanding of the process of normal language development.

Let us consider two case studies drawn from the files of Ms. Karen Saywitz. The first case is a 3½-year-old Caucasian male, Paul. Paul's mother brought him in because of what she regarded as a "language problem." The mother described her son's problem to the doctor in this way:

> Something is wrong with the way my son talks, Doctor. We really can't understand him. His friends understand even less of what he says. He sometimes doesn't even understand his friends either. Paul was such a late talker. He has a younger brother who is 2 years old, and Paul doesn't really talk any better than his younger brother, even though he is a year and a half older.

The doctor then interviewed the mother:

Doctor: When did he first walk?
Mother: One year old.
Doctor: When did he first start to talk?
Mother: Two and a half years of age.
Doctor: When did he first use sentences?
Mother: Not 'til 2 years 9 months of age. When he was 1½ years, he became very sensitive to sounds from others, so we decided to whisper to him. We kept on whispering for an entire year but it did not help at all.
Doctor: How did you know he was sensitive to sounds?
Mother: He would have tantrums whenever he heard loud sounds. He still has tantrums when he doesn't get his way. Very violent ones. In fact, we have to keep everything in our house off the ground and elevated. We took everything out of his room except his crib and boarded up the lower half of the window. He's the only one out of the five kids who is so upsetting to the family. I think he's always frustrated when we don't understand him.

The doctor noted that in the office Paul was very talkative, cheerful, attentive and friendly, but his speech was nearly unintelligible. The child frequently looked up questioningly as if he were bewildered, even though he knew when he was being addressed by the doctor or the mother. Paul spent most of his time playing silently with a few toys in the doctor's office. The doctor administered the Denver Developmental Scale. According to the Denver norms, a 3½-year-old child should be able to tell you his first and last names. Paul could not do this. A 3½-year-old child should use plurals, and Paul could not do this either. From the results of the Denver we concluded that Paul's language was not commensurate with his age. Paul had skills possessed by most 2-year-olds. On the Denver this means that he knew three words other than "momma" and "dadda" and could combine two different words in a single utterance. The results from the Denver did not tell us that no one understands 80 per cent of what Paul says; that Paul did not understand 60 per cent of what was said to him. The test also did not indicate whether Paul would outgrow the delay and catch up with other 3-year-olds, or if he needed referral to a specialist, such as an audiologist, neurologist or speech/language pathologist. The Denver told us nothing about the nature of the problem; in fact, it did not even indicate if there was a disorder. Thus, the results of the Denver added little to what the doctor had already gathered from observations and listening to a distraught parent. If we were attuned to children's language development, we could make three conclusions about this child:

1. He appeared to be delayed in talking.
2. He seemed overly involved in imitating the communication style of his younger, 2-year-old brother; thus, Paul spoke in an imitative style for a 3-year-old.
3. In responding to an early stage of his language development, *whispering,* Paul's parents overly relied upon this stylistic aspect of speech. Their behavior unnecessarily prolonged this primitive stage of his language development.

The second case is a 3-year, 1-month-old Mexican-American male, Allen. The mother brought her son to the pediatrician because of the child's overall delay and failure to develop as normally as other children. It is important to note that the presenting complaint did not refer specifically to language.

The following interview occurred:

Mother: Allen is a very quiet, shy child. He plays by himself most of the time. He was very slow at everything; a late talker, late walker, and late learning to feed himself. Is he retarded? He's so afraid of strangers. It's hard to leave him with sitters or take him with me to new places.
Doctor: Does he have any brothers and sisters at home?
Mother: No, he is an only child.
Doctor: Who lives in the home with him?
Mother: Just me; his father and I are recently divorced.

The doctor observed that Allen cried when attempts at separation from the mother were made. The child said practically nothing during the examination, and when he did speak, his utterances were unintelligible. Yet Allen seemed to respond to the doctor's instructions. The Denver revealed a developmental delay in all milestones of fine/gross motor, social, perceptual and language skills. This child had a great many problems which needed treatment. It is likely, in a case such as Allen's, that the child's language difficulties may be overshadowed by the other problems and the lack of information available about language.

Normal Language and Communicative Development

As we have seen from these two cases, the typical assessment, which involves parent report, the doctor's observation and interview in the office, and the use of the Denver, does not provide a great deal of information for the sensitive assessment of potential and already existing language problems in preschool children. Pediatricians can become more effective in both assessing and recognizing problems in language and communication with infants and toddlers. It is necessary to take a closer look at four important issues in language development: (1) Why should doctors know more about normal development? (2) What is language and communicative knowledge? (3) How do language and communicative knowledge develop normally? (4) How can doctors more sensitively assess whether their patients are normal?

Why Should Doctors Know More About Normal Development?

The study of normal development provides a standard with which the pediatrician can compare deviant or abnormal development. In addition, a firm knowledge of normal language development can serve as a guide for treatment and intervention in collaboration with a speech/language pathologist.

What Is Language and Communicative Knowledge?

Language knowledge has been described as "communicative competence" (Hymes, 1972). It includes knowledge about the structure, content and functions of language (Bloom and Lahey, 1978). We can think of language competence, then, as a set of rules about structure, function and content. Each of us acquires the rules about his native language. We do not memorize a list of sentences. Rather, research has shown that we learn a set of rules about how to produce sentences and how to understand other people's sentences. By rules, we do not mean the regulations in, say, an English grammar book. But we do know the rules of English in that we know how to pronounce words and how to put words together to form English sentences. Linguists refer to knowledge of language rules as "tacit knowledge," that is, unconscious knowledge. We know the rules because we speak English fluently and grammatically and effectively. We do not know them in a conscious way in the sense that we can recite the rules of English grammar.

The structure of language consists of rules about: the sounds of language, phonology, forming words from sounds, morphology; and forming sentences from words, syntax of the language. Morphology and syntax are referred to as grammar. The content of the language consists of the rules which relate objects in the world to the signs or lexicon of the language. Content is referred to as semantics, the system of meaning in language. Rules about how to use language effectively and appropriately, that is, the functions of language in social contexts, is called the pragmatics of the language.

Children acquire all these rules about their native language; some children and adults acquire many language rule systems and are bi- or multilingual. When we talk about a child who is not developing normally, we mean that the child is either *delayed* in the acquisition of these rules or else *disordered* in their acquisition, in which case certain rules or combinations are not acquired, or the child invents his own inappropriate rules. Typically, a disordered child creates one or two inaccurate rules and that pervade the child's speech.

Let us survey what we know about normal language development. We will then consider what is meant by delay and disorder as well as how to identify these problems.

How Does Language Develop Normally?

We know a great deal about how language develops normally in preschool children. We know how the content, function and structure are different and how they progress for children of different ages and stages during the preschool years. In addition, we know something about what this development involves, including both the biological and environmental influences.

First of all, we believe that *language development occurs within* what Lewis and Cherry (1977) have called *the unified model of human development, which assumes that language, cognitive and social capacities are interrelated and interdependent.* These aspects of individual development are investigated in a unified approach to human development so that observable human behavior can be explained. Individual development includes language, social and cognitive knowledge, and the unified model implies that all human behavior is to be understood, not just that regarded as language. There are social and cognitive skills which are necessary for language development. Table 1 summarizes some of these skills and provides suggestions for exploring children's performance.

A second principle is that *language development begins at birth and continues throughout life,* even though the most dramatic development is seen in the first four or five years. For example, Halliday (1975) investigated the developing language and communicative functions in the speech of his son Nigel from 9 to 18 months. He observed three phases in the development of his son's speech. He characterized the first stage as a "content-expressive system," or protolanguage in which the child used language to satisfy material needs, control behavior, establish and maintain contact with others, express himself, comment on his environment, and construct a fantasy world. Halliday saw the second stage as transitional. In the third stage Nigel added dialogue and grammatical structure as well as informative function to language, that is, the use of language to provide information. In this third stage, then, the child makes the transition to the adult system. From here on, the child will gradually abandon his own language structure as he creates the rules which govern speech that he hears. He will increase his vocabulary, articulate speech more conventionally, and be able to sustain increasingly longer conversations. It is possible that

TABLE 1   Cognitive and Social Skills Related to Preschool Language Development

Are the conceptual foundations which are necessary for language learning established?	Use history and observation to determine if child has skills
Is conceptual development commensurate with age?	The child knows body parts, colors, how to count, prepositions?
	There is a difference between nonverbal and verbal IQ?
How does the child modulate meaning with language?	The child uses word order only until 2½ years; inflections appear at 2–2½ years and are mastered by 4 years in following order:

–ing	present progressive tense
–s, –es	plurals
–ed	past tense
the, a	articles
my, 's	possessives
he likes it	3rd person singular agreement
is, am, have	auxiliary verb, copula

Are the auditory perception skills necessary for language learning established?	
How does the child process auditory information?	
Auditory memory	How many commands can child follow from memory?
	How many numbers can he/she repeat in a row?
	How many words in a list can he/she remember?
Auditory sequencing	Can child follow several commands in sequence given?
	Does child repeat a list of unrelated words in sequence given?
Auditory discrimination	Does child confuse similar sounding words, (like pot/cot, moon/soon) in listening? In speaking?
Are the social foundations which are necessary for language learning established?	
(Ask parent and/or observe:)	
Does child prefer verbal or silent play?	When given dolls, a child should narrate his/her play, pretend to speak for other characters.
Is language used creatively?	Does child use memorized phrases, limited routine expressions only to express needs? Does child echo others?

TABLE 1   (Continued)

How is language used and for what purposes?	Determine if language is used for the following functions or if child relies on gestures, context clues or significant others.
	a. to locate/name objects b. to describe events c. denote possession, negation, recurrence d. to qualify or modify ideas, to elaborate e. to command and demand desires f. to question (yes–no type; wh–type, e.g., when, where, why, etc.)
How is language used socially?	Is it used to attract attention, manipulate others? Is there sufficient opportunity for communication development in home (is it bilingual, one parent deaf, or only child)? Does the child initiate and/or enjoy conversation?
Can child imitate grammatical constructions he does not use in spontaneous speech?	Usually, a child will not repeat constructions in a sentence that he does not know or understand. What the child deletes from his/her repetition is a clue to his/her knowledge

language problems occur in the earliest months of the child's life as well as into adolescence. Table 2 provides an overview of the main characteristics of the language and communicative development of preschool children.

A third principle about language development is that *it involves certain maturational factors which seem to be universal.* In addition to these biological time-clocks is the strong influence of environmental factors. Language development begins when a child is born into a social world and when he interacts with other people. In infancy communication modulates the care-giving process, as the mother becomes aware of the success and failure of her behavior and the child, in turn, develops rules in the context of these communications. In the early years the child takes the alternate roles of speaker and listener as he participates directly in communication with others. These are the most important experiences for the child as they provide him with opportunities to test language and communicative rules and to receive information about the adequacy of these rules from the person he is speaking to.

For example, parents of toddlers often play the "naming game" with their children. In the following example a mother and child are playing with a "pop" toy, and the mother maintains the flow of conversation by asking the child a series of "naming" questions:

Mother: What's that?
Child: Uh.

TABLE 2 Normal Language Development

	1 month	2 months	5–6 months	8 months	10–18 months
Form	*Reflexive crying* *non-cry comfort sounds* (k, l, g) Vowels (V) and consonants (C)	Sounds in front of mouth (m, b) Play with pitch	5 vowels (V) 5 consonants (C) *CVCV combinations* 2-syllable repetitions (dada, papa)	Midmouth sounds (g, d, n, l) *Intonation* contouring added to vocal play	*Echolalia* imitation *First words*
Use	Practice vocalizing Crying	*Private and social babbling* Practices a variety of sounds Majority is solitary practice	*Vocal play* Uses sound to attract attention Public practice increases Solitary practice decreased	Crying decreases	Communicates needs in gestures Uses speech to locate and name objects, people
Content	None	None	Uses *facial expressions* to communicate (smiles, laughs) Purpose of sound both pleasure and reflexive	*Intonation patterns* (questions, commands) *Understand gestures*	*Holophrastic speech* – a word stands for meaning of a whole sentence Spurt in *comprehension* Vocabulary = 10–20 words
Possible disorder if:	*Feeding problems* High palatal arch leads to later lalling and excessive lip-rounding (wabbit for rabbit)	*No opportunity to practice;* vocalizing alone needed to develop oral-facial musculature			

	18–24 months (1½ yrs.)	2 years	2½ years	3 years	4 years
Form	*Jargon* *Practicing fluency* Echolalia Pronunciation poor (mo for snow) Speech 25% intelligible Single word utterances	*Joins two words* 60–70% speech poor pronunciation Speech rhythms broken Jargon gone *Word endings* – 's, ing	*Three-word utterance* Vowels 90% intelligible; uses i, c, n, k, g, ng correctly	*Compound sentences and phrases* All vowels correct Uses b, p, m, n, w, t, d, n, h correctly Short sentences 3–4 words Articulation errors still common but 70% of speech is intelligible	Uses sh, zh, th correctly; sentences over four words long; articulation errors still normal on l, r, s, z, sh, ch, j, th. Nonfluencies appear
Use	Communicates needs and desires Locates and names objects Uses speech for attention getting	Meaningful social control with language Denotes possession (mine!); questions; commands	Uses speech to modify and qualify; demands desires; describes events; questions (yes–no type); negation, recurrence (more); nonexistence (all gone)	Social control, request announces action Whispers, likes to hear whispers, gives full name and sex Explains happenings	Likes extremes, both whispers and yells Seeks information, relates experiences

TABLE 2   (Continued)

Content	Understands simple commands with gesture and intonation Vocabulary = 50 words Speaks in present tense only One word represents many unrelated objects (doggie means all 4-legged animals)	Vocabulary = 50–250 words Telegraphic speech – omits function words (want cookie, where kitty?) Inflections – to modulate meaning (possession, present progressive verb tense)	Vocabulary = 400–500 words Nouns, verbs, adjectives, junction words (is, am, were), pronouns Understands some prepositions	Vocabulary = 900–1000 words Pronouns, adjectives, plurals, (you, me) Sentence types: agent–action; action–object; agent–object Expands noun phrases with tense, gender, number Conjugates verb 'to be'	Past tense, comparatives (bigger, biggest) Uses all sentence types and relative clauses ("He did what he could") Complex sentences like "I think it's the wrong way"
Possible disorder if:	There has been no vocal play, echolalia, jargon; speech may be developmentally delayed Suspect later deviations to arise	– child doesn't yet realize language is meaningful – vocabulary has not increased in number and kind of words (nouns, verbs, adjectives) – speech is only used to locate and name objects and not for social control – child relies on gesture, people, context rather than speech to communicate needs		Between ages 3–4 most speech/language disorders become fixed and noticeable (voice quality, lisps, stuttering, comprehension problems, auditory perception, memory and sequencing skills) Most can be remediated if referred early	

5 years

Form	Intelligibility has some distortion on articulation like r, s and blends (gl, sn) Now uses z, th, r, ch, j correctly in speech
Use	Asks permission Gives excuses Questions actions of others Uses please, thank you Maturity of speech use gives child freedom and pleasure
Content	Knows common opposites Uses adverbs, future tense Counts to 10, counts four objects Boastful
Possible disorder if:	*Persistent misarticulations* of early developing sounds Grammar still *telegraphic* Nonfluencies still exist Speech or voice quality *distorted* (slurred, hypernasal, etc.)

> Mother: What is that?
> What do we call it?
> Child: A pop-pop.
> Mother: Yes, a pop-pop.

Communication breakthroughs and breakdowns provide opportunities for modifying the rules of language. Both the pressure associated with the breakdowns and the rewards associated with the breakthroughs are believed to motivate this process. Thus, the child develops language and communicative competence as an adaptation to the pressures generated by conversations in which he participates with others such as parents (Cherry, 1979).

A fourth principle about normal language development is *paradoxical.* Research has shown that even though almost all children learn their native language, parents are not explicitly involved in teaching it to their preschool children (Brown, 1972; Cazden, 1974). Also, any conscious attempts to teach rules of language structure, content and function have failed, particularly if the long-term effects are examined (Cazden, 1974).

A fifth principle involves *two myths parents often believe about how children develop language.* It is commonly thought that children learn language through imitation and reinforcement, two psychological constructs that refer to the way people acquire new behavioral systems. Children are believed to imitate the language they hear around them, from parents, teachers, siblings and others. It is also assumed that children are rewarded for grammatical speech and are corrected by parents for errors. Both of these myths have been explored by extensive research in the last two decades (Cazden, 1972). Imitation accounts for some aspects of language acquisition, such as pronunciation or articulation of sounds, but this mechanism cannot explain all of the child's language development, for two reasons. First, anyone who has spent time with young children knows that they often say things that they could not possibly have heard from others. Children never cease to surprise us in their imaginative and creative use of language.

What everyone who has had contact with a toddler probably remembers is the child's invented words and overgeneralization of the rules of language. Overgeneralization involves applying a rule in appropriate as well as inappropriate situations, as for example, in the toddler's use of "foots" instead of "feet," or "goed" instead of "went." The child in the first instance is using a rule about regular plural formation in an irregular case, and in the second case is applying a rule about regular past tense verb formation in an irregular case. Toddlers do not hear "foots" and "goed" from the adults around them. The children have created these expressions themselves, from their own rule-based systems. These systems, individual for each child, evolve to approach eventually the adult model.

Children do not learn language by being rewarded for "correct" language; nor do parents behave like grammar teachers. Parents and children are busy interacting with one another, attending largely to what each person says rather than how it is said. Furthermore, toddlers seem to be impervious to imitating a correct form given by their parents before the children have developed that form in their own rule system. In the following exchange a child is commenting on a toy in which balls pass down a slide:

Child: No ball.
            No ball.
            No ball.
Father: No more balls.
Child: No ball.
(Several minutes elapse)
Child: No ball.
Father: No more balls?
Child: No ball.

We infer that this child has not yet acquired the adult rule for forming regular plurals in English. Although the father incorporates that rule in his speech, which could serve as a "correct" model for the son, the model seems to have no effect on the son's speech.

Even though environmental influences upon children's language acquisition are substantial, *the processes of imitation and reinforcement do not account for children's normal language development to any large extent.* Children's conversations with others contribute to the gradual acquisition of language, and responsive and productive parents, who will attend to the child's communicative efforts, are very important. The child's experience as speaker and listener is vital for language development. As can be seen in the following example taken from a conversation between a father and his 2½-year-old son, the parent interest in his son's chosen topic as well as the responsiveness to his son's utterances is a key to the success of their exchange:

Child: A doggie.
Father: Oh, is the doggie going for a ride?
            Is he going 'round and 'round?
Child: Yes.
            Dog.
            Dog fe dow.
Father: The dog fell down?
Child: Yeah.

As with other aspects of human development, including social and cognitive knowledge, children need responsible adults who can interact with them, guide them and provide them with the stimulating experiences and opportunities to put into practice what they have learned.

A sixth principle is that language develops in a sequence, that is, there is a basic order to the development of language rules. Halliday (1975) believes that the first stage is a protolanguage followed by transitional stage. Other psycholinguists have formulated models of the acquisition of language structure and function. Brown (1972) has postulated that there are five stages of language. The first stage of basic semantic and syntactic relations consists of the "major meanings of language" and a very primitive structure for constructing language to express these meanings. Stage two involves the elaboration of these major meanings through the grammatical system, including the acquisition of 14 new grammatical elements. By and large, most of the previous research has focused on the earliest stages of the grammatical acquisition (Bloom and Lahey, 1978; Brown, 1972; Halliday, 1975). A common theme in all these studies is that there is a basic sequence to the development of language and communicative rules. Table 3 summarizes the basic developmental sequence of language.

How Can Doctors Become More Sensitive
In Assessing the Language Development
of Preschool Children?

One possibility is for doctors to resort to some of the techniques used by psychologists to assess children's language knowledge. Psychologists study children's

TABLE 3   Developmental Sequence of Language

	Months	Years
Nonlinguistic development		
Reflexive crying and noncry comfort sounds	1	
Private and social babbling	2	
Vocal play	5–6	
Echolalia (imitating self and others)	10	
Jargon (practicing fluency)	18	
Linguistic development		
First words – holophrastic speech	10–12	1
Telegraphic speech – joining two words	24	2
Three-word utterances, inflection appears	30	2½
Simple complete sentences with pronouns	36	3
Compound sentences – three- to four-word utterances	42	3½
Mastery of inflections	48	4
Articulation 90% intelligible	60	5
Compound–complex sentences	72	6

language acquisition by observing what the children say, what they understand, and by attempting to elicit responses which indicate what they know about language. There is a crucial distinction between speech and language, or performance and competence. What we want to know about is children's knowledge about language. However, we can only know this by observing performance, comprehension, speech. Just because the child does not say something does not mean that he does not know that word, grammatical structure, function. Your task, as our's, is to try to find out if the child knows language appropriate for his age and to create a situation that encourages effective and appropriate use.

A Second Look at Paul

Having considered normal language development, let us take a second look at Paul and see whether we can now more sensitively assess what he is doing with his language knowledge. From our interviews with Paul we observe that he avoids using language creatively. Rather than make his own contribution to a conversation he seems to use memorized utterances or partial repetitions. Paul also uses language for only the most primitive function of naming objects, expressing a need or indicating a possession, such as box, want box, it mine. Paul relies on gesture, context clues, and other people for the more advanced language functions such as describing an event or modification, qualification and questioning. At 3½ years of age Paul should be able to use language and grammar for these more sophisticated purposes.

His poor intelligibility is due in part to his poor grammar. He follows his own grammatical rules which allow him, for example, to omit the first person pronoun in all speech: "I want cookie" becomes "wants cookie." He also omits the verb of a sentence at will, believing that the other speaker will know what he means. For example, "want cookie" now becomes only "cookie" sometimes. When asked to imitate sentences, Paul reveals a greater knowledge of grammar than he uses in his own speech, repeating constructions that he does not usually produce spontaneously.

Paul's problems appear to be those of deviance and not mere delay which he could eventually outgrow. It is likely that aspects of his home situation are contributing to this deviance. Members of Paul's family respond to his needs, and he is exposed constantly to a deluge of language fluency. The only exception to this general pattern of "overcompensation" is Paul's younger brother, who is still at the very primitive stage of language development. Paul imitates his brother's speech in order to get attention from the family. Paul's mother described that the family whispered to him for an entire year. All children go through a whispering stage; however, it is difficult to hear the ends of words and certain sounds, like consonants with an aspiration, when whispering. Thus, at a critical point in language development, Paul did not receive the needed linguistic information from his environment about sounds and how they are pronounced. As a result, Paul has a disorder in which he omits all final consonants and all endings on plurals and possessives, thus rendering his speech unintelligible.

This unintelligibility is Paul's worst problem with regard to language form. He has invented two inaccurate phonological rules which prevent others from understanding him. First, he omits all terminal consonants. "Cake" becomes "k," "pot" becomes "pa." This rule is so pervasive that Paul's speech is unintelligible about 50 per cent of the time. Second, Paul omits the sound "s" wherever it occurs in a word. When "s" appears in a cluster or a blend, as in "snow" or "slow," the entire blend is omitted and "snow" becomes "o." Paul also displays several errors in articulation which are quite common in normal speech development. Yet because he commits these errors much more frequently than most children, they can no longer be considered to be normal misarticulations. In general, Paul does not discriminate between different terminal consonants in his speech or in his listening. Most of his articulation errors are considered normal, to be outgrown eventually by a child under five. However, it is not normal for one child to possess all these misarticulations, especially at any one point in development. Paul's auditory perceptual skills are also very weak, and this is why he had so much trouble understanding the speech of others, including his doctor. His auditory memory, sequencing, and discrimination of sounds have not evolved sufficiently to permit normal language development. Thus, his comprehension of what others say is not much better than his comprehension of what he says. Paul does not complete sentences and leaves out words and concepts as if his intent was already known to the listener. He does seem to know much more about the grammar and the lexicon of English than he uses in his speech, but even this knowledge does not seem commensurate with his age. In addition, the length of his sentences is far below average. Paul's problems of form, then, are deviant and delayed. The quantity and pervasiveness of his problems are most critical and not to be outgrown, even though an untrained observer would judge him merely a late talker.

With regard to content, Paul does not understand prepositions or verb tenses, and he can only follow a command when two critical elements are contained. That is, he can respond to an utterance like "get the blue ball," but not to the command to "get the big blue ball." Paul's vocabulary of useful words is much more meager than it should be for a child of his age. Also, he does not use adjectives. Paul does not use abstract concepts and does not understand many abstract concepts. His language thus reflects a fact about his cognitive development: his thinking remains largely at the concrete level. Paul consistently overextends conceptual categories by referring to many unrelated objects with one term. This is a stage of normal language development which typically occurs much earlier. Paul's problem in content appear to be those of delayed development and not any real deviance, as with form and use. This is not surprising when one considers that he did not begin talking until two and a half years, that is, one year ago, and did not use sentences until age three, that is six months ago. Paul's problems in content probably would be outgrown if they were the only concern. However, his problems in both form and use are of a deviant nature and could not be outgrown without remediation. In general, Paul's expressive speech and language are developmentally delayed by one to one and a half years in terms of articulation or form, grammar and morphology as well as vocabulary, content and function.

Paul displays symptoms of developmental aphasia of an unknown etiology. His delay in content was corroborated by a psychologist's report of normal nonverbal and depressed verbal IQ scores. Combined with his delay in talking and specific language and speech disorder, these are critical factors in the diagnosis. Paul has also displayed deficits in auditory perception and sequencing typically associated with developmental aphasia.

Paul appeared to be an excellent candidate for remediation. In fact, six weeks after he left the Neuropsychiatric Institute at which he was evaluated, he had advanced six months in development of speech and language. Had his parents been told he would outgrow the problem, he would have been sent home and would no doubt have fallen deeper into frustration and confusion.

Clinical Applications

Four tables are included in this chapter which chart the basic course of normal language development during the preschool years. They may help you to apply basic theoretical and empirical knowledge about early language development to your practice. Table 4 represents normal milestones in language form, use and content. This chart can be used to determine whether a child's speech or language development is delayed beyond hope of being outgrown. The chart can also guide history taking to determine how early the problem began and how settled it has become in a child's speech. The question to ask is whether the speech and language milestones are developmentally delayed.

Conclusion

In this chapter we have attempted to acquaint you with some of the theories and facts of normal language development. As you know, your task as pediatricians is not solely to intervene in a crisis, to heal sick children but also to foster and maintain normal development. Parents typically are unaware that their child may be delayed or even deviant in language and communication. It is possible

TABLE 4 Developmental Milestones

Question	Normal response
When were the child's first words?	10–12 months
How long are the child's utterances? Is length commensurate with age?	2 years – 2 words 2½ years – 3 words 3 years – 3–4 words 4 years – 5 words
Did the child babble and play with sounds in the first six months?	Yes
Did the child imitate sounds, words and intonation patterns and gestures?	Yes, all
Was the size of the child's vocabulary commensurate with age?	1½ years – 10–20 words 2 years – 50–250 words 2½–3 years – 450 words 3½ years – 800 words 2½ years – all vowels 3½ years – *p, b, m, h, w, n, ng* 4½ years – *k, j, g, f, d* 5½ years – *t, r, sh, v, l, s* 8½ years – *occasional* misarticulation of: *tw, dw, bl, kl, fl, gl, pl, sl, br, kr, dr, fr, gr, pr, tr, thr, sk, sm, sn, sp, st, sn, kw*
Is the child's understanding of how words are put together into sentences commensurate with age?	2 years – telegraphic 2½ years – phrases 3 years – complete simple sentences with pronouns 3½–4 years – compound sentences 6 years – compound, complex sentences

Brown, R. *A first language: The early stages.* Cambridge, Mass.: Harvard University Press, 1973.

Dale, P. *Language development.* Seattle: Holt, Rinehart, & Winston, 1976.

Templin, M. C. *Certain language skills in children: Their development and interrelationships.* Minneapolis: University of Minnesota Press, 1957.

and necessary for pediatricians to be sensitive to these early problems, which may manifest themselves very subtlely in infancy and toddlerhood, and to intervene through treatment and/or referral as early as possible.

References

Bloom, L. and Lahey, M. *Language Development and Language Disorders.* New York: J. Wiley and Sons (1978).

Brown, R. *A first language: The early stages.* Cambridge, Mass.: Harvard University Press (1973).

Cazden, C.B. (ed.) *Language in Early Childhood Education.* Washington, D.C.: National Association for the Education of Young Children (1972).

Cazden, C.B. Two paradoxes in the acquisition of language structure and function, in Connolly, K. and Bruner, J. (eds.), *The Growth of Competence.* London: Academic Press (1974).

Cherry, L.J. A sociolinguistic approach to language development and its implications for education, in Garnica, O. and King, M. (eds.), *Language, Children, and Society.* New York: Pergamon Press (1979).

Collins, A.W. (ed.) *Children's Language and Communication: The Minnesota Symposia on Child Psychology* (Vol. 12). Hillsdale, N.J.: Lawrence Erlbaum Associates, Publishers.

Dale, P. *Language Development.* Seattle: Holt, Rinehart, and Winston (1976).

DeVilliers, J. and DeVilliers, P. *Language Acquisition.* Cambridge, Mass.: Harvard University Press (1978).

Fraser, C. and Bellugi, V. Control of grammar in imitation, comprehension, and production. *J. Verbal Learning and Verbal Behav.,* 2:121–135 (1963).

Halliday, M. *Learning to Mean.* London: Edward Arnold (1975).

Hatch, E. (ed.) *Second Language Acquisition.* Rawley, Mass.: Newbury House Publishers (1978).

Hymes, D. On communicative competence, in Pride, J. and Holmes, J. (eds.), *Sociolinguistics.* Baltimore: Penguin Books (1972).

Ingram, D. Phonological rules in young children. *J. Child Lang.,* 1:49–64 (1974).

Lewis, M. and Cherry, L.J. Social behavior and language acquisition, in Lewis, M. and Rosenblum, L. (eds.), *Interaction, Conversation, and the Development of Language: The Origins of Behavior* (Vol. V). New York: J. Wiley and Sons (1977).

Slobin, D. *Psycholinguistics.* Glenview, Ill.: Scott, Foresman, and Co. (1971).

Templin, M.C. *Certain Language Skills in Children: Their Development and Interrelationships.* Minneapolis: University of Minnesota Press (1957).

Van Riper, C. *Speech Correction: Principles and Methods.* Englewood Cliffs, N.J.: Prentice-Hall, Inc. (1972).

19

Clinical Appraisal of Language Functions in the Preschool Child

PEGGY C. FERRY

Clinical assessment of language development in the preschool child is not easy. Rapin vividly describes the difficulties in evaluating language in a nonverbal child who is uncooperative, pushes away toys offered to him, and remains silent except when an attempt is made to test his reflexes, look in his eyes or detach him from his mother (Rapin, 1978). Yesterday's "hard-to-test" child has become today's routine patient in many pediatric clinics (Singh, 1978). However, the same clinical skills which have enabled pediatricians to evaluate other medical, developmental and neurological disorders in the young child can be used successfully in diagnosing and managing language disorders. I will review the three basic aspects of diagnostic evaluation: the history, physical examination and the use of ancillary laboratory and special language tests. The role of *office evaluation* by the practicing physician is stressed since most parents of children with delayed language development initially consult their child's doctor for advice.

The History

With the vagaries and limitations of physical and laboratory examinations, use of the medical history assumes even greater importance. The history should be taken carefully, in private, with sufficient time allowed for elaboration of pertinent facts. Check lists and written forms are not as useful as the face-to-face interview.

Chief Complaint and Present Illness

Elicit initially the parents' major concerns and reasons for referral. Is the child not talking at all, able to be understood only by close family members, understanding but not speaking, or not doing either? Is he "in his own little world" or "slow" in other areas? Does he gesture or use nonverbal means to communicate with family members? How does he react if frustrated at his inability to communicate his wants and needs? Does his language development seem to be out of proportion to his social, affective, cognitive and motor development?

Obtain additional information about the age of onset, type of speech or language difficulties and their progression. Did the child babble as an infant, use single words at one year, and speak in short sentences at two years? Can he follow simple, two-step commands? Does he know the names of family members, pets and common objects in his environment? Is he improving in his speech development or is his language becoming more deviant? Did the child suddenly "stop talking" when seizures began at age two? (characteristic of acquired auditory verbal agnosia, Ferry, 1978)

Ask the parents to illustrate the child's communicative skills with examples and vignettes. For example, information about his use of language at the dinner table, on family outings, at birthday parties, watching television, or in relating an amusing event when Daddy comes home from work will be useful. Parents should be asked about the percentage of the child's speech which is intelligible to them as opposed to strangers.

Prenatal

Inquire about the pregnancy history, including possible "TORCH" infections, bleeding, drug ingestion, Rh incompatibility, or preeclampsia.

Birth

Review data on gestational age, birth weight, onset (induced or spontaneous) and duration of labor, presentation, medications, Apgar scores and immediate postnatal course. Perinatal asphyxia and complications of prematurity are high-risk situations which may predispose to language problems.

Postnatal

In addition to the developmental history, ask about hyperbilirubinemia, meningoencephalitis, head injuries, vascular occlusion (the "acute infantile hemiplegia syndrome"), seizures, coordination problems, visual difficulties or any other central nervous system problems. Historical information about oromotor functions may be helpful: has the child had any difficulty sucking, chewing or swallowing? Was prolonged or excessive drooling noted in infancy? Can he suck through a straw and lick an ice cream cone without difficulty? Children with dysarthria due to pseudobulbar palsy or oral dyspraxia may have difficulty in these activities, along with their "poor speech" (Ferry, 1975).

Genetic/Family History

While the specific genetic patterns of most childhood language disorders are not fully known, a positive family history of speech, language or reading problems is found more commonly than not in children with delayed language development (Ferry, 1979). Familial cerebellar syndromes, chromosomal anomalies, genetic hearing loss, seizures and mental retardation may all be associated with language disorders. In all cases obtain a careful family history to include the languages spoken in the home. Selected cases may require pedigree analysis and genetic counseling.

The Physical and Neurologic Examinations

All children with delayed language development should undergo a complete physical examination even though it will be normal in the majority of cases. Height, weight and head circumference measurements should be plotted on standard pediatric growth charts. Small head circumference and delayed language development may be due to congenital rubella or another of the TORCH agents. Conversely, hydrocephalic children may show particular patterns of "cocktail party speech" (Schwartz, 1974). Somatic malformations may be seen in chromosomal anomalies. Congenital aortic stenosis, elfin facies and delayed speech development associated with mental retardation are seen in the infantile hypercalcemia syndrome.

    Neurologic examination should assess gait, coordination, cranial nerves, motor function, tendon reflexes, cerebellar integrity and, when possible, sensory functions. For specific attention to perioral neuromotor functions, including (1) jaw jerk; (2) snout reflex; (3) tongue diadokinesis; and (4) gag reflex. A cotton-tipped applicator to elicit tongue movement and lateralization may be helpful. A hyperactive jaw jerk or snout reflex indicates an upper motor neuron lesion involving the pyramidal tracts and may be associated with dysarthria, even in the absence of other neurologic abnormalities ("cerebral palsy of the mouth"). Observation of the child chewing a cracker, sucking through a straw, and drinking from a cup permits assessment of functional aspects of oropharyngeal integrity.

Finally, the mental status examination should be included in the medical-neurologic evaluation. This is usually done best in a playroom setting by playing games with the child, standing on one's head, or taking him for a walk or to get a drink of water. His affect, general level of intelligence, ability to relate, selection of toys, conversational speech, response to commands, and ability to organize thoughts can be evaluated informally. The presence or absence of associated autistic behavior, mental retardation, personality or thought disorder, or even frank psychosis may be appraised in this fashion. In fact, if the examiner is pressed for time, this is probably the most valuable portion of the examination.

Ancillary Diagnostic Tests

Additional laboratory tests should be selected only on the basis of findings from the history and physical examination. There are no "routine" tests in the medical work-up of a child with delayed language development.

Blood and Urine Studies

TORCH titers, thyroid function studies, anticonvulsant blood levels, chromosomal analysis (karyotype) and urine amino acids may be useful in selected cases.

Skull X-rays

Except in cases suggestive of intrauterine infection (with intracranial calcifications) or megalocephaly (hydrocephalus), skull radiographs are rarely indicated.

Electroencephalogram (EEG)

If there is any history suggesting seizures, an EEG would be helpful. Also, if the child has an *acquired* language disorder, an EEG should be performed in the waking and sleep states, looking for subclinical seizure activity (Ferry, 1978). In most cases of language disorder, however, an EEG would not assist in diagnosis or management and should not be performed.

Computed Tomographic Brain Scan (CT Scan)

The CT scan is a new, noninvasive, quick, painless and accurate scanning device for evaluating intracranial structures. Previous studies have documented the presence of structural brain damage, particularly left temporal horn atrophy, in children with developmental language disability (Dalby, 1975; Hauser, 1975). While it would be intriguing from a research or theoretical standpoint to perform CT scans on children with impaired language development, it would not alter management or therapeutic planning in most cases. Furthermore, the expense ($200–250) and the need for sedation, particularly in the preschool child, make it impractical to recommend this test on a routine basis. The author has found that CT scans done on 12 children with development dysphasia showed no abnormalities.

Brain Stem Auditory Evoked Potentials (BSER)

In recent years measurement of brain stem potentials evoked by auditory clicks has been used to assess the integrity of the auditory pathway beyond the cochlea, including the auditory nuclei, and tracts from the medulla, pons, mid-brain and diencephalon. Latencies of the sequential, individual components vary with developmental age and signal intensity. BSER has the advantages of being noninvasive, painless, showing uniformity irrespective of the stage of sleep, and demonstrating the integrity of the auditory pathway independent of motor responses.

In adults BSER has proven to be useful in evaluating a variety of brain stem lesions, including demyelination, infarction, edema and neoplasia. Preliminary data suggest its usefulness in evaluating neonates who lack a startle or blink response to a loud noise (Knauss, 1975). Specific absence of one of the wave forms has been associated with neonatal asphyxia (Hecox, 1978). No studies are available that indicate its clinical value in children with language disorders; however, research in the area is certainly warranted. Given the apparent selective vulnerability of the central auditory pathway to injury, this new technique offers a precise mechanism of investigation and correlation with clinical syndromes. At the least, it provides adjunctive information to conventional audiologic assessment which is so critically important in these children.

Speech and Language Assessment

With completion of the medical and neurologic assessment of the child with a suspected language disability, the physician should consult with colleagues in psychology, speech/language pathology and audiology, who are skilled in early child language assessment. If general language delay is suspected, psychological testing should precede speech and language evaluation. The field of child language assessment is a relatively young one, with rapid development of knowledge, trained professional personnel and new diagnostic tests and techniques.

Physicians should know about these developments in order to collaborate in planning rational therapeutic programs for children in their practices.

Characteristics of the Examiner

With the inherent difficulties present in working with nonverbal, preschool children, it is important to stress the qualifications of the examiner who is involved in language assessment. *It is not a task for the beginner or amateur or those with outdated training.* Lynch has outlined some of the characteristics of a competent examiner: (1) a good observer and skilled listener; (2) patience; and (3) flexibility (Lynch, 1978). A sense of humor, genuine love for children, knowledge about basic brain function, and experience with a broad range of handicapping conditions (cerebral palsy, mental retardation, autistic behavior, hearing impairment, emotional disturbance) are also essential. There is no substitute for "hands-on," direct experience with hard-to-test children.

Given this background, the examiner will select the appropriate tests for use with a particular child. Repeated or multiple examinations may be necessary in some cases, although, with the long clinic waiting lists and the expense of evaluation, as much of the testing as possible should be completed in a single visit. Not every test need be given to every child: the "no-frills," essential aspects of the problem should be assessed to enable formation of rational therapeutic plans. Collaboration between the psychologist and speech/language pathologist may enable joint testing.

Three primary aspects of language may be assessed: (1) form (syntax, morphology and phonology); (2) content (semantics, vocabulary); and (3) use (pragmatics) (Bloom and Lahey, 1978). Specific test batteries are available to assess content and form (see Appendix and Bloom and Lahey, 1978). Assessment of language use is done best by observation, as no reliable, standardized batteries are available for preschool children.

General language development measures, receptive-expressive language levels, measures of specific language functions (semantic, phonologic and syntactic), language functions elicited during informal play sessions, spontaneous language sampling and elicited imitation tests can all be used (Emerick, 1979).

More comprehensive approaches to specific aspects of language assessment, e.g., comprehension, are being developed currently (Rees, 1978). It is no longer sufficient simply to assess the literal meaning of sentences; rather, one must also analyze presuppositions (presupposed information), inferences and elocutionary acts (how the speaker intends the sentence to be conveyed).

Remember that detailed, specific, in-depth language assessment of the preschool child *is* possible and that intervention techniques are available, even for young children. It is no longer appropriate to say, "Don't worry, he'll grow out of it" to parents of a child with delayed language development. Collaboration among the physician, psychologist and speech/language specialist will enable correct diagnosis in the majority of cases. Such accurate diagnosis is the essential first step in rational therapeutic planning for the language-disabled child.

Acknowledgment

The author is indebted to Noel D. Matkin, Ph.D., Jean B. Glattke, M.A., and Peter F. Norlin, Ph.D. for their help in the preparation of this paper.

References

Bloom, L. and Lahey, M. Identifying Children with Language Disorders, in Bloom, L. and Lahey, M. (eds.), *Language Development and Language Disorders.* New York: John Wiley and Sons, pp. 340–367 (1978).

Cooper, J. and Ferry, P. Acquired verbal agnosia and seizures in childhood. *J. Speech Hear. Disord.*, 43:176–184 (1978).

Dalby, M.A. Air studies in language-retarded children: evidence of early lateralization of language function. Presented at The First International Congress of Child Neurology, Toronto, Ontario (1975).

Emerick, L.L. and Hatten, J.T. (eds.) *Diagnosis and Evaluation in Speech Pathology.* Englewood Cliffs, N.J.: Prentice-Hall, pp. 140–156.

Ferry, P., Hall, S. and Hicks, J. Dilapidated speech: developmental verbal dyspraxia. *Devel. Med. Child Neurol.*, 17:749–756 (1975).

Ferry, P., Culbertson, J., Fitzgibbons, P. and Netsky, M. Brain development and language disability. *Int. J. Pediatr. Otorhinolaryngol.*, 11:13–24 (1979).

Hauser, S.L., DeLong, R. and Rosman, N.P. Pneumographic findings in the infantile autism syndrome: a correlation with temporal lobe disease. *Brain*, 98:667–688 (1975).

Hecox, K. and Blau, M. Application of brain stem evoked responses to the diagnosis of neurological disease in infancy. Presented at the Child Neurology Society Meeting, Dillon, Colorado (1978).

Knauss, T.A. More than a startle and a blink. *Pediatrics*, 60:934–935 (1975).

Lynch, J. Evaluation of linguistic disorders in children, in Singh, S. and Lynch, J. (eds.), *Diagnostic Procedures in Hearing, Speech, and Language.* Baltimore, Md.: University Park Press, pp. 335–339 (1978).

Nation, J.E. and Aram, D. *Diagnosis of Speech and Language Disorders.* St. Louis, Mo.: C.V. Mosby Co., pp. 386–408 (1977).

Rapin, L. and Wilson, B.C. Children with developmental language disability: Neurological aspects and assessment, in Wyke, M.A. (ed.), *Developmental Dysphasia.* New York: Academic Press, pp. 32–33 (1978).

Schwartz, E.R. Characteristics of speech and language development in the child with meningomyelocele and hydrocephalus. *J. Speech Hear. Disord.*, 39:465–468 (1974).

Singh, S. and Lynch, J. Evaluation of "hard-to-test" children and adults, in Singh, S. and Lynch, J. (eds.), *Diagnostic Procedures in Hearing, Speech, and Language.* Baltimore, Md.: University Park Press, pp. 105–106 (1978).

APPENDIX Speech and Language Tests for Pre-School Children

Name	Age Range	Assesses	Available From
Assessment of Children's Language Comprehension	3–7 yrs.	Auditory comprehension	Foster, R., Giddon, J. J., Stark, J. Manual for the Assessment of Children's Language Comprehension. Palo Alto, CA: Consulting Psychologists Press, 1972.
Wepman Auditory Discrimination Test	5–8 yrs.	Auditory comprehension	Wepman, J. Auditory Discrimination Test. Chicago: Language Research Associates, 1958.
Carrow Elicited Language Inventory	3–7 yrs.	Auditory comprehension, syntax	Carrow-Woolfolk, E. Carrow Elicited Language Inventory. Austin, Tex.: Learning Concepts, 1974.
Deep Test of Articulation	No age limit	Motor speech, phonetic structure, phonology	McDonald, E. T. A Deep Test of Articulation. Pittsburgh: Stanwix House, Inc., 1964.
Detroit Tests of Learning Aptitude	3–19 yrs.	Word recall, symbolic comprehension	Baker, H. J., and Leland, B. Detroit Tests of Learning Aptitude. Indianapolis: The Bobbs-Merrill Co., Inc., 1974.
Developmental Sentence Types, Scoring, and Analysis	2.3–6.6 yrs.	Expressive language (syntax)	Lee, L. Developmental Sentence Analysis. Evanston, Ill.: Northwestern University Press, 1974.
Fisher-Logemann Test of Articulation Competence	No age limit	Articulation, motor control, phonetic structure, phonology	Fisher, H. B., and Logemann, J. A. Fisher-Logemann Test of Articulation Competence. Boston: Houghton Mifflin Co., 1971.
Goldman-Fristoe Test of Articulation	6–16 yrs.	Articulation, motor control, phonetic structure, phonology	Goldman, R., and Fristoe, M. Goldman-Fristoe Test of Articulation. Circle Pines, Minn.: American Guidance Service, Inc., 1970.
Goldman-Fristoe-Woodcock Test of Auditory Discrimination	3.8–7.0 yrs.	Auditory perception and comprehension	Goldman, R., Fristoe, M., Woodcock, R. Goldman-Fristoe-Woodcock Test of Auditory Discrimination. Circle Pines, Minn.: American Guidance Service, Inc., 1969.

APPENDIX (Continued)

Name	Age Range	Assesses	Available From
Hiskey-Nebraska Test of Learning Aptitude	3–8 yrs.	Non-verbal intelligence	Hiskey, M. Hiskey-Nebraska Test of Learning Aptitude. Lincoln, Neb.: University of Nebraska Press, 1966.
Houston Test for Language Development	6 mo.–6 yrs.	General language functions (receptive and expressive)	Crabtree, M. Houston Test for Language Development. Houston Test Co., 1963.
Illinois Test of Psycholinguistic Abilities	2.4–10.3 yrs.	Language age, memory; receptive, associative, expressive performance at various levels	Kirk, S. A., McCarthy, J., Kirk, W. D. Illinois Test of Psycholinguistic Abilities. (rev. ed.) Urbana, Ill.: University of Illinois Press, 1968.
Miller-Yoder Test of Grammatical Comprehension	3–6 yrs.	Auditory comprehension	Miller, J. F., and Yoder, D. E. The Miller-Yoder Test of Grammatical Comprehension: Experimental Edition. Madison, Wisc.: Department of Communicative Disorders, University of Wisconsin, 1972.
Northwestern Syntax Screening Test	3.0–7.11 yrs.	Language comprehension and expression phonology	Lee, L. Northwestern Syntax Screening Test. Evanston, Ill.: Northwestern University Press, 1969.
Peabody Picture Vocabulary Test	2.9–18.5 yrs.	Auditory comprehension (vocabulary)	Dunn, L. M. Expanded Manual for the Peabody Picture Vocabulary Test. Circle Pines, Minn.: American Guidance Service, Inc., 1965.
Pre-School Language Manual (Zimmerman)	1.6–7 yrs.	Auditory comprehension, verbal ability	Zimmerman, I., Steiner, V., Evatt, R. Pre-School Language Manual. Columbus, Ohio: Charles E. Merrill Publishing Co., 1960.
Receptive–Expressive Emergent Language Scale (REEL)	Birth–3 yrs.	Receptive–expressive quotients (mainly interview techniques)	Bzoch, K., and League, R. Assessing Language Skills in Infancy. Gainesville, Fla.: Tree of Life Press, 1971.

APPENDIX   (Continued)

Name	Age Range	Assesses	Available From
Test for Auditory Comprehension of Language (TACL) (Carrow)	3.0–6.11 yrs.	Auditory comprehension	Carrow-Woolfolk, E. Test for Auditory Comprehension of Language. Austin, Tex.: Learning Concepts, 1970.
Token Test	3.0–12.5 yrs.	Auditory comprehension	DeRenzi, E., and Vignolo, L. A. The Token Test: A sensitive test to detect receptive disturbances in aphasia. *Brain* 85:665–678 (1962).

Modified from: Nation, J. E., and Aram, D. Tests and tools available for designing the diagnosis: a tool–retrieval source. Appendix III. In: Diagnosis of Speech and Language Disorders. St. Louis; C. V. Mosby, 1977, pp. 386–408.

20

Early Language Intervention: When and How

JON F. MILLER

The goal of early language intervention is to teach children the community language resulting in a functional communication system. This enterprise presumes the early identification of children at risk for impaired communication development and strategies that sustain facilitation of language acquisition when initiated early in life.

Early language intervention requires specifying the physiological, environmental and psychological factors that would identify a child at risk and documenting effective early language intervention for a variety of deficits associated with language delay. The basic question to be asked, then, is: is early language intervention effective and for whom?

Is Early Intervention Effective?

Results from early intervention programs have been described in review articles by Bronfenbrenner (1975) and Haskins *et al.* (1978). These reviews reveal that most programs document at least short-term gains in a variety of skill areas including social, cognitive, motor and language. More important, reviews point out the difficulties in documenting gains which are attributable to intervention alone. Factors contributing to the problem of documenting the effects of early intervention include: heterogeneity of populations, specificity of program goals, carefully constructed measurement devices capable of documenting developmental change while validly reflecting program content, differentiation of teaching impact from program content, and research designs capable of documenting nonlinear development that do not require control groups.

Despite the complexities of intervention research, a number of programs impressively demonstrate the effectiveness of early intervention in enhancing language and cognitive development. In a day care setting Robinson and Robinson (1971) report significant gains for children through the first two years of life. With a more comprehensive approach combining educational and home programming, Heber and Garber (1975) and Ramey *et al.* (1976) document significant gains for children of low socioeconomic status (SES) at risk for sociocultural retardation through five years of age. These projects have accumulated longitudinal data that continue to support program effects.

Objective evidence of the structure and longitudinal impact of early intervention programs for children with moderate to severe developmental disabilities is scant (Bricker *et al.,* 1978). Bricker and Carlson (1979) point out that while gains can be documented for a number of language training programs, the nature of the gains falls short of interventionist's expectations. Although most children show progress in developing some communication skills, they frequently do not develop complete linguistic systems.

The most notable problems which consistently emerge in intervention research include generalization, nonapplication of skills acquired in direct teaching contexts in other daily living activities, and maintaining attention and motivation in repetitious teaching contexts. Problems in generalization of training across a number of behavioral domains including language have a long history in behavioral teaching programs. A frequent solution has been to develop separate training sequences that promote generalization of skills acquired in direct training contexts. In reviewing these training studies Stokes and Baer (1977) reveal that a number of approaches do promote generalization. Examples include the use of multiple contexts (laboratory, home, school), multiple exemplars (using balls of different sizes and colors in vocabulary training), and multiple trainers teaching the same skills. These approaches focus on manipulating the program format where changes in program content, i.e., what skills are to be taught and in what contexts, are determined by remedial logic (Guess *et al.,* 1977).

Basic to remedial logic is the premise that any behavior can be taught if the learning environment is structured properly to include explicit antecedent, response conditions with appropriate reinforcement. In remedial logic the child's needs for functional behavior should determine the skills to be taught. Skills can be identified in a number of contexts such as the home, where communication around basic self-help skills of eating, dressing and toileting may be deficient. While this approach was developed to meet the training needs of older mentally retarded children, the power of behavioral programming has prompted its application to early intervention as well, particularly with more severely involved populations.

As intervention programs for moderately and severely retarded children began to focus on younger subjects (under five years), programming strategies changed. The task, then, became one of teaching the child an effective language system rather than eradicating deficiencies in a deviant system. Achieving this goal prompted interventionists to turn to developmental theory and data for assistance. The resulting intervention programs combined behavioral technology with an alternative approach to selecting program content. This approach, termed developmental (Graham, 1976), recognized that language develops systematically over time and that sequences of linguistic behaviors identified in the speech of young children would provide a logical starting point in teaching a complex hierarchical system leading to functional communication. Early programs reflected the developmental literature at the time and focused primarily on teaching syntax (Bricker, 1972; Miller and Yoder, 1972a,b).

Basic research in normal development has continued to expand our understanding of the complexity of language and communication and at the same time has begun to document the relationships between language and social and cognitive development. Early intervention programs have incorporated these advances in developmental theory and data. As a result, several shifts in program emphasis have occurred, each leading to more impressive outcomes. With the recognition of the role of cognitive theory in language acquisition, Bricker and Bricker (1973, 1974) incorporated the teaching of cognitive prerequisites in their early intervention programs. The shift in theory from syntax to a semantic-cognitive basis for early language acquisition is reflected in the program described by Miller and Yoder (1974).

Throughout this period came the recognition that traditional models of clinical and educational language intervention were deficient where results documented lack of generalization of training. Children's failure to generalize was traced to several factors including: limited amount of training, time usually ranging from one twenty-minute session a day to twice a week for an hour; artificial training contexts (child and trainer isolated in small room with trainer presenting stimuli and child responding with no conversational contexts); and the content although developmentally sequenced not functional for the child's everyday environment.

The Brickers' programs have reflected a number of changes over the years to overcome these difficult problems (Bricker and Carlson, 1979). Bricker and Carlson make two guiding principles implicit in their and others (Miller and Yoder, 1974; McDonald and Blott, 1974) early programs:

1. A recognition of the interrelated nature of early developmental processes, cognitive, social and linguistic.
2. The reciprocal interactive nature of the child with his parent and environment.

The fundamental change in programming strategies for infants and young children brought about by these principles is the shift from teacher or clinician as agent of change to mother. This shift has potential for addressing the problems related to content appropriateness and generalization identified previously. Mothers spend the most time with their children, with an opportunity for increased training time. Training, moreover, is conducted in the child's natural environment, the home or other natural settings, providing a chance to teach functional language for everyday experiences. In addition, the child's natural environment allows him frequent interactions as initiator as well as respondent, providing the basis for the development of conversational skills.

Recently Reported Early Intervention Research

Recently, four early intervention projects have documented significant gains in communication skills (Fowler, 1979; Ramey *et al.*, 1979; Kysela *et al.*, 1979; Hart and Rogers-Warren, 1978). Each of these projects reflects recent developmental research recognizing the reciprocal interactive nature of functional language use and the central role of parents/caretakers in fostering developmental change. Each program was developed for a different population and to answer different research questions. However, each employs parents as agents of change, and each focuses on existing parent-child relationships as the vehicle for facilitating the child's communication skills.

Fowler (1979) reports a series of research projects demonstrating that 12 to 21 months of early, directed stimulation with normal infants results in significant increases, over test norms, in language, cognitive and motor skills. Moreover, longitudinal follow-up revealed these gains are maintained at five years of age. These impressive results indicate that intervention initiated between three and twelve months of age significantly advances performance at age five. Fowler argues that these studies demonstrate the effects of the environment on development; that is, directed stimulation provides the child with the means to realize his biological potential more efficiently than environments left to chance.

Fowler's program is based on two principles. First, program content is planned and systematically ordered to reflect current developmental sequences. Second, it is professionally mediated, i.e., professionals design programs and transmit training techniques in writing or through personal guidance to parents or teachers. While the program is both formal and systematic, the strategy for implementation is adaptive and clinical. The program for each child is not fixed in advance; rather, child stimulation and care-giver guidance are constructed and modified according to the developing styles of the child and care-givers in the home or day care setting.

Fowler's very impressive results demonstrate consistent long-term effects from early intervention that focuses on enhancing and strengthening parent/caretaker commitment to children's development. In demonstrating that environmental manipulation produces lasting developmental advances in cognitive, linguistic and motor skills, Fowler's research raises important issues about developmental theory and the application of his program to deviant children.

The first issue is: what specific processes were altered by early intervention? Were the child's perceptual-cognitive systems tuned up as a result of consistent and frequent stimulation presented at or just above developmental status? Or, were parents tuned in to the child's level of performance with training to foster social and communicative interactions that were continued beyond the formal intervention period? These questions cannot be answered with existing data, but they demonstrate how intervention research can provide data relevant for developmental theory.

The answers to these questions are also germane to the issue of whether Fowler's programs be applied to developmentally disabled children. The resolution of this second issue depends upon your theoretical point of view. If you believe the child's ability to learn has been accelerated by early intervention, then you would seriously consider direct application of Fowler's stimulation programs to children with perceptual, neurologic and cognitive deficits. If, on the other hand, you believe the parent/caretaker-child training strategies continued to adapt beyond the formal training period, then the child's environment has been significantly altered over time and not the child himself. The latter view raises questions about what constitutes early intervention, duration of training and generalization. While this line of argument may seem circular it comes down to whether the child or the environment altered over time?

In application to developmentally disabled populations, the former argument would predict improving deficit performance at the perceptual-cognitive level. The latter argument would demand continual environmental manipulation to maintain and foster developmental change. The obvious third alternative is that both occur to some extent.

Ramey *et al.* (1979) report on a project specifically aimed at preventing the association of sociocultural mental retardation with low socioeconomic status. The studies of Ramey and his colleagues, as well as others, document that race and the mother's educational level at the time of the child's birth significantly predict child's IQ, academic achievement and teacher's opinion of him in the first grade (Ramey *et al.*, 1978). These studies confirm what has been historically presumed—that relative social disadvantage is associated with slow development and subsequent school failure. Ramey *et al.* argue that to the extent that there are general variables, like the mother's educational level, that are predictive and part of a causal chain, there must be specific parental practices directly affecting the disadvantaged child different from those of more advantaged parents. They suggest that educational level may be associated with different nutritional habits, forms or content of teaching or an abnegation of parental responsibility (Ramey *et al.*, 1979).

In pursuing this line of research, Ramey and his colleagues recognize the mother-child relationship as fundamental to the developmental process. Also, while socioeconomic status is associated with failure to develop, significant numbers of children from low SES families do develop appropriately and are successful in school. Ramey and Smith (1977) have developed criteria for identifying families as "at risk" for school failure from low SES populations.

The Ramey (1979) paper reports on a study of 24 families identified as high risk for school failure. This study was designed to determine if the early mother-child interaction could be positively modified toward more mother involvement with the child through a parent education program. Intervention began before the children were 12 weeks old, and mother-child interactions were evaluated at six months. Results showed that mothers of the parent education group spent significantly more time holding their infants, less time away from them and were more frequently involved in mutual play than control dyads. In addition, control group mothers spent more time reading to themselves and had infants who spent more time playing alone or not being involved in any discernible activity. Ramey stressed that the mothers' greater involvement is mediated by their significantly greater frequency of joining ongoing child activity and staying with the activity longer. The researchers argued that these results are particularly encouraging in light of past research (Farran and Ramey, 1979) documenting that dyadic involvement at six months was related to developmental status at four years of age.

The Ramey project documents that parent-child interaction can be modified through parent education. The specific effects of these changes on children's communication status in later years must await follow-up studies of this population. Explanation of future outcomes will require careful documentation of the mother's performance as well as the child's. Generalization of parent training over time is central to discovering specific processes controlling development within mother-child exchanges. In addition, these data will have direct bearing on when intervention should be initiated, its duration and specific parent-training procedures.

The important link between the Fowler (1979) and Ramey (1979) papers is that both demonstrate the relationship between extensive parent-child interactions early in the developmental period and advanced cognitive and language development in later years. While the specific interactional processes affecting development are yet to be identified, these studies demonstrate that such mechanisms must exist. Further, future longitudinal research shows promise in revealing them. Preventing communication and cognitive deficits in children suspected of not receiving necessary parental interaction appears possible in the not-too-distant future.

The impact of early intervention on parent-child interaction for populations with cognitive deficits has received little attention (McDonald and Blott, 1974). Bricker and Carlson (1979) point out several factors contributing to the lack of data including: the changing nature of our understanding of language acquisition, development of teaching-intervention technologies and, most important, the nature of the population itself.

There are numerous programs for teaching communication skills to retarded children (Graham 1976 and Fristoe 1976). The formulation of these programs has been fundamentally guided by population characteristics related to severity of retardation. For example, children with moderate to severe handicaps have noticeable deficiencies in attention, memory and generalization of learned skills. In addition, these children do not actively interact with their environment in infancy, as evidenced, among other things, by low rates of communicative attempts.

These population characteristics required carefully structured programs usually based on behavior modification principles. The programs consisted of a teaching strategy or technology and the content or sequence of skills to be taught. In addition, they frequently had separate training sequences for generalization. Historically, these programs were first developed for older, school-age, retarded children. Recent trends toward programming for younger children with significant developmental delays have resulted from federal and state legislation (PL 94-142), improved techniques for identifying developmental disabilities early, and advances in our understanding of the processes underlying language acquisition.

This progression is best represented by the intervention research of the Brickers who over the past 15 years have implemented an impressive series of state-of-the-art intervention projects. Recently, these projects have focused on early intervention of cognitive and language skills in severely and profoundly retarded children. Their programs have increasingly used parents as the agents of change in order to expand training time and to improve the likelihood of the child generalizing learned behaviors. In addition, their recent programs have included sequences of cognitive skills to be taught as prerequisites for language development. These have been derived from the Piagetian perspective of the language-cognition relationship and include such skills as the functional use of objects. This expansion of content as well as the emphasis on reciprocal interaction reflects the impact of basic research on intervention through specification necessary and sufficient conditions for language development.

A primary difference in programs for severely and profoundly retarded children is the belief that these children will not acquire communication without intervention. Several reasons can be offered for this belief: (1) these children often have multiple handicapping conditions which do not allow access to environmental stimuli available to normal children; or (2) since the child is relatively unresponsive to environmental stimuli, interactions with him decrease, resulting in decreased linguistic input; or (3) cognitive deficits are so severe that the number of trials or presentations necessary for skill acquisition are significantly higher than for less affected populations. Therefore, the environmental consistency presumed necessary for these children to learn is simply not available in the natural environment. All of these arguments for the failure of this population to acquire communication skills spontaneously are likely to be true to some extent. Regardless of point of view, the result is the overwhelming task of teaching the entire language communication system.

The movement toward earlier intervention has prompted shifts in programming strategies since programs developed for higher functioning children were not appropriate for lower functioning children. The significant shift has come in performance requirements. In programs requiring children to be respondents only, they learned to respond to specific linguistic stimuli but failed to initiate utterances of similar form and content. Similarly, exposure to increased linguistic stimuli without specific initiation or response requirements failed to provide participatory communication which appears necessary for language acquisition. Current language acquisition theory and past intervention research and experience suggest that programs that incorporate a positive parent-child relationship with parents counseled in teaching specific skills will increase efficiency in training communication skills (Bricker and Carlson, 1979).

A recent early intervention project reported by Kysela *et al.* (1979) documents significant gains with a systematic approach to training that incorporates consistent replicable methods and carefully sequenced content within specific training contexts. They compared two groups of mild to severely developmentally disabled children, one group participating in a home training program, the other in a school-based program. Both programs emphasized improving parent and teacher skills and isolating program deficiencies for individual children. In addition, the programs sought to establish generalizable parent/teacher teaching skills for new behaviors as well as generalized child responses. Both programs incorporated direct and incidental teaching models developed from experimental and applied behavior analysis research conducted within a learning framework.

Both programs produced significant gains in language and cognitive skills with no significant differences in language skills between groups. Parents were able to acquire the skills necessary to train their children, who evidenced remarkable rates of acquisition. It is important to point out that documented gains were in relation to test performance at baseline. No control group was included in this study. At present, legal and ethical considerations make it virtually impossible to employ control groups in longitudinal intervention research projects.

In addition, the expected outcome of no training for retarded populations is decreased performance on tests with increasing age resulting in what are termed cumulative deficiencies. The advances by developmentally disabled infants 2 to 16 months of age are indeed impressive when parents served as agents of change.

Early intervention programs which employ teaching methods adapted to child performance and specific content in variable contexts with parents as agents as well as teachers significantly advance language development in developmentally disabled populations. While these programs are highly systematized and adapted to individual deficits, there is a striking resemblance in early intervention techniques to the behaviors exhibited by mothers of normal children. This is obvious, since some intervention techniques have been derived from developmental research while others have come through experience in attempting to teach children language. While it is impossible to unravel the time between experience and basic research, Chapman (1979) reviewed the literature documenting the language mothers addressed to children and found that it changed with the child's level of productive language development.

In general, mothers' speech directed to children under two is less complex in all linguistic domains, phonological, syntactic, semantic and pragmatic. Chapman identifies two major problems encountered by the language learning child: first, the segmentation of linguistic input, i.e., recognition of the various sound, meaning and grammatical elements in the stream of speech; second, the identification of the referent, i.e., what object, event or relationship is being talked about in the environment. She then documents a number of devices mothers use to help the child overcome these problems. For example, segmentation appears to be facilitated by the use of pauses at utterance boundaries and a higher frequency of single word utterances. Children's identification of referents is facilitated by restricting topics to immediate here-and-now context. The speech addressed to children two and younger is almost exclusively about the immediate situation. In addition, the consistent use of dialogue cycles, getting the child's attention, asking a question, e.g., "what's that?" and providing the label are reminiscent of teaching strategies employed in early intervention programs. Mothers also use consistent feedback to children, always correcting incorrect labels and confirming correct ones, but rarely correcting incorrect grammatical form.

Detailed studies of mothers' speech to young children reveal consistent interaction styles, restricted, sequenced content, responsiveness to child-initiated utterances and context-specific behaviors. These studies reveal a much more ordered environment that appears more conducive to language learning than was thought possible 10 to 15 years ago. Yet, many of these documented patterns have been employed in early language intervention programs before their discovery in studies of normal children.

We have come full circle in our search for the processes associated with linguistic growth and change. Interventionists have traditionally looked to basic research for ways to advance development in deviant populations. At present, early intervention appears to be highly productive for designing experiments to document causal relationships identified in naturalistic, observational research. In the development of the science of language disorders, intervention, particularly early intervention, is no longer the stepchild of observational study but the cornerstone of scientific method in developmental research.

Early Intervention, When and How

All evidence suggests that intervention can proceed as soon as conditions associated with delayed communication development have been identified. A variety of neuropsychological, physiologic and environmental factors have been isolated which affect language acquisition and use (Table 1). Table 1 reveals that some variables affect production of language and not comprehension. Speech motor control, for example, does not affect language comprehension but will influence intelligibility in varying degrees with significant delays related to respiratory control deficits. Children with general motor deficits, cerebral palsy for example, are at risk for oral communication development due to physiologic limitation of motor movements necessary for productive speech.

Fowler (1979) presents the only data available on the impact of intervention initiated at different times in infancy. He reports that intervention begun at 3 months and continuing to 15 months results in immediate significant gains which continue to accelerate through the training period. Training initiated at 12 months and continuing through 24 months shows similar accelerated rates of development. These results demonstrate that intervention begun at three months is as effective as when initiated at 12 months. These effects may not be generalizable to conditions where basic parenting skills are suspect. The results of the Ramey (1979) and Thoman (1979) papers argue that early reciprocal interactions between mothers and their children are essential for fostering developmental growth and change. Intervention, to have maximal impact, should begin as soon as children are identified, the earlier the better.

As to the design of effective intervention strategies, it should be clear that early intervention must focus on parent/caretaker skills fostering reciprocal interaction. Programs should emphasize the following: (1) mothers should respond to child-initiated communicative attempts; (2) mothers should repeat and expand child utterances, adding one or two words; (3) mothers' speech should be directed toward immediate ongoing events, i.e., describing, commenting on child's ongoing activities, maintaining joint attention to objects and events when talking about them; (4) mothers should expect children to comprehend more

TABLE 1 Variables in Language Acquisition and Use

Variables Affecting Language Acquisition and Use	Effect Seen in Language Comprehension Reception	Effects Seen in Language Production (Expression)	Effects Seen in Use of Language For Communication

Neuropsychological Factors
1. Cognitive Development
2. Central Processing
  A. Auditory
  B. Visual Perception/Discrimination
3. (Speech) Motor Control
4. Attending, relating, motivation
	1. Delayed onset – slow development
	2. Does not develop (severe) to Delayed onset (minimal) – auditory –
	3. Not affected
	4. Does not develop to delayed onset depending on severity
		1. Delayed onset – slow development
		2. Sound production diminished at 6 Mos. (auditory) – Delayed onset (visual)
		3. Intelligibility of speech poor to fair (dysarthria)
		4. Delayed onset or failure to develop; Dysfluency (stuttering and cluttering)
			1. Delayed onset – slow development
			2. Motor and motor Vocal Vocal (auditory)
			3. Not affected
			4. Disordered or nonexistent nonexistent

Structural and Physiological Factors
1. Sensory
  A. Auditory
  B. Visual
    Acuity end
    Organ dysfunction
2. Cranial facial anomalies
3. Laryngeal anomalies
	1. Delayed onset (minimal to moderate)
	2. Poor to fair in intelligibility (auditory)
	3. Not affected
	4. Not affected
		1. Delayed onset – auditory
		2. Intelligibility of speech related to structures affected and severity
		3. Limited voicing including voicing intensity frequency and quality disorders
			1. Motor and motor Vocal expression
			   Delayed onset (visual) minimal
			2. Not affected
			3. Motor and Motor vocal expression –

Environmental Factors
1. Social and Cultural
  A. SES
  B. Language and Dialect
2. Physical
  A. Experience
  B. Linguistic input (living situation)
	1. Delayed onset (bilingual home)
	2. Delayed onset
		1. Delayed onset, dialect reflectant of culture and community
		2. Delayed onset
			1. Not affected
			2. Delayed onset, few communication needs

language than they can produce; (5) mothers need to recognize and develop routines and conversational games like pat-a-cake and peek-a-boo; and (6) fundamentally, mothers must recognize that communication needs to be fostered in all of the child's activities throughout his daily routine. Communication cannot be taught through simple accelerated stimulation; more is not necessarily better. Direct stimulation, modifying mothers' patterns of speech, and increased responsiveness to child performance, emphasizing conversational exchange, will facilitate the child's acquisition of language and result in functional communication.

Identification, The Missing Link to Prevention

We have seen effective interventions employed with normal middle-class children (Fowler, 1979), low SES children of families identified as "at risk" for sociocultural retardation (Ramey *et al.,* 1979), and developmentally disabled children varying in severity (Kysela *et al.,* 1979). These programs demonstrate positive accelerated developmental change when parents are trained early in the child's life to interact positively and frequently with their children. The positive effects have been demonstrated with a variety of populations. No deleterious effects of early parent training programs on children have been reported. While research in early intervention continues to discover improved strategies and identify processes associated with developmental change, findings to date can have an impact on existing service delivery systems.

At the center of the health care system is the pediatric office. As the first professional in contact with the infant and family, the pediatrician is responsible for the early identification and referral of children with known or suspected developmental delays. There are a variety of neuropsychological, physiologic and environmental conditions associated with delayed communication development (see Table 1). The relationship of these conditions to the development of language skills is not well understood in all cases. With the identification of each condition comes the expectation for significantly delayed communication development unless intervention is initiated. On the other hand, children identified early with delayed language development may be suffering significant physiologic, neuropsychological or environmental deficits. Communication behavior is a sensitive indicator of the integrity of the child and his environment.

While the importance of early identification is well recognized, the means to detect early developmental delay have emerged slowly. Significant improvements are being made in detecting problems at birth with the development of various high-risk registers. Several developmental scales are available, each evaluating a variety of behaviors emerging in infancy and each including some items evaluating communication. In most cases these scales do not include sufficient items to independently judge the child's developing skills in language comprehension, language production and emerging conversational competence. More exhaustive developmental scales focusing on language employ formats difficult or too time-consuming to use in pediatric offices.

One of the tests most widely used by pediatricians for screening developmental performance is the Denver Developmental Screening Test. In Table 2 the language items are listed by the specific aspect of language evaluated, phonology, syntax, semantics and pragmatics, in both comprehension and production. An examination of Table 2 reveals a number of significant deficiencies. For example, little attention is paid to the sound system and the items evaluating comprehension do not begin until 17 months when the item is a frequent routine played by mothers and children. Such routines do not provide sufficient evidence of linguistic understanding given their frequency of occurence, order of presentation and visual cues. Even the items at 20 months are questionable, since the child is only required to understand one word—the last word—to comply with the direction. The child, given the block, understands the implied action and gives the block to mommy. The result is that children with significant problems in comprehension cannot be identified with this test until well over two years of age.

What is required is a set of items developed around times when children are likely to visit pediatric offices for routine examination or immunization. These items should be few in number and readily observable or easily elicited. Ideally, they could be administered in 5 to 10 minutes in conjunction with other routine tasks. Table 3 is an example of behaviors expected at each point, from birth to 1 month, 6, 12, 18 and 24 months. Where possible, the implications of absent performance for each item are included. Each age period represents an independent developmental scale which is short but provides sufficient detail to recommend follow-up evaluation of language behavior or related characteristics.

The development and implementation of a scale like that in Table 3 is essential for identifying, monitoring and following up communication development in children with known deficits and as a symptom of significant medical problems. At least as important is the early identification of children who at three evidence significant developmental delays in language and who have no other physiologic, neuropsychological or environmental deficits. This population has been estimated to be as high as 5 per cent of children three years of age. At present, there is no systematic way to identify them early in infancy. The major problem is distinguishing the children at the slow end of the developmental continuum from those whose rates of development will result in significant delays at three years of age.

These children, if identified, would be excellent candidates for an intervention of the type described by Fowler *et al.* (1979). With the documented effects of early intervention through parent training, preventing these developmental deficits at three years appears to be a very real possibility.

TABLE 2 Language Items from the Denver Developmental Screening Test

Age At Which 50% Pass	Production				Comprehension			
	Phonology	Syntax	Semantics	Pragmatics	Phonology	Syntax	Semantics	Pragmatics
1 Month	Vocalizes not crying							
2 Months	Laughs Squeals							
7 Months	Mama or Dada Nonspecific Imitates speech sounds			Peek-a-boo (6) Pat-a-cake (9)				
10 Months			Mama or Dada specific					
13 Months			3 words other than Mama or Dada	Indicates wants (requests) (12)				

Age				
17 Months				Points to body part named (routine)
20 Months	Combines two different words	Names one picture	Interactive Play (24)	[Follows two of three directions] 1. *Give the block to mommy* 2. *Put the block on the table* 3. *Put the block on the floor*
2 years–6 Months	Uses Plurals			
2 years–9 Months				Gives 1st and last name
3 years				Comprehends cold, tired and hungry Prepositions 3 colors
3 years–9 Months		Defines 6 words		

TABLE 3 Sample Developmental Scale for Identifying Communication Deficits in the First Two Years of Life

Age	Physiological/Behavioral Indices	Implication
Birth–At One Month	Feeding Problems Weak Cry Congenital Anomalies	At Risk for Communication Development At Risk — Developmental Delay
	Syndrome	At Risk — Developmental Delay
	Orofacial Anomalies	Medical Decisions: Surgery — Timing
	Laryngeal Anomalies	Implications for Speech Motor Control
	Motor Deficits — CP At Risk — Low Birth Weight	Long-Term Considerations
6 Months	Productive Vocalization Stops or Diminishes	Hearing, Note Other Developmental Milestones
	Orient To Sound	Hearing
	Production Characteristics Syllable Repetition (Ba Ba Ba)	*Developmental Delay* Respiration
	Duration of Cooing, Singing and Babbling 2–3 Sec.	Respiration, Laryngeal
	Variable Intonation, Both During Crying and Cooing	Laryngeal
	Voiced/Voiceless Contrast P vs. B/	Laryngeal
	Discrete Tongue Movements /D/ /N/ /G/	
12 Months	*Production* Produces Mama or Dada, pet name referentially. Low frequency and intelligibility Imitates Speech Sounds	*Implication* Developmental Delay Cognitive Deficits Minimal Hearing Loss
	Comprehension Understands own name Present familiar people, familiar objects	
	Use of Language for Communication Turn taking vocalizations in communication games, Peek-A-Boo, Pat-A-Cake	

TABLE 3 (Continued)

Age	Physiological/Behavioral Indices	Implication
18 Months	*Comprehension* Single Words, Object Names within Visual Field	*Implication* Developmental Delay Hearing Loss
	Production Few Intelligible Words Familiar People and Objects /CV/ Frequency of Productions Increasing	
	Use of Language for Communication Requests, Comments Rejects with Motor and Vocal or Vocal Behavior Hi and Bye with Gesture or Vocal Behavior	Absence of Intention to Communicate
24 Months	*Comprehension* Two-Word Utterances "Mama's Book" Possessor Possession "Throw Ball" Action Object Single Words Action Verbs Absent Objects	*Implication* Developmental Delay Specific Communication Delay
	Production Vocabulary Increase to 20 Words — Minimum Two-Word Utterances At Least Two Intelligible Utterances	
	Use of Language for Comprehension Request names, locations "What's that", "Where's that" Ritualized Use Words for Multiple Functions	

Summary

In this chapter we have demonstrated that early intervention programs directed at modifying parent-child interaction patterns have resulted in positive developmental gains in a variety of populations. Further, longitudinal follow-up has revealed that these gains are sustained over time. Remediation programs based on positive, frequent parent-child exchanges show promise as an efficient means of preventing communication handicaps. Therefore, the pediatrician's role in the early identification of impaired communication development is crucial to the prevention of communication handicaps in school-age children.

References

Bricker, D. Imitative sign training as a facilitator of word-object association with low-functioning children. *Am. J. Ment. Defic.,* 76:509–516 (1972).

Bricker, D. and Carlson, L. *Issues in Early Language Intervention.* Paper presented at the conference entitled "Early Language Intervention," Sturbridge, Massachusetts, May (1979).

Bricker, D., Seibert, J. and Scott, K. *Early Intervention: History, Current Status and the Problem of Evaluation.* Paper presented at Gatlinburg Conference on Mental Retardation Research, March (1978).

Bricker, W. and Bricker, D. Behavior modification programmes, in Mittler, P. (ed.), *Assessment for Learning in the Mentally Handicapped.* London: Churchill Livingstone (1973).

Bricker, W. and Bricker, D. An early language training strategy, in Schiefelbusch, R.L. and Lloyd, L.L. (eds.), *Language Perspectives—Acquisition, Retardation and Intervention.* Baltimore: University Park Press, pp. 431–468 (1974).

Bronfenbrenner, U. Is early intervention effective? in Guttentag, M. and Struening, E. (eds.), *Handbook of Evaluation Research, Vol. 2.* Beverly Hills, California: Sage Publications (1975).

Chapman, R. *Mother-Child Interaction in the Second Year of Life: Its Role in Language Development.* Paper presented at the conference entitled "Early Language Intervention," Sturbridge, Massachusetts, May (1979).

Farran, D. and Ramey, C. *Social Class Differences in Dyadic Involvement During Infancy.* Paper submitted for publication (1979).

Fowler, W. *A Strategy for Infant Learning and Developmental Learning.* Paper presented at the conference entitled "Early Language Intervention," Sturbridge, Massachusetts, May (1979).

Fristoe, MaCalyne. Language Intervention Systems: Programs Published in Kit Form, in Lloyd, L. (ed.), *Communication Assessment and Intervention Strategies.* Baltimore: University Park Press (1972).

Graham, L. Language programming and intervention, in Lloyd, L. (ed.), *Communication Assessment and Intervention Strategies.* Baltimore: University Park Press, pp. 371–422 (1976).

Guess, D., Sailor, W. and Baer, D. A behavioral-remedial approach to language training for the severely handicapped, in Sontag, E. (ed.), *Educational Programming for the Severely Handicapped.* Reston, Va.: CEC (1977).

Hart, B. and Rogers-Warren, A. A milieu approach to teaching language, in Schiefelbusch, R. (ed.), *Language Intervention Strategies.* Baltimore: University Park Press, pp. 193–236 (1978).

Haskins, R., Finkelstein, N. and Stedman, D. Infant-stimulation programs and their effects. *Pediat. Ann.*, 7:2, 123–144 (1978).

Heber, R. and Garber, H. The Milwaukee Project: A study of the use of family intervention to prevent cultural-familial retardation, in Friedlander, B., Sterritt, G. and Kirk, S. (eds.), *Exceptional Infant, Vol. 1.* New York: Brunner/Mazel (1975).

Kysela, G., Hillyard, A., McDonald, L. and Ahlsten-Taylor. *Early Intervention: Design and Evaluation.* Paper presented at the conference entitled "Early Language Intervention," Sturbridge, Massachusetts, May (1979).

McDonald, J. and Blott, J. Environmental language intervention: The rationale for a diagnostic and training strategy through rules, context and generalization. *J. Speech and Hear. Disord.*, 39:244–256 (1974).

Miller, J. and Yoder, D. On developing the content for a language teaching program. *Ment. Retard.*, 10:9–11 (1972a).

Miller, J. and Yoder, D. A syntax teaching program, in McLean, J., Yoder, D. and Schiefel-busch, R. (eds.), *Language Intervention with the Retarded: Developing Strategies.* Baltimore: University Park Press, pp. 191–211 (1972b).

Miller, J. and Yoder, D. An ontogenetic teaching strategy for retarded children, in Schiefel-busch, R. and Lloyd, L. (eds.), *Language Perspectives–Acquisition, Retardation and Intervention.* Baltimore: University Park Press (1974).

Ramey, C., Collier, A., Sparling, J., Loda, R., Campbell, F., Ingram, D. and Finkelstein, N. The Carolina Abecedarian Project: A longitudinal and multidisciplinary approach to the prevention of developmental retardation, in Tjossem, T. (ed.), *Intervention Strategies for High-Risk Infants and Young Children.* Baltimore: University Park Press, pp. 629–665 (1976).

Ramey, C. and Smith, B. Assessing the intellectual consequences of early intervention with high-risk infants. *Am. J. Ment. Defic.*, 81:318–324 (1977).

Ramey, C., Sparling, J. and Wasik, B. *Creating Social Environments to Facilitate Language Development.* Paper presented at the conference entitled "Early Language Intervention," Sturbridge, Massachusetts, May (1979).

Ramey, C., Stedman, D., Borders-Patterson, A. and Mengel, W. Predicting school failure from information available at birth. *Am. J. Ment. Defic.*, 82:525–534 (1978).

Robinson, H. and Robinson, N. Longitudinal development of very young children in a comprehensive day-care program: The first two years. *Child Devel.*, 42:1673–1683 (1971).

Stokes, T. and Baer, D. An implicit technology of generalization. *J. Appl. Behav. Anal.*, 10: 349–367 (1977).

Thoman, E. *Non-Linguistic Communication as the Prelude and Context for Language Learning.* Paper presented at the conference entitled "Early Language Intervention," Sturbridge, Massachusetts, May (1979).

PART V

Affective/Temperament Development

This section on affective/temperament skills delineates the most unappreciated and unstudied areas of childhood development. Only recently has attention been focused away from motor, language and cognitive development and toward affective and temperament problems. The present state of the art indicates that individual differences in temperament exist from birth and that these differences can be assessed. Understanding and assessment of these differences in temperament makes guidance to parents and caregivers possible so that better matches between individual differences and environment demands can be developed. This procedure constitutes one important way in which assessment can lead to intervention, not necessarily by attending to the child's temperament itself, but by modifying environmental styles.

The study of affective and emotional development focuses our attention on the development of feelings, moods and individual differences in expression. We now know the role of affective dysfunction on other aspects of development. For example, failure to thrive may be caused as much by affective disorders such as depression as by biological insult. In this final section theoretical discussions of affect and temperament are followed by assessment procedures designed to measure individual differences and other developmental courses. These procedures, while being concurrently developed, hold great promise. Traditional intervention strategies around affective demands are discussed.

21

Theoretical Perspectives on Emotions in Developmental Disabilities

CARROLL E. IZARD
S. BUECHLER

In order to understand the way emotions figure in developmental disabilities it is necessary first to review their functions in normal, healthy development. With a theoretical framework for viewing the role of the emotion system and discrete emotions in personality and development, it should be possible to delineate the interactions between affective development and growth in the other personality systems in the developmentally disabled child. This exploration will be largely theoretical and speculative, since empirical research with a clear focus on the emotions is still relatively scarce. There have been some significant beginnings in the empirical investigation of emotions in normal and deviant development and these will be reviewed.

The major theories of child development have little to say about emotions. Piaget (Piaget and Inhelder, 1969) views emotion as the energy source or motivation for cognitive development. He recognized, too, that the young child tended to view emotion and emotion expression as causal agents. That is, for the infant emotion expression is what makes things happen (1927, 1960). Aside from these provocative and insightful observations, Piagetian theory offers little for the student of emotions.

Classical psychoanalytic theory has also failed to present an adequate conceptual framework for understanding emotions and affective development. Freud first viewed affect as transformed libido, a derivative of instincts or drives. The drives themselves were used to explain much of human behavior. For example, the sex drive was seen as a basis for intellectual curiosity. However, in this early view affect (e.g., anxiety) was seen as a motivating force, one that is inherently primitive and disorganizing. Later, Freud described anxiety as a signal—a perceived danger. Thus, the anxiety affect was a cognitive phenomenon arising in the ego and thus lacking the motivational power.

Some contemporary psychoanalytic theorists address the issue of emotions more directly. Helen Lewis's (1971; 1978a,b) seminal work on shame and guilt is a prime example. She argues convincingly that these affects figure prominently in the development of the self and the functioning of the superego. She maintains that both positive and negative affects express human social connectedness. Her ideas of the role of shame and guilt in the development of psychopathology will be discussed later. Other psychoanalytic thinkers who give discrete emotions a prominent role in motivation and personality development include Emde (1976), Dahl (1979) and Singer (1978). These investigators contribute to differential emotion theory, defined as a conceptual orientation with the motivational properties of discrete emotions and the role of each emotion and of patterns of emotions in the development of adaptive and dysadaptive personality and social behavior.

Both Freud and Piaget propose a kind of parallelism between affect and cognition. The early Freudian position like Piaget proposed that affects were the energy source for cognition, but neither saw affects as directing cognitive development. Freud's reluctance to give affects a prominent role in cognition is clear in his final view of anxiety as signal arising in the ego and hence without power to control consciousness. Differential emotions theory proposes an interactive or feedback-feedforward model of the relationships between affects and perceptual-cognitive processes. Although the emotions provide the motivational thrust, they interact and bond with cognitions and are readily triggered by perceptual-cognitive processes, including appraisal, imagery and anticipation. The feedback-feedforward model, however, holds that some affect is always present in consciousness. Thus, one affect or pattern of affects motivates the cognition that may in turn activate another affect or affective pattern. The bonds between affect and cognition affective-cognitive structures acquire trait like characteristics that structure personality and social behavior.

As discussed earlier (Izard and Buechler, 1979), the very process of personality integration is dependent on the emotion system. First, on the assumption that experience—the feeling state of joy, sadness, anger, fear or any emotion—is the same throughout life, then the invariance of emotion experiencing provides continuity of consciousness and self-awareness. Second, emotion experiences have an organizing effect on the processes of consciousness. During infancy, when the infant is primarily an affective being, the organizing effects of affective experience are central to the emerging sense of a separate, experiencing self. Third, the emotions provide the motivation for integrative processes that engage and interrelate the various personality systems.

What is the relevance of these theoretical disabilities, for example, a learning disability? Following Piaget, one could say that a child who is slow to learn has a deficiency of energy or affect. This idea of the relation between emotion and cognition may be implicit in views of the slow learner as lazy. His affect is not sufficiently "powering" his cognitive progress. Freud's view suggests that the infant's cognitive explorations are born out of its deficiencies (or tension about deficiencies). If all its tensions or needs were completely satisfied, there would be no force for cognitive growth. This pictures the child as avoiding the effort of cognitive growth unless forced to by its libidinal or instinctual needs.

In contrast, in differential emotions theory some slow learners may have maladaptive emotion-cognition bonds, or affective-cognitive structures, lack needed interest or interest/joy experiences with learning. Some may not have had the experience of overcoming intellectual hurdles (frustration/anger directing behavior in a positive, constructive sense). Some may have purely cognitive deficits that have resulted in shame experiences. Shame in learning situations can narrow the child's awareness of self-as-a-learner to a concept of self-as-a-poor-learner. Some may be limited in their ability to concentrate (focus) on cognitive tasks because they elicit fear or anxiety patterns. The possibilities for discrete emotion-cognition interactions and therefore for difficulties in learning and cognitive development are highly variable and complex and must be approached with much finer diagnostic tools than have been used in the past.

The Emotions as a System Affecting Development

Differential emotions theory defines personality as a grand system of systems. Constituent, partly independent, highly interactive, these systems are the homeostatic, emotional, physiologic need (drive), motor, perceptual and cognitive systems (Izard, 1971, 1977). Broadly speaking, healthy adaptive development is a function of two sets of processes: normal development of the separate systems and balanced, harmonious interactions among systems. Dysadaptive development results from deviant or retarded development within a system and/ or imbalance and dysfunction among systems. For example, delayed development of the emotion system would reduce responsiveness to environmental stimulation sufficiently to retard cognitive and even motor development. Likewise, a congenital cognitive deficit would tend to reduce social stimulation that contributes to early learning opportunities. Severe punishment of emotion-expressive behaviors would constrict responsiveness in general, particularly in novel (optimal learning) situations where the consequences of expression are unpredictable.

There is the possibility that delayed motor development or even delayed exercise of motor functions may retard emotional development in certain situations. The work of Campos *et al.* (1978) suggests that locomotor experience may be a prerequisite for fear of heights or fear of falling.

As development proceeds, the emotion system changes in several ways. There is an increase in the number of emotions. Izard *et al.* (in press) and Izard *et al.* (in preparation) have shown that a situation (inoculation) that included playful interaction, acute pain and soothing and amends by mother and nurse elicited an increasing variety of negative affect expressions after four–six months of age. This stimulus situation elicited a total of discrete emotion expression and the affect expression of discomfort-pain in infants one–nine months of age.

The developmental increase in the number of discrete affect expressions paradoxically parallels a decrease in the infant's dependence on facial and non-linguistic vocal expressions of emotion as virtually the sole means of social communication, a topic that will be pursued later. That is, while facial and vocal expression of emotion remains the principal vehicle for social interchange for some time, these modes are at seven–nine months increasingly complemented by the motor system wherein body language (gesture, etc.) and locomotion are emerging. With the emergence of multiple means of emotion communication, facial and nonlinguistic vocal expressions of emotion are expected to be modulated, and all emotion communication is expected to become more specific and more subtle.

Of course, as the cognitive-affective development gives rise to language, the communication systems change drastically, and the child is expected to give priority to symbolic or affective-cognitive communication rather than purely emotional expression. Inadequate development of the motor and cognitive system leads to overdependence on the emotion system for social communication. If the resultant overdetermined or delayed emotion expressive behavior is punished and inhibited, severe communication deficits are more likely to emerge.

There is need for more evidence on several questions regarding the relationship of the emotion system to different aspects of development. Of greatest importance is the questions as to causal relations among systems of the personality.

1. Are there prerequisites in other systems (e.g., cognitive) for the emergence, full expression and regulation of an emotion? If so, then a delay in development of that system would result in lags in emotional development.
2. Does the experience of an emotion promote growth in other (perceptual, cognitive, motor) systems? If so, we would expect that a cognitive delay may be the result of emotion-system abnormalities.

3. Are there particularly important emotion-other system bonds or "critical periods" for developing these bonds? For example, if an infant does not develop a link between joy and interactions with the care-giver during a specifiable period, how does this lack affect subsequent perceptual, cognitive, social or emotional development? What if the interest affect is deficient and does not focus perceptual behaviors when the visual system becomes capable of focusing on objects close at hand?

Investigators have typically looked at a "known" cognitive disability (e.g., Down's syndrome) to see whether abnormalities in emotional development can also be discerned. It is often subtly assumed that the cognitive deficit caused the abnormality in the emotion expression. This framework must itself be the subject of future inquiry.

In order to study just what lags behind in the handicapped child's development, we need a much more focused approach than has generally been employed. Previous work has suggested that affect expression may be "slow" and "dampened," for example, in the Down's syndrome infant. Good descriptions are available of the "flaccid" body, dampened smile, etc. of the Down's child (Emde *et al.*, 1978; Cicchetti and Sroufe, 1978). But is the Down's child simply harder to "read" because its smiles aren't accompanied by coos and other signals of joy? And are its other emotional expressions also less easily read than the normal child's? Is this due simply to fewer parts of the face expressing the expectable movements for a particular emotion, or is this due, in part, to a lack of covariance between facial, vocal and other motor expressions of emotion? In general, what is suggested here is that it is possible that the Down's syndrome infant's emotions are harder to read because one looks for certain normal covariances that are absent or delayed in this child. It may be the coordination of behavioral elements of expression that is delayed that makes "reading" this child more difficult.

A major question to be addressed is: if, at certain points in development, major changes in the organization of emotion system occur, how do these relate to cognitive growth? For example, if fear does not emerge on schedule, how does this relate to the ability to anticipate, which underlies a good deal of cognitive growth in the latter part of the first year? What this would suggest is that the new "organizers" are not just "marked" by the emergence of new emotions (Spitz, 1959; Emde *et al.*, 1976) but are the new discrete emotions and the consequent new emotion-cognition bonds. Certain developmental delays would be seen as the failure of a particular emotion to emerge at a critical point. Clearly, that is not a tenable explanation for all developmental delays. Some deficits are probably purely organic, purely perceptual, purely motoric, etc., until socialization adds interpersonal meaning to them. But what if an infant is less able to narrow its conscious awareness to include only those aspects of the environment that are required for its next cognitive leap? Wouldn't that leap take longer to make?

Cicchetti and Sroufe's (1978) study of the Down's child's response on the visual cliff may illustrate how the emotional system influences other systems and development as a whole. Their sample of Down's versus normal children were equated for DQ, yet the Down's children did not show "distress" where the normal children did. It may be that the response of the Down's syndrome infants to the visual cliff is different from average not because of cognitive lag nor even because of "a problem of extracting meaning from their experience" (p. 37) but because they are slower to develop affective-cognitive structures and coordination between affective and motor processes.

We must also investigate how the emotion system is affected by a deficit in another system (homeostatic, drive, perceptual, cognitive, motor). Once again, each emotion and each type of deficit needs to be considered separately. The answerable type of question is not "does slower or faster motor development slow or speed affect development?" but rather a question such as "how does the inability for self-locomotion at nine months affect the experience of fear of falling from heights?"

We need to investigate the effect of optimal and nonoptimal system interactions on interpersonal interactions. It is reasonable to hypothesize that the infant in whom every available body system is expressing anger or rage is difficult to communicate with or relate to. The originally damaged child or the one who for other reasons has difficulty modulating emotion expression may be more likely to elicit inappropriate negative affect and abuse from the caregiver.

The Emotional System and the Development of Social Competence

If we consider interpersonal communication as an integral part of social competence, then the emotion system must be given a significant place in its ontogeny. There is now considerable agreement that in the early months of life the infant is primarily an affective being (Escalona, 1969; Sroufe, 1979; Stechler and Carpenter, 1967; Tennes *et al.,* 1972) who communicates principally by means of affect expression (Emde *et al.,* 1976; Izard *et al.,* in press). The importance of these characteristics of the infant and its social relationships was eloquently described by Darwin (1872, 1965):

> The movements of expression in the face and body, whatever their origin may have been, are in themselves of much importance for our welfare. They serve as the first means of communication

between the mother and her infant; she smiles approval, and thus encourages her child on the right path, or frowns disapproval (p. 364).

Though recognized as important by Darwin and countless caregivers before and since, the nature and significance of the system of nonverbal signal between infant and caregiver, composed mainly of affective expressions, is just now becoming systematically researched.

One function of the affect system is to keep the mother abreast of the infant's changing feelings. Further, the mother's expressions apparently provide even the very young infant with information important to its well-being. This was demonstrated in a study by Brazelton *et al.* (1975) in which they had mothers maintain a poker face for three minutes during a face-to-face interaction. The infant reacted to the mother's still face as follows:

> When she violates his expectancy for rhythmic interaction by presenting a still, unresponsive face to him, he becomes visibly concerned, his movements become jerky, he averts his face, then attempts to draw her into interaction. When repeated attempts fail, he finally withdraws into an attitude of helplessness, face averted, body curled up and motionless. If she returns to her usual interactive responses, he comes alive after an initial puzzled period, and returns to his rhythmic cyclical behaviour which has previously characterized their ongoing face-to-face interaction (p. 137).

While this maternal behavior was a bit extreme, it may not be very far from the end of a continuum of individual differences in caregiver expression that provides a source of individual variations in infants' well-being and social development.

Only a few studies focus on the role of caregiver affect expression in infant social development. Main (1977) and Tolan (1975) (cited in Ainsworth *et al.*, 1978) found that caregivers rated as more expressive were likely to have infants more securely attached. Type of attachment was assessed in the Ainsworth-Wittig (1969) strange situation procedure which classifies infants as young as 12 months old as secure, ambivalent or avoidant in their attachment to their caregivers.

In a discussion following a recent presentation of research with the strange situation (Waters, 1979), the participants developed the idea that this procedure may measure an important aspect of social competence. In fact, Waters *et al.* (1979) have shown that type of attachment as measured in the strange situation at 18 months predicts ratings of competence in the peer group (nursery) at three years. Studies are now under way in our laboratory to determine precisely what emotions the infant expresses during the various episodes of separation, stranger interaction, and reunion in the strange situation. Preliminary data suggest that the emotion expression and the patterning and sequencing of emotion expressions are different for securely and insecurely attached infants. We are just inaugurating a project designed to determine the patterns of infant-caregiver emotion expression in early infancy that predict type of attachment at one year of age.

This section would seem truncated without a word about synchrony. The term has been used by a number of investigators (e.g., Lewis and Goldberg, 1969; Sander, 1969; Stern, 1974; Thoman, 1975) to describe effective, coordinated, mutually responsive mother-infant interaction. The notion is that appropriately sensitive mothers act or react in synchrony with their infants. Studies attempting to measure synchrony have focused on vocal and visual behavior and their concomitants.

It is difficult to extract a concise definition of synchrony from the literature. It is generally assumed to be a desired, favorable condition for healthy development and one that refers mainly to noncognitive aspects of dyadic interaction. Brazelton *et al.* (1975) used the term "affective synchrony" and suggested that it is the goal of many of the infant's actions. By implication it is also the goal of many of the caregiver's actions.

The term synchrony overlaps somewhat with the concept of empathy, one definition of which involves the concurrence of identical or similar feelings. When one considers these terms in relation to expressions and communication of emotion, they lack differentiation and specificity. That is, the concurrence of smiling may reflect appropriately sensitive care-giving and a healthy interaction for mother and infant, but concurrence of the same emotion is not always desirable. It would generally be inappropriate for the caregiver to scream when the infant experiences pain. But would it be inappropriate for the mother to cry in this case or to express mild anger toward a barrier that frustrates and angers the infant? The answer is not immediately obvious, especially in relation to intensity of expression and appropriate concomitant behaviors of such caregiver emotion signals.

Synchrony can be considered as mutually adaptive, coordinated responsiveness in a dyadic feedforward (signal-interaction) and feedback (response-to-signal) system of affective communication. Such a definition may be broad enough to incorporate most of the connotations of synchrony as the term has been used in the literature. Still, it needs differentiation. One possibility is to work toward specifying the types of synchrony that involve emotions (or expressions) of like valence and those that involve emotions of different valence.

The requirements of a mutually adaptive, synchronous emotion communication may differ, depending on the predominant emotion being expressed and the age or status of the infant. In the earliest months of life the infant who is perceived by the mother to be expressing rage or anger needs a response that says that the mother is in tune with the source of the frustration, rather than a "mirroring" of the frustration itself. Thus, for mother and infant to be communicating in a synchronous, mutually adaptive manner when the infant is very young and is expressing anger, mirroring is nonadaptive. While empirical evidence is scarce in this area, some data (Buechler *et al.,* 1979) suggest that mothers are aware of this need and perceive themselves as responding with frustration-reducing behaviors and positively toned affect to infant anger expressions during the first year of life. After the first year, however, synchronous, mutually adaptive functioning may begin to require a more "mirroring" style of response to anger expressions. Mothers of infants older than one year were less likely to respond positively to expressions that they perceived as anger. One might speculate that as the caregiver begins to expect the infant to be able to regulate expression of a particular emotion, she changes the quality in her (synchronous) emotional responses. Thus the mother of a five-month-old enraged infant might well respond with a soothing smile, interest in what is causing the anger and efforts to alleviate any discomfort. But if the mother of a two-year-old in an uncontrolled temper tantrum smiles her acceptance of this expression, with no negative feedback to communicate her expectation that the infant attempt to regulate anger, her response may not be mutually adaptive. The enraged toddler may perceive the caregiver's positive expression not as a sign of tolerance but as a signal of its own failure to communicate and influence the social surroundings or as a sign of rejection.

The situation changes entirely for synchronous, mutually adaptive responses to perceived fear. Mothers also seem to recognize that their response to perceived fear expressions should differ, depending on the infant's age (Buechler *et al.,* 1979). Once the infant is old enough to regulate anger, it might be adaptive to express a negative response to uncontrolled rage, but could it ever be adaptive to respond negatively and mirror the infant's fear?

Briefly, then, much research is needed to clarify the meaning of synchronous or mutually adaptive caregiver-infant emotion expressions, but our view is that the quality of this interaction will differ, depending on the emotion being expressed and the capacity of the infant for regulating its expression. Even though the very young infant may not "regulate" its expressions of joy and interest, a mirroring of these expressions may be experienced as a pleasurable, synchronous or "in tune" response. For these emotions this may be true throughout life in that, regardless of its age, the child whose joy and interest elicit similar expressions from the caregiver and social environment will feel "understood" and experience synchronous, adaptive communication. For other emotions the requirements of a synchronous, mutually adaptive response may be much more complex, and entail accurate reading of the emotion being expressed, the emotion-regulation capacities of the expressor, the intensity of the affect as it is experienced, and the current potential for modulating the emotion through reciprocal expression of other emotions or affective-cognitive bonds.

Emotion Communication and the Development of Social Competence

The infant's first experience of affecting another human being is through its affect expressions. Its cries, smiles, and interested gazes evoke different responses from the caregiver. Learning that its emotion expressions have an impact on others may be even more important than learning precisely how they impinge. This would suggest that for the normal development of social competence the infant must first experience some differentiated responding to its emotion signals. Unless it can affect the caregiver differently, depending on the particular emotion it is signaling, it may not develop a sense of itself as causal agent in social interactions. It may develop a sense of social impotence that leads to social incompetence. The eventual development of social competence may thus depend on early experiences that one's emotion signals are read or understood and effect different responses depending on the emotion being expressed.

Mutually adaptive, synchronous responses at this earliest level may entail the caregiver's reflection, in a consistent manner, of the differences between the infant's positive and negative affect states. The behavioral response may be less important than whether the infant experiences that its discomfort or sadness elicits a relatively consistent response that differs from the caregiver's response to its signals of joy or interest. The infant's most pressing need may be to feel that its negative affect signals have an impact on the caregiver. A study by Bell and Ainsworth (1972) suggests that latency to respond to infant distress directly affects length of cry and that infants who received prompt responses to their cries in the early months of life tended to cry less in later months and to develop other (verbal) modes of communication earlier. This seems consistent with the notion that in the earliest months of life the experience of social competence can be equated with the experience of prompt responses to one's affect signals. It may suggest that the infant whose distress, interest and joy have received consistently different responses feels that it has an impact on the human environment, that it can make its needs and affective experiences known, and that it is a locus of interpersonal influence. Later, higher levels of social competence could not develop or would be retarded without this initial experience of the self as causal agent in interpersonal exchanges. As the infant grows, and new emotion expressions emerge in conscious experience, social competence involves more complex emotion interactions with the caregiver.

The signals of emotion expression in the developmentally delayed infant may be qualitatively different as well as delayed in appearance. The cry and face of the developmentally disabled infant have been shown to arouse different emotional responses in caregivers, and perhaps to be implicated in the child's interpersonal difficulties, since the delayed youngster may not give the full, expectable positive emotion response (see Emde *et al.,* 1978) and may have a more disturbing cry (Ostwald and Peltzman, 1974; Lester, 1976). Several hypotheses come to mind:

1. That some developmentally disabled infants' emotion signals differ from the normal in intensity only.
2. That others differ in quality of discrete emotion or emotion-blends conveyed.
3. That they differ in intensity, in discrete emotion(s) conveyed, and in proportion of voluntary:involuntary empathy-arousing elements (Hoffman, 1978).

Actually, all infants' expressions may fall on a scale of intensity, clarity of emotion display and compelling quality of signals, but in certain types of developmental disability the infant may be on an extreme end of one or more of these scales. Detailed analyses of the facial expressions of developmentally delayed infants, analyses of the acoustic properties of their cries, and studies of caregivers' physiologic and phenomenologic responses to these expressions would address this question.

Emotion Expressions and Communication in the Developmentally Disabled Child

While the study of emotions in the developmentally disabled child requires much more empirical investigation, the differential emotions theory suggests certain specific guidelines for this research. The discussion below presents some of the principles that have implications for the future study of emotion development in the atypical infant.

Differential emotions theory maintains that the emotion and perceptual/cognitive systems have some independence but are frequently interacting and interdependent. This suggests that there will be specifiable limits to the differences between the development of emotion systems of the developmentally disabled and normal infants. Since an emotion experience can occur without prior cognitive appraisal, and since there may not be cognitive "pre-requisites" for emotion experiences, the ontogeny of emotion expressions in the developmentally disabled child cannot simply be predicted to be "slower" than normal, as though the emergence of an emotion expression were a cognition-dependent task or response similar to the development of the object concept.

Certain milestones in the affective development of the disabled child will differ predictably from normal development, but others will show much more individual variation. More specifically, we can predict that since the ontogeny of discrete emotion expressions proceeds generally according to a maturational timetable, the initial emergence of, say, anger in the Down's child should show some consistency across individuals. It seems likely that the emergence of emotion expressions in a Down's child will differ from the normal less than will event-specific emotion thresholds and the development of event-specific regulation of each emotion.

While caregivers may expect normal infants to begin regulating their anger expressions by a relatively predictable point in time—this is partially determined by the caregiver's experience with other children—the parent of the developmentally disabled child is in a more ambiguous situation. Given this ambiguity some parents may form demanding standards, expecting their disabled child to control anger expressions at the same age as they would expect such behavior in the normal child (perhaps partially as a reflection of their refusal to acknowledge differences between this child and others). At the other extreme, some parents may abandon all expectations of emotion control for their "different" child, giving the infant little encouragement or direction in the development of emotional regulation. Furthermore, to the extent that emotion regulation is a process that utilizes cognitive, perceptual and motor skills, the developmentally disabled infant will show more variability in its attainment. The rationale for this hypothesis is not that the developmentally disabled child shows greater than average cognitive individual differences (these may actually be less than average, depending on the disorder) but that the development of adequate coping devices and "substitutes" for lagging skills will be more variable. Assuming, hypothetically, that anger is most easily regulated in the normal infant through the recruitment of interest-motivated activities, normal development of skill in these activities should present the average infant with an avenue for anger regulation. When such a child, for example, is frustrated by a distance barrier to a desired object, emotion-motivated activities to overcome the barrier may help attenuate the anger. That is, not only will the normal child be able to do more about the barrier, but he may become more interested in the problem of overcoming the obstacle and the interest itself, as well as the cognitive, perceptual and motor activities it motivates, will contribute to anger regulation.

The disabled child is likely to show more-than-average variability in the expression of interest and its related activities to regulate the expression of negative emotions, such as anger. First, development of interest and interest-motivated activities and skills will be more variable. Perhaps more important, there may be wide differences in developing the capacity for regulating one emotion by recruiting another. That process, dependent as it must be on interpersonal contributions and, perhaps growing awareness of the self as a coping, choosing being, must be subject to a greater degree of variability in the developmentally disabled. The feedback the atypical child receives about himself as being able to create solutions for frustrating situations may differ widely.

Furthermore, the atypical child's range of interest-related activities may be smaller, so that the frustrating situation will be less likely to evoke the anger-attenuating emotion of interest. This would seem to suggest the hypothesis that developmentally disabled children will be predictably less able to regulate anger expressions than normal children.

But the regulation of emotion may be much more complex than such a hypothesis implies. It may be, for example, that for some normal and developmentally disabled infants interest/joy-motivated social interchanges help regulate anger expressions even without interest/anger-motivated activities. The developmentally disabled child may be just as able as his normal peer to use this interest/joy-motivated social avenue for anger regulation, so that for some developmentally disabled children anger regulation would proceed at a pace not significantly different from normal. In brief, while the emergence of discrete emotions, largely dependent on maturational factors, may be relatively predictable in some developmentally disabled children with consistent differences from (or similarities to) the normal pattern of emotion ontogeny, emotion regulation in atypical children will show greater-than-average variability.

The developmentally disabled child's atypical emotion development will likely have significant consequences in the caregiver-infant relationship. A recent paper by Thoman (1978) stresses the interactive nature of this relationship and presents some evidence that the social interchanges between the caregiver and the developmentally disabled infant may differ from normal. Describing her extensively detailed observations of mother-infant dyads, Thoman found that, compared to average, "the three special subjects showed similar patterns of interaction during the first five weeks: there was overall less interaction of a purely social nature, that is, when the infants were awake and the mothers were not engaged in caretaking activities; and during social interaction, there was much less visual attention to the infants and less stimulation, including patting, rocking, caressing, and moving the infants" (p. 27). It is intriguing that these observations made during the first five weeks of life preceded any diagnosis of the infants as atypical. The infants did not differ from the rest of the group in amount of wakefulness, fussing or crying.

Differential emotions theory might interpret Thoman's data as indicating that it is in the realm of the positive emotions (interest and interest/joy-motivated social exchanges) that these dyads differed from normal, while other discrete emotions showed no disparity. This suggests that the study of the developmentally disabled child's emotion development and emotion-related social development must examine each emotion separately, focusing attention on its emergence, its regulation in various situations, and its effects in interpersonal interactions. It is interesting to speculate why Thoman's special infants received less social attention well before their diagnosis of disability and without any obvious signs that they were difficult to care for or more irritable. One can surmise that the reciprocal and nonreciprocal expressions of emotion form an interpersonal matrix. Some of these matrices (e.g., those related to interest) may be more subject to interpersonal cues that are affected by developmental disabilities. The weak and dampened smile of the Down's syndrome child may have a greater effect on the infant-caregiver interest/joy interchanges than on their interactions relative to negative affects. But other developmental factors (e.g., extreme prematurity) may impinge more in infant-caregiver distress-related interactions, since the cry of the premature infant may have properties that greatly affect their caregivers. In short, for each type of disability, the emergence, expression and regulation of each of the fundamental emotions and emotion-motivated social interchanges must receive separate study.

To illustrate this approach, let us briefly examine the role of fear in the experience of the developmentally disabled child. The study of the emergence and regulation of fear in the normal infant has been complicated by discrepancies in the experimental situations and criteria for judging the presence of the emotion across investigations (see Izard and Buechler, 1979, for a review of these issues). Since few studies have attempted longitudinal investigation of infantile emotional responses to a variety of possible fear-evoking situations, more data are available on, for example, the emergence of fear of heights than on the emergence and regulation of fear as a fundamental emotion experience.

Many investigators have assumed that emergence of fear depends on specific cognitive prerequisites. Schaffer (1966) suggested that, "the establishment of the object concept is therefore a precondition to the onset of fear of stranger . . ." (p. 103). This viewpoint has had many adherents, despite the paucity of tangible evidence that any particular cognitive attainments must precede the emergence of fear expressions (see Campos *et al.*, 1978).

It seems likely that different maturational, cognitive, social and motor variables influence the emergence versus the regulation of fear. As discussed earlier in this section, it seems consistent with differential emotions theory to hypothesize that emergence of fear will be less variable, and less affected by the cognitive, social, perceptual and motor concomitants of developmental disability, than its regulation. That emergence of fear is not a simple result of cognitive level is consistent with the data of Cicchetti and Sroufe (1978) on the emergence of fear in the Down's infant. These investigators found that Down's infants cried less than normal infants on perceiving an object (shadow) looming toward them, even when the infants were equated for developmental quotient. The data can be considered consistent with the concept that emergence of emotion is largely independent of cognitive level and dependent more on maturational than on environmental factors.

Fear can be hypothesized to play an adaptive role in fostering awareness of the vulnerability of the self and in motivating motor development (allowing successful escape from threatening situations and perception of the self as able to escape harm). Fear also promotes bonding to the parent and motivates activities that increase the ability to anticipate events and to learn cause and effect relations in traumatic situations. To the extent that fear ontogeny is delayed or deviant in the developmentally disabled child, all of these other areas of growth can be expected to be affected. The new awareness of vulnerability of the self (in situations that elicit fear, such as the approach of a stranger) promotes flight to the caregiver. Differential responsiveness to particular caregivers (e.g., being soothed only by nearness to mother or father) probably augments the social bonds between infants and caregivers. The emergence of fear as a conscious experience probably increases alertness to cues of impending events, such as mother's preparations for leaving the house. Focusing awareness on these details may well contribute to development of the infant's ability to use its perceptions and cognitions to anticipate future events. By attempting to change the course of events (e.g., fear-motivated efforts to keep mother from leaving) the infant learns something of the extent of its impact, its vulnerability to the effect of behavior controlled by another, its separateness, and the nature of social and physical cause-effect relationships (e.g., that its tears may or may not stop mother from leaving, but the ring of the telephone always will).

In summary, the emergence of fear as a part of the infant's life experience motivates important social, perceptual and cognitive developments. The delayed emergence of fear in the experience of the Down's infant may retard advances in these other areas, slowing the process of bonding to a special protective caregiver, of learning to anticipate events, and perhaps even attenuating awareness of the vulnerability of the self, the self as capable of escape from harm or of influencing others and recruiting help.

The differential emotions perspective suggests that, rather than concentrating on the "prerequisites" for emotional experiences, a more fruitful line of research would be studying the interaction of each fundamental emotion with social, perceptual, cognitive and motor development in the disabled (as well as the normal) infant. Emotions presumably play an adaptive role in development, so their delayed or attenuated emergence and their "dampened" or less "readable" expression, are assumed to affect the interpersonal relationship to the caregiver and growth in all personality systems. The empirical task for the future is to establish the baseline of normal development of the emergence, significant event-specific expressions and regulation of each of the fundamental emotions in the infant's life. Then, for each fundamental emotion it will be important to study differences in the growth of the developmentally disabled child. Such comparisons will yield important information about the fundamental nature of emotion expressions and experience of emotion. Just as we may learn much about the adaptive function of the normal infant-caregiver bond from studying the effects of its absence in the autistic child, investigations of emotional development in disabled and normal infants are complementary, helping to elucidate the variables that affect the emergence of each emotion and the part each emotion plays in personality development.

368 IZARD and BUECHLER

References

Ainsworth, M.D. and Wittig, B.A. Attachment and exploratory behavior of one-year-olds in a strange situation, in Foss, B.M. (ed.), *Determinants of Infant Behavior IV*. London: Methuen (1969).

Bell, S. and Ainsworth, M.D. Infant crying and maternal responsiveness. *Child Devel.*, 43: 1171–1190 (1972).

Brazelton, T.B., Tronick, E., Adamson, L., Als, H. and Wise, S. Early mother-infant reciprocity. *Parent-Infant Interaction*. Amsterdam: CIBA Foundation, Associated Scientific Publishers (1975).

Buechler, S., Huebner, R.R., Coss, C. and Izard, C.E. Mothers' expectations in regard to their infants' emotion expressions. Department of Psychology, University of Delaware, unpublished study (1979).

Campos, J.J., Hiatt, S., Ramsay, D., Henderson, C. and Svedja, M. The development of fear on the visual cliff: Effects of experience, cognition, and context, in Lewis, M. and Rosenblum, L. (eds.), *The Development of Affect*. New York: Plenum Press (1978).

Cicchetti, D. and Sroufe, L.A. An organizational view of affect: Illustration from the study of Down's syndrome infants, in Lewis, M. and Rosenblum, L. (eds.), *Origins of Behavior: Affective Development*. New York: Plenum Press (1978).

Dahl, H. The appetite hypothesis of emotions: A new psychoanalytic model of motivation, in Izard, C.E. (ed.), *Emotions in Personality and Psychopathology*. New York: Plenum Press (1979).

Darwin, C.R. *The Expression of Emotions in Man and Animals*. London: John Murray (1872). (Chicago: University of Chicago Press, 1965).

Emde, R.N., Gaensbauer, T.J. and Harmon, R.J. *Emotional Expression in Infancy: A Behavior Study*. New York: International Universities Press (1976).

Emde, R.N., Katz, E.L. and Thorpe, J.K. Emotional expression in infancy. II. Early deviations in Down's syndrome, in Lewis, M. and Rosenblum, L. (eds.), *The Development of Affect*. New York: Plenum Press (1978).

Escalona, S.K. *The Roots of Individuality*. Chicago: Aldine (1968).

Hoffman, M.L. The arousal and development of empathy, in Lewis, M. and Rosenblum, L. (eds.), *Origins of Behavior: Affective Development*. New York: Plenum Press (1978).

Izard, C.E. *The Face of Emotion*. New York: Appleton-Century-Crofts (1971).

Izard, C.E. *Human Emotions*. New York: Plenum Press (1977).

Izard, C.E. and Buechler, S. Emotion expressions and personality integration in infancy, in Izard, C.E. (ed.), *Emotions in Personality and Psychopathology*. New York: Plenum Press (1979).

Izard, C.E., Huebner, R.R., Risser, D., McGinness, G. and Dougherty, L. The young infant's ability to encode discrete emotion expressions. University of Delaware, in press.

Izard, C.E., Hughes, K.L., Nelson, G.M., Huebner, R.R., Dougherty, L., O'Reilly, L.S. and Buechler, S. Developmental changes in one-week to seven-month-old infants' facial responses to pain. University of Delaware, in preparation.

Lewis, H. *Shame and Guilt in Neurosis*. New York: International Universities Press (1971).

Lewis, H. [a]Reasons for the neglect of the phenomenology of shame and guilt. [b]Distinctions between shame and guilt, in Izard, C.E. (ed.), *Emotions in Personality and Psychopathology*. New York: Plenum Press (1979).

Lewis, M. and Goldberg, S. Perceptual-cognitive development in infancy: A generalized expectancy model as a function of the mother-infant relationship. *Merrill-Palmer Quarterly*, 15:81–100 (1969).

Main, M. Analysis of a peculiar form of reunion behavior seen in some daycare children: Its history and sequalae in children who are home reared, in Webb, R. (ed.), *Social Development in Daycare*. Baltimore: Johns Hopkins University Press (1977).

Piaget, J. *The Child's Conception of Physical Causality*. Totawa, New Jersey: Littlefield, Adams (1960). (Originally published, 1927.)

Piaget, J. and Inhelder, B. *The Psychology of the Child*. New York: Basic Books (1969).

Sander, L.W. The longitudinal course of early mother-child interaction-cross case comparison in a sample of mother-child pairs, in Foss, B.M. (ed.), *Determinants of Infant Behavior IV*. London: Methuen (1969).

Schaeffer, H.R. The onset of fear of strangers and the incongruity hypothesis. *J. Child Psychol. and Psychiat.*, 7:95–106 (1966).

Singer, J. Affect and imagination in play and fantasy, in Izard, C.E. (ed.), *Emotions in Personality and Psychopathology*. New York: Plenum Press (1979).

Spitz, R.A. *A Genetic Field Theory of Ego Formation: Its Implications for Pathology*. New York: International Universities Press, Inc. (1959).

Sroufe, L.A. Socioemotional development, in Osofsky, J. (ed.), *Handbook of Infant Development*. New York: John Wiley and Sons (1979).

Stechler, G. and Carpenter, G. A viewpoint on early affective development, in Hellmuth, J. (ed.), *The Exceptional Infant*. Vol. 1. Seattle: Special Child Publications (1967).

Stern, D. Mother and infant at play: The dyadic interaction involving facial, vocal, and gaze behaviors, in Lewis, M. and Rosenblum, L. (eds.), *The Effect of the Infant on Its Caregiver*. New York: Wiley (1974).

Tennes, K., Emde, R., Kisley, A. and Metcalf, D. The stimulus barrier in early infancy: An exploration of some formulations of John Benjamin. *Psychoanal. and Contemp. Sci.*, 1:206–234. New York: Macmillan (1972).

Thoman, E.B. How a rejecting baby affects mother-infant synchrony. *Parent-Infant Interaction*. Amsterdam: CIBA Foundation, Associated Scientific Publishers (1975).

Thoman, E.B. Infant development viewed within the mother-infant relationship, in Quilligan, E. and Kretchmer, N. (eds.), *Perinatal Medicine*. New York: John Wiley and Sons (1978).

Tolan, W.J. Maternal facial expression as related to the child-mother attachment, in Ainsworth, M.D., Blehar, M.C., Waters, E. and Wall, S. (eds.), *Patterns of Attachment*. Hillsdale, New Jersey: Erlbaum (1978).

Waters, E. A method for measuring attachment in infants and preschool children. Paper presented at the Second SSRC Conference on Measuring Emotions in Infants and Children. Princeton, New Jersey (1979).

Waters, E., Wippman, J. and Sroufe, L.A. Attachment, positive affect, and competence in the peer group: Two studies in construct validation, in Osofsky, J. (ed.), *Handbook of Infant Development*. New York: Wiley (1979).

_____**22**_____

Clinical Appraisal of Temperament

WILLIAM B. CAREY

Let us make quite clear at the outset that in obtaining temperament data on children we are not screening for disabilities in the same sense that one does with vision, hearing or development. What a temperament profile gives the clinician is information about the child's contribution to the parent-child interaction, and this may possibly be useful in managing that relationship. There are no specific temperament characteristics or clusters that call routinely for professional intervention. The clinician should consider intervention only when there are problems in the parent-child interaction or in the child's health or psychosocial adjustment.

Definition

The best definition of "temperament" is the behavioral style or emotional reactivity in interacting with the environment. Temperament describes *how* the child behaves, rather than *what* he can do, which reflects abilities or level of maturation, or *why* he does it, which is a matter of motivation or psychosocial adjustment (Thomas *et al.*, 1968).

Various ideas about temperament have been popular throughout the course of Western civilization. The Hippocratic humoral theory, in vogue from the fourth century B.C. into the nineteenth century, has undoubtedly the longest history. While the first half of the twentieth century was largely a period of environmentalism in the behavioral sciences, the modern scientific study of temperamental differences was beginning slowly.

Probably the most widely known and applied view of temperament is that introduced by Thomas *et al.* (1963, 1968) in their New York Longitudinal Study (NYLS) over 20 years ago. On theoretical and clinical grounds they decided upon nine variables for study: activity, rhythmicity of biological functions, initial approach/withdrawal, adaptability, intensity, mood, persistence, distractibility and sensory threshold. From these nine characteristics they derived three clinically significant clusters: (1) the difficult child (arrhythmic, low in approach and adaptability, intense and predominantly negative in mood); (2) the easy child (opposite traits: rhythmic, approaching, adaptable, mild and positive); and (3) the slow-to-warm-up child (low in activity, approach and adaptability and negative, but variable in rhythmicity and mild in intensity). The approximately 40 per cent of children not falling into one of these groups have been designated intermediate high (difficult) and intermediate low (easy) (Carey, 1970).

The other interpretation of temperament best known in the United States is that of Buss and Plomin (1975), which consists of emotionality, activity, sociability and impulsivity.

Measurement

Behavioral qualities such as mood or adaptability are not as readily measured as physical growth or blood chemistries. On the other hand, current determinations of temperament are not as inprecise and subjective as some critics claim. Familiarity with the measurement technique makes it possible to avoid the three "maternal perceptions" fallacies prevalent at present. The extreme form of this thinking is that intrinsic differences between children are all in the mother's mind and do not really exist in the child. This point of view was expressed by the pediatrician who could not understand how a mother with her pre-existing attitudes could possibly have rated her two children differently.

The second form of this fallacy allows that perhaps individual differences are real but that parental reports are so hopelessly tainted by emotion as to render interview or questionnaire data useless for clinical or research applications. This attitude betrays a lack of clinical experience or unfamiliarity with the available techniques and their validation.

The third fallacy does not distinguish between clinical diagnoses derived from questionnaire scores and maternal impressions—two entities not necessarily the same. Researchers who refer to diagnoses from questionnaire scores as "maternal perceptions" of difficult temperament without any idea of the mother's actual impression are confusing themselves and their readers.

The three current techniques for measuring children's temperament are parent interviews, parent questionnaires and observations.

Parent interviews, used by the NYLS group, obtained from the mother detailed descriptions of the child's reactions to a variety of situations, avoiding her general impressions and reactions to the child. The interview, dictation and rating took at least two hours per child, making it impractical for clinicians (Thomas *et al.*, 1963, 1968).

A parent questionnaire seemed like a reasonable solution if it could obtain comparable data and be psychometrically sound. My original Infant Temperament Questionnaire was the first published attempt to convert the NYLS research interview into a practical clinical instrument (Carey, 1970). Eight years later my revision, done with Sean McDevitt, improved its psychometric properties, particularly the internal consistency (Carey and McDevitt, 1978a).

Similar parent questionnaires (about 95 items rated on a 6-point frequency scale) for older children have followed. The one- to three-year period is now covered by the Toddler Temperament Scale (Fullard *et al.*, 1978) and the three- to seven-year span by the Behavioral Style Questionnaire (McDevitt and Carey, 1978). Work is just completed on a Middle Childhood Temperament Scale for 8–12 year old children (Hegvik *et al.*, 1980).

Thomas and Chess (1977) have also developed both parent and teacher questionnaires for the three- to seven-year group and are completing one for young adults. Several other researchers, such as Mary Rothbart, Frank Pedersen and John Bates, have been refining other questionnaires primarily for the infancy period. Reports of the questionnaires of Persson-Blennow and McNeill (1979) and Buss and Plomin (1975) are published. These other scales evidently have been used only in research and have not been introduced into any clinical setting.

Some data are available on the psychometric characteristics of our three completed instruments: the ITQ, the TTS and the BSQ. The level of internal consistency and one-month retest reliability was acceptable at about 0.85 for all three. The MCTQ is similar.

Demonstrating the external validity of these scales has been difficult because there are no standardized techniques for observing temperament characteristics against which they can be compared. There are two approaches to establish validity. Academicians from the behavioral sciences tend to disbelieve parents, to regard their reports as "maternal perceptions," and to value as scientific data only what they themselves observe in children, usually in their laboratories. If their findings, usually based on observations of only one or two hours, disagree with maternal reports, the mother is regarded as wrong. On the other hand, we clinicians trained to rely on histories know that, while we cannot believe everything we are told, the right questions asked in the right way will produce data sufficiently valid for responsible, effective clinical management. As in any other clinical appraisal, we should use both parental reports and our own observations in evaluating children's temperament. We should discard parental reports only when our own observations have been long enough to compare adequately with the vast experience of parents with their child.

For both the Denver Prescreening Developmental Questionnaire (PDQ) of Frankenburg *et al.* (1976) and the developmental questionnaire of Knobloch *et al.* (1979), validity studies have shown that properly collected parental data yielded results very close to formal developmental testing by standardized instruments.

Billman and McDevitt (1980), studying 78 nursery children, found significant correlations (0.18 to 0.46, median 0.38) for six out of seven characteristics between mother's ratings on the BSQ an average of six months earlier and independent observers' evaluations, done intermittently over several weeks, using the Teacher Temperament Questionnaire of Thomas and Chess (1977). Berberian (1979) studied the reactions of 60 infants to strangers in a laboratory setting and found that infants with more difficult temperaments, as rated by their mothers on the revised ITQ, demonstrated "more fearful and fewer friendly reactions to the stranger" than the easier ones, especially those rated with low approach ($r=0.40$). Searls *et al.* (in press), employing the revised ITQ, rated 20 babies on selected items suitable for her 90-minute home observations and obtained significant correlations with mothers' ITQ ratings in four out of eight categories. Using this technique with longer observations would undoubtedly have raised the correlations. Two other studies have included observations that more difficult babies cried more (Campbell, 1977; Sarett, 1976).

I have found it impossible to make adequately valid observations during routine pediatric office visits. The time is too short, too much else is going on, and the sample of behavior may be quite atypical. Instead, it was possible to compare simultaneous but independent ratings by the two parents. Problems with this scheme include insufficient contact between father and infant and prior parental discussions of the child. The couples tended to describe the same pattern in their infants with category correlations ranging from 0.37 to 0.72 with a median of 0.54, all highly significant. The consistently higher agreement between parents' ITQ category scores than their general impressions of the characteristics supports the view that many detailed questions produce a more accurate picture of a child than comprehensive statements (Carey, 1981).

Other criteria for the adequacy of clinical test instruments are cost and acceptability. The cost is negligible, and only about 15 minutes of professional time is needed to score and interpret each questionnaire. Parents need about 25 minutes to complete the forms. The acceptability of this technique appears to be borne out by the fact that 95 per cent or better of the mothers in my practice have returned them properly completed even though there has usually been no clinical problem or other expectation of benefit to them. (Those interested in obtaining sample copies of these instruments are referred to the instructions at the end of the chapter.)

Origins and Stability of Temperament

An extensive discussion of the origins and stability of temperament is not within the scope of this presentation. In brief, it appears that characteristics of temperament are partly derived from genetic factors and influenced both by prenatal and postnatal environment. There is no clear evidence at present of consistent effects from perinatal complications or from confirmed brain damage or dysfunction.

Temperamental traits are not fixed at any point but interact constantly with the environment with mutual modifications. However, their stability has been established to a greater degree with the use of better instruments and measurement of the same variables as the two points. The reader is referred elsewhere for more extensive reviews of the studies supporting these conclusions (Carey, 1981; Carey and McDevitt, 1978b, 1979; Thomas and Chess, 1977).

Clinical Usefulness

Knowledge of temperamental differences enhances the clinician's effectiveness in three ways. First, it is valuable to be aware that these differences exist and to discuss this fact with parents. For example, parents are interested in knowing that children who persist at unacceptable activities usually persist at more socially desirable ones, too. Also, some normal children are highly active; this trait does not necessarily mean overstimulation or brain dysfunction.

Second, the clinician sometimes finds it helpful to be able to define in detail the temperamental characteristics of a particular child. Parental impressions may be distorted, but not so much the clinical diagnoses based on extensive behavioral descriptions from interviews or questionnaires. With such detailed information at hand the clinician has a far better grasp of the child's contribution to the parent-child interaction and is in a much better position to facilitate the adjustment between the two. Parents often need help in recognizing difficult temperament for what it is and are greatly relieved to learn that the infant's behavior is not due to inadequate or inappropriate parenting. At later ages parents and teachers often confuse behavioral style with motivations and environmental effects, as when teachers call a slow-to-warm-up child "insecure" or parents label a low-activity child "lazy" or urge consumption of vitamins.

Should a pediatrician, preschool teacher or other professional routinely assess temperament in children under his care? Since they are doing this informally anyway, the question is really whether they should use a test instrument. Further experience will be necessary to determine whether the benefits justify the effort. In the meantime, I routinely ask parents to complete an Infant Temperament Questionnaire at about six months but later only when the data will help to deal with a specific clinical concern.

Others considering the clinical use of temperament questionnaires should remember that they are not screening devices for abnormal behavior but for behavioral style. If there is a problem, it is not in the child's temperament but in the parent-child interaction; a difficult child and a difficult interaction are not necessarily the same. Therefore, there is no specific temperamental characteristic or profile that routinely calls for action by the clinician. Questionnaire results reported to parents should be in general, descriptive terms only; labels are to be avoided. Finally, questionnaires should be used by professionals and only according to directions to avoid the risk of misinformation.

Third, several areas of clinical concern, once thought to be entirely due to organic or environmental factors, now appear to have important components of temperament-environment interaction. These are: behavioral problems, school performance, the physiologic disturbances of colic and night walking, the incidence of accidents and illness and minor developmental delay. It seems likely that a role for temperament will become evident with further investigation in child abuse, failure to thrive, obesity and other psychosomatic problems. There is no evidence to date that any developmental disability brings with it a specific temperamental profile. However, we may speculate that such characteristics as adaptability and persistence could strongly influence the behavioral outcome in the child, particularly the success of rehabilitative measures (Carey, 1972, 1974, 1981).

Let us discuss two areas of special clinical concern: behavior problems and scholastic performance.

Behavior Problems

The principal finding of the New York Longitudinal Study (Thomas *et al.*, 1968) was that certain temperamental patterns, particularly those of the difficult child, predispose to behavior problems, often requiring professional intervention. Two later projects by Graham *et al.* (1973) and McInerny and Chamberlin (1978), while smaller and less elegant in design, support the earlier conclusions. From these investigations one might conclude that certain children can be identified early as being at risk for behavior problems. Some zealous persons have even proposed that preventive screening for difficult temperament would be a major contribution to mental health.

However, matters are too complex for that approach. Identifying difficult temperament by questionnaire does not mean that one has discovered a disharmonious parent-child interaction. While more problems generally attend difficulty of temperament, many mothers report being very happy with difficult babies. Obviously, they are somehow adapting to each other satisfactorily, at least at that time. The clinician should interfere only when excessive stress results from a mismatch.

There is also the problem of determining when the child with difficult temperament has developed a behavior problem. The best solution seems to be to remember that difficult temperament is a matter of style, while the behavior problem is more one of content and an unsatisfactory psychosocial adjustment. Getting angry easily is one thing; having no friends because of the temper is another.

If difficult temperament leads to the development of a behavior problem, how does this affect the goals of therapy? Even with successful therapy one should expect that the difficult child would still be difficult. A reasonable objective would be to alter the parent-child relationship so that the child's reactive symptoms disappear but also to help parents and teachers become more understanding and flexible with the less modifiable temperamental characteristics.

Scholastic Performance

A child's school performance is presently explained in terms of his past experience, neurological status, intelligence and psychosocial adjustment, but a growing body of evidence substantiates the view that the child's temperament is also a factor. Gordon and Thomas (1967) demonstrated that the traits of approach and adaptability in preschool children affected their teachers' judgments of their intelligence. Chess *et al.* (1976) established that the same two characteristics correlated significantly with higher academic achievement scores in the early school years regardless of ratings on intelligence tests. Teacher judgments of school adjustment were related to the pupils' adaptability in another recent study (Carey *et al.*, 1977). Finally, in a group of 30 children referred by schools to a pediatric neurologist for problems in learning and behavior and diagnosed as having minimal brain dysfunction (MBD)—based on present standards including the presence of at least two "soft signs"—the commonest characteristic was low adaptability (Carey *et al.*, 1979). It is evident from these studies that the child with difficulty modifying his behavior in a socially desirable direction (i.e., low in adaptability) is going to encounter problems in school.

An important finding of this last study was that all groups of children referred to the neurologist by the teachers tended to be low in adaptability and persistence (or attention span) and high in activity, regardless of whether their final diagnosis was MBD, adjustment problem or something else. This not only raises doubts as to whether MBD—if indeed such a syndrome exists—can be diagnosed by behavior alone but suggests that it is children with these characteristics who are of greatest concern to teachers. Since these traits are all variations of temperament, one must wonder whether their management should not be behavioral rather than, as is so often the case, pharmacologic—unless we are ready to propose that it is acceptable to medicate children for individual differences in personality.

A reasonable way out of the present diagnostic and therapeutic confusion generated by the vagueness of the terms MBD and hyperactivity is to stop using these labels and describe children instead in terms of a neurobehavioral profile. Such a profile organizes all objective data about the child under six headings: general physical, neurological, maturation, information processing abilities, temperament and psychosocial adjustment. Findings in one area, such as temperament or information processing, would not lead to unsupported conclusions in other areas, such as neurological status. This clear separation of objective findings and an elimination of imprecise comprehensive labels would advance our professional competence and be a genuine kindness to children and their families (Carey and McDevitt, 1980).

Summary

One may summarize what has been said about clinical measurement of temperament by saying that the recently devised set of questionnaires offers the best combination of simplicity and psychometric sophistication. The absence of standardized observation techniques has made external validity hard to demonstrate and has provided academic critics with a target for their doubts. However, accumulating studies demonstrate what clinicians have known all along—that properly asked questions get data valid enough for responsible clinical action.

References

Berberian, K.E. *Infants' Reactions to Strangers: The Effects of Memory Development and Temperament.* Unpublished doctoral dissertation, Bryn Mawr College (1979).

Billman, J. and McDevitt, S.C. Convergence of parent and observer ratings of temperament. *Child Development,* 51:395–400 (1980).

Buss, A.H. and Plomin, R. *A Temperament Theory of Personality Development.* New York: John Wiley and Sons (1975).

Campbell, S.D. *Maternal and Infant Behavior in Normal, High Risk, and "Difficult" Infants.* Paper presented at meeting of the Society for Research in Child Development, New Orleans, March (1977).

Carey, W.B. A simplified method for measuring infant temperament. *J. Pediat.,* 77:188–194 (1970).

Carey, W.B. Clinical applications of infant temperament measurements. *J. Pediat.,* 81:823–828 (1972).

Carey, W.B. Night waking and temperament in infancy. *J. Pediat.,* 84:756–758 (1974).

Carey, W.B. The Importance of Temperament-Environment Interaction for Child Health and Development, in Lewis, M. and Rosenblum, L. (eds.), *The Uncommon Child.* New York. Plenum Press, 1981.

Carey, W.B., Fox, M. and McDevitt, S.C. Temperament as a factor in early school adjustment. *Pediatrics,* 60 (suppl.):621–624 (1977).

Carey, W.B. and McDevitt, S.C. Revision of the infant temperament questionnaire. *Pediatrics*, 61:735–739 (1978a).

Carey, W.B. and McDevitt, S.C. Stability and change in individual temperament diagnoses from infancy to early childhood. *J. Child Psychiat.*, 17:331–337 (1978b).

Carey, W.B. and McDevitt, S.C. *M.B.D. and Hyperkinesis. A Clinical Viewpoint. Amer. J. Dis. Child*, 134:926–929 (1980).

Carey, W.B. and McDevitt, S.C. *Continuity and Discontinuity of Temperament in Children.* Paper presented at meeting of International Society for the Study of Behavioral Development, Lund, Sweden, June (1979).

Carey, W.B., McDevitt, S.C. and Baker, D. Differentiating M.B.D. and temperament. *Develop. Med. and Child Neurol.*, 21:765–772 (1979).

Chess, S., Thomas, A. and Cameron, M. Temperament: Its significance for school adjustment and academic achievement. *New York Univ. Educ. Rev.*, 7:24–29 (1976).

Frankenburg, W.F., Van Doornick, W.J., Liddell, T.N. and Dick, N.P. The Denver Prescreening Developmental Questionnaire (P.D.Q.). *Pediatrics*, 57:744 (1976).

Fullard, W., McDevitt, S.C. and Carey, W.B. *The Toddler Temperament Scale.* Unpublished test form (1978).

Gordon, E.M. and Thomas, A. Children's behavioral style and the teacher's appraisal of their intelligence. *J. School Psychol.*, 5:292–300 (1967).

Graham, P., Rutter, M. and George, S. Temperamental characteristics as predicators of behavior disorders of children. *Am. J. Orthopsychiat.*, 43:328–339 (1973).

Hegvik, R., McDevitt, S.C. and Carey, W.B. *The Middle Childhood Temperament Scale.* Unpublished test form. 1980.

Knobloch, H., Stevens, F., Malone, A., Ellison, P. and Risemberg, H. The validity of parental reporting of infant development. *Pediatrics*, 63:872–878 (1979).

McDevitt, S.C. and Carey, W.B. The measurement of temperament in 3–7 year old children. *J. Child Psychol. and Psychiat.*, 19:245–253 (1978).

McInerny, T. and Chamberlin, R.W. Is it feasible to identify infants who are at risk for later behavior problems? *Clin. Pediat.*, 17:233–238 (1978).

Persson-Blennow, I. and McNeill, T.F. A questionnaire for measurement of temperament in six-month-old infants: Development and standardization. *J. Child Psychol. and Psychiat.*, 20:1–13 (1979).

Sarett, P.T. *A Study of the Interaction Effects of Infant Temperament on Maternal Attachment.* Unpublished doctoral dissertation, Rutgers (1976).

Searls, E., Fullard, W. and McDevitt, S.C. *Relationship Between Infant Temperament Questionnaire Ratings and Observations During a Short Home Visit. Infant Behavior and Development.* In press.

Thomas, A. and Chess, S. *Temperament and Development.* New York: Brunner/Mazel (1977).

Thomas, A., Chess, S. and Birch, H.G. *Temperament and Behavior Disorders in Children.* New York: New York University Press (1968).

Thomas, A., Chess, S., Birch, H.G., Hertzig, M.E. and Korn, S. *Behavioral Individuality in Early Childhood.* New York: New York University Press (1963).

Appendix A

Information on Obtaining Temperament Questionnaires

The addresses from which our three temperament questionnaires may be obtained are listed below. Since these instruments were developed without any financial support, please send a contribution of $5.00 for each scale to help us cover expenses. The forms may be photocopied as much as you wish from the one you receive.

1. Infant Temperament Questionnaire (4 to 8 month old infants) revised 1977 by W.B. Carey and S.C. McDevitt.

    William B. Carey, M.D.
    319 West Front Street
    Media, Pa. 19063, USA
    Telephone: (215) 566-6641

    Reference: Revision of the Infant Temperament Questionnaire. Pediatrics 61:735-739, 1978

2. Toddler Temperament Scale (1-3 year old children) developed in 1978 by W. Fullard, S.C. McDevitt, and W.B. Carey

    William Fullard, Ph.D.
    Department of Educational Psychology
    Temple University
    Philadelphia, Pa. 19122, USA
    Telephone: (215) 787-6102

    Reference: submitted for publication

3. Behavioral Style Questionnaire (3-7 year old children) developed in 1975 by S.C. McDevitt and W.B. Carey

    Sean C. McDevitt, Ph.D.
    Devereux Center
    6436 East Sweetwater
    Scottsdale, Az. 85254, USA
    Telephone: (602) 948-5857

    Reference: The measurement of temperament in 3-7 year old children. Journal of Child Psychology and Psychiatry 19:245-253, 1978

All three scales assess the 9 New York Longitudinal Study temperament characteristics by eliciting parent responses to about 97 behavioral descriptions. Internal consistency was 0.83, 0.85, and 0.84 respectively for the three scales; one month retest reliability was 0.86, 0.88, and 0.89. Some external validity data are available.

4. Middle Childhood Temperament Questionnaire (8–12 year old children) developed in 1979–80 by R.L. Hegvik, S.C. McDevitt and W.B. Carey available on the same terms as of Nov. 1980 from:

> Ms. Robin L. Hegvik
> 307 North Wayne Avenue
> Wayne, Pa. 19087, USA
> Telephone: (215) 687-6058

23

Theoretical Issues in Temperament

MARY KLEVJORD ROTHBART
DOUGLAS DERRYBERRY

The past two decades have seen a resurgence of interest in a very old topic in psychology: individual differences in temperament. The interest reflects a reassessment of the child's role in early parent-child interaction (Bell, 1968; Lewis and Rosenblum, 1974). Socialization is no longer seen as a unilateral process in which children, initially alike, are shaped into different human beings through the reinforcements of their parents and teachers. Instead, children are seen as active social agents from the very first, influencing others as they are influenced. One effect of this reassessment has been an increasing concern with individual differences in children. We are asking the questions: what are the dimensions of variability in infants? How do parental treatments interact with child differences in social development? Is it possible that there may be no single "right way" to bring up children, but that our child-rearing should be influenced by the characteristics of the individual child?

Origins of Temperament Study

The recent interest in temperament becomes appended to an intellectual tradition going back over 1,600 years to the work of Vindician, who developed a four-fold typology of temperamental characteristics based upon Hippocrates' ideas about the humoral constitution of the body (Diamond, 1974). Indeed, the term "temperament" derives from the Latin temperamentum, meaning a proportionate mixture presumably denoting the relative preponderance of one or another humors in the individual's constitution. In Vindician's typology the *melancholic* person, quiet and moody, was seen as having a predominance of black bile; the *choleric,* touchy, aggressive and active, a predominance of yellow bile; the *sanguine,* sociable and easygoing, a predominance of blood; and the *phlegmatic,* calm and even-tempered, a predominance of phlegm. Vindician's classifications persisted in Western Europe well into the Middle Ages, and quotations from Vindician were repeated in medical manuscripts during the medieval period (Diamond, 1974). Analogous temperament typologies reportedly developed in eastern cultures such as China and India. During the twentieth century, the four-fold typology has remained alive through Pavlov's (1935) early work relating types of individual differences to the nervous system and in Eysenck's (1947) four-fold classification of individuals according to their scores on the dimensions of introversion-extraversion and neuroticism.

There are several criteria by which the temperament tradition may be identified in the study of individual differences. First, temperament has been closely linked to the individual's physiology or constitution, as in the case of the early humoral theory, and therefore has been closely associated with a psychobiological analysis of behavior. We will define "constitutional" as "the relatively enduring biological makeup of the individual, influenced over time by the interaction of heredity, experience, and maturation." Second, temperament has been particularly associated with postulated or observed individual differences in nervous system function. Pavlov's system of temperament, for example, was based upon the nervous system characteristics of strength and mobility of excitatory and inhibitory response. Third, temperament, since it is closely associated with the biology of the organism, has application even to the very young. Therefore, the study of very early individual differences has involved the study of infant temperament.

To date, however, little theoretical work other than Escalona's (1968) has been attempted by students of infant temperament. Most researchers have used the nine temperament categories which Thomas, Chess and their associates (Thomas *et al.,* 1963; Thomas and Chess, 1977) extracted from parent interviews about infant behavior. Much of this research has had a descriptive rather than an integrative focus.

We would therefore like to begin to develop a broad conceptual framework allowing consideration of possible dimensions of infant temperament. This framework will permit us to delineate the complexity of response systems involved in individual temperament and at the same time to suggest some of the integrative properties that may coordinate these responses. The paper will thus approach infant variability from two necessary and mutually interacting perspectives. Although we will separate the two perspectives for purposes of this discussion, we feel that ultimately they will be understood as a single process. The first approach, which views the infant primarily as a "reactive" organism, is concerned with establishing the range and organization of temperament, and in so doing it focuses on variability in the structural components of response and the temporal patterning of response systems. The second approach, which establishes the essentially "active" nature of the infant, emphasizes the self-regulatory behaviors which interact with the temporal and structural dimensions of response. Following this attempt to differentiate and then, to some extent, integrate the behaviors and response systems relevant to temperament, we will suggest some ways in which maturation and experience may influence infant temperament. Finally, we will present our own views as to whether extreme scores on temperament measures should be viewed as developmental disabilities.

Multiple Response Systems

To begin with, let us approach the infant as a reactive organism. Reactivity generally refers to the overall excitability, responsivity or arousability of the individual. Although it is often theoretically useful to speak of a "net level" of excitation or arousal within a given situation, at first we would like to focus upon reactivity in terms of its component response systems. Approached in this way, reactivity can be seen to be a complex and interesting phenomenon, revealing vast potential for the existence of individual differences.

Reactivity is a function of coordinated cortical, autonomic, motor and endocrine processes with potential for variability in the relative strengths and resultant patterning of these response systems. Given such complexity, individual differences in reactivity can be approached at a number of different levels. In behavioral reactivity, for example, infants appear to react to intense and novel stimuli with varying degrees of excitation. Birns (1965) found cross-modality individual differences in neonates' intensity of behavioral response to auditory, tactile and oral stimulation. Moreover, these differences were stable across four sessions between the second and the fifth days of life. In an attempt to extend and broaden these findings of stability, Birns *et al.* (1969) examined a number of temperamental dimensions across the first four months of life. Here, vigor of response was not found to be stable, although the related dimensions of sensitivity, irritability and tension in reaction to stimulation were stable across the four months.

In addition to the variability observed by Birns *et al.*, individual differences have been noted in behaviors such as vocalization (Kagan, 1971) and attention (McCall, 1971; Horowitz, 1974). In our initial laboratory presentations of intense and novel stimuli to infants, we have observed that infants differ in the frequency, the intensity and the duration of their sequences of vocalization. Similar variability emerges with attentional behavior; infants appear to differ in the intensity and duration of their orienting responses. Perhaps the most striking aspect of these observations has involved the extent to which infants vary in the patterning of their motor, vocal and attentional reactions. Some infants appear to react primarily through motor activity, others through facial expressions or vocalization, and others chiefly through their attentional processes. Given such diversity in response, no single response system will be necessarily representative of reactivity as a whole. It is therefore essential that reactivity be approached in terms of its expression through a number of different response systems. In this way, an integrated assessment can more adequately reveal the full range and organization of temperament.

That infant reactivity is important to early social development has been observed by both Escalona (1968) and Korner (1973), who have argued that individual differences in infants' sensitivity to stimulation are likely to have a long-range influence on development. In addition, Escalona (1968) has proposed that some children may be especially sensitive to stimulation in a particular modality (e.g., the tactile or auditory mode). Escalona extends this argument to include reactivity to interoceptive sensation, suggesting that some infants are more reactive than others to internal physiologic signals. Thomas *et al.* (1963) have also proposed that infants differ in their threshold for reaction, distractibility and intensity of reaction.

Reactivity via multiple response systems, with all the potential for complexity it allows in individual temperament, provides only part of the picture. We also feel it is important to approach reactivity in terms of its temporal dimensions. We see reactivity as more than simply an attained level of response, since it involves phasic response to stimulation, processes which rise in strength, peak and subside across time. Each of these three parameters appears to be influential in an infant's individuality. For example, some infants seem to build rapidly to a high peak of motor excitement and recover quickly, while others rise more gradually, peak at lower levels and recover slowly. In addition, there appear to be differences in the sequential arrangement of processes through which reactivity unfolds. Some babies become distressed through a gradual cumulative process in which motor agitation initiates the sequence, is then augmented by facial distress and later also includes negative vocalization. In other infants the motor and facial components may occur simultaneously, followed in close sequence by a burst of crying. In connection with these fluctuations, Brazelton's (1973) Neonatal Assessment Scale assesses individual variability along a "rapidity of build-up" scale, "peak of excitement" and "consolability" scales.

The rising phase of reactivity has been to some extent overlooked in infant research. Brazelton *et al.* (1975), however, provide an example in which a toy monkey is suspended within a young infant's reach: "this state of intense, rapt attention built up gradually to a peak which was disrupted suddenly by the infant's turning away from the object, becoming active, and flailing his extremities." The authors reported that marked differences in the infants' duration of orienting, buildup of excitement, disruption of attention and state activity were evident as early as three weeks of age. Such differences in the rate with which a reaction grows will have important influences upon the infant-parent interaction and the child's experience. For example, the infant who rises gradually in excitement offers the parent greater opportunity to facilitate or alleviate the reactivity before its peak. Moreover, such an infant may be in a better position to effectively regulate his own increasing excitement and may thus be less likely to experience overwhelming levels of excitation.

In contrast, the falling phase of excitement has received considerable attention over the past few years. A number of studies have reported individual differences in the rate at which infants recover from a distressed state when various soothing procedures are applied. Birns *et al.* (1966), for example, observed neonates showing differential behavioral and cardiac quieting when irritable, with the differences consistent across two days. In a later study, Birns *et al.* (1969) found a dimension of soothability to be consistent across the first four months of life. More recent work has provided evidence that in addition to differences in how quickly infants recover when soothed, they also vary in how successfully they soothe themselves (Korner and Thoman, 1972; Freedman, 1971). Again, such differences will be very important to both the infant and the parent. Infants who recover rapidly from a peak of excitement may require relatively little intervention from the parent and may in fact become quite efficient in the use of self-soothing behaviors. Other infants who do not recover quickly may require large amounts of soothing from the parent, who in turn may come to question his or her own effectiveness. Infants who rarely experience soothing in connection with others, because they are either rarely distressed or able to soothe themselves, may be less likely to associate other human beings with comfort than infants who have been frequently soothed by a parent.

As can be seen, our reactive approach to infant temperament has already begun to reflect the active, self-regulatory dimensions of behavior inherent in the infant's self-soothing. Before giving full attention to active components, however, we would like to mention a few of the constitutional elements which may accompany the behavioral patterning. By briefly discussing the autonomic, endocrine and cortical dimensions of reactivity, we can consider possible additional sources of diversity in temperament.

Within the autonomic nervous system, Lacey (1950, 1967) has demonstrated that people show stable differences in their response to a specific stimulus or situation. For example, when faced with a difficult mental task, some persons react primarily through cardiac activity, others through electrodermal activity, and others through vasomotor activity. Although the patterning of autonomic reactivity has received little attention in infant research, evidence indicates that infants differ in their extent of responsiveness within a single modality. Lipton *et al.* (1961) examined cardiac reactivity to an air puff in a group of infants during the newborn period and again at two and a half and five months. Individual differences in magnitude of response were not consistent from the newborn to two and a half months, but stability was found from two and a half to five months, perhaps due to maturation of cardiac control mechanisms (Steinschneider, 1971). In addition to differences in peak magnitude, Richmond *et al.* (1962) found variability in time to peak and time to recover measures of heart rate. These findings are complemented by a number of other studies, including work by Richmond and Lustman (1955), Bridger *et al.* (1965) and Lewis *et al.* (1970), which provide evidence of autonomic individuality during infancy.

Body neurochemistry also consists of a number of interacting subsystems which appear to form differential patterning across individuals. Focusing on one of the endocrine systems, the catecholamines, Frankenhaeuser (1975) argues that individuals differ in their basal epinephrine levels, in the epinephrine output to a particular stimulus, and in the time required for epinephrine excretion to return to baseline levels. She reports that following a difficult mental task, rapid epinephrine decreasers had higher epinephrine secretion during inactivity, better performance scores on a sensory-motor task, and lower neuroticism scores than slow "decreasers." Porges (1976), in considering the central balance between the neurotransmitters norepinephrine, acetylcholine and serotonin, has provided an interesting approach to constitutional differences possibly underlying behavioral dimensions of activity, inhibition and reactivity. Porges proposes that imbalances between these neurochemicals may be related to such disorders as hyperactivity, psychopathy and infantile autism.

Individual differences in reactivity become especially interesting when approached at the level of the central nervous system. Here we find very little empirical evidence but some provocative theories. For example, the hypothetical model of temperament developed by Pavlov (1955), Teplov (1964) and Nebylitsyn (1972) is concerned with the equilibrium between excitatory and inhibitory processes and also with their temporal characteristics. Thus, properties such as "mobility" (the speed with which an excitatory process is transformed into an inhibitory process), "lability" (the speed with which responses are initiated and terminated), and "dynamism" (the ease with which responses are generated) interact with the "strength" of excitatory and inhibitory processes in describing reactivity (Teplov, 1972). Other theorists have hypothesized variability in the relative reactivity of central neural systems. The reticular formation and the limbic system, for example, have been related to behavioral dimensions such as introversion/extroversion (Eysenck, 1967; Gray, 1972) and sensation-seeking (Zuckerman, 1974).

Self-regulation

We have thus far presented a view of infant temperament as a complex organization of structurally and temporally overlapping response systems. Such a view is valuable in that it demonstrates both the complexity of temperament and the need for an integrated assessment of that complexity. This perspective is somewhat misleading, however, in that it neglects the fact that the infant is an experiencing organism, and such experience is central to his or her behavior. In other words, the infant often experiences reactivity, and behavior is modulated in relation to the affective tone of that experience. It is at this level of experience and modulation that we will set aside the multidimensional approach to reactivity and focus instead on an overall level of activation. Within such a framework the active nature of the organism emerges, which includes individual differences in approach, withdrawal and self-regulation.

The term "arousal potential," introduced by Berlyne (1960), is particularly helpful in relation to an experiential, unitary conception of reactivity. It denotes the extent to which a stimulus or situation can be expected to elicit activation. Berlyne has related arousal potential to felt affect through an inverted-U function: positive affect is seen to increase to an optimal level as activation increases to moderate levels, and then to become more and more negative as activation increases to still higher levels. In addition, several personality theories propose that individuals differ in their optimal levels of arousal (Fiske and Maddi, 1961; Eysenck, 1967). Thus, some infants, possibly because they are relatively less reactive, will approach and/or tolerate higher levels of stimulation. More reactive babies, on the other hand, may surpass their optimal levels sooner and may be likely to avoid or become distressed at the higher stimulation levels. Although optimal range may be solely a function of extent of reactivity, it may be independent; further research will determine the extent of correlation. Infants' optimal ranges can be assessed through convergent measures of activity level, attentional behavior, positive and negative affect, and perhaps most closely through more subtle arousal-modulating behaviors such as self-stimulation and self-soothing.

The concept of self-regulation is represented in the "dual process" theories of affect and motivation. Schneirla (1959) has provided the basic dual-process model: "approach" systems are activated in response to low and moderate intensities of stimulation, while "withdrawal" systems are activated at high intensities. Related versions have included the "reward versus aversion" systems (Berlyne, 1971), the "stimulus-intake versus stimulus-rejection" systems (Lacey, 1967), and the "orienting versus defensive reflexes" (Sokolov, 1963). From the present perspective, these approaches are relevant in that individual differences in the "intensity level" of stimulation at which approach and withdrawal responses are activated appear to be a function of temperamental constraints.

Differences in the level of intensity or novelty, the duration of stimulus exposure, and the attained level of reactivity at which infants demonstrate approach and avoidance behaviors are therefore of special interest in our laboratory observations. In some instances, such as following an extended presentation of a relatively uninteresting toy, infants initiate behaviors which appear to serve an arousal-increasing function. For example, they may lean forward, visually scan the room, look toward the experimenter and bang on the table, as if they are seeking additional stimulation. Needless to say, infants differ greatly in the conditions under which they become bored and also in the intensity with which they attempt to correct this condition. In the case of other, more intense stimuli, behaviors such as leaning back from the stimulus, gaze aversion and hand-to-mouth contact appear to dampen the arousing effects of stimulation such that continued interaction with the stimulus can occur (Pien and Rothbart, in press). These behaviors, which may indicate that an infant is moving beyond a tolerable level of activation, are again utilized quite differently by various infants. Some will react to a moderately intense stimulus with rapid, successive gaze aversions, and may eventually become overwhelmed and distressed by the situation. Others will suck on their fingers, thumb or hands while maintaining contact with the stimulus over an extended period. Still others will initiate arousal-decreasing behaviors only at the highest intensities of stimulation and even then will demonstrate little negative affect.

These arousal-increasing and arousal-decreasing behaviors involve the self-regulation of reactivity and as such they reflect the organism's active, controlling capacity. Stern (1974a, 1974b) has observed arousal modulation in the social behavior of three- to four-month-old infants. He describes the following "game" engaged in by infants and their mothers:

> It consists of the infant looking at the mother, smiling, vocalizing, and showing other signs of mounting arousal and positive affect, including increasing motor activity. As the intensity of his state increases, he begins to show signs of displeasure, momentary sobering, and a fleeting grimace, interspersed with the smiling. The intensity of arousal continues to build until he suddenly averts gaze sharply with a quick but not extensive head turn which keeps the mother's face in good peripheral view, while his level of 'excitement' clearly declines. He then returns gaze, bursting into a smile, and the level of arousal and affect build again. He again averts gaze, and so on. The infant gives the clear impression of modulating his states of arousal and affect within certain limits by regulating the amount of perceptual input (Stern, 1974b, pp. 208–209).

An important aspect of Stern's observations involves the extent to which the infant's attentional processes are involved in the modulation of arousal. By *actively* shifting attention away from the arousing stimulus, the infant initiates a recovery process which allows for a continuing engagement of the stimulus. The argument could be made that attentional processes provide the infant with his or her primary means of self-regulation. In this respect the infant can direct his or her attention toward or away from objects so that reactivity is initiated (by looking toward), enhanced (by looking intently), maintained (by extended orienting), reduced (through gaze aversions) or terminated (by looking away). As the child grows older and acquires the capacity for imagery and language, attention takes on even greater and more flexible self-regulatory functions. For example, the one-year-old may be able to attend to the image of an absent parent or remind himself or herself that the parent will return as a means of alleviating separation distress or an older child may "not think" about an approaching stressful event in order to avoid the anxiety connected with it.

To the extent that there are individual differences in the mechanisms related to attention, variability will appear in the styles and efficiency of self-regulation. Thomas *et al.* (1963) suggested that important differences exist in the deployment of attention and proposed the temperamental categories of attention span, persistence and distractibility. Distractibility can be seen to be important to both care-giver- and self-regulation. Infants are often soothed through distraction, i.e., by directing their attention to an object, the sound of the parent's voice, and so on. Thus, children who are more distractible may be more readily soothed and may also more readily soothe themselves. They may also be relatively adept at actively disengaging their attention from an unpleasant stimulus and refocusing upon a less arousing or more comforting object.

Attention span or duration of orienting may also be important in relation to an infant's self-regulation. Several researchers have noted that infants reliably differ in their rate of habituation, i.e., in decrease of their attention toward a stimulus over successive repetitions. McCall (1971) and Cohen (1975) have identified "slow" and "rapid habituators," and Horowitz (1975) has described a subgroup of "short lookers." Beyond the reflection of differing rates in the formation of cognitive structures, these differences in habituation rate may reflect variability in infants' ability to disengage themselves from a stimulus. The relation between self-regulation and such attentional behavior may help to provide a link between temperament and the styles of cognitive control which emerge as the child grows older.

Although persistence may be treated primarily as an attentional variable, our own approach has been concerned with the individual differences in behavioral persistence which appear when an infant's goal-directed activity is blocked. Such interruption results in increased arousal, and infants appear to differ in both the extent of reactivity to frustration and in their manner of regulating it. For example, Kramer and Rosenblum (1970) studied the reactions of one-year-olds when a glass barrier was placed between the child and an attractive toy. They observed three kinds of infant reactions to the barrier: some infants were persistent and managed to obtain the toy; others gradually shifted their interest to some other environmental focus without securing the toy; and a third group became distressed and abruptly lost interest in the toy. In our observations of the attempts of six-month-olds to secure an out-of-reach object, variability has also been evident. Some infants become motorically and vocally agitated—frowning, fussing and pounding on the table as they continue to reach for the toy—while other infants quietly persist in reaching. Of additional infants who show little persistence, some abandon their efforts with an intense display of negative affect, while others appear to desist with little indication of distress.

We might expect that such differences in reactivity and regulation related to frustration would have important interactions with the infant-parent relationship. Infants, particularly when they are in the process of mastering emerging motor skills, are subject to a great number of potentially frustrating situations, and the parent is often in a position to intervene. The parent may be able to either facilitate or weaken the child's capacity for persistence by the amount and frequency of this intervention. For example, the child's persistence may be limited to the extent that he understands the parent's potential as a means to obtaining a goal and also to the extent that the parent does in fact assist the child. The child's persistence may be facilitated to the extent that the parent is able to support the child without taking over the task completely.

The infant's active, self-regulatory nature also becomes apparent when the temperamental dimension of activity level is considered. The dimension of activity level has been central to most studies of infant temperament (e.g., Escalona, 1968; Buss and Plomin, 1975; Thomas *et al.,* 1963), but questions remain concerning its stability across time. Although Birns *et al.* found consistency of activity for infants between the ages of one to four months, Buss and Plomin (1975) have concluded that the characteristic shows stability only after infancy. One reason for this apparent inconsistency may involve differences in the regulatory nature of motor activity during the early and later months of the first year. Early motor activity, before the acquisition of manipulative skills, appears to be a relatively direct reflection of the infant's ongoing reactivity. As the child develops manipulative and locomotive skills, however, these capacities take on important self-regulatory functions. For example, approaching and actively interacting with objects may serve to increase arousal, whereas avoidance and inactivity may serve to contain an already high level of arousal within an optimal range. Thomas *et al.* have identified approach/withdrawal as an important temperamental dimension. It therefore seems reasonable to expect that a highly reactive two-month-old may in the later months of the first year be less likely to further increase his or her level of activation through extensive interaction with objects. Bell *et al.*'s (1971) findings of a reversal in intensity of motor reaction between the newborn and preschool periods may support this prediction.

Once again, we expect that the child's activity level will greatly affect the nature of the infant-parent relationship. For example, the active infant who continually approaches and "gets into" things around the home may require extensive monitoring. A less active child may be satisfied with a more limited number of proximal and familiar sources of stimulation and will not require constant watching. We expect that the experience of both parent and child will be affected by the activity level and stimulation-seeking of the infant. The active child, who is often thwarted in his or her efforts to seek out additional stimulation, may come to construe parents as potentially frustrating agents, and the parents, in turn, may view the child as something of a "nuisance." In contrast, the less active infant may not be subject to the same amount of frustration and scolding, and the parents are likely to appreciate his or her relative contentment, even though at a later age they might wish the quiet child were more energetic at household and other tasks.

In our approach to infant temperament we have proposed that infants differ in socially important ways in their reactivity to and recovery from arousing stimulation and that they also differ in their optimal range of stimulation. Now we will discuss some of the ways in which early maturation and experience may affect infant temperament.

Early Maturation and Experience

We have talked about Berlyne's (1960) concept of arousal potential which points out that *intensity* of stimulation is not the only possible source of phasic activation in the infant. Other sources of arousal potential include the rate of presentation and size of the stimulus. In addition, Berlyne (1960) has identified a set of arousing stimuli which he calls *collative,* i.e., which involve a person's collation or comparison of stimuli with a representation in memory (an expectation). Activation results from a discrepancy between what is expected and what is experienced, i.e., from surprise. Berlyne included in this category of collative arousal novel or discrepant events, and we would also include the interruption of a goal-directed activity. In addition, activation can result from the "meaning" or "significance" of a stimulus to the child. To the extent that a previously relatively neutral stimulus has been paired with a stimulus of significance, e.g., the presentation of food or of a distressing event, the neutral stimulus may come to elicit activation in itself. When we combine Berlyne's arousal potential view with our concept of temperament, it should be clear that individual differences would be an additional major contribution to the arousal potential of a stimulus.

Given this approach, it should be clear that increasing sources of arousal potential will become available during the child's rapid physical maturation in the first years of life. For example, increasing maturation of the nervous system appears to be related to fixation time for complex visual patterns (Karmel and Maisel, 1975), and perception of higher levels of complexity represents an increasing source of activation. The infant's increasing memory capacities create the possibility for more sources of expectations and therefore of collative activation. Bronson (1978) has argued that older infants react to the meaningfulness of stimuli associated with distressing situations, and this would be an additional source of activation. Certainly at a much earlier time we will have seen the association of positive excitement with preparation of food. To the extent that older infants come to understand means-ends relations, they may also become more distressed to the experience of limitations. At the same time, the maturation of inhibitory mechanisms may allow the infant increasing means for modulating these various sources of activation (Peiper, 1963; Scheibel and Scheibel, 1964; Parmelee and Michaelis, 1971). It should be clear that in order to understand temperament conceived as individual differences in reactivity and self-regulation, we must also understand the infant's rate of maturation and level of cognitive development, and we have much to learn in this area.

Theorists working in the area of infant development have proposed major biobehavioral transitions during the early months of life. Benjamin (1965), for example, has proposed that infants show a marked and relatively sudden increase in sensitivity to exogenous and possibly endogenous stimulation at the age of three to four weeks, with this increase associated with a shift in the waking EEG from a relatively flat, undifferentiated, neonatal pattern to distinct periodicity with an increase in amplitude. At about three to four weeks, and until about eight to ten weeks of age, according to Benjamin, the infant is especially vulnerable to distress, as evidenced in bouts of paroxysmal crying and general fussiness. By eight to ten weeks, however, a "stimulus barrier" is established in which a maturing cortex acquires increased inhibitory control over subcortical input.

Emde (1977) and his associates have studied in more detail the changes occurring after two months. They propose that the marked increase in quiet sleep and decrease in activation of transitory reflexes occurring at this time are correlates of the maturation of forebrain inhibitory centers. Emde notes the decrease in fussiness and increase in smiling to exogenous stimuli during the two- to three-month period. He also notes changes in visual scanning patterns (Bergman *et al.,* 1971; Haith, 1976; Maurer and Salapatek, 1976) with greater fixation of facial features, especially the eyes.

A second transition in reactivity has been observed at seven to nine months (Emde, 1977; Kagan *et al.,* 1978; McCall *et al.,* 1977) in connection with such behaviors as fear of strangers, separation distress, wariness and latency of approach to novel objects. If there is variability in the timing of this transition (Wilson, 1978), we might expect that individual differences in the time these shifts occur may result in major differences in temperamental behavior and experience at any given point. For example, infants who are maturationally advanced might show distress and latency to approach novel stimuli at an earlier age than less advanced children. Though slower maturers might develop the advanced behavior patterns later, we might expect that the quality of experience of early- and late-maturing infants would vary in the intervening period. The later-maturing infants might be expected to experience greater interaction with and habituation to novel objects during this period than the earlier-maturing infants.

We also suspect that strong environmental factors may influence stability of temperament. One of Pavlov's (1935) early observations of temperament in dogs was that he could produce timid or "melancholic" behaviors by highly restricting the dog's early experience. The optimal level concept also has been related to experience. Fiske and Maddis' (1961) "optimal level" is actually a "customary" level of activation and thus very much a function of experience.

Developmental Disabilities

Finally, we would like to consider whether extreme scores on temperament measures should necessarily be viewed as developmental disabilities. In our own observations of normal infants we have decided that each behavioral characteristic has both its good and bad points. Perhaps a better way of saying this is that there are both costs and benefits connected with a given characteristic, depending on the task demands of a given situation. For example, Thomas *et al.* (1968) have pointed out that highly distractible infants may be seen as "good babies" because they are so easy to soothe by presenting a toy or walking around with the child and so reactive to their parents' playful approaches. At the age of seven, however, a distractible child may be difficult to get off to school in the morning because too many other activities interfere with getting out of the house. The child may also show problems in completing reading assignments and getting homework done. Similarly, a child who shows an early defensive reaction as an infant may later be very cautious and planful, a child who controls situations early in order to avoid unpleasantness. Teplov (1964) has offered an analogy in which he compares the highly reactive individual to a very sensitive photographic plate: "Such plates demand specially careful treatment: more than any others they must be protected from strong light or over-exposure. This is, of course, a negative property: but it is a consequence of a highly positive one—great sensitivity" (pg. 71).

The individual patterns of temperament do not, themselves, have positive or negative value. What matters is the interaction between the temperament and the environment, what Thomas and Chess (1977) have referred to as the "goodness of fit." Value emerges out of this interaction and is best thought of in terms of the quality of growth (in both affective and cognitive development) which is fostered. All temperaments involve both capacities and limitations, and it is the relation between these aspects to the requirements of a given situation which is important. To focus too closely on either the child or the parent as the source of developmental difficulties is to oversimplify a highly interactional process of adjustment occurring over years of development.

For example, much emphasis has recently been placed upon the mother's role, in particular upon her sensitivity to the infant's signals, in the development of "felt security" and effective attachment (e.g., Ainsworth, 1973). We would suggest, given the temperament concept, that much more is involved in the attachment process than the mother's sensitivity and flexibility. Infants may differ in their optimal levels of stimulation, their relative reactivity, their rapidity of buildup and their rate of recovery, while mothers vary along parallel lines and also in the styles through which they attempt to regulate the child's behavior. Even though the mother's sensitivity and flexibility in adjusting her ministrations to the infant's needs will be very important, the role of the child's constitutional capacities and limitations in shaping her behavior should not be underestimated. Nor should the sensitivity and flexibility of the infant be neglected, for infants vary greatly in their capacity to augment or reduce their own reactivity. It therefore seems essential that the mother-infant interaction and the resulting attachment be viewed as a function of two intricate and flexible interactional systems, which can achieve a "balance" in a number of different ways. The quality of the balance will be reflected in the affective and cognitive development of the child and the parent.

Acknowledgments

This paper was partially supported by grant 5RO1MH26674-04 from the National Institute of Public Health. The authors wish to thank the following persons for their helpful comments on early drafts of the paper: Michael I. Posner, Benson Schaeffer, Diana Pien, Myron Rothbart, and Susan Hoffman.

References

Ainsworth, M.D.S. The development of infant-mother attachment, in Caldwell, B.M. and Ricciuti, H.N. (eds.), *Review of Child Development Research*. Chicago: University of Chicago Press, pp. 1–94 (1973).

Bell, R.Q. A reinterpretation of the direction of effects in studies of socialization. *Psychol. Rev.*, 75:81–85 (1968).

Bell, R.Q., Weller, G.M. and Waldrop, M.F. Newborn and preschooler: organization of behavior and relations between periods. *Monographs of the Society for Research in Child Development*, 36 (1 and 2, Serial No. 142) (1971).

Benjamin, J. Developmental biology and psychoanalysis, in Greenfield, N. and Lewis, W. (eds.), *Psychoanalysis and Current Biological Thought*. Madison: University of Wisconsin Press, pp. 57–80 (1965).

Bergman, T., Haith, M.J. and Mann, L. Development of eye contact and facial scanning in infants. Paper presented at the SRCD Convention, Minneapolis, Minnesota, April (1971).

Berlyne, D.E. *Conflict, Arousal, and Curiosity*. New York: McGraw Hill (1960).

Berlyne, D.E. Arousal and reinforcement, in Levine, D. (ed.), *Nebraska Symposium on Motivation*. Lincoln, Nebraska: University of Nebraska (1967).

Birns, B. Individual differences in human neonates' responses to stimulation. *Child Devel.*, 36.249–256 (1965).

Birns, B., Blank, M. and Bridger, W.H. The effectiveness of various soothing techniques on human neonates. *Psychosom. Med.*, 28:316–322 (1966).

Birns, B., Barten, S. and Bridger, W. Individual differences in temperamental characteristics of infants. *Transactions of the New York Academy of Sciences*, 31:1071–1082 (1969).

Brazelton, T.B. *Neonatal Behavioral Assessment Scale*. Clinics in Developmental Medicine, No. 50. Philadelphia: Lippincott (1973).

Brazelton, T.B. and Freedman, D.G. Manual to accompany Cambridge Newborn Behavioral and Neurological Scales, in Stoelinga, G.B.A. and Van der Werff Ten Bosch, J.J. (ed.), *Normal and Abnormal Development of Brain and Behavior*. Leiden, The Netherlands: Leiden University Press, pp. 104–132 (1971).

Bridger, W.H., Birns, B. and Blank, M. A comparison of behavioral and heart rate measurements in human neonates. *Psychosom. Med.*, 27:123–134 (1965).

Bronson, G. Aversive reactions to strangers: a dual process interpretation. *Child Devel.*, 49: 495–499 (1978).

Brazelton, T.B., Koslowski, B. and Main, M. The origins of reciprocity: The early mother-infant interaction, in Lewis, M. and Rosenblum, L.A. (eds.), *The Effect of the Infant on Its Caregiver*. New York: Wiley (1975).

Buss, A.H. and Plomin, R. *A Temperament Theory of Personality*. New York: Wiley (1975).

Carey, W.B. and McDevitt, S.C. Revision of the infant temperament questionnaire. *Pediatrics*, 61:735–739 (1978).

Clifton, R.K. and Graham, F.K. Stability of individual differences in heart rate activity during the newborn period. *Psychophysiol.*, 5:37–50 (1968).

Cohen, L.B. Infant visual memory: A backward look into the future, in Ellis, N.R. (ed.), *Aberrant Development in Infancy*. New York: Wiley (1975).

Diamond, S. *The Roots of Psychology*. New York: Basic Books (1974).

Emde, R.N. Two developmental shifts in infant biobehavioral organization: two months and seven-nine months, in *Qualitative Transitions in Behavior During Infancy*. Symposium presented at the meeting of the Society for Research in Child Development, New Orleans (1977).

Emde, R.N., Gaensbauer, T.J. and Harmon, R.J. Emotional expression in infancy. *Psychol. Issues, Monograph 37* (1976).

Escalona, S.K. *The Roots of Individuality: Normal Patterns of Development in Infancy.* Chicago: Aldine (1968).

Eysenck, H.J. *Dimensions of Personality;* a record of research carried out in collaboration with H.T. Himmelweit and others. London: Routledge and K. Paul (1947).

Eysenck, H.J. *The Biological Basis of Personality.* Springfield, Illinois: Thomas (1967).

Fiske, D.W. and Maddi, S.R. (eds.) *Functions of Varied Experience.* Homewood, Illinois: Dorsey Press (1961).

Frankenhaeuser, M. Experimental approaches to the study of catecholamines and emotion, in Levi, L. (ed.), *Emotions—Their Parameters and Measurement.* New York: Raven Press, pp. 209–234 (1975).

Freedman, D.G. Genetic influences on development of behavior, in Stoelings, G.B.A. and Van der Werff Ten Bosch, J.J. (eds.), *Normal and Abnormal Development of Behavior.* Leiden, The Netherlands: Leiden University Press, pp. 208–229 (1971).

Gray, J.A. The psychophysiological nature of introversio-extraversion: A modification of Eysenck's theory, in Neblitsyn, V.D. and Gray, J.A. (eds.), *Biological Bases of Individual Behavior.* New York: Academic Press (1972).

Haith, M. Visual competence in early infancy, in Held, R., Leibowitz, H. and Teuber, H.L. (eds.), *Handbook of Sensory Physiology VIII.* New York: Springer-Verlag (1976).

Horowitz, F.D. (ed.) Visual attention, auditory stimulation, and language discrimination in young infants. *Monographs of the Society for Research in Child Development,* 39 (5–6, Serial No. 158) (1974).

Kagan, J., Kearsley, R.B. and Zelazo, P. *Infancy: Its Place in Human Development.* Cambridge, Massachusetts: Harvard University Press (1978).

Karmel, B.Z. and Maisel, E.B. A neuronal activity model for infant visual attention, in Cohen, L.B. and Salapatek, P. (eds.), *Infant Perception: From Sensation to Cognition.* New York: Academic Press (1975).

Korner, A.F. and Thoman, E.B. The relative efficacy of contact and vestibular-proprioceptive stimulation in soothing neonates. *Child Devel.,* 43:443–452 (1972).

Korner, A.F. Individual differences at birth: implications for early experience and later development, in Westman, J.C. (ed.), *Individual Differences in Children.* New York: Wiley (1973).

Kramer, Y. and Rosenblum, L.A. Responses to "frustration" in one-year-old infants. *Psychosom. Med.,* 32(3):243–257 (1970).

Lacey, J.I. Individual differences in somatic response patterns. *J. Compar. and Physiol. Psychol.,* 43:338–350 (1950).

Lacey, J.I. Somatic response patterning and stress: Some revisions of activation theory, in Appley, M.H. and Trumbull, R. (eds.), *Psychological Stress: Issues in Research.* New York: Appleton-Century-Crofts (1967).

Lewis, M. and Rosenblum, L.A. *The Effect of the Infant on Its Caregiver.* New York: Wiley (1974).

Lewis, M., Wilson, C., Ban, L. and Baumel, L. An exploratory study of the resting cardiac rate and variability from the last trimester of prenatal life through the first year of postnatal life. *Child Devel.,* 41:799–811 (1970).

Lipton, E.L., Steinschneider, A. and Richmond, J.B. Autonomic function in the neonate: Individual differences in cardiac reactivity. *Psychosom. Med.,* 23:472–484 (1961).

Lipton, E.L., Steinschneider, A. and Richmond, J.B. Autonomic function in the neonate: VII. Maturational changes in cardiac control. *Child Devel.,* 37:1–16 (1966).

McCall, R.B. Attention in the infant: Avenue to the study of cognitive development, in Walcher, D.N. and Peters, D.L. (eds.), *The Development of Self-Regulatory Mechanism.* New York: Academic Press (1971).

McCall, R.B., Eichorn, D.H. and Hogarty, P.S. Transitions in early mental development. *Monographs of the Society for Research in Child Development,* 42 (3, Serial No. 171) (1977).

Mason, J.W. Emotion as reflected in patterns of endocrine integration, in Levi, L. (ed.), *Emotions: Their Parameters and Measurement.* New York: Raven Press (1975).

Maurer, D. and Salapatek, P. Developmental changes in the scanning of faces by young infants. *Child Devel.,* 47:523–527 (1976).

Nebylitsyn, V.D. *Fundamental Properties of the Human Nervous System.* New York: Plenum (1972).

Parmelee and Michaelis. Neurological examination of the newborn, in Hellmuth, G. (ed.), *The Exceptional Infant.* New York: Bruner/Mazel, Inc., pp. 3–24 (1971).

Pavlov, I.P. General types of animal and human higher nervous activity. *Selected Works.* Moscow: Foreign Language Publishing House (1955). (Originally published, 1935.)

Pien, D. and Rothbart, M.K. Incongruity humour, play and self-regulation of arousal in young children, in Chapman, A. and McGhee, P. (eds.), *Children's Humour.* Wiley, 1980.

Pieper, A. *Cerebral Function in Infancy and Childhood.* New York: Consultants Bureau (1963).

Porges, S.W. Peripheral and neurochemical parallels of psychopathology: A psychophysiological model relating autonomic imbalance to hyperactivity, psychopathy, and autism, in Reese, H.W. (ed.), *Advances in Child Development and Behavior,* pp. 35–63 (1976).

Richmond, J.B., Lipton, E.L. and Steinschneider, A. Autonomic function in the neonate: V. Individual homeostatic capacity in cardiac response. *Psychosom. Med.,* 24:66–74 (1962).

Richmond, J.B. and Lustman, L.Q. Individual differences in the neonate. *Psychosom. Med.,* 17:269–280 (1955).

Scheibel, M.E. and Scheibel, A.B. Some neural substrates of postnatal development, in Hoffman, M.L. and Hoffman, L.W. (eds.), *Review of Child Development Research.* Vol. 1. New York: Russell Sage Foundation (1964).

Schneirla, T.C. The evolutionary and developmental theory of biphasic processes underlying approach and withdrawal, in Jones, M.R. (ed.), *Nebraska Symposium on Motivation.* Lincoln, Nebraska: University of Nebraska Press (1959).

Sokolov, E.N. *Perception and the Conditioned Reflex.* New York: Macmillan (1963).

Steinschneider, A. Determinants of an infant's cardiac response to stimulation, in Walcher, D.N. and Peters, D.L. (eds.), *The Development of Self-Regulatory Mechanisms.* New York: Academic Press (1973).

Stern, D. The goal and structure of mother-infant play. *J. Am. Acad. Child Psychiat.,* 13: 402–421 (1974a).

Stern, D. Mother and infant at play: The dyadic interaction involving facial, vocal, and gaze behaviors, in Lewis, M. and Rosenblum, L. (eds.), *The Effect of the Infant on its Caregiver.* New York: Wiley, pp. 402–421 (1974b).

Teplov, B.M. Problems in the study of general types of higher nervous activity in man and animals, in Gray, J.A. (ed.), *Pavlov's Typology.* New York: Macmillan (1964).

Teplov, B.M. The problem of types of human higher nervous activity and methods of determining them, in Nebylitsyn, V.D. and Gray, J.A. (eds.), *Biological Bases of Individual Behavior*. New York: Academic Press (1972).

Thomas, A. and Chess, S. *Temperament and Development*. New York: Brunner/Mazel (1977).

Thomas, A., Chess, S., Birch, H.G., Hertzig, M.E. and Korn, S. *Behavioral Individuality in Early Childhood*. New York: NYU Press (1963).

Thomas, A., Chess, S. and Birch, H.G. *Temperament and Behavior Disorders in Children*. New York: New York University Press (1968).

Wilson, R.S. Synchronies in mental development: an epigenetic perspective. *Science,* 202: 939–947 (1978).

Zuckerman, M. The sensation seeking motive, in Maher, B.A. (ed.), *Progress in Experimental Personality Research*. Vol. 7, New York: Academic Press (1974).

24

Developmental Disabilities: Intervention Strategies in the Affective Domain

DAVID B. FRIEDMAN

Careful diagnostic exploration and treatment planning are necessary in order to develop effective therapeutic intervention as it is germane to the affective component of developmental disabilities. The strategies for implementing the therapeutic plan must be based on dynamic principles of human action and interaction. In addition they should encompass the idea that behavior has meaning and that physical and psychological symptoms may often be a means of communication. The discussion which follows relates to the affective component of all developmental disorders, impairments and disabilities as well as to the primary affective disorders (Cohen, P., 1979; Cohen, R., 1979; Ornitz, 1977; Rutter, 1978; Seidel, 1976).

Children's behavior and development are determined by four major factors: their inheritance, including temperament; what children and adults in their world teach them; how they react to their life experiences; and, probably most important, how their parents, siblings and other figures in their extended family think and feel about them and about themselves. The behavior and development of a child with a physical, developmental or emotional handicap or disability is further influenced by how child and parents perceive the handicap or disability (Freud, A., 1977; Grossman, 1979; Kessler, 1977).

In assessing the developmentally disabled child for the purpose of therapeutic intervention a number of factors must be considered (Committee on Child Psychiatry, Group for the Advancement of Psychiatry, 1973). The first of these is the degree of physical and neurological impairment, particularly as the impairment relates to the areas of healthy functioning in the child (Lemkau, 1961).

Next is the young patient's ability to tolerate pain, discomfort, frustration and anxiety. It is important to measure the child's current neurological, psychological, behavioral and cognitive developmental status as well as his or her personality and temperament. The child's capacity for conceptualization, communication and relating to others should be explored. The proportion of reactive to intrapsychic elements in the developmental disability must be weighed. Lastly a look at the way both family and child view and feel about the disability will provide useful data for developing a successful therapeutic strategy (Freud, A., 1977).

A paper published in 1967 (Augenbraun *et al.*) pointed out the unique therapeutic opportunities provided by family interviewing:

1. To facilitate and interpret family communication
2. To bring to the awareness of parents the meaningfulness of child behavior by interpreting the child's many ways of communicating
3. To observe and explore the effects of parental behavior on the child as well as the reciprocal effects upon the parents
4. To demonstrate appropriate parenting
5. To prepare one or more members of the family group for psychiatric referral

A follow-up paper in 1968 on family therapy in pediatrics (Friedman, D., 1968) related these therapeutic opportunities and strategies to the everyday work with families in the pediatrician's office. Family interviewing and family therapy are especially helpful in working with the families of children with developmental disabilities.

The following outline can serve as a guide for observing and evaluating family dynamics:

Communication

How do the members of this family communicate with each other? What is their capacity for verbal and non-verbal interaction? Is this a stable, cohesive family? Are the individual family members open or evasive, close or distant? Does there appear to be a family secret? Does the family interact with the outside world?

Handling of Affect

How do individual family members handle feelings? How do they use and cope with anger, guilt, anxiety, tenderness, hostility, overactivity and passivity? What is the family mood? How psychologically-minded is this family? What is the degree of mental health of individual family members and the family as a whole? What is the family life style? What are the characteristic family patterns in the areas of sleep, food, meals, toileting, sex, discipline, punishment, illness, safety, accident prevention, television, friends, relatives and daily routines?

Intrafamily Alignments and Schisms

In most families there is a favorite or a scapegoat, a clown or a brain, a hero or a villain, a tease or a teased, a protector or a protected one. Is there specific role behavior in this family? What is the role of the child or the child's disorder, disability or handicap in the psychic economy of this family? Does the family or do individual members of the family use the child and his or her disability for their own gain? What, if any, is the disabled child's secondary gain from his or her handicap?

Expectation of Development or Behavior

Is the psychological climate in this family accepting and encouraging or rejecting and discouraging for the child? Is the family milieu independence-granting and achievement-inducing or is it overprotective and unrewarding? How does the handling of independence reflect the subcultural values dominant in this family?

Reaction to Stress Situations (Coping Style)

How do individual family members react to illness, death, separation and decision making? What is their coping style? Do they meet the challenge, behave reasonably and express appropriate feelings or do they fall apart, evade or deny? Do they tend to somatize difficulties and express their feelings in somatic complaints? What is the capacity of this family for cooperating with treatment plans? Does any individual member have a need to sabotage any plan agreed upon by the group? Will the family members follow advice or instructions and accept referral in the context of a healthy doctor–parent–patient relationship?

Adults' View of Own Childhood

How do the adults in the family view their own childhood and childhood in general? How does their "inner child of the past" (Missildine, 1963), their childhood experiences in their own family, affect their parenting style? It is well known that parents who have been treated harshly by their own parents, to the extent that they have developed a poor self-image and become isolated people, are high risk for abusing their own children.

The success of any treatment plan also depends on community response and attitudes (Committee on Child Psychiatry, Group for the Advancement of Psychiatry, 1973) including the response of school personnel, who have their own investment in the child, and the attitude of the juvenile justice system when that is relevant. Another factor is the attitude of the child's peers who are always an important influence. Geographic factors (urban, suburban or rural setting), economic, cultural and religious factors must also be weighed, as must the community social and recreational opportunities. The range of accessible helping facilities and therapeutic resources is especially important. The availability or unavailability of appropriate clinics, therapists, groups, camps, self-help groups, social agencies and recreational organizations which meet the needs of the developmentally disabled child and his or her family is a crucial issue in therapeutic planning.

It is obvious that no one therapeutic or intervention strategy will meet the affective needs of all developmentally disabled children. The helping professional must borrow from a number of models (Lazare, 1973) and develop a broad, eclectic approach. A review of potential models will serve to clarify this point.

The Medical Model (Health and Disease)

In this model the health professional begins with problem identification or diagnosis and proceeds to problem-solving or treatment through developing a data base, which includes a social history and personal profile, and makes his or her decisions based on this data base and that difficult to define entity, clinical judgment. This model also includes patient and family health education with the health professional assuming an empathic stance and an appropriate distancing of himself or herself to achieve a healthy doctor–patient relationship.

The Social Model (Functioning in a Social System)

In this model the professional studies the child in his or her family and community and notes the responses of the child and his or her family to the milieu, the setting, the situation and the problem. He or she then attempts to reorganize the milieu and the setting as well as the child's and the family's response to the situation and to the problem. The goal is to effect appropriate behavioral change.

The Behavioral Model (Social Learning Theory)

In this model the professional determines the behavior to be modified, studies it and establishes the conditions under which it occurs. He or she then determines the factors responsible for the behavior (here and now) and selects a set of treatment conditions. The professional then arranges a schedule of retraining and conditioning or deconditioning.

The Psychological Model (Psychodynamic Theory)

In this model the professional explores and examines early and recent psychologic determinants. He or she then clarifies events, feelings and behavior using himself or herself and the relationship with the child and the family as a therapeutic tool to enhance growth and maturity. This model is especially effective in reducing parental anxiety which, in turn, helps the child by improving his or her self-image and coping skills.

The Developmental Model
(Maturational Level or Stage in Life Cycle)

In this model the professional determines the phase or stage of the child's development and compares these levels with chronological, sociocultural and/or situational norms. The criteria used for assessment are simply the skills and behavior expected of normal children. The child is evaluated in terms of how close he or she comes to the normal expectations. In working with developmentally disabled children criterion-referenced assessment measures are often used in preference to norm-referenced tests.

The Educational Model (Teaching and Learning)

In this model the professional develops goals and objectives which are usually stated in terms of expected response or behavior. A teaching or lesson plan is then formulated based on these objectives. The educator then instructs according to this plan using an appropriate format and setting. Evaluation is an essential feature of the model with resultant continuing reassessment and revision of goals and objectives.

The Eclectic Model (Unified Concept)

This model includes methods and approaches borrowed from the other models. It is an expanded version of Engel's concept that there are biological, social and psychological components in every health professional–patient encounter and that all of these components must be considered together and included in therapeutic planning to achieve optimal results (Engel, 1960). In the affective area the treatment of the developmentally disabled child requires the use of this eclectic model to achieve optimal results. The issue of when and how other professionals should refer to a mental health professional (Swinger and Sandler, 1977) is beyond the scope of this discussion. In part the resolution of this problem depends on the interests, orientation and skills of the professional involved. Some of the strategies which follow are clearly in the domain of the mental health professionals. Others may be implemented by one or more of the professionals working with the family.

Therapeutic intervention in the affective domain falls into four main categories (Committee on Child Psychiatry, Group for the Advancement of Psychiatry, 1973): intra-psychic modification, alteration of family functioning, alteration of peer group interaction and environmental manipulation. Therapeutic modalities which attempt intrapsychic modification include psychodynamic therapy (psychotherapy, play therapy, music, dance and movement therapy and developmental stimulation), behavior modification, analytic therapy, nondirective or structured counseling of parent and child, parent group therapy (professionally-led or self-help or combination) and peer group counseling. Therapies attempting to alter intrafamily function fall into two primary categories, family therapy and marital counseling. Modalities directed toward the alteration of peer group interaction include the head start, day care, nursery school, preschool constellation, the therapeutic school or day treatment center, the specialized educational program and the community service group. Lastly, therapeutic intervention may involve environmental manipulation through parent education, changes in living arrangements (even, as a last resort, removal from the home), and providing home and family support services such as homemakers, child care and other parent-support modalities.

No discussion of therapeutic strategies for children would be complete without some mention of parenting and parent development. Parents progress through five stages of development in relation to their children (Friedman and Friedman, 1977). Briefly these stages are (1) learning cues (infant), (2) accepting development (toddler), (3) allowing separation (preschooler), (4) tolerating rejection (school-ager) and (5) restructuring life (teenager). Parent development has special meaning in relation to the handicapped or developmentally disabled child. Utilizing this conceptual framework in the diagnostic and therapeutic process may be very rewarding. Kessler, in an excellent paper, "Parenting the

Handicapped Child" (1977), discusses the role of the pediatrician and other health professionals working with the parents of handicapped and developmentally disabled children.

All disciplines working with developmentally disabled or handicapped children can play a role in the affective therapeutic process. Child and parents need continuing reassurance and education relative to the subtleties and inherent limitations of the young patient's handicap and therapy. There is a continuing need to allay guilt and anxiety in parent and child. There is also a need for free expression of ideas and feelings by all members of the family including siblings. Parents have a continuing need for guidance as they develop insights relative to their child at each developmental level. There is a continuing need to discourage the neurotic use of the handicap or disability by the child and/or any family member. There is a continuing need to help the child set and reach his or her own potential and limits. There is a continuing need to encourage appropriate limit-setting by everyone working with child and parent. Lastly and probably most important there is a continuing need to encourage the development of a healthy self-image in parent and child.

These needs can be met only if everyone working with child and family is aware of, knowledgeable about and cooperative with the intervention strategy. This is important whether one is working with a primary affective disorder such as depression or autistic behavior or with the affective components of developmental disorders or disabilities. The intervention strategy can then be truly multi- and interdisciplinary and an effective, eclectic diagnostic–therapeutic model can be implemented for the benefit of child and family.

References

Arnold, L. (ed.) *Helping Parents Help Their Children.* New York: Bruner/Mazel (1978).

Augenbraun, B., Reid, H. and Friedman, D. Brief intervention as a preventive force in disorders of early childhood. *Am. J. Orthopsychiat.*, Vol. XXXVII, No. 4 (July 1967).

Cohen, P. and John, J. Followup study of patients with cerebral palsy. *Western J. of Med.*, 130:6–11 (Jan. 1979).

Cohen, R. Case formulation and treatment planning (pp. 633–640) and Interpretation conference and communication with referral sources (pp. 640–647), in Noshpitz, J. (ed.), *Basic Handbook of Child Psychiatry.* New York: Basic Books (1979).

Committee on Child Psychiatry, Group for the Advancement of Psychiatry, *From Diagnosis to Treatment*, Vol. VIII, Report No. 87 (Sept. 1973).

Engel, G. A unified concept of health and disease. *Perspect. in Biol. and Med.*, 3:459–485 (1960).

Freud, A. The role of bodily illness in the mental life of children, in Solnit, A. (ed.), *Physical Illness and Handicap in Childhood.* New Haven: Yale Univ. Press (1977).

Friedman, A. and Friedman, D. Parenting: A developmental process. *Pediat. Ann.*, 6:9 (Sept. 1977).

Friedman, D. and Hansen, H. Family therapy in pediatrics. *Clin. Pediat.* Vol. 3, No. 11:665–669 (Nov. 1968).

Grossman, H. et al. (eds.), *The Physician and the Mental Health of the Child.* Chicago: Amer. Medical Assn. (1979).

Kessler, J. Parenting the handicapped child. *Pediat. Ann.,* 6:10 (Oct. 1977).

Lazare, A. Hidden conceptual models in clinical psychiatry. *New Engl. J. Med.,* 288:345–351 (1973).

Lemkau, P. The influence of handicapping conditions on child development. *Children,* pp. 43–47 (Mar./Apr. 1961).

Missildine, H. *Your Inner Child of the Past.* New York: Simon and Shuster (1963).

Ornitz, E. and Ritvo, E. The syndrome of autism, in Chess, S. and Thomas, A. (eds.), *Annual Progress in Child Psychiatry and Child Development.* New York: Brunner/Mazel (1977).

Rutter, M. Brain damage syndromes in childhood, in Chess, S. and Thomas, A. (eds.), *Annual Progress in Child Psychiatry and Child Development.* New York: Brunner/Mazel (1978).

Seidel, V., Chadwick, O. and Rutter, M. Psychological disorders in crippled children, in Chess, S. and Thomas, A. (eds.), *Annual Progress in Child Psychiatry and Child Development.* New York: Brunner/Mazel (1979).

Swinger, H. and Sandler, A. Mental health referral. *Pediat. Ann.,* 6:10 (Oct. 1977).

25

Using Our Emotions: Some Principles for Appraising Emotional Development and Intervention

ROBERT N. EMDE
THEODORE GAENSBAUER
ROBERT J. HARMON

A four-month-old boy gives a beaming smile and begins cooing as his mother approaches. His eyes sparkle, and as he looks into her eyes, he becomes excited. Even though he is in an infant seat, his arms and legs begin to exercise in a bicycling motion while his face lights up. At times he looks away from Mom, and the excitement diminishes but soon he looks back to her. Quite naturally, she smiles and speaks endearingly. She also carries on her other activities.

A one-year-old girl cries when mother leaves the room but is comforted when she returns. Although she shows initial inhibitions and possibly even some fearfulness when a stranger approaches, there is a "warming up" and she eventually makes friends, while intermittently looking at mother.

A young toddler is "into everything," exploring, fingering, looking, making noise and moving about. Mother is obviously watching and available. When a flower vase is about to be grasped, she says "no!" Her toddler stops, evidences frustration and briefly whimpers. He then recovers and goes about again. Later, mother gives what seems like a casual acknowledgment through a glance, a smile and a gentle pat on the head as her child comes to her before happily venturing out again.

Imagine that you have made these observations in your pediatric office. Whatever else is involved in the consultation, you have a good feeling. Behavioral development is on track. In each instance the child's emotions indicate an active, curious and, on the whole, pleasurable engagement with the world. Emotional expression is regulated and the child can express displeasure as well as pleasure. Further, the mother (we could as well have said father) is available and responsive. She may express concern during the consultation, and particularly during times of her child's distress, but overall she reflects a balance of good feeling. While she seems pleased that her child expresses love for her in a special way, she takes pride in the developing evidence of an expanding interest in the world beyond her.

Now let us consider three other observations.

A four-month-old boy is in an infant seat as his mother approaches. However, smiling is weak and eye-to-eye contact is not sustained; there is no crescendo of excited activity and vocalization. Instead, as mother looks, his eyes wander off. Although the infant is not frankly lethargic, there is not an atmosphere of zest or involvement. The parents seem vaguely worried and somewhat distant but upon inquiry deny concerns about a problem with their infant.

A one-year-old girl cries when mother leaves the room, but when she returns, the girl seems to avoid mother's looks and comforting overtures. Mother comments: "You didn't miss me!" At first it seems there is little difference between the child's response to an unfamiliar person and response to mother. Later, when the stranger leaves the room, the infant seems more distressed than when mother had left.

Finally, a young toddler remains with mother. In spite of many attractive toys in the room and the warm coaxing of an unfamiliar person, he does not explore but remains clinging to mother. There is intermittent whining and she refuses to pick him up. Mother's smile seems somewhat mechanical as she talks with another adult. She adds that this behavior is typical.

These observations with children of comparable ages are also made in your office. This time, however, no matter what else has occurred, you do not have that good feeling. Behavioral development may not be on track. The child's emotions do not indicate a balance of curiosity and pleasurable engagement with an expanding world. Instead, evidence suggests a restrictiveness and a "turning off." This seems reflected in parental behavior where there is a swing away from pleasurable engagement and expansion. Instead of pride, one suspects parents may often feel uncertain, embarrassed, isolated and defensive. In these observations our emotions tell us that there is a need for understanding and help. (Of course, you would want more information about usual behavior with father and other family members before making any definitive clinical judgments. But you are concerned.)

In this essay we as clinician-researchers will review some principles important for assessing emotional development in the infant and toddler. Most of these principles, we hope, will be familiar, since we believe they are part of what is enduring and human in the art of medicine. By discussing cases of emotional assessment in the context of these principles, we hope to convince you of the adaptive importance of emotions for learning and for social development, and of the value of using your own emotions as a guide for understanding and treatment.

The Communicative Value of Emotions

For a long time most of psychology labored under the belief that emotions were maladaptive, largely disruptive and disorganizing aspects of experience that should be "gotten rid of" or avoided. Today, the predominant scientific view is otherwise. While peak emotions can sometimes be disruptive, emotions on the whole are appreciated as ongoing, organizing and useful aspects of everyday functioning. Aside from their motivating properties (for arousing, sustaining and terminating certain kinds of behavior), emotions orient us to our general state of being and facilitate communication. As we will show, these ideas not only have a strong common-sense basis in clinical practice and in parenting but also a basis in current evolutionary thinking.

Clinicians have long found emotions to be at the center of everyday work. Patients come for consultation of affective discomfort; they tell us they want to "feel better." Further, in any therapeutic intervention, whether with children or adults, emotional expressions permit ongoing assessment; both patient (through feeling) and doctor (through observation and empathy) "monitor" the progress of treatment.

As every parent knows, emotional expressions are the "language of the baby." Not only are they prominent, but they guide care-giving by allowing the infant's current state of need or satisfaction to be monitored. Some expressions are unequivocal and their survival value for the infant is also clear. *Crying*, for example, communicates distress or pain to the adult and gives a universal per-emptory message: "Come, change something"; *smiling* communicates pleasure and conveys: "Stay, keep it up, I like it" (Stechler and Carpenter, 1967). Beyond this, the baby's expression of interest reveals a readiness for learning. The expression of surprise may indicate the beginning of assimilating new in-formation (Charlesworth, 1969). Similarly, expressions of fear, anger and sad-ness communicate compelling messages, especially during later infancy and early childhood.

Evolutionary considerations underscore the wisdom inherent in the common-sense view about the communicative value of emotions. Darwin (1872) originally set forth the adaptive, communicative role of emotions, although its scientific influence remained dormant until recently (Ekman, 1973). Hamburg (1963), in reviewing the course of primate evolution, concluded that human emotions evolved because of a selective advantage in facilitating social bonds. He speculated that group living operated as a powerful adaptive mechanism, and the formation of social bonds came to be experienced as pleasurable and their dis-ruption as unpleasurable. Myers' research (1976) with free-ranging and labora-tory monkeys has provided some experimental evidence for a close connection between emotions and social life. Emotional and social behaviors were found to be controlled by the same forebrain areas. When these regions were surgically ablated, facial expressions and vocalization of emotion were unavailable for social communication. Upon release from captivity ablated animals wandered through their social groups without interacting and probably did not survive.

The face, which is so central for emotional expressiveness, evidences increasing complexity as one moves from prosimians through monkeys, apes and man. Evidence suggests an evolution of primate facial expressiveness which corresponds to an increasing use of vision and social communication signals in group-living animals (Chevalier-Skolnikoff, 1973).

In the evolutionary step to man facial muscles became further differentiated with speech, and as Chevalier-Skolnikoff emphasizes (1973), social communication of subtle internal states occurs more often through language than facial expression of emotion. However, crosscultural evidence that discrete facial expressions of emotion are universally recognized and expressed throughout the human species, and that there are regularities in ontogeny, indicates that facial expressions have continued adaptive importance (Ekman, 1972; Izard, 1971, 1977; Sroufe, 1979; Emde, 1979; Izard, this volume). We believe that this adaptive importance consists in providing us with a universal "language," one modulated by speech but guiding us to what is both universally human and individually meaningful (Emde and Gaensbauer, 1981).

Some General Principles
for Assessment and Intervention

It should not surprise us that some common principles apply to assessment and intervention. Understanding is not merely the basis for all help, the understanding of another encourages confidence and is, in a very human sense, helpful in itself. Recently, we were reminded of five principles in talking with an articulate young mother and father who reviewed the pediatric care given their chronically ill infant daughter. The parents described what was meaningful for them during many times of turmoil, uncertainty and pain. These principles all have to do with sensitivity; at the same time, they have to do with understanding and with what is helpful.

The first principle we might label as *temporal sensitivity*. A diagnostician knows the importance of multiple observations over time. One observation of a distressed infant and a harassed mother during a pediatric office visit may be misleading. Certainly, it would be an error to attempt a definitive judgment about emotional development based on any single observation cited in the opening of this paper. Further, assessment is an ongoing process. Development creates change and circumstances vary. But temporal sensitivity applies to treatment as well as diagnosis. In terms of what is helpful, there is nothing more important than the availability of the helping professional.

In talking with us, the parents contrasted their experience with two attending pediatricians in two different hospitals. One pediatrician came and went unexpectedly, was difficult to reach by telephone and sometimes shifted their daughter's care to a colleague without telling them. Their conviction was strong that this doctor did not know or understand their daughter, and they doubted his interest or ability to help either her or them. This contrasted with the feeling of confidence they had in the other attending pediatrician who was available. This physician may not have spent more time with their daughter, but she visited regularly and allowed time for talking with the parents, for sharing her observations and current thinking as well as for answering questions. She was available by telephone (although they called her only twice during a two-month period). When she left town for an extended period while their daughter was hospitalized, they knew of her plans and before she left were introduced to a colleague who was covering.

A second principle is *empathic sensitivity*. The couple not only spoke of the importance of pediatricians "being there" in times of crisis, but "being there with feelings." If the first principle is that of "availability," the second can be thought of as "emotional availability." That the professional can use his own feelings as a diagnostic tool will be illustrated in the case histories to follow. That emotional responsiveness in the professional is humanizing and important was emphasized by the parents who appreciated the essential virtues of warmth, feelings and caring amid the technological complexities of modern hospital care.

Dynamic sensitivity is the third principle. These parents especially appreciated the second pediatrician who could "understand our struggles." Not only was she there, but she seemed to appreciate their conflicts about expressing anger at the hospital staff and their intermittent struggles with admitting disappointment and sadness about having a handicapped infant. It is often important to understand not only what a child or family is doing or not doing but also what they are struggling against; in particular, what conflicts may be occurring in matching the realities of an illness or crisis with expectations and wishes.

A fourth principle follows quite naturally from the first three. We might call it *individual sensitivity*. The couple was most explicit about the value of "understanding us as individuals." Each had had particular experiences with loss of loved ones and illness; thus, each had strong feelings and memories reactivated by their daughter's life-threatening illness. They were grateful for the individual attention and respect of the second pediatrician which added comfort and dignity to their difficult times. When the health care professional pursues what is individually meaningful and imposes a minimum of assumptions and prejudices, the patient and family feel respected and understood. They may then see new options beyond the restrictions that illness imposes. After all, the human being is extraordinarily complex, the meaning of experience unique, and possible adaptive solutions to problems posed by varied environments are multiple. It also follows that we need sensitivity in appreciating particular needs and interests of *families* and of *special environments* or communities. If patients could, they might say "not only appreciate us as individuals but also appreciate us as families and appreciate where we live."

This leads us to a fifth principle, *systems sensitivity*. This involves the appreciation of complexity, that there are multiple meanings and multiple causes of distress and happiness (Fleming and Benedek, 1966). Further, in approaching a clinical problem one must be aware of factors beyond the individual patient. The parents realized that their daughter's prolonged hospitalization was a stress they were somehow coping with individually but which was jeopardizing their marriage. The second pediatrician was sensitive to this and made special allowances for talking with the couple about family concerns. She also encouraged their use of the more flexible visiting hours available at the hospital. In retrospect they felt this was helpful and that after a time of marital crisis, they had probably come together under the stress rather than drawing apart. The pediatrician's sensitivity to potential family disruption may have been a factor which allowed this family to survive as a unit. A number of studies have indicated that there is an increased incidence of marital disruption associated with prematurity (Caplan *et al.*, 1966; Leifer *et al.*, 1972). An ongoing longitudinal study of prematures and their families also reveals that this time of crisis presents an opportunity for strengthening family ties (Harmon, in preparation).

All of these principles imply that an onging diagnostic attitude is therapeutic. It may be worth mentioning some other attitudes which combine diagnosis and treatment. One such attitude has been referred to as "nonjudgmental." It involves appreciating that people are doing their best, often under difficult circumstances and with limited resources. There are many ways of solving problems, and what at first seems a problem may in fact be a response to a problem or the beginning of a solution.

Another attitude is an *optimism about development*. This seems obvious and probably has something to do with why we are in this field, but there are some subtleties worth bearing in mind. The developmental process is creative and there are strong self-righting tendencies. If there is a deviation or deflection from a developmental pathway, caused by trauma or disease, for example, there will be a strong tendency to get back on the path, to develop competence in achieving biologically prescribed developmental goals (Waddington, 1940; Sameroff and Chandler, 1975). Further, among handicapped infants and children there are creative self-righting tendencies which can be encouraged and many possibilities for developing a sense of self-worth and fulfillment.

Pleasure, "Turning Off" and Depression in Development

We have paid particular attention to pleasure because we have found it a useful indicator in assessing behavioral development. If development is going well, there will be some sense of sustained pleasure as well as a range of expressed emotions. One expects to see evidence of this in a child, in the parents and in their interaction. Our opening examples have highlighted this. If behavioral development is not going well, the clinician can often see evidence of a "turning off." There is little pleasure and the range of emotional expressiveness is restricted. In extreme instances there may be sadness and depression.

As Brazelton and his coworkers have shown, and as the Neonatal Behavior Assessment Scale demonstrates so vividly (Brazelton, 1973), the newborn not only has the capacity to take in and process information but also to "turn off" stimulation by regulating behavioral state. Further, when things are not going well over a period of time, because of illness or a continually stressful environment, for example, the newborn can become lethargic, excessively sleepy or difficult to engage in wakeful attentiveness. Such behavior may alert the sensitive pediatrician to an early problem.

Soon after two postnatal months one normally expects to see the infant's pleasure system in full blossom with social smiling, sparkling eye-to-eye contact and cooing. Interestingly, this is accompanied by more sustained wakefulness and by enhanced exploratory "playfulness" with objects and people (Emde *et al.*, 1976). Again, if development is not going well, there is apt to be less pleasure and less engagement with the world. Lethargy or social avoidance may characterize extreme cases.

Certainly by seven to nine months the infant increasingly shows preference for one or more primary care-givers. For example, not only is there obvious pleasure in greeting mother, but there is apt to be specific displeasure when she leaves (separation distress) or when a stranger initially approaches (stranger distress). Toward the end of the first year and on into the second the infant increasingly uses mother as a "secure base" from which to explore (Ainsworth *et al.*, 1978). There is a surge of exploratory activity in early toddlerhood with periodic returns to mother for "emotional refueling," as Mahler and her colleagues have termed it (Mahler *et al.*, 1975). If development is not going well, one may see manifestations of what Ainsworth has called "anxious attachment" in the infant to its mother, with lack of positive preference for mother or with avoidance of mother or resistance to being comforted by her during a reunion after a brief separation. Further, one might also see a "turning off" with restriction of emotional expressiveness and of exploration or "defensive" use of play which feels driven, stereotypic and less than joyful (Harmon *et al.*, 1979).

From the parents when development is going well, one expects to see a predominance of pride and pleasure with elements of renewed excitement following developmental accomplishments. Research has shown that parental perceptions and attitudes about their children's development are important for indicating risks for emotional problems. This is true for mothers who judge their newborns as less than average on simple traits (Broussard and Hartner, 1971), mothers who make negative comments about their infants in the delivery room (Gray *et al.*, 1977) or mothers who perceive their infants over time as "difficult" (Thomas and Chess, 1977).

We believe the pediatrician should be aggressive in finding out how parents feel about their children's development and in assessing what we might call the "pleasure/distress quotient" in parental activities. In addition to direct inquiry about this, we have found responses to questions about the baby's personality generally revealing (Does your baby have a personality yet? If so, what is it like?) We have also found it useful to ask how the mother perceives her infant's emotions. Reports of a lot of anger, fearfulness or guilt during the first year, for example, may indicate problems that are worth pursuing. Our research program is currently documenting normal and deviant maternal perceptions of infant emotions at different ages in an attempt to provide useful background information for the clinician (Emde, 1979).

When development is on track, pleasure and a range of emotional expressiveness should be evident in reciprocal functioning between parent and infant. Further, observed interactions should not be stereotypic but should show flexibility and should increase in complexity as the infant matures. In observing interactions one can note the clarity of emotional signaling, that is, the extent to which each partner is able to express what interests, what pleases and what is being asked for. In assessing reciprocal functioning one might also ask about "games" the baby will play with mother. Toward the end of the first year can the baby demonstrate peek-a-boo and back-and-forth games? We find it useful to think about assessing emotional availability via this reciprocal functioning. Parents as well as infants need to be happy, and when there is deprivation of rewarding interaction both will be involved no matter how a deprivation might have begun (Gaensbauer and Sands, 1979). From this vantage we can appreciate the ongoing reciprocal adjustments which may characterize an interaction. If one partner is less emotional or less active, the other may adjust with more emotional expressiveness or more activity. This kind of situation is particularly prominent with parents of Down's syndrome children who may be less emotionally expressive or with premature infants who may be less active (Goldberg, 1978).

Finally, we must emphasize the importance of being aware of grief, sadness and depression in development. That grieving and depression in parents can interfere with emotional availability is well known, and clinicians who know about a recent loss in families can often help facilitate grieving. What seems to be less well known, however, is that infants and young children can also be sad and depressed. In one of our research programs in which we observed and evaluated infants and mothers (Gaensbauer *et al.,* 1979), sadness proved to be one of the most difficult affects to rate. Often new raters of videotapes missed the component behaviors relating to sadness (facial expressions and posture, for example)—a phenomenon which does not happen nearly so much with other emotions. This seems explainable in terms of our not wanting to see sadness in young children. Depression is perhaps the emotional problem most often missed. This is true not only in the clinical setting but also in other settings. Even in school, the quiet, depressed child is not the one referred for evaluation. More often it is the "hyperactive" child who makes his wants and disappointments more obviously known. One of our case examples will carry this discussion further.

Using Our Own Emotions and Understanding— Clinical Examples

These examples from our recent experience illustrate how the clinician might use his emotional availability in understanding and assessing problems of emotional development.

Emotional Assessment of a Two-Year-Old After Severe Trauma

A 26-month-old girl had been sexually abused by her uncle and, following this, her mother was hospitalized briefly for depression. After a week's separation, mother and daughter were reunited and evaluated several days later. Protective Services needed information as to whether, in view of the trauma, the child's emotional development showed evidence of chronic abuse, and whether there was a satisfactory mother-infant relationship.

A playroom observation included free play between mother and infant, interaction with an unfamiliar male, a brief separation from mother, reunion with mother and some developmental testing. Happily, there was clear evidence for a warm and mutually satisfying relationship between mother and daughter. The child initiated a variety of interactions, sometimes showing and handing mother particular toys and sometimes checking back with her while smiling and verbalizing in enthusiastic play. At no time did she evidence fearfulness or anger at mother. Mother seemed to be a source of pleasure and security in the midst of an uncertain playroom situation. Looking at mother and occasionally coming near her seemed to enable her to explore toys in a distant part of the room.

When the unfamiliar male entered the room, she seemed somewhat reluctant but did accept being held by him; she then became distressed when held closely. At this point she reached for mother, and when put down went immediately over to be hugged. During separation from mother she cried but was comforted by the stranger and soon began playing with him. When mother returned, both infant and mother seemed pleased with the reunion. After greeting the mother positively, the child began playing with her, and mother responded to the child's initiative quite naturally.

This child's capacity to show organized affection and play were considered evidence of a relatively stable environment. She showed none of the affective indicators which often appear in conjunction with an abusive or chaotic environment. She did not show the marked fearfulness, watchfulness, tendency to freeze or propensities towards marked anger and low frustration tolerance typical of infants from such pathological settings (Gaensbauer et al., 1981). Instead, the examiner noted that she seemed to expect good things of people. She was able to use the stranger as a source of comfort in mother's absence, and she also played with him. It was only when she was held close that she began crying, suggesting the possibility of a reminder of the specific abuse situation. Although there was sustained pleasure, the child's predominant mood was noted to be somewhat subdued, with sadness during lulls in activity and during the developmental testing when toys were removed. The sadness was concluded to be related to the recent mother-infant separation. In view of the pleasure and range of affects displayed, there did not seem to be evidence of chronic depression.

Unusual Pleasure in a Nine-Month-Old

During a longitudinal research observation a new member of our team was struck with a very unusual interaction between a mother and her nine-month-old Down's syndrome infant. Mother demonstrated a special way that her infant "knew" her. She held him in a seemingly awkward position with her arms under his back and his side against her body while she gently patted his buttocks. The infant stretched his neck, looked at her and smiled. In spite of the awkwardness both mother and infant seemed to get pleasure from this. The new observer felt a sense of uneasiness and asked mother more about what was happening. In response, mother was clear about the special significance of this posture and the patting. She recalled that as a newborn, when he was in the Intensive Care Unit fighting for his life, this was the only manner in which she could touch and comfort him because of the wires and tubes positioned so delicately. Amid his pain and enforced immobility she could help him get to sleep when no one else could. She felt they were both remembering when that was the only way in which he could be held, touched and comforted. What was once interaction for survival was now playing.

This case is documented in more detail in a previous report (Emde and Brown, 1978). The vignette illustrates that parents of handicapped infants develop special adaptations. As it turned out, although this infant had a dampened affective display system, as do so many with Down's syndrome, mother adjusted by becoming more sensitive in responding. The pediatrician might occasionally be surprised by some of the affective adjustments between parents and such infants. Inquiry will often reveal an interesting history of mutual regulation.

Parents Who Are Not Bonding

The nursing staff noted that the mother of a premature infant seemed reluctant to touch her baby. Out of concern that she was not "bonding" properly to her newborn, consultation was requested from the child psychiatry liaison service. This revealed that mother's behavior had been misinterpreted. The parents conveyed a sense of sadness. Both mother and father had been anticipating with pleasure the delivery and birth of their first child. They had attended childbirth preparation classes and were eagerly awaiting the "perfect" natural delivery. Unfortunately, medical complications necessitated cesarean section and a preterm infant was born. It became clear that reluctance to touch and hold the infant had less to do with a bonding problem and more with a need to grieve for the loss of the birth experience they had expected but not received. Mother and father seemed relieved to talk about their disappointment to an empathic listener. Soon they were able to become involved in the nursery, and touching and holding their infant followed naturally.

This example illustrates that not only can behavior be misinterpreted but that we need to appreciate what may happen when parental expectations are not met. The couple needed to undergo a "mini-grieving process" following the loss of an experience which had been anticipated with pleasure and excitement. Currently, particularly in middle-class populations, expectations around the delivery process are quite high. These include the assumption that attending childbirth preparation classes will ensure a relatively easy delivery of an alert and active newborn with whom one can interact in the first hours of life. Unfortunately, medical necessity may preclude an uncomplicated delivery. The pediatrician is often in a position to help families get "back on track." Should the birth experience have been marred by difficult labor or a sick infant, it is probably important to explore the parents' disappointment and, if it seems substantial, to help in the grieving process. Such a process need not be long, but some parents may feel that "all is lost" when they are unable to have a natural delivery and an early excited contact with their infant.

Depression in the Hospital

A three-year-old boy was referred for psychiatric evaluation because of increased withdrawal in the hospital after he had been accidentally burned over his legs and feet. Although the burns were severe, they were not considered life-threatening, and the staff was disturbed by the contrast between their optimistic view and the child's attitude which seemed to express "giving up." Upon seeing the child it became clear that he was severely depressed. He had been transferred from home to the burn center, and his parents were not able to visit regularly. The nurses had noticed that he was less irritable and did not whine when left alone as compared with times when someone was with him. Consequently, he was left alone for long periods. A self-perpetuating cycle then developed wherein occasionally people tried to interact with him but did not persist when he became more irritable. Many felt they should leave him alone. What was difficult to appreciate was that he was becoming severely depressed and that his protestations were an attempt to engage the environment around him. As this became apparent in the course of consultation with a child psychiatrist, he was assigned a primary care nurse and a consistent foster grandmother in addition to being seen by the psychiatrist and a developmental specialist. When the foster grandmother noticed that he became more upset when his legs were uncovered, the staff became aware of the shame he felt about his burns when others were around. Exploration uncovered a deeper humiliation he felt about having to wear a diaper and have it changed by others in spite of having mastered toilet training over a year ago. He was reassured that once his legs were better he could again use the toilet; everyone understood his need for diapers now because of the physical problem. His spirits lifted as a result of these interventions.

Depressed children often seem to drive away those who attempt to respond to their depression. In this "protest phase" of depression irritable behavior is often misinterpreted as "making the child worse," when in fact the child is trying to interact in the only way the depressed state will allow. Certainly, one should not be driven away by such children but should sustain interaction. Sadness and depression are difficult (and perhaps painful) for us to recognize in children. Too often the quiet child who may be depressed is not seen as withdrawn or in need of intervention but rather as compliant and well-adjusted to the present situation. The case also illustrates that even in a three-year-old the loss of a developmental function which has just been mastered may be experienced as overwhelming and humiliating. As the child's aloneness and separation from parents contributed to his depression, being put back into diapers without explanation or reassurance contributed to his shame.

A Two-Year-Old Who Is Eager To Please

A two-year-old boy had been placed in a foster home following documentation of parental abuse involving an older sibling. A playroom evaluation, similar to that described above, was carried out. It yielded a picture of considerable dysynchrony in adult-child emotional interactions. Even though both foster mother and child seemed to be making efforts to interact positively, one had a sense that things were forced. The child seemed to look to the foster mother for cues on how to react rather than for pleasurable stimulation. The foster mother seemed quite concerned about having a child play with the toys in age-appropriate ways, but her interventions had the effect of getting the child to do what she wanted rather than allowing him to pursue his own interests. On several occasions she interrupted his play with a particular toy, directing him to play with another. For example, when the child rolled a truck along the floor, she told him to put a toy in it. The observer felt discomfort and some anger at the foster mother in the face of this insensitivity. Further, one became aware that while the child was superficially obedient, he showed a tendency to withdraw from social contacts.

The child's vigilence and eagerness to please carried over to the examiner. His initial shyness to the stranger seemed different from what one might expect. When the stranger offered to pick him up, he held his hands out stiffly. He allowed himself to be held but clearly did not enjoy it. A propitiating style became evident during developmental testing with a forced smile that did not convey pleasure. His response to a verbal prohibition ("no-no") was striking. He developed a worried look, a frozen posture, and after eyeing the examiner for about 20 seconds gave an uncertain smile.

In talking with the foster mother after the session, one became aware of a background for her behavior. She did not see the child's obedience and tendency to withdraw as problematic; rather, they were virtues, indicating more independence and responsibility.

Using his own feelings, the observer became aware of a blocking of empathy by the foster mother. Her attitudes and expectations, while possibly appropriate under ordinary circumstances, were problematic in relation to the needs of this vulnerable child. Because of previous traumatic experience the child had developed a hypervigilence and an eagerness to please. In addition, there was a pattern of emotional withdrawal interpreted by the foster mother as independence. The observations made it clear that the child needed to be drawn out in order to develop renewed confidence in his caretakers. An infant stimulation program was recommended which included a series of consultations with the foster mother to help her respond more effectively to this child's particular needs. She was helped to understand that her efforts to direct the child's activity toward mature play were intimidating to him rather than openly received. At the same time, she was encouraged to be active in engaging and comforting him when he showed a tendency to withdraw.

Summary and Conclusions

We have used case examples to present some principles for assessing emotional development in the infant and toddler. These principles apply to intervention as well as to assessment, since the process of understanding is not merely the basis for help but is likely to be helpful in itself. Principles involving temporal, empathic, dynamic, individual and systems sensitivity were outlined.

Our approach to assessment is based on the assumption that emotions are adaptive features of everyday functioning, central in the "language of the baby" and vital for motivating engagement with an expanding world. Our approach also emphasizes the concept of "emotional availability" in the parent-child system. If development is going well, there is apt to be a sense of sustained pleasure and a range of emotional expression in the child, the parents and in their interactions. If development is not going well, there is likely to be a deficit of pleasure, a "turning-off," and, in marked instances, a mood of depression. Implicit throughout our approach is the value of the clinician's emotional availability—a professional competence in the use of his own emotions to guide understanding and treatment.

Acknowledgments

Dr. Emde is supported by Research Scientist Award #5 KO2 MH 36808 and NIMH Project Grant #2 RO1 MH 22803. Dr. Gaensbauer is supported by Research Scientist Award #KO4 HD 00214-05. Dr. Harmon is supported by Research Scientist Award #1 KO1 MH 00281 02 and NIMH Project Grant #1 RO1 MH 34005 02.

Part of the work on which this chapter is based was supported by the Developmental Psychobiology Endowment Fund of the Department of Psychiatry, given by the Grant Foundation.

References

Ainsworth, M.D., Blehar, M.C., Waters, E. and Wall, S. *Patterns of Attachment.* Hillsdale, New Jersey: Lawrence Erlbaum Associates (1978).

Brazelton, T.B. *Neonatal Behavioral Assessment Scale.* London: William Heinemann Medical Books Ltd., Philadelphia: J.B. Lippincott Co. (1973).

Broussard, E.R. and Hartner, M.S. Further considerations regarding maternal perception of the first born, in Hellmuth, J. (ed.), *Exceptional Infant. Studies in Abnormalities,* Volume 2. New York: Brunner/Mazel (1971).

Caplan, G., Mason, E. and Kaplan, D.M. Four studies of crisis in parents of prematures. *Comm. Ment. Health J.,* 1:149–161 (1965).

Charlesworth, W.R. The role of surprise in cognitive development, in Elkind, D. and Flavell, J.H. (eds.), *Studies in Cognitive Development.* New York and London: Oxford University Press (1969).

Chevalier-Skolnikoff, S. Facial expression of emotion in nonhuman primates, in Ekman, P. (ed.), *Darwin and Facial Expression.* New York: Academic Press (1973).

Darwin, C. *Expression of Emotion in Man and Animals.* London: John Murray (1904) (1872-original publication).

Ekman, P., Friesen, W.V. and Ellsworth, P. *Emotion in the Human Face.* New York: Pergamon Press, Inc. (1972).

Ekman, P. *Darwin and Facial Expression.* New York and London: Academic Press (1973).

Emde, R.N. Levels of meaning for infant emotions; a biosocial view. Collins, W. Andrew (ed.) *Minnesota Symposia on Child Psychology.* Vol. 13 (1979).

Emde, R.N., Gaensbauer, T.J. and Harmon, R.J. Emotional expression in infancy: A biobehavioral study, in *Psychological Issues, A Monograph Series,* Vol. 10, #37. New York: IUP (1976).

Emde, R.N. and Gaensbauer, T. Modeling emotion in human infancy, in Immelmann, K., Barlow, G., Main, M. and Petrinovitch, L. (eds.), *Early Development in Animals and Man.* West Germany: Zentrum für interdisziplinare Forschung, University of Bielefeld (1981).

Fleming, J. and Benedek, T. *Psychoanalytic Supervision.* New York: Grune and Stratton (1966)

Gaensbauer, T.J., Mrazek, D. and Emde, R.N. Patterning of emotional response in a modified "strange situation" paradigm. *Inf. Behav. and Devel.,* 2:163–178 (1979).

Gaensbauer, T. and Sands, K. Distorted affective communication in abused/neglected infants and their potential impact on caretakers. *J. Amer. Acad. Ch. Psychiat.,* 18: 236–250 (1979).

Gaensbauer, T.J., Mrazek, D. and Harmon, R.J. Behavioral observations of abused and/or neglected infants, in Frude, N. (ed.), *Psychological Approaches to the Understanding and Prevention of Child Abuse.* London: Batsford Academic, 1980.

Goldberg, S. Prematurity: Effects on parent-infant interaction. *J. Pediat. Psychol.,* 3:137–144 (1978).

Gray, J.D., Cutler, C.A., Dean, J.G. and Kempe, C.H. Prediction and prevention of child abuse and neglect. *Ch. Abuse and Negl.,* 1:45–58 (1977).

Hamburg, D.A. Emotions in the perspective of human evolution, in Knapp, P.H. (ed.), *Expression of the Emotions in Man.* New York: IUP (1963).

Harmon, R.J., Suwalsky, J.D. and Klein, R.P. Infants' preferential response for mother versus an unfamiliar adult: Relationship to attachment. *J. Amer. Acad. Ch. Psychiat.,* 18:437–449 (1979).

Izard, C. *The Face of Emotion.* New York: Appleton-Century-Crofts (1971).

Izard, C. *Human Emotions.* New York: Plenum Press (1977).

Izard, C. (this volume)

Leifer, A.D., Leiderman, P.H., Barnett, C.R. and Williams, J.A. Effects of mother-infant separation on maternal attachment behavior. *Ch. Dev.,* 43:1203–1218 (1972).

Mahler, M.S., Pine, F. and Bergman, A. *The Psychological Birth of the Human Infant.* New York: Basic Books, Inc. (1975).

Myers, R.E. Cortical localization of emotion control. Invited lecture, American Psychological Association, Washington, September (1976).

Sameroff, A.J. and Chandler, M.J. Reproductive risk and the continuum of caretaking casualty, in Horowitz, F.D. (ed.), *Child Development Research,* Vol. IV. Chicago and London: The University of Chicago Press (1975).

Sroufe, A. Socioemotional development, in Osofsky, J.D. (ed.), *Handbook of Infant Development.* New York: John Wiley and Sons (1979).

Stechler, G. and Carpenter, G. A viewpoint on early affective development, in Hellmuth, J. (ed.), *Exceptional Infant, Vol. 1. The Normal Infant.* New York: Brunner/Mazel (1967)

Thomas, A. and Chess, S. *Temperament and Development.* New York: Brunner/Mazel (1977).

Waddington, C. *Organizers and Genes.* London: Cambridge University Press (1940).

INDEX